RS
The Faster FORDS

RS

The Faster FORDS

Jeremy Walton

MRP

MOTOR RACING PUBLICATIONS LTD
Unit 6, The Pilton Estate, 46 Pitlake, Croydon CR0 3RY, England

First published 1987

Second edition, revised and extended, 1990

British Library Cataloguing in Publication Data
Walton, Jeremy *1946-*
    RS — the faster Fords.–2nd ed.
    1. Ford RS cars, history
    I. Title
    629.2222

    ISBN 0-947981-51-9

Advertising: Boland Advertising, 71 Bondway, Vauxhall, London SW8 1SQ

Printed in Great Britain by Amadeus Press Ltd,
Huddersfield, West Yorkshire

CONTENTS

INTRODUCTION

This story of 20 years of fast European Fords takes us from the Escorts and Capris which founded the RS legend in the 1970s to the latest cars like the Sierra RS Cosworth and the Fiesta RS Turbo. An RS badge was first used in Britain to identify 'Rallye Sport' products from the Ford Advanced Vehicle Operations factory of 1970-74. During the 1970s the spelling of 'Rally' was anglicized to delete the final 'e' in press releases concerning the cars, though the parts operation tended to retain the final 'e' in their material. After 1974 most, but not all, of the RS cars were designed and developed by some of the engineers who had worked at Ford Advanced Vehicle Operations, regrouped in the Special Vehicle Engineering unit. Post-1975 RS Fords, while often using UK-sourced power units, were usually assembled abroad, in either German or Belgian Ford plants. Exceptions were the RS200 which was constructed at the Reliant factory in Staffordshire, and the Anglo-Belgian RS500.

I decided that wherever possible we needed to present the history of these cars in context with how their owners felt today. In that respect you will see that I owe a special debt to the Ford RS Owners Club, with whose co-operation I was able to carry out a mini survey. In the particular case of pre-1974 RS Fords, where the Ford AVO Owners Club have a special expertise, I have used comments from that source. In a few cases running reports from the staff of specialist magazines have been called on to top up the results of the survey, but basically I aimed to get two to four differing accounts of each model from those who have had to pay from their own pocket to run them. . .

My general rule for the contents of this book has been that the cars should carry external RS badges for admission to our pages. The exception is the Mk1 Mexico, so closely a part of the RS story that it

could not be omitted in spite of its 1600GT badges. It was one of the biggest selling RS products to date, joining the second generation RS2000 over the 10,000 sales barrier.

The rarest RS types? Only just over 100 RS1800s are recorded as having been sold, with a few works team rally cars to be added to that total. The RS200's short span covered just 200 units built for homologation inspection, and the Capri RS3100 managed little more — 248 according to FAVO totals, 249 according to the man who liased between Aveley and Halewood in the course of their production.

In all, 17 RS cars come under scrutiny in these pages. Some of these models are long out of production, some still undergoing engineering development as this is written. The list begins with the Escort variations: Escort RS1600; Escort Mexico Mk1 and Mk2; Escort RS2000 Mk1 and Mk2; Escort RS1800; Escort RS1600i; and two generations of Escort RS Turbo. There are two Capris, RS2600 and RS3100. There is the dramatic mid-engined RS200, furthest removed of all from mainline production Fords. There are the exciting 140mph-plus Sierra RS Cosworths; even in the short production spell since 1985 Ford have produced four Sierra RS derivatives — some 5,000 three-door hatchbacks; a further 500 'evolution' cars in the same body for Group A racing; the refined and understated Sapphire-style four-door version; and the 4 × 4 development announced in 1990. The most recent use of the RS badge (now only on RHD models) is for the Fiesta RS Turbo, another 1990 arrival that we describe.

Before looking at the cars themselves, we examine the emergence of the RS lineage from the high performance Fords of an earlier period, the Cortina GT, Lotus Cortina and Escort Twin Cam, as well as recounting the stories of the Ford Advanced Vehicle Operations and Special Vehicle Engineering departments which conceived the majority of the RS models. The history of the 16-valve BDA engine and some of the non-production cars in which it found a home, like the flame-spitting Zakspeed turbo Capris, is reviewed, along with the important ancillary activity of Ford RS/Motorsport parts sales.

Appendices include technical specifications for each production type, a comprehensive collection of performance figures including those of representative competition cars, sales figures where available, and club contacts.

ACKNOWLEDGEMENTS

I cannot pretend the RS Ford book was my idea. Within the same week, Rod Mansfield at Ford Special Vehicle Engineering and Nigel Fryatt (then editing *Sporting Cars* magazine) both said, *Why don't you do something about all the RS models, right from the start to today?* Since Rod Mansfield had always been a source of valued advice for myself and other journalists, it was not a comment to be ignored. Working on the **RS = Right Stuff** project for Nigel Fryatt underlined how much work would be needed to cover a rapidly expanding model list...one still growing at press time, which always makes life difficult for the book author.

Further stimulus came from Jesse Crosse and Ian Wearing at AGB Specialist Publications, publishers of **Performance Car.** They commissioned a magazine format publication, **The RS Fords,** which appeared in October 1986. I'm told 25,000 copies were sold in three months, clearly establishing the interest in the subject and the following Ford have for their top-performance range. Space limits allowed only the germ of this book within those pages, and among much new material I have been able to add are the owners' comments, appropriate competition coverage, and six RS types that were not in the magazine at all — two generations of Mexico, three further versions of the Sierra RS Cosworth and the turbocharged Fiesta.

AGB also commissioned several photographic sessions at considerable cost and there was not enough room in that 1986 glossy for even a fraction of those specially commissioned pictures. I hope you will agree that we have made good use of some creative pictures; one of the photographers had taken over 400 shots of the RS3100 Capri alone, so I was somewhat spoiled for choice!

Because some of the RS Fords detailed had not yet been released when I was researching the book our publisher had to be particularly discrete before publication. John Blunsden of MRP was the natural choice — my thanks to him, his editor and all who worked on the tight production timetable.

My thanks to the following individuals who made this work possible, many of them contributors to our owner survey: Peter Nixon, RSOC publicity officer, for guidance and assembling key RS owners to help; Steve Rockingham, RS concours ace; Steve 'Tickford Capri' Saxty; Peter Williams, AVOOC secretary and source of much Mk1 Escort knowledge; Geoff and Steve George, for two generations of RS expertise; Peter de Frere, RS1600i and RS Turbo owner; Martin Castick, AVOOC Mexico registrar; Colin Beverley, RS1800 restorer; John Carter and Mark Rennison, operators of the DSRM rallycross RS200; Kevin Shortis, RS Turbo owner and RSOC secretary; I. McNicoll, RS Turbo owner; Stuart Adams, RS2000 owner; Jacques le Clainche, RS2600 owner and RSOC membership secretary; Steven Reid, RS1600i owner; Simon P. Sage, Mexico Mk2, RS2000 and RS1600i owner; M. J. Parkinson, RS3100 owner; Tom Chaplin, secretary RSOC of Australia; Dennis Sellars, RS3100 expert; Norm Walls, Australian Capri expert; and all the other RS owners who have discussed their cars with me.

It would be ungracious not to acknowledge also my debt to some key Ford personnel who have always encouraged my efforts. Stuart Turner illuminated the RS200 tale in particular, but has also opened my mind to many other facets of working and leisure life. Peter Ashcroft, Mike Moreton and John Wheeler at Ford Motorsport worried conscientiously about my BMW and Audi enthusiasms but never did anything but assist my research. John Southgate and Harry Calton of Public Affairs allowed generous access, whilst Barry Reynolds displayed his customary sporting Ford knowledge and shuttled me into the various departments I needed with aplomb.

Bob Howe looked back over 30 years of company service and more than two years consultancy on the RS200 and other projects to make me think again about some early aspects of the RS story, especially providing a candid insight to the establishment of Ford Advanced Vehicle Operations. Charles Mead and Bill Meade proved as cheerfully helpful in 1987 as they had during my employment at Ford in the 1970s.

Photographically much of the material has come from that AGB connection acknowledged earlier, and I should add that the bulk of the work is from **Performance Car's** senior photographer, Peter Robain, or freelance Tim Andrew. I also relied on Steve Clark and Sheila Knapman at Ford photographic; London Art Tech's superb sporting and road test archives; and — in emergency only — my own Canon/Pentax capabilities.

Jeremy Walton
Bix, Oxfordshire
April 1990

RS competition highlights 1970-90

1970: Circuit of Ireland Rally, RS1600, Roger Clark — first RS International win.

1970: World Cup Rally, 1.8-1itre Mexicos, Mikkola leads Escort 1, 3, 5, 6, 8 and team prize.

1971: Salzburgring ETC, RS2600, 1, 2, 3, — first RS Capri win.

1971: Holland, RS1600, Gilbert Staepelaere, first Continental rally win.

1971: European Touring Car Championship for drivers, Dieter Glemser, RS2600. German title to Jochen Mass, RS2600. South African manufacturers' championship to RS Ford.

1972: Hong Kong Rally, RS1600, Makinen leads Escort 1, 2, 3.

1972: Nurburgring 1,000km sports car race, RS2600, 1, 2 in class, 7, 8 overall.

1972: East African Safari Rally, RS1600, Mikkola scores first non-local win, Escorts also 3, 4 and 8.

1972: Le Mans 24 hours, RS2600, 1, 2 in class, 10, 11 overall.

1972: Spa 24 hours ETC: RS2600, 1, 2, 3. Capri RS drivers win European, German and Belgian championships.

1972-79: RAC Rally, RS1600/1800 wins 8 times (Clark 1972 & 1976; Makinen 1973-75; Mikkola 1978 & 1979; Waldegard 1977).

1973: Scottish Rally, first ten places taken by RS Escorts.

1973, 74, 76, 77, 81: 1,000 Lakes Rally, Finland, RS1600/1800 wins 5 times.

1973: European Rallycross Champion, RS1600, John Taylor.

1973-76: German Touring Car Championship, Zakspeed RS1600/1800s win 4 times (Glemser 1973 & 1974; Heyer 1975 & 1976).

1974-76: Tour of Britain, RS2000 wins 3 times (Clark, Marshall 1, 2 in 1974; Pond 1975, Vatanen 1976).

1974: Nurburgring 6 hours ETC, RS1600, Heyer/ Ludwig, outright winners.

1975: Scottish Rally, Clark scores RS1800's first international win.

1975, 76: Hungarian Rally, RS1800, Staepelaere wins twice.

1976-78, 80: British Open Rally Championship, RS1800 wins 4 times (Vatanen 1976 & 1980; Brookes 1977; Mikkola 1978).

1977, 79-81: Acropolis Rally, RS1800 wins 4 times.

1977: East African Safari Rally, RS1800, Waldegard wins.

1978, 79, 81: New Zealand Rally, RS1800 wins 3 times.

1978, 79, 81: European Rallycross Championship, RS1800, Martin Schanche wins 3 times.

1979: Portugal Rally, RS1800, Mikkola leads Escort 1, 2.

1979: World Rally Championship for Makes, Ford Escort RS1800; World Rally Championship for Drivers, Waldegard.

1980: Cyprus Rally, RS1800, Clark wins.

1981: World Rally Championship for Drivers, RS1800, Ari Vatanen.

1985: European Rallycross Championship, Group A, and 1,000 Lakes Rally, Group N, Escort RS turbo wins.

1986: British Open Rally Champion, RS200, Mark Lovell.

1987: Circuit of Ireland Rally, Sierra RS Cosworth, Jimmy McRae wins.

1987: World Touring Car Championship Eggenberger Sierra RS Cosworths win manufacturers' title for Ford.

1988: Tour de Corse, Sierra RS Cosworth, Didier Auriol wins — first Sierra World Championship rally win.

1988: German National Racing Championship, drivers' title to Klaus Ludwig, RS500.

1989: Bathurst, Australia, RS500, Dick Johnson/ John Bowe win.

1989: Cartel Rally (British international series), Sapphire RS, Colin McRae wins (youngest ever winner at 22).

FOREWORD

As exemplified by the outstanding results listed opposite, successful participation in competition by factory or factory-backed teams, or by privateers able to draw on the factory's expertise and specialized parts supply, has been an essential element in the RS story. The other side of the coin is the RS model as the enthusiast's road car, and for an overview of the many aspects of owning the most exciting and emotive machinery from a company famous for its colourful and competitive history I am delighted to offer the observations of Geoff George, Chairman of the Ford RS Owners Club 1983-87, summing up his two decades of varied RS motoring.

Having owned Escorts since 1969 and RS types from a couple of years later, my experience covers many years and models. My lasting impression is not of the differences between individual models but that between marks, as in the three generations of Escorts. I am fortunate that I have grown older whilst successive marks became more refined.

In my younger days I was very enthusiastic about rallying at Club level. I graduated to Escorts from Anglias and Cortina GTs. Then, I was only interested in how fast a car went round corners. The subsequent deterioration in ride quality after uprating the suspension was of no consequence. My priorities have changed with age, and I now require a more refined ride, one consistent with reasonable roadholding.

Ford created tremendous goodwill among the motor sporting fraternity throughout the 1970s. Unless they liked Minis, most enthusiasts drove Fords of some description. By comparison with my modified competition cars the standard Mk1 Escort was perfectly acceptable as a road car, and the first RS2000 was a great improvement in refinement over the Mexico.

Some of my Mk2 Escorts were also modified, but the standard Mk2 RS2000 was a considerable improvement over the first RS2000 as a road car. Considerable work on cutting down Noise, Vibration and Harsh-

ness (NVH), as well as the restyled front, made a very desirable vehicle that retains considerable popularity to this day. From April 1980 until June 1984, I was completely happy with my last RS2000. Unfortunately my son wrote it off at a Goodwood test day and I liked neither the asking prices nor condition of possible replacement RS2000s.

Feeling a bit depressed, I decided to wait for the Escort RS Turbo, even though I would have preferred rear-wheel drive. I took delivery in February 1985 and am very happy, granted its occasionally strange steering characteristics. Again this later RS is much more refined than its predecessors, and I would not return to the RS2000 of either mark as my main road car. However, I am pleased that we do keep examples of each in the family!

It was a joy to own each RS model when it was a current model. I leave aside the desirable and collectable Escort RS1600 and RS1800 models, because they are not really suitable as everyday cars. An RS2000 is almost as fast in standard form, and is much cheaper and easier to maintain for the average enthusiast.

The earlier RS cars used tried and trusted components from the Ford range. This made them very reliable, and also very easy to maintain. The latest cars with electronic engine management, fuel injection and turbocharging make home maintenance difficult. After many years of working quite happily on my earlier cars, I opened the bonnet of my new Turbo, had a look around, and quickly shut it again! I hope it can remain shut for some time.

*The supply of parts to keep earlier RS types in good condition already causes concern. Mechanically we have few worries, but body and interior trim is another matter. Ford stop supplying interior trim about two years after a model ceases manufacture, so RS owners have to rely on places such as Withers of Winsford in Cheshire and others who advertise in **Motoring News**.*

More and more RS Fords are returned to concours condition and lead cosseted lives with occasional summer outings. This promises a good long term future — provided they are not stolen and broken up, a worrying and persistent problem — but such concours cars pose a very interesting question.

Does the RS enthusiast purchase the model of his choice and use it as everyday transport? Used thus, it is bound to suffer the ravages of time and our winter roads, with no hope of keeping it in concours condition. Or does he regularly drive a Mk3 Cortina or 1100 Escort, bringing out his pristine RS for summer club events? Personally, as I want to drive my RS all the time, I align myself with the everyday RS drivers. But, as I am also concerned for the longer term future of the RS, I am very, very, glad that there are enthusiasts to support the concours approach.

Finally what of the future? If I were to consider a change I would go for the Sierra RS Cosworth, which I think is a brilliant car and a worthy addition to the RS range. On the horizon appears the new Sapphire-bodied RS Cosworth, with toned-down exterior, maybe a challenger in the BMW and Mercedes market.

Is this the way Ford intend to go with the RS marque? Only time will tell, but I feel the RS marque belongs with the enthusiast.

In concurring with Geoff George's closing remarks I would add my view that the RS name should be earned by exceptional dynamic prowess from any model, and the right to wear the RS motif ought to be associated with factory competition participation. However, I have no desire to see the resulting supply of RS cars aimed at a purist elite or simply at the wealthy. I hope the cars continue to appeal broadly to enthusiasts and I hope, too, that the RS content is not diluted to the point where it becomes just another marketing badge. Here's hoping the next generation of RS Fords will be equally enjoyable.

1

Origins and ancestors

There has been a Ford presence in Britain since the very early days of the motor industry, but only in the 1960s did the identifiable predecessors of the RS cars begin to emerge. Managing Director of Ford of Britain since 1986 is Roger Humm; in the manner of the legendary and apocryphal Henry Ford quotation about history and bunk, he confesses: *There are big blocks of history I don't recall, inside and outside our company. But I do know where the RS inspiration came from in my reading of our company history in Britain. It was the GT Cortina, no doubt about it. That car just set the people alight at a time when Austin Cambridges still existed.* The eyes roll expressively to the ceiling of the large corner office on the top floor of Ford's HQ at Warley.

When I spoke to him in the spring of 1987, 76 years after the incorporation of the Ford Motor Company (England) Ltd on March 8, 1911, Ford's British sales were at record levels. The Escort, Fiesta and Sierra, the latter soon to be reinforced by the arrival of the three-box Sapphire version, were 1-2-3 in a strong UK market, and Ford's total market share was very close to 30%. By 1990, arch-rivals GM had gained some ground and 25% was a more realistic UK Ford market share.

An important turning point for the British Ford Motor Company had come in late 1960 when the American parent stepped up its holding from 54.6% ownership to 100%, planning greater operational flexibility and the coordination to a greater degree of worldwide Ford operations, hinting already at the multinational, and particularly European, form that the company's future activities would be taking.

In September 1962, when the first Ford Cortina was announced, Ford employed 52,665 people and made an annual total of 529,127 cars and commercials in Britain. By June 1967 Ford of Europe had been created to coordinate forthcoming production facilities across Europe, particularly in the development of the high technology, lower labour cost Spanish factories, which came on stream with the 1976 Fiesta, Ford's first multi-million selling front-drive design.

By 1985 the effect of those multinational policies could be felt. Against the increasingly effective Japanese competition, Ford pitched an increasingly unified European production, with centres in Spain (Valencia), West Germany (Cologne and Saarlouis), and Belgium (Genk, under Ford Germany's production management) joining Britain's Dagenham and Halewood plants. Less product was 'Made in Britain' than in 1962, with output down to 455,147 units (317,689 of that total were cars). Fewer people were employed — 'over 45,000' was the company quote — yet Ford sold 485,620 cars in the UK. Over half were assembled in Britain but 139,675 came from Germany, over 45,000 from Belgium and 30,697 from Spain.

Thus did the Ford world change between the 1960s and 1980s. The model which spanned those years was the Cortina, in five best-selling but progressively larger and less sporting bodies. It was the Cortina that brought the belief that Ford could build a sporting car for Europeans, and the company were not slow to realize that the racing and rallying prestige of the Lotus and GT Cortinas benefited the complete range by association.

Roger Humm again: *The GT Cortina took us out of the mould as providers of workaday transport only. Then the Lotus Cortina and Cortina Lotus/Twin Cam series generated fantastic excitement and reinforced that GT image both on the road and with their competition results. They created new opportunities for ourselves and our dealers to become involved with a completely different type of Ford customer. We couldn't quantify the effect of these models just by their sales, for inside the company we knew these cars were giving us a real opportunity to break open new sales areas for Ford in Britain.*

What kind of cars were those sporting Cortinas, and what did they contribute to the first RS, the Escort RS1600 of 1970?

As is normal Ford practice, the Cortina inherited some of its running gear from earlier models, and shared some hardware with forgotten sisters such as the Capri-Classics and Corsairs. In essence it was a light, conventional, rear-drive car, but it was the two-door 118E 1500GT version, launched in April 1963, that opened Ford eyes to the commercial worth of sporting performance, making it possible for the later RS types to emerge. Officially the Lotus Cortina also went into production at the same time, but the Lotus version of 'production' at their factory in Cheshunt, Herts, drove Ford to distraction. There were vast changes in the specification of the Mk1 version and for the Mk2 'Cortina by Lotus' or Cortina Twin Cam of 1967-70 production was transferred to Dagenham.

Roger Humm, Managing Director, Ford of Britain. The company's UK sales rose steadily through the 1980s to reach record levels by 1989.

Ford's first British manufacturing plant opened at Trafford Park, Manchester, in October, 1911. In its first full year the factory made 3,000 Model Ts. Production continued there until September, 1931, ceasing a few days before the Dagenham plant in Essex came into operation.

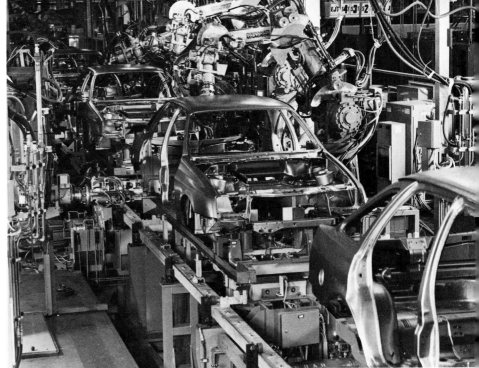

Manufacturing techniques have certainly moved on a bit since the Trafford Park days! The sparks are flying from metal finishing operations on a 1967 Mk 2 Cortina, below, in contrast to the robotic welding, devoid of humans, for the 1982 Sierra, right. It was the Sierra which followed several generations of Cortinas, and eventually brought the RS label to Ford's middle-range saloons.

What were the mechanical ingredients for the GT and Lotus Cortinas? A cynical Ford old-timer told me: *The GT and the later Cortina Lotus can be described with some confidence, but I reckon every Cortina that Lotus made was different to its mates!*

The basic Cortina GT, the existence of which made it possible for the Lotus version to be made, was outstandingly simple by the standards of the 1980s, a fact reflected in a kerb weight around 1,960lb. There was the formerly traditional front engine driving through a four-speed gearbox to a leaf-sprung axle. This axle assembly did sterling duty on Lotus Cortinas, Escort Twin Cams and the rear-drive RS Escorts of the 1970s, with a variety of final drive ratios of which 3.77:1 was most popular. The Cortina GT also had IFS provided by the MacPherson struts that were then something of a Ford speciality, though virtually universal in mass-production car design today.

The four-cylinder pushrod OHV Cortina 1500 engine had a bore of 80.97mm, a dimension shared with the 105E Anglia engine as well as the 1200 Cortina and some later power units used in RS products in the 1970s, and a stroke of 72.75mm to give a capacity of 1,498cc. In standard form, with a single-choke carburettor, it produced 59.5bhp at 4,600rpm and 81.5lb/ft at 2,300rpm, but for the GT version it was uprated to 78bhp at 5,200rpm and 91lb/ft at 3,600rpm. The increases were obtained as the result of consultancy work by Cosworth, the most obvious modification being the use of a Weber compound twin-choke downdraught carburettor.

The Cosworth connection also inspired a more vigorous camshaft that went on to serve the first 1300GT Escort and the later Mk2 1600GT Cortina, a tubular steel four-branch exhaust system and a 9:1 compression ratio where 8.3:1 was the standard 1500 specification. So customers could have had the first Cosworth-badged Ford road car in 1963, long before the sports Cortina's spiritual successor, the Sierra RS Cosworth of 1985. . .

Although the first GT Cortinas bore little external evidence of their increased power (and 78bhp was enough to top the output of the legendary 1275S Mini-Cooper), Ford did discard the 1500's usual four-wheel drums for 9.5in diameter front discs and 9.0in × 1.75in back drums, the latter an inch up on diameter and 0.25in wider than those of less powerful models. From October 1964 radius arms were fitted from underbody to rear axle.

Such radius rod axle location came and went on mass production Fords according to who was winning the engineering and marketing battles over the NVH (Noise, Vibration, Harshness) issue in the 1960s and 1970s, but all rear-drive RS Escorts were to feature these proven axle-hop restraints. Wider wheels were evident from the start of the GT Cortina's life too: 4.5in steel rims wearing the usual crossply rubber were specified.

The Cortina GT was available with either two or four-door body, but the Lotus Cortina came only as a two-door and was a lot further from being a normal production Ford, particularly in its earliest form. The engine, shared with the Lotus Elan, had the Ford 1500 block, bored out to 80.96mm but retaining the standard 72.75mm stroke for a capacity of 1,558cc, and fitted with an alloy twin-cam eight-valve cylinder head designed by Harry Mundy. The camshaft drive, conventionally enough, was by roller chain, and the compression ratio was 9.5:1. Fitted with two sidedraught Weber 40DCOE twin-choke carburettors, the unit produced 105bhp at 5,500rpm and 108lb/ft of torque at 4,000rpm.

The first Lotus Cortinas were homologation specials produced to satisfy an FIA Group 2 requirement for production of 1,000 units a year, but you can be absolutely sure that nothing like

that total existed of the car in its original radical form. Radical? I think the word is justified, because Lotus re-engineered the rear axle layout to take an A-bracket and coil springs, whilst the body featured aluminium panels for the bonnet, boot and doors. Additional axle location links were provided between the forward spring hangers and the damper-to-axle mountings. Searching for body stiffness with competition in mind brought reinforcements to the Cortina's boot area. Forged track control arms replaced the pressed steel ones and they were elongated to aid the provision of negative camber. Continuing a thorough job, Lotus extended the front anti-roll bar and shortened the steering arms.

The disc-drum braking system was shared with the Cortina GT, but the interior equipment was much improved. Whereas the GT had only a stick-on rev-counter and a skimpy centre console for extra instruments in its first incarnation, the Lotus Cortina had an outstanding six-dial display in a purpose-built facia beneath the period three-spoke, woodrim steering wheel. Aside from the famous green sidestripe, the Lotus Cortina was also identifiable by its lowered suspension, 5.5in × 13in steel wheels with 6.00-section crossplies, and the first use of the quarter front bumpers that would pass on to the Escort era.

The performance of the Lotus Cortina benefited from a 112lb weight reduction to around 1,848lb and naturally showed a considerable advance over the 1500 GT's performance. *Motor* timed the pushrod-engined car at 91.5mph and

The first Cortina's low weight and simple layout made it an excellent basis for a rallying and racing saloon, and much of the RS hardware of the 1970s could be traced back to the GT and Lotus versions of 1963-66. The second Cortina, and particularly the twin cam Cortina Lotus, bottom right, which was redeveloped by the Motorsport department at Boreham for production by Ford rather than Lotus, formed a direct foundation for the RS effort. Bill Meade, active on RS projects in the 1980s including the RS200, was among those who worked on that car.

The Ford Anglia 105E, left, was raced on the factory's behalf by both Superspeed and Broadspeed, the latter team providing the car with which John Fitzpatrick won the British Saloon Car Championship in 1966. The Anglia's engine was the first of a four-cylinder line which was to power many generations of Ford including the Escort from which the 1970 RS1600 was developed. The 105E power unit also proved a suitable basis for Cosworth's 1-litre Formula 3 engine, while the tuners who put 1,650cc and even 1,800cc twin cam engines in Anglias for road and club competition use first proved the popularity of the comparatively large engine in a small car which was to make the later Escort TC and RS types so successful.

0-60mph in 12.1 seconds, while the first-generation Lotus Cortina went from 0-60mph in 10.1 seconds and ran up to 108mph. You paid at the petrol pumps with 20.1mpg overall in the Lotus and 26.1mpg from the GT, all figures courtesy of **Motor**. The same source tells us that later Cortina by Lotus variants were not so quick (at 1,949lb kerb weight without the alloy bits, and the same power, this was no surprise) and when the Cortina Mk2 body came along maximum speed was reduced to 105mph.

Although the first Lotus Cortinas were exotic concoctions that won races and rallies but could be temperamental, the later versions, particularly after the deletion in June 1965 of the A-bracket rear suspension (which was fine in theory but proved a weak link for road use and rallying in practice) were more dependable. They took Ford's ability to sell performance cars to the general public far beyond the first tentative unofficial steps that had led to the creation of these sporting machines.

Motorsport honours were pretty evenly divided between GT and Lotus derivatives, particularly bearing in mind that the Ford Competitions Centre at Boreham tended to rip off the Lotus A-bracket assembly for rallying (if they did not, rough roads did the job for them!) creating in effect a kind of halfway-house Lotus-powered GT for competition.

Principal international victories that cannot be forgotten included the 1964 East African Safari Rally (first and third, plus team prize) for the 1500GT, whilst the Lotus fought both BMW and Alfa Romeo to win the 1965 European Touring Car Championship for Sir John Whitmore amongst its many track conquests. The Lotus Cortina also won the 1966 Acropolis and Geneva internationals as well as the RAC Rally.

The Mk2 Cortina GT and Lotus variants were a lot more than simple re-shelling jobs. As noted, Ford took over the production of the Lotus in 1967, and Competitions mechanics from Boreham performed the practical transformation that was also to provide the basis for the 1968-71 Escort Twin Cam, and thence the running gear beneath the RS1600.

In April 1966 Boreham received a pair of Cortina GTs in the Mk2 body for development into the second-generation Cortina Lotus. The new GT differed not only in its heavier and less aerodynamically efficient body, but also in the important details that the engine was now of crossflow layout and was coupled to what became known as the 2000E gearbox. The box was to serve both the first Mexico and the RS1600 in the 1970s. It traced its ancestry back to the 105E Anglia, but that model had no first-gear synchromesh. When the Cortina came along in 1962 it did have four synchronized forward ratios, but there was an enormous chasm between second and third. This was rectified in the unit which first appeared in the Corsair 2000E V4 of 1965 and was then transferred into the Cortina GT, later serving the Cortina Lotus and Escort TC before entering the RS era.

The crossflow pushrod engine had a slightly taller cylinder block than the earlier version. The stroke was lengthened to 77.62mm but the bore remained the traditional 80.97mm for a capacity of 1,599cc. The big change was in the cylinder head, now of Heron design with the combustion chambers recessed into the tops of the pistons, and with the exhaust ports on the opposite side of the engine to the inlet ports to provide the crossflow layout for better breathing. Designated the 'Kent' engine, it is still in production in the 1980s as an industrial power unit and continues to be the force behind Formula Ford. It has appeared in many vehicles including the Cortina 1600GT and the Mk1 Escort Mexico, and was also adapted for transverse mounting to provide its blend of lusty and reliable motivation for the first Fiesta XR2 of 1981.

In that front-drive role the Kent engine was rated at 84bhp, but in the 1967-70 1600GT Cortina, with a 9:1 compression ratio, tubular exhaust manifold and downdraught Weber carburettor, it was credited with 88bhp at 5,400rpm and 96lb/ft of torque at 3,600rpm. **Motor** found that the Mk2 1600GT could just top 96mph with its extra 10bhp, but a kerb weight around 2,000lb meant 0-60mph occupied just three tenths less than the 1500GT at 11.8 seconds.

Boreham's first task, over 20 years ago, was to take out those GT pushrod fours and install the Lotus Ford DOHC unit. Still 1,558cc and still based on the earlier 1500 block, it had been uprated to Elan SE specification, for which a gross 115bhp was sometimes claimed. A more realistic 109.5bhp was more usually quoted, at 6,000rpm. With a 9.5:1 compression ratio, the unit was also credited with 106.5lb/ft at 4,500rpm. The SE unit's power had been increased primarily by

The careful conservation of these Twin Cam Escorts in the 1980s demonstrates the continuing regard in which this immediate predecessor of the RS1600 is held. The two cars were very similar in specification – indeed some early RS1600s were round-headlamp Escort TC models with transplanted power plants.

replacement camshaft profiles that raised the peak revs moderately, up 300rpm for maximum bhp and 500rpm for the best torque figure.

Ford at Boreham made further engine changes, fitting a thicker-gauge exhaust system, replacing strap location with O-rings and dwarfing the Lotus Twin Cam alloy rocker cover with a two-barrel air cleaner feeding the usual pair of sidedraught Weber 40 DCOEs.

Working under the managerial flair of the innovative Henry Taylor, Boreham's Bill Meade, Ken Wiltshire and Mick Jones put the new Cortina Lotus concoction through a short development programme that emphasized both rough road durability and those engine improvements. The bulk of their running gear ideas were to be carried on to the Escort RS types in the 1970s, particularly the employment of export specification heavy-duty welding around the front strut mountings, and banishing the battery to the boot. Lowered suspension around simpler Ford strut and leaf-sprung axle components than the first Lotus Cortina worked well enough to pass on to the Escorts, as did the installation of a hydraulic clutch. That 3.77:1 ratio axle was strengthened during Boreham's development mileage (including the inevitable inversion on the Bagshot tank testing track!) too, uprated with high-tensile bolts. At first this axle ratio was reserved exclusively for the Cortina Lotus.

Braking was based on the servo-assisted Corsair 2000 disc/drum layout and would also be passed into the RS Escort specification. 9.62in diameter solid front discs and 9in × 1.75in rear drums were used.

Weighing a little more than the standard 1600 GT's 2,000lb, the Cortina Lotus kept to the tradition of two doors only, but had full-width front bumpers in Mk2 trim. It could be ordered with the Team Lotus white and green stripe livery, but plenty of other standard Ford finishes were also available, making the 105 to 108mph Cortina an excellent Q-car. Overall, the engine seemed to have gained in efficiency in its new home, and the independent testers' fuel consumption figures I have seen range from 22 to over 24.6mpg.

The second Cortina Twin Cam was not as widely used in competition as the original, for the arrival in January 1968 of the Escort range, including a Twin Cam variant, abruptly curtailed its career as a works team car, one necessarily abbreviated anyway by the cancellation of the

The international debut of the Escort Twin Cam came with X00 355F's outing on the 1968 Sanremo Rally: Ove Andersson and John Davenport finished third. Ancestor of the RS Capri was this Weslake-tuned 2.4-litre 2300GT campaigned across Europe in 1970, below. Front spoiler (cum oil cooler) and flared wheelarches are beginning to appear.

1967 RAC Rally because of a foot-and-mouth disease emergency.

The factory-backed Team Lotus racing appearances lasted most of the 1967 season in Britain, with Graham Hill, John Miles, Paul Hawkins and Jacky Ickx making spectacular appearances in Group 5 Cosworth FVA-engined Mk2s that proved faster than Vic Elford's AFN Porsche 911 on occasion, though not so reliable!

Later racing Cortina Twin Cams had just over 200bhp rather than the 180bhp of the BRM-developed engine in the racing Mk1. Rallying engines had an output of 160 to 165bhp, and were usually built by Ford Boreham employees including the present competition manager Peter Ashcroft, David Wood, subsequently ARG Motorsport engine designer, and rally engine specialist Terry Hoyle.

Although rally successes for the Mk2 Cortina were almost uncommon by the standard of the previous Cortina GT/Lotus, the car was well accepted on the UK market, at an initial price of £1,068 2s 11d. It stayed in production on the Dagenham lines until the Cortina was reborn in Mk3 'Coke bottle' style during 1970.

The direct predecessor of the first RS Escort was the Escort Twin Cam of 1968-70. Conceived at a brainstorming session chaired by Henry Taylor on January 25, 1967, the cocktail of Lotus Cortina running gear in an Escort package was irresistible to the Boreham-based factory competition centre. They obtained a plastic replica of the 1968 Escort in March 1967 and levered the 1.6-litre 110bhp Twin Cam unit into the space usually reserved for a 70bhp crossflow 1300.

Surrounding the engine, which had to be installed at a slight angle to clear the confines of its new home, were all the Cortina Lotus trimmings: lowered radius rod suspension; 9.62in discs and 9.0in drums; 3.77:1 final drive; 5.5 × 13in steel wheels with 165 tyres; rear-mounted battery (spare wheel on the floor, rather than the Cortina's upright position); 2000E four-speed gearbox and associated hydraulic clutch.

For competition purposes, with 160 to 180bhp available from the proven Twin Cam, it was a must, for the Escort shell was lighter, at 1,730lb, and nearly a foot shorter than the Mk2 Cortina. But how could they make enough cars to satisfy the sports authorities?

The people at Boreham found allies in Bob Howe, of the mainstream Product Planning department, and Dick Boxall, who was a production manager at the Halewood factory as well as a motor sport supporter. Somehow they badgered the Twin Cam Escort into a corner of the Merseyside complex, lots of willing volunteers completing each car from a basic Escort 1300GT. Insiders estimate that approximately 450 such Escort Twin Cam road cars were constructed in this manner, while a further 25, including pre-production cars for the press, came from Boreham's small workforce to get the car into the public eye and smooth its homologation into Group 2, which was achieved in March 1968.

That car did even more for us, and more importantly for the new Escort, in competition than even the Cortina's example could have let us hope, recalled Roger Humm. Even prior to homologation, Boreham took a pair of prototype Twin Cams with no more than 165bhp and gave them a winning debut in front of the ITV cameras for a **World of Sport** Rallycross at Croft, near Darlington, in wintry February conditions.

From the moment it was homologated, the Escort TC looked a winner. Ove Anderson/John Davenport were third in the Sanremo Rally, Roger Clark ruled the Circuit of Ireland in April, and other major race and rally wins quickly followed.

On the race track, Frank Gardner was overall winner in the 1968 British Saloon Car Championship, and in rallying, the Escort won the 1968 and 1969 International Championship, a series that predated today's World Championship and was built around many of the same classic rallies. For example, Escort Twin Cams won the Finnish 1,000 Lakes from 1968 to 1970, and the rough Acropolis fell to a 'Twink', too, in 1968. . .

It was the Twin Cam which introduced the stocky, competition-bred sporting Escort look back in the days before the opening of Ford Advanced Vehicle Operations. With its flared wheelarches and quarter bumpers, it usually shared the significantly tougher Type 49 body of the RS1600 and subsequent RS Escorts, although something like 25 pre-production Twin Cams had a BB48 chassis plate instead of BB49 for the heavy-duty body used in all FAVO-production RS Escorts.

I am indebted to Peter Williams of the Ford AVO Owners Club for reminding me that the very first RS1600s were actually Escort Twin Cams with 16-valve Cosworth-Ford power units replacing the older Lotus-Ford. Hence the fact that my first road test RS1600 was badged TC. Incidentally the same kind of process later saw slower-selling RS1600s lose their engines in favour of Mexico pushrod units in a hurried bid to capitalize on the London-Mexico Marathon win, so the first Mexicos were literally RS1600s in all but their transplanted engines and associated ancillaries.

Thus the Escort Twin Cam, theoretically on sale at £1,080 in January 1968, though it was actually in June of that year and at more than £1,123 that the TC began its sales run, is the most direct predecessor to the RS Fords which are our subject in this book. Looking back over the RS years, how did Roger Humm feel these specialized Fords had fitted into this mass-production manufacturer's repertoire?

It attracted entirely new Ford customers, that's for sure. Those first RS Escorts pulled in doctors and many other professionals who would never have considered a Ford previously. At first we just had to get a grip on this new opportunity and create a cohesive RS Dealer network. That is unique to Britain, and always has been: no other European Ford company has an RS Dealership system, but we think the cars need specialist training and service.

I received some violent criticism of the RS network during the preparation of this book, with a small number of dealers on the other hand warmly praised for their service. Roger Humm was naturally not inclined to dwell on any shortcomings that might or might not exist in his view, but he too pointed out a small number of outlets who are providing premium service. It seems the RS owner has to pick and chose very carefully. Owners of the older cars will almost certainly exist on specialist suppliers anyway for the bulk of those special items no longer in production, particularly in respect of body trim.

Asked in 1987 about the worst period in the development of the RS identity, Roger Humm had no hesitation in picking — *four to five years ago. About 1979 through to 1983, when we were out of rallying and there was no new product to offer in the showroom. We got pretty twitchy about the whole thing at that time. There were moments when I worried that the whole RS thing would go, particularly as Ford in Europe was switching the Escort over to front drive.*

I am totally convinced Ford has to be in both Formula 1 racing and rallying to succeed because they are different audiences. Rallying gives us a chance, along with saloon car racing, to demon-

Strong sales of Series X modifications like these wheelarches, front spoiler and wide wheels in FAVO four-spoke style were to encourage Ford to use the RS name in this area again.

The original RS symbol, far left, has undergone a number of changes of style over the years, while remaining a potent marketing force. The entwined monogram on these lamp covers was echoed on RS Escorts of the late 1970s.

strate the high technology of production-based cars. I call them cars with a future and I think high technology cars play a vital role in the RS story.

Nobody else in the UK makes such a commitment to technology and making use of features like turbocharging, ABS anti-lock braking and viscous couplings is important in the technical appeal of the RS types.

In Britain this appeals to a particular type of customer, but in Germany the hi-tech content is right up front for every sector of the market, making it a very tough place to get your message across. In Britain we've been building the RS thing nearly twenty years and it is a particularly British success. Five years ago a lot of people said that was the end of RS, but now it's just so strong. These are not cars that are generally discounted, never mind what some motoring journals say!

For example, the Sierra RS Cosworth was exactly on sales schedule. We planned to run out of the pre-evolution model in June 1987 and that is exactly the way it's turning out. Each of those cars has gone for good money. The RS badge brings prestige, but have no doubt it is also profitable, highly profitable. . .

What kind of customers buy RS today, and how do they compare with those of the 1970s? Roger Humm replied: The general level of consumer affluence has grown up since models like the RS1600 and 2000 appeared. There is a greater demand for comfort beyond the kind of rubber mat originals we sold. For instance, the Escort Turbo research showed we could offer a softer ride and more comfort features, so that is what we did. The RS still has to perform of course, we'll always be interested in outright performance, but the buyer is demanding more from this kind of car, and that's why we're going along the route we've followed with the Sapphire RS Cosworth where the customer wants far more than a stark interior,

powerful engine and no ride quality, characteristics that might have been accepted ten years ago.

An RS customer today is not a yuppie, because he is not likely to be happy with a mass identity, which does mean that we have to be careful not to go overboard on RS volume. Our potential RS customer can afford, and will buy, the RS for its individuality. Sometimes simply because it is not so freely available as our XR performance variants. Some of these are so successful — XR3i is still over 12.5% of all Escort sales — that potential customers cite the car's sales success as reasons not to purchase. . . And that's the kind of Ford customer, who wants something of an ultimate, that the RS appeals to so strongly.

Answering criticism that the RS Turbo Escort lacks visual identity compared to an XR3i today, Roger Humm admitted: Yes, we could do more to identify the RS in this case, but there's no lack of customers.

Looking to the future of the RS range within a range, Roger Humm predicted: I see no sense to splitting up RS and Cosworth. Some have suggested we may drop RS in favour of Cosworth, but both names have been seen so widely in racing and rallying that I think that is crazy. I see them staying together and I can assure you we'll look at the merits of such variants across the range from Fiesta to Scorpio in years to come.

One more pointer to possible future directions came in this hint with which Ford of Britain's amiable Managing Director concluded his review of the RS story: Anyone who uses their eyes can see there are a lot of women driving our XR2s and XR3s at present. I really hope the natural pattern of RS development and sales evolution, plus the consumer-targeted marketing that I believe in (and for which others often mock me!) will bring women to recognize the merits of the RS Ford in significant numbers too. . .

2

FAVO and SVE

In September 1969 Ford of Britain began to recruit key staff for a new specialist manufacturing operation to be located at Arisdale Avenue, South Ockendon, Essex, RM15 5TJ.

During 1986 one of FAVO's founder members recalled the atmosphere that led to Ford's establishing this 'factory within a factory'. Speaking from his office at Boreham Airfield, where he was acting as a consultant on the RS200 sales programme after more than 30 years of Ford employment, Bob Howe explained: *Alex Trotman — then Product Planning Director, now President, Ford of Europe — vowed that we would never do another J25 Escort Twin Cam project inside the mainstream factories.* This senior Ford executive's opinion was one shared by the majority of those concerned in Ford's primary business — the mass production of the maximum number of cars for the lowest unit costs possible. Although many of the production workers loved specials like the Escort Twin Cam which served to break the monotony, their inclusion ran contrary to the whole production-line principle.

To tackle this basic incompatability between mass-production models and limited-run performance variants Bob Howe, then a product planner who had intimate knowledge of the problems which had been created when the Escort Twin Cam was produced, received an instruction from Ford director Walter Hayes in April 1969: *Go out and find some suitable premises . . . a place where we could centralize production of all our performance and custom cars.*

This reference to 'custom cars' was indicative of Ford's legendary sensitivity and speedy reaction to changing market tastes; at the time the monthly magazine **Custom Car** was achieving impressive circulation growth and was destined to become the top selling motoring magazine in the UK during 1975-77, with peak sales of more than 150,000 copies monthly.

Bob Howe searched all over the Essex lowlands for an ideal site. *There was a plant at Romford that looked good, but I eventually identified the South Ockendon site as most satisfactory for our needs.* Always colloquially known as Aveley, after the nearby Essex suburb, its sprawling and capacious buildings had housed part of Ford Research and Development's engineering staff in the late 1950s and early 1960s, but it was perhaps better known as a warehousing facility and pilot production plant.

Aveley was such a large site that FAVO (Ford Advanced Vehicle Operations), as the new unit was to be known, fitted in easily, and activities like the Motorcraft parts operations, Ford Photographic, Ford Industrial Products and others continued there whilst FAVO was at its peak. The operation was split into two main groups, separated by about a quarter mile of non-FAVO activities. Manufacturing and the bulk of the administration offices were clustered alongside the acres of car park that are used today by the Ford AVO Owners Club for weekend driving tests and club meets, while engineering for FAVO products and RS components was located almost as far away as possible, at the other end of the site. The RS parts operation had been transferred from Ford Competitions at Boreham, and it prospered into the 1980s, a story recounted later in the book.

Bob Howe continued: *Finding the site was not sufficient, for there was still considerable opposition within the company at the highest levels — especially from a Vice President of engineering at the mainstream Dunton site — to the idea of having any kind of in-house Ford operation like this. I got approval for Aveley, but there was still a lot of pressure to have FAVO off-site: some senior executives said they were scared fartless at the thought of 'a goddam Mickey Mouse factory' inside our gates!*

About September 1969 there was approval from Ford of Europe for the project to begin, but there was another hurdle to face in what had already proved a very controversial proposal. Ford's European approval had come about 14 days before Henry Ford II came over on a visit. Walter Hayes took our proposal papers over to him at Grafton Street (a Ford business office hidden away in the side streets between Piccadilly and Park Lane) *and got the ultimate approval in mid-October.*

Only then could we start to recruit personnel and spend some of the allocated budget that had been raised amongst all those committees and approvals meetings. From memory I reckon Ray Horrocks (later to become better known for his management role at Austin Rover) *was the first appointment. It was Ray who managed FAVO from its inception to his departure from the company, a period followed by Stuart Turner's reign from 1972 to closure.*

Bob Howe was an obvious choice for secondment to the Aveley operation, and equally early appointments were performance engineer Rod Mansfield (much more about him later) and former Boreham competitions manager/driver Henry Taylor. But, important though each of these FAVO luminaries was in his own right, the benefit of hindsight allows us to highlight former Halewood production manager Dick Boxall as *the key* appointment. Dick was not the most popular character around senior Ford mainstream management of the period, for it was his tough-talking dynamism that had pushed the Escort Twin Cam through the inertia of large scale plant production. *It was also Dickie who insisted on the overhead 'carousel' roundabout line that we used at FAVO,* recalled Bob Howe.

The Architect. Behind virtually any Ford performance or racing project since the 1960s lay the presence of Walter Hayes. Like the establishment of Ford Advanced Vehicles (FAV) to build the GT40 at Slough, the creation of a complete performance car and components plant, Ford Advanced Vehicle Operations (FAVO), had the enthusiastic backing of Hayes. He was appointed Vice-Chairman, Ford of Europe, in 1984 and retired in 1989.

Outwardly not amongst the most beautiful establishments, the competitions department, Ford Motorsport, at Boreham airfield has supplied the motivation behind most RS projects between 1970 and 1990.

The original plan was for FAVO to have production based on individual service bays. Dickie Boxall simply said he would not come down and work for us if we persisted with that idea! So the round-about line was used. Both it and Dickie were fantastic in my opinion, putting some discipline into the whole operation. That, and the paint booths we installed to get a higher level of finish and quality about these more expensive products, were perhaps the best features of FAVO, concluded Howe.

The Arisdale Avenue operation was Ford's second venture into specialist car building in the UK, the first Advanced Vehicles factory having produced the legendary GT40 at Slough in the 1960s under the directorship of John Wyer and Walter Hayes; Mr Wyer later bought that establishment from the company after the requisite number of GT40s had been made.

On January 14, 1970 the existence of Ford Advanced Vehicle Operations was made public. Production, centred entirely around Ford Escort derivatives, the RS1600 and its pushrod cousin the Mexico, began on November 2, 1970 and settled down initially at a rate of 12 cars per day. In 1971 the staff level was quoted as 250.

The compact engineering department, some of its staff subsequently to graduate to today's Special Vehicle Engineering unit, developed a series of vehicles, most of which were produced elsewhere. The list comprised RS1600; RS2000 Mk1 and Mk2; Escort Mexico, pushrod Mk1 and overhead camshaft Mk2; RS1800; and two Capri versions, the fuel injection RS2600 and the RS3100. In addition to the catalogued models, they tackled a number of interesting prototypes that were not put into production, such as the Frua-bodied Mexico, Mexico Estate, four-wheel-drive Capri, and turbocharged V6 Granada and Cortina.

In organization, FAVO contained all the essential elements of the parent Ford company, from cost accounting, labour relations, product planning and engineering to production line workers. There were five main departments when I worked at FAVO between 1972 and 1974. Engineering was managed by Rod Dyble, production by Dick Boxall and finance by Ron Owers. Mike Bennet, a Reliant executive in the 1980s, was in charge of sales, and when he departed Graham Bridgwater replaced him; Graham later worked over a long period for another former Ford employee, Barrie Gill, when he moved into sports promotion and

Currently managing Special Vehicle Engineering, Rod Mansfield has been a source of inspiration for the faster Fords for over 20 years, often acting as ambassador for the RS products within the company. Formula Ford and Formula 3 champion Gerry Birrell, below, spent a lot of time testing FAVO cars before his death at Rouen in 1973. Another Scot, Tom Walkinshaw took over the driver/development engineer role before establishing his own successful business, TWR.

The first RS2000, not yet registered, parked near the entrance to the FAVO administrative office in December 1974.

By 1971, FAVO had established this training centre on the Aveley site. To the right are two BDA engines, while the well-used Mexico rests in company with a special-build Escort in the background, its wheelarches cut away ready to receive flared extensions.

24

Ford Advanced Vehicle Operations was an assembly rather than a manufacturing plant, Escort two-door bodyshells to Type 49 heavy-duty specification being shipped in direct from Halewood for the RS mechanical underpinnings to be added. By 1971 the overhead carousel line was primarily occupied with the production of Escort Mexicos. Average daily production was below 30 units, and less than 20 a day by no means a rarity. Engines – below is a 1600GT pushrod Mexico unit – joined their assigned bodies in unit with their four-speed gearboxes.

sponsorship. The fifth primary FAVO department was run by Keith Verran and dealt with parts supply.

Successful in many ways, Ford Advanced Vehicle Operations was nevertheless closed after four years, partly because the fixed cost overheads per car made were extremely high. Single-shift production rarely exceeded 20 per day, although I certainly saw days when 28 cars — Mexicos, RS2000s and rare RS1600s — were assembled.

When the fuel crisis of 1973-74 came along, Ford of Germany lost their Motorsports department and Britain then sacrificed the FAVO manufacturing facility. Officially, the last FAVO-produced Escort was completed on January 24, 1975: there is statistical evidence of several hundred RS Escorts being sold during 1975 from existing stocks.

Many elements of FAVO lived on, particularly

25

the work of engineers like Rod Mansfield, Boreham's Bill Meade, Harry Worrall and RS200 product planner Mike Moreton, who also wrote the paper that outlined the specification of the Capri RS3100. Other FAVO engineers remembered for one RS reason or another included three Mikes — Smith, Hillman and Cadby — Allan Wilkinson and Richard Martin-Hurst. Most of them will pop up again later in this book in relevant places. But it is worth reporting here that Smith and Wilkinson both worked on different aspects of Mitsubishi's Starion Group A activities in 1986 (Wilkinson from his Ralliart base at Maldon, Smith for BBW Motorsport at Brackley) and that Martin-Hurst's initiative might well have saved the RS2600 Capri at a crucial juncture. An extrovert character, he used to rally a Rover V8-engined Escort of such violence that it once threw the **Motoring News** fifth wheel halfway into one of Silverstone's grandstands!

The supply of RS Motorsport parts continues from Arisdale Avenue to this day, run by Charles Mead, who performed many of the same tasks for FAVO in the 1970s — more details of that operation later in the book. There were many more Ford Advanced Vehicle Operations employees, and my only regret is that I cannot mention all of them. They created something of a legend, one that seems more revered today than it was at the time. . .

Following FAVO's closure there was a confused period during which some key engineers and product planner Mike Moreton had to work without a formal system to produce the RS2000 and Mk2 Mexico. It should be made plain that the engineering came from that FAVO nucleus — as did the little conversion work carried out to make the few RS1800 road cars that were constructed.

From the late 1970s onward FAVO's engineers were split up and ceased to be a unit, Rod Mansfield even working in Public Affairs at one point. Between 1975 and 1980 it looked as though new RS products were doomed, for there was no particular department or division intent on their manufacture. Ford Competitions at Boreham ran the RS1800 until 1979, winning the World Rally Championship for Makes, and then retired from active participation as production Escorts went front-drive with the hatchback Mk3. The RS1800 defied obsolescence though, rallying its way into the 1980s against all odds, and the David Sutton Motorsport Rothmans team used it

to capture the 1981 world title for Ari Vatanen and Dave Richards.

There were, of course, other labels apart from RS to designate Ford performance. The old GT tag had become *passé*, along with Sport (a marketing designation for cars that at least looked as though they 'did the business'). But new identities were created: in particular, Ford concentrated on the Escort XR3 as the epitome of performance in answer to the influential and successful VW Golf GTI, the introduction of which in 1976 had far-reaching effects on the production-based performance car market.

An expanding demand for vehicles of this type meant that, sooner or later, Ford would need some kind of specialized development facility again. On February 1, 1980 Rod Mansfield became the manager of the Special Vehicle Engineering group. SVE attracted many former FAVO engineers as it grew from an original dozen or so to over 30 regular employees. This time Ford mainstream engineering wanted any performance offshoot firmly in their sight, and Ron Mellor (effectively the boss for all Ford engineering in Europe by 1986) ensured that SVE was found house room at the Basildon Research and Development centre, home to thousands of Ford engineers and usually nicknamed Dunton, after a local village.

The new unit did not start off with an RS product, nor was it to become exclusive to the RS badge, but most enthusiasts are aware of SVE's existence today through the two generations of front-drive Escort RS Turbo cars and their work on both three and four-door Sierra/Sapphire RS Cosworths. For the record, SVE did not perpetrate the original carburettor-equipped Escort XR3 (that came from Ford Germany) but started their specialist engineering labours with the Capri 2.8 Injection, an RS in all but name and representing a decade's progress from the RS2600.

SVE then tackled some truly diverse projects including the Fiesta XR2 in two bodies; the Escort XR3i (first generation — in the second shell it went back to mainstream engineering); Escort Cabriolet production and suspension engineering for Karmann; and the four-wheel-drive Sierra XR4 × 4 (the rear-drive XR4i biplane came from Germany). Like the XR3i, the Sierra went back to the mainstream for its second set of clothes, but, unlike the Escort, it was left substantially alone in respect of its running gear. So, although the RS types are often regarded as the exclusive property of Ford Advanced Vehicle Operations, immediately followed by Special Vehicle Engineering and involving many of the same personnel, the true story was rather more complicated.

It could fairly be said that the Escort nameplate has always received the bulk of RS attention and it was an Escort derivative — the rear transaxle, front engine, turbocharged RS1700T — that was intended to regain the RS competition initiative in the early 1980s. As detailed later, the Escort RS1700T occupied much Boreham and some SVE development time between 1980 and 1983, until rapidly changing circumstances in international rallying led to the project's abandonment.

However, when it was obvious that the RS badge and sporting intention were still as relevant to Ford in the 1980s as they had been in the 1970s, the first front-drive RS, the German Ford Motorsport department's RS1600i, soon appeared. That strong seller encouraged the subsequent generations of front-drive Escort

Turbos, engineered by SVE, and the similarly conceived rear-drive Cosworth Sierra RS. Both types of turbocharged Fords emerged from the current three-stage pattern of development: inspiration from Ford Motorsport; input from Product Planning and SVE; engineering by SVE.

Over the years from the 1968 Escort Twin Cam to the most recent RS200 and evolution Cosworth Sierra RS types, it has been Ford Competitions/ Motorsport (the same Boreham-based department, but carrying different logos) that has kept the RS faith through thick and thin. They *had* to have something better than a straight production Ford to win against the best internationally. Those sporting activities, from the Safari to Silverstone and from the Welsh forests to the Nurburgring, have provided the stimulus for technical development and in return have invested the RS nameplate with the glamour and prestige which have established it amongst the most emotive — and commercially profitable — 'designer labels' for cars.

This RS3100 was displayed at many shows and forums, as well as being used to answer desperate calls for 'a fast Ford for our club night this evening!' It dozes here in the FAVO car park in December 1974, the month FAVO's closure was publicly announced.

Left: just some of the people who contributed to the Sierra RS Cosworth development schedule at SVE in 1985. The longest serving RS figure is not SVE boss Rod Mansfield (in dark glasses beside the car) but Bill Meade, second from left. The distinguished gent in a city suit, fourth from left, is homologation expert and engineer John Griffiths. Like Meade, Griffiths was assigned from the Motorsport department for specific projects such as this.

Below: Keith Duckworth, the celebrated engineer without whom none of it would have happened, in jovial mood, leaning on the tailplane of the first Ford road car to carry a Cosworth badge, though not the first with a Cosworth-developed power unit.

3

Escort RS1600

This is a very rapid little saloon with the ability to leave anything but the Lotus Elan or the exotic GTs a very long way behind. It is also a saloon of considerable character with a unique engine sound similar to that of a supercharged unit, a delightful gearbox (probably the best made in any saloon today) and very agile handling. These qualities, combined with the adequate, if not inspired, braking from a disc/drum arrangement, must put it near the top of the list for the man who must get around Britain in the quickest possible times, without attracting attention. **Motor Sport,** May 1970.

The 'very rapid little saloon' was GNO 420H, a Ford Escort RS1600 on long-term test, and the words are my own. They serve to show that the first RS was an eminently usable road car, not just a homologation special. But less than 1,200 examples of the model were made, between 1970 and 1975, according to sources within Ford. Indeed, one insider told me, *First estimates that we would make and sell 1,000 Escort RS1600s annually proved wildly optimistic. If it had not been for the pushrod Mexico and the later RS2000, we would never have achieved even the modest volumes recorded by FAVO.* At the time of writing, just 22 Escort RS1600s are registered with the Ford RS Owners Club.

Consequently it is for its competition appearances that most enthusiasts remember the RS1600. For this extraordinary amalgam of conventional saloon and high performance 16-valve engine, the latter a pioneer in production terms, proved to be a world-class winner. Its conquering principles were passed on to the boxier Mk2

Escort, the RS1800, which succeeded it and the two models between them established a decade and more of supremacy in rallying in the British Isles and beyond.

Whilst I was revelling in that loaned RS road car's abilities to romp to both Snetterton and Thruxton over the Easter weekend in 1970, March 26-30 had seen Roger Clark and Jim Porter debut the factory RS1600 rally car. Boreham-built, it was a conversion of an Escort Twin Cam that had failed to finish the 1970 Monte. For the tough 60-stage Circuit of Ireland it was in prototype (Group 6) trim, its 1.8-litre iron block BDA delivering 180bhp.

Unsurprisingly, the white and matt black works Ford stomped over the opposition on that event, but its Twin Cam badgework was a reminder that the era of the Twin Cam in rallying was not quite over. This applied equally at the race track, for the RS1600 was not homologated for international competition as a production-based (Group 2) car until October 1970. Thus the Broadspeed 1300GT/1600TC Escorts continued to compete through 1970, whilst the factory rally team confined themselves to sporadic outings for the newcomer that included an overwhelming number of failures to finish, including Clark's lone RS amongst the works TCs for the 1970 RAC Rally, that car having 200bhp at 7,500rpm.

For 1971 the RS Escort, now homologated, took over as the front-line factory rally machine, though Boreham initially opted to stay with the known durability of the Twin Cam on African events including the Safari. But their confidence in the new car quickly grew as it began to prove

Underbonnet view of an immaculate RS1600, NEL 637M, reveals that the BDA power unit was just as tight a fit in the Escort engine bay as the earlier Lotus Twin Cam had been. Production power output was only slightly higher than the later Lotus engines, but the BDA had tremendous development potential for competition. The camshaft drive-belt cover has been removed for this shot.

Most notable detail difference between this early Ford press fleet car and the one shown above is the use of Weber carburettors rather than the Dellortos fitted to the later machine. This example has its belt cover in place, and also illustrates a change in brake servo design.

successful. 1972 brought an unexpected win for Roger Clark and Tony Mason on the RAC Rally in an Esso-sponsored car fitted, unusually for rallying, with Lucas fuel injection. Other 1972 victories included the three home internationals, the Welsh, Scottish and Manx, as well as the East African Safari (Hannu Mikkola was the first non-local resident to achieve this feat) and the Tour of Belgium.

Competition inevitably stimulated the development of the car. Most of those 1972 wins used the BDA engine in its 1800 form with thick-walled iron cylinder block. But Clark's RAC Rally car had the Brian Hart aluminium block which became standard RS1600 wear from October onwards. For road cars it kept the nominal 1,601cc capacity, but the works rallying machinery was bored to 90.4mm to produce a nominal 2-litre that actually measured 1,993cc. Such a specification became the standard rallying engine first in the Mk1 RS1600 and subsequently in the Mk2 RS1800. Power grew from the initial level of 235bhp in 1972 to 255bhp at 8,500rpm by 1979.

So far as I am aware the majority of works engines (I hesitate to say all, but would not be suprised to hear it was thus . . .) were the work of the specialist engine tuners who had developed the light alloy block, Brian Hart Ltd at Harlow. Ferrari fanatic and former Boreham engine man Terry Hoyle has been credited with some of the works engines in other recent accounts, but so far as I know that did not occur during the rear-drive Escort's life as a factory team rally car.

In 2-litre form, with a ZF five-speed gearbox, limited-slip differential and disc brakes on all four wheels, the RS1600 built up a formidable rallying record. Timo Makinen followed up Roger Clark's 1972 RAC Rally success by heading an Escort 1-2-3 on the 1973 event in a car carrying Milk Marketing Board sponsorship and winning again in 1974 in Colibri colours.

An outing to Monte Carlo in 1973 proved that the RS1600 was not invincible on the world stage, but Hannu Mikkola did manage fourth behind the rear-engined Alpine-Renault squad, equalling the best result ever recorded by a Mk1 Escort on the

Uncluttered and rounded lines of the Mk 1 Escort were lent distinction in the RS version by slightly flared front wheelarches and quarter bumpers. The style of the spoked alloy wheels added to this car is a reminder that some RS1600s were supplied with optional Tech Del Minilite magnesium alloy wheels of the type much used in competition.

33

Six-dial instrument pack shared with all the first sports Escorts combined 7,000rpm tachometer and 130mph speedometer with four smaller gauges for temperature, volts, fuel level and oil pressure. Inside the RS1600 boot are the battery and floor-mounted standard steel spare wheel. RS1600 interior had plastic seats as shown, unless the customer specified one of several cloth-covered options, and the flat three-spoke RS steering wheel typical of the period.

classic. Other events abroad suited the car better, and successes included winning the 'Finnish Grand Prix' — the Rally of the 1,000 Lakes — in 1973 and 1974, and events in New Zealand (first and second in 1973) and Belgium (the Boucles de Spa and the Ypres 12 Hours).

Those results represent only an outline of the RS1600's rallying prowess, for many Ford sales companies ran their own successful competition programmes, and the privateers went on winning for years after the works team made the transition to the Mk2 bodyshell and RS1800 in 1975. The home internationals in particular were dominated by Escorts throughout the 1970s — including an incredible first 10 places on the Scottish Rally in 1973 — and as late as 1980 and 1981, in the Ari Vatanen/David Sutton era, the RS1800 could still show the others the way.

In circuit racing trim too the RS Escort was widely successful, able to encompass both short distance 'sprint' races in the UK and longer endurance events at Continental tracks. Early on there was a fleeting pre-homologation non-championship appearance for the jovial, fast-

talking Aussie, Frank Gardner. Frank forsook his Boss Mustang for an August 1970 Thruxton outing in a prototype RS1600 racer; it set pole position time against some reasonable V8 opposition, but the rear axle failed before it could race to glory.

The famous names in circuit racer preparation nearly all had a hand in the legend, but two teams in particular really mattered in RS Escort racing results: Broadspeed, based at Southam in Warwickshire, and Zakspeed of Niederzissen, West Germany. At Broadspeed, Ralph Broad, using Cosworth components, seemed to find the right answer immediately, fielding a 1.7-litre RS1600 in white and Castrol livery for John Fitzpatrick in the 1971 British Championship, with a similar car in silver also making regular European Championship appearances.

Straight out of the box, 'Fitz' took an outright win against the Chevrolet Camaro 5.7-litre V8 opposition of the period. Uprating that superb example of the flared arch Escort racing art from 235bhp to more than 250 by the close of the year, safe to 9,000rpm, was not enough to repeat the

Competition RS1600s inherited the development already carried out on the Twin Cam, so replacement items such as the ZF five-speed gearbox, disc brakes on all four wheels and revised suspension were already familiar competition Escort hardware. But even a successful 1969 Twin Cam, such as the Roger Clark/Jim Porter 1.8-litre car seen here on its way to victory in the Circuit of Ireland, was unlikely to have more than 180bhp, whereas the rallying RS1600s started out with more than 200bhp available and the same basic layout progressed to a reliable 250 to 265bhp in Mk 2 RS1800 guise. Ever stronger transmission components were required to accompany the BDA's prodigious appetite for higher revs and more bhp.

Best known and most successful of the British RS1600 circuit racers were the Broadspeed cars like this 2-litre version in the hands of Andy Rouse, class winner in the 1973 championship.

Chevrolet-killing act but it did give Fitzpatrick a class win in the championship. Broadspeed followed this up with class titles won by BDA-engined Escorts each of the next two years, a reign only ended by the termination of Group 2 racing in favour of Group 1 in 1974, when Broad switched to the Triumph Dolomite Sprint 16-valve with equal success.

Best known 2-litre RS1600 Broadspeed racers were Andy Rouse (1973 class champion) in a car entered by Vince Woodman, and Dave Matthews, the 1972 class winner. Vince Woodman himself took the ultimate RS Escort homologation special, 'RS1300' to the 1.3-litre British saloon car honours in 1973. In that season Les Nash got the 1-litre BDA 'RS1000' Escort concept to a sufficiently reliable pitch to win the smallest class in the UK series as well.

But the RS Escort never equalled Frank Gardner's Escort Twin Cam record of securing the outright British title, as that went to small capacity cars in all the relevant years save 1973 (when Frank did the job again in, umm, dare I say it, a Chevrolet).

Another very well known RS racer was David Brodie. The Escort that made him famous was the 2.1-litre club racing 'Tin Can' in black and gold, rather than his 2-litre RS1600, the latter destroyed in that infamous 1973 Silverstone GP-supporting event when Matthews (in Broad's trick Capri RS2600) and Brodie went cartwheeling at over 140mph after an incident with a backmarker Mini.

By 1974 another club racer was doing wonders for the Escort RS image, Nick Whiting in the All Car Equipe machine facing up to Gerry Marshall in the General Motors/DTV Firenza, amongst others. That yellow Escort was a 16-valver all right, but employing Cosworth FVC power at 1.9 litres, later switching to a full 2 litres.

On the race tracks of the Continent the RS1600 showed the Capri RS2600 that 'Ford leads the way', a contemporary marketing slogan, had a new meaning, though politics prevented more than the occasional win for the smaller car during 1971. For outstanding victories against all odds, I have to nominate the exploits of Zakspeed with their racing RS1600s of 1974. In green and white Castrol livery with additional support from Radio Luxembourg, the Zakspeed Escorts were in astounding form that season.

Hans Heyer, the veteran German racer with a taste for Tyrolean hats and McLarens as *objets d'art*, did not stop at a string of European class wins from Monza to Jarama and back via Zandvoort and Vallelunga . . . No sir! Herr Heyer and Erich Zakowski's 150mph Escort RS won outright against the big BMWs (and the Capri RS3100) in the best-attended event of the year, the Nurburgring 6 hours. To fill the Ford cup of joy, Jochen Mass stepped across from dying Capri to flying Escort so that third place was also recorded for the RS1600.

The reward for that outright 1 and 3 finish at the Nurburgring, and a second overall at Jarama, was for Zakspeed driver Hans Heyer to win the 1974 European Touring Car Championship of Drivers, and the marques title also went to Ford. This in a year that was billed as the battle of Capris and titanic 24-valve BMWs, until the fuel crisis cut budgets, resulting in a series of non-appearances and a number of cancelled races.

The Zakspeed Escort RS1600 racers, in 2-litre 270bhp-plus trim, were multiple winners in the German national championship and had considerable international success too. In 1974 they gained the European Touring Car Championship driver's title for Hans Heyer and the overall marque title for Ford, results that season including an overall win against the big BMWs at the Nurburgring (inset) and second overall at the decisive round in front of Jarama's almost deserted grandstands in October.

Zakspeed were also the moving force behind the RS1600's fabulous German Championship record, providing the champion driver's mount from 1973 to 1975 . . . Yes, the Mk1 did go into 1975 as a winner, even though Zakspeed also fielded the second-generation RS1800 as well.

The *Deutschen Rennmeisters* in the 2-litre Escort were former Capri RS2600 star and rose-grower Dieter Glemser (1973 and 1974) with Hans Heyer snatching the 1975 title using Glemser's 1974 season car.

In 1973 the Zakspeed RS 1600 was credited with slightly under 2 litres (specified with an 89.9mm bore instead of 90mm), 11.5:1 compression ratio, 250bhp at 8,500rpm and 170lb/ft

torque at 7,000rpm. This was enough to propel its 1,826lb to 146mph.

When Heyer won the 1975 title the RS1600 served up by Zakspeed's faithful band (some of whom originally worked 'underground' at the truck dealership, rather than at the better known Niederzissen Ford franchise) deployed a claimed 275bhp at 9,000rpm with an 11.8:1 compression ratio. Peak torque went unreported, but the machine, now weighing 1,936lb, produced acceleration reported at 0-62mph in 4.7 seconds, 0-100mph in 10.1 seconds and 0-124mph in 17.4 seconds. Today you'll find it takes a 48-valve V12 Lamborghini Countach with a claimed 455bhp to equal that 0-62mph sprint. . .

But what of the road car which formed the basis for these prodigious competition machines? Central to the plot, of course, was the engine. The background story of the Cosworth-developed BDA power unit is recounted later in the book: suffice it here to recall that it was a road-going cousin to the FVA Formula 2 racing engine, with an alloy 16-valve twin overhead camshaft head mounted initially on an ordinary iron Kent-series cylinder block as used in crossflow pushrod form in the contemporary Cortina and lesser Escorts. Whereas the FVA had gear-driven camshafts, the BDA employed a toothed belt drive better suited to a road car because it was lighter, cheaper and much quieter.

The BDA had an unusual official cubic capacity of 1,601cc. This came from a bore and stroke of 80.98mm × 77.72mm instead of the usual pushrod engine dimensions of 80.97mm × 77.62mm. This was really just a competition expediency, emphasizing maximum tolerance decimal points to ensure the engine was eligible for a bigger capacity class than 1,600cc, because Ford knew they would rally and race at more than 1.6 litres, having already enlarged the Lotus Twin Cam considerably (for example, to 1.8 litres for Roger Clark to win the 1969 Circuit of Ireland Rally in an experimental factory Escort). The shallowness of the 1,601cc story could be gauged from the use of identical reciprocating components in the pushrod 1600, whether for Formula Ford, the Escort Mexico or contemporary Cortina and Capri models, all quoted as 1,599cc.

The redundant pushrod camshaft was retained for the BDA engine to drive the fuel and oil pumps and the ignition distributor. Other features included twin sidedraught Weber 40DCOE carburettors, then as ubiquitous in performance car use as Bosch fuel injection became in the 1980s. The compression ratio was 10:1 and the simple inlet manifolding was matched with a curvaceous and large bore four-branch exhaust manifold.

Certain details changed during production: some hand-assembled prototypes had a dynamo instead of the officially listed 35amp alternator of 1970. Also, I understand that some late RS1600s, particularly those sent overseas, could have Dellorto, rather than Weber, sidedraught twin-choke carburettors.

Altogether, the BDA was an extremely sophisticated roadgoing 1.6-litre by 1970 standards. Its 120bhp (net) at 6,500rpm, with 110lb/ft torque at 4,500rpm, compare very well with Honda and Toyota 1.6-litre 16-valve units of 17 years later (119-124bhp for Toyota, 125bhp for Honda Integra/CRX).

At its most basic, the BDA had production Cortina 1600 crossflow bottom end components, but included a Tuftrided iron crankshaft. In much the same way, the earlier Lotus Twin Cam head had topped the Cortina 1500 block, and much more recently Volkswagen installed a 16-valve head on the Golf GTI engine to extract 139bhp from 1.8 litres. Substituting a light alloy cylinder block for the original iron one moved the BDA a step further away from its mass-production base and when it came to compete as an international

rally or race engine many high specification steel moving parts from Cosworth came into play to ensure life over 6,500rpm. In production some later RS1800s had a steel crankshaft and improved connecting rods.

The public debut for the BDA came in a Capri, not an Escort. The Capri was announced to the public in January 1969, and for the press launch in Cyprus a little earlier, Ford deployed eight Boreham-built Capri GTs converted to carry the brand new Ford-Cosworth engine. This was simply to cover up the lack of more powerful Capris in production, the planned 3-litre Ford coupe taking until September 1969 to arrive.

Contemporary comments on the BDA-engined Capri were most favourable: *With 6in rim Minilite magnesium wheels the handling was well able to cope with the increased power. It was the way the power manifested itself, rather than the number of horses that was so impressive. With an engine so directly descended from a 140bhp per litre racing unit, and with so many valves and cams, I was expecting plenty of noise and harshness, but this new twin cam is a delightful road unit.*

It pulls smoothly and perfectly happily from 2,500rpm, and from 4,500rpm upwards there is a hard surge of power which obviously went on long after the red sector on 'my' car's tachometer, which was in fact a 1600GT instrument (6,000rpm redline). On the straight, narrow, road from Nicosia to Famagusta, the 16-valver swept along at over 100mph through the rain, with little more noise than the 1600GT made at 80, and a quick change down to third to sweep past any traffic and back up to cruising speed was delightful.

Those words, the best description I have read of driving one of those rare Capri-BDAs, came from **Autosport,** on January 24, 1969, and were penned by the late and deservedly legendary John Bolster. They were accompanied by a fine action picture of one such prototype, TLN 18G, in opposite-lock action on mountain snow. By a coincidence which seemed particularly ironic to me, Peter Newton (then editing **Cars & Car Conversions**) took very similar action pictures, at the same Troodos ski resort location, when Toyota let us loose in their rear-drive 16-valve coupe, the Corolla — but that was some 16 years later! If only Ford and Cosworth had taken more joint commercial advantage of their head start in quad-valve technology. . . .

But the Capri-BDA was a red herring, for it

The factory team RS1600s really did compete in all corners of the world. YEV 207L achieved no result on the snows of the 1974 Arctic Rally in the hands of Hannu Mikkola and John Davenport but had won the 1973 1,000 Lakes in Finland crewed by Timo Makinen and Henry Liddon, the latter tragically killed in an air crash in 1987.

Amid the East African dust, PVX 400K was one of a team trying unsuccessfully in 1973 to repeat Hannu Mikkola's Safari victory of the previous year and is seen here on a reconnaissance run with Mikkola driving the freshly appointed competitions manager Peter Ashcroft.

was obvious to Ford competition manager and former GP driver Henry Taylor and Boreham rally engineer Bill Meade that the Escort was the machine best able to benefit from this new Ford-Cosworth 16-valve development. What did a road-going RS1600 offer the customer at a launch price of £1,447 and a pre-decimal 11s 2d?

Exactly as for the majority of Escort Twin Cams, a white Type 49 heavy-duty bodyshell was employed. The heavy-duty components were: strengthened longitudinal chassis rails from engine bay to back crossmember; stronger flitch plates surrounding the front strut legs; rear sheet metal protected with additional plates to prevent stone damage; reinforced top mounting plates for the MacPherson struts; and mounting points for two short rear axle location radius rods. Apart from the new BDA engine, the mechanical under-

British favourite in action. Bristolian Nigel Rockey was one of a number of rallymen tipped to succeed Roger Clark in the feverish search to find home-grown talent. He and Ron Channon finished 11th on the 1973 RAC Rally in this factory-prepared 2-litre RS1600.

pinnings were also initially drawn from the Escort Twin Cam: indeed some of the first RS1600s *were* Twin Cams with BDA engine transplants. Much of the same equipment also served on Escort Mexicos and the RS2000.

A single-plate clutch was unusual for Escorts in having hydraulic instead of cable operation, again a direct legacy of the earlier Escort Twin Cam and Cortina. The gearbox with its three-rail shift mechanism and ratios was descended directly from the Corsair 2000E and had previously been used in Cortina GTs and Lotus Cortinas during the 1960s.

The back axle, with Timken bearings, did not have a Salisbury limited-slip differential as standard, but many were optionally fitted. So far as I am aware, all rear-drive RS Escorts shared this drum-braked axle, whatever the model, from 1970 to 1980. Basically the same axle can also be found under 1960s Cortinas, GT or Lotus, but remember that the track dimension was different for the Mk1 version. Also, the very first Lotus Cortinas had an A-bracket for location, later deleted for durability.

Front disc brakes of just over 9.5in diameter were also as found on Escort and Cortina Twin Cams, along with the 9in diameter back drums. All the RS Escorts of 1970-80 had vacuum servo assistance, but you will notice variations in rear brake drum dimensions for the RS2000.

Rack-and-pinion steering was fresh to Ford when the Escort was announced and all the RS Escorts featured this excellent system; the official turning circle was just under 30ft and *Autocar* made the lock-to-lock figure a sporting three turns. Competition cars, or those owned by very keen

drivers, may have had the RS 'quick rack' installed, requiring half a turn less lock-to-lock.

All 1970-80 RS Fords shared a MacPherson strut front end with an anti-roll bar jointed into the lower track control arms (TCAs), but spring rates and damper settings varied amongst models. During the production life of the Aveley RS types a fundamental switch was made from the oversteer-biased handling of the original Boreham competition development legacy to a more predominantly understeering mode favoured by the two Scottish racing drivers contracted by Ford as development testers, Gerry Birrell (who died in June 1973) and Tom Walkinshaw.

At the rear the live axle was suspended on leaf springs and located by short radius arms from body to axle casing. It is worth noting that the Ford Escort, RS or otherwise, underwent a fundamental running production change on the rear suspension in November 1973, when the telescopic dampers were shifted from a 'sea leg' inclination of 65.5 degrees to a vertical stance, in anticipation of the layout that would be standard throughout the Mk2 Escort range.

Incidentally, factory competition Escorts had vertical rear damper mounting from the very early days as a 'demon tweak' which provided better axle control and allowed the dampers a more efficient working stroke. All RS1600 works rally cars featured such rear suspension, along with a variety of location rods. This upright rear damper modification could be applied to any Escort by using what was colloquially called a 'turret kit', successfully sold by the Ford RS parts operation over the years along with all the other hardware

Notable victory. LVX 942J kicks up the leaves during a typical Sunday public park outing as Roger Clark and Tony Mason head for a win on the 1972 RAC Rally.

One for the number-plate buffs. LVX 942J is always thought of as Roger Clark's RAC Championship winner, but in its 1971 incarnation it served on the East African Safari for local rally star Joginder Singh.

In 1972 Hannu Mikkola and Gunnar Palm scored the first victory on the East African Safari by anyone other than a local resident, underlining the versatility of both the RS Escort and the Finnish school of rally drivers.

needed to make a near replica of a factory rallying RS1600.

No rear anti-roll bar was specified for roadgoing RS1600s, and the standard dampers, both the front strut inserts and the telescopic rears, were all-hydraulic. FAVO offered Bilstein gas damping with some option packs, and these West German units were frequently purchased as extras by keener owners.

Early RS1600s tended to be in white only, but the other colourful FAVO paint options (including blue, orange, black and red) were also offered during the 1971-74 period. External RS1600 recognition points included quarter bumpers at the front, a style carried over from both the original Lotus Cortina and the Escort Twin Cam. There was also a black grille, an RS badge on the bootlid beside the Escort motif and one RS1600 silver and blue badge per front wing. Headlamps were round, 7in diameter, quartz iodine 110/55 watt units, the same spec as late Escort TCs but markedly better than the small rectangular units chosen for the more expensive versions of the normal Mk1 Escort.

The front wings were distinguished from mundane mass-production Escorts by a modest flare to the wheelarches. In 1971 the mainstream Ford production plants picked up this feature for the 1300GT-engined Sport. Originally the flare was felt necessary because the Escort had been

designed to operate on 12in diameter wheels, whereas both Escort TC and RS1600 employed strong steel 5.5 × 13in rollers, but I have seen Mk1 Escorts running around today on 13in diameters without visibly flared front arches, so perhaps it was as much a matter of style as of practicability.

The Type 49 heavy duty body could at first also be identified inside the boot, for the battery was moved from the engine bay aft (again as in the Lotus Cortina and Escort TC) and mounted alongside a semi-upright spare wheel. In October 1972 the Mexico had its battery moved back into the engine bay, allowing vertical spare wheel mounting, but the RS1600 retained rear battery location throughout production and the spare stayed on the floor.

An RS1600 cabin could feature a number of genuine factory finishes, according to year and option pack. All these RS Fords used the six-dial instrumentation that came from the Escort 1300GT and included 8,000rpm tachometer (redline at 6,500); 140mph speedometer; plus smaller dials for water temperature, battery conditions, fuel contents in the 9-gallon/40.9-litre tank and oil pressure, the latter uprated to 60lb/sq in.

The steering wheel featured in all the early publicity shots and most press cars was a dished three-spoke Springalex, often carrying the Ford badge or the symbol of Ford Sport, the defunct factory-backed sports motor club. By 1971 this

GVX 883N was the Colibri-sponsored RS1600 freshly built for Timo Makinen and Henry Liddon to win the Lombard RAC Rally in 1974, middle of the hat-trick years for Timo. Detail shots illustrate the comprehensive preparation of the works-team cars, every modification the result of lessons learned the hard way in the heat of competition. Among the more obvious features are the brace between the front strut top mounts and the oil tank in the boot for the dry-sump system.

'thick leather rim' item was listed amongst standard RS1600 features, along with inset reversing lamps, dipping mirror and grab handles. Subsequently a flat three-spoke steering wheel, shared with other RS products, became the norm.

An RS1600 owner could also specify either a Custom or Clubman Pack when ordering a car from one of the 70 or so British RS dealers amongst the Ford network in the 1970s. The Custom Pack appeared in October 1971 priced £108.44 tax-paid and included an effective sound insulation kit, deep pile carpet, cloth seat trim (standard specification was a chunky, split-prone plastic), a compact centre console, map reading lamp, electrically heated rear screen and cloth trim for the back seats. Such items were rendered partially redundant in October 1972 when the company installed carpets as standard and, later, trim plushness generally improved in the wake of the RS2000's debut in 1973.

A Clubman Pack was offered from July 1971 at £145.24 and comprised four auxiliary lamps and brackets, a simple hoop-style rollover bar, wraparound bucket seats in cloth trim, Bilstein gas front damping with stiffer coil springs, and a map-reading lamp that later became standard equipment. Other popular options at the period were a sump guard at £49.02, a sump shield and oil cooler at £67.36 and chunky 165 × 13 Dunlop SP44 rally tyres at £17.30 the set, when ordered on a new car.

The vehicle number within the engine bay (part of the main black and white Ford product plate, riveted to the front rail that the bonnet closes on) should display the Ford code BFAT (B = Britain; F = Aveley; A = Escort; T = Two door), carry a five-figure ID number, and should record a production date between November 1970 and December 1974, although RS Escorts were assembled during 1975 after FAVO's official closure.

Any Ford engineering prototype (quite a rarity for this model!) should really have been destroyed by the company under an Inland Revenue agreement, or reworked for another model option and then faced with the knacker's yard. Some did get away via employees, but the company usually caught up with them!

Additional new information about the early days of FAVO and the RS1600 occasionally still comes to light. From a chance meeting with a former colleague, Kevin Cooney, I gathered some fascinating snippets about the production and launch of the first RS1600s. Today, Kevin runs Impulse, an Abingdon marketing company, but in 1970 he was amongst the first FAVO employees, placed in charge of a small customer service and advice department. Also in this area were Martin Sharp, now Deputy Editor of *Cars & Car Conversions* magazine, and Bob (not Rod) Mansfield, who still works for Ford.

On the subject of the early manufacture of the RS1600, before the Aveley production line began in late 1970, Kevin recalled: *Myself and Ric Lee from Sales used to go up on the overnight sleeper from London to Liverpool to collect the early RS1600s from Halewood.*

Because of the way the production lines were arranged up there, they would actually build a complete J25 Twin Cam, then remove the engine and install the BDA. So all those early cars really were Escort Twin Cams with BDA power. I remember our tour around the country to meet our dealers with those GNO-registered RS1600s labelled 'Potent Mix'...particularly as some of the cars at the back would have their bonnets wired down and a Twin Cam still installed, because there were so few RS1600s around in the earliest days!

I can also remember us taking the 'Potent Mix' show to Silverstone one day when March were sorting out a very, very sick Can-Am car — really evil, it looked, with those great ram-stack trumpets. As our dealer demos came to an end, Chris Amon was spluttering round in the March and Ronnie Peterson was watching, Colin Crabbe having brought him up to try and get him a ride in the Cam-Am car.

Ronnie was a really nice bloke to have around, quiet and polite, so when he asked if he could drive an RS1600 we agreed. He came back so chuffed...Yes, he really had gone round faster than Amon in the sick March! I went for a ride alongside him — that RS was not in a straight line for very

long! It was really a fabulous experience. I hadn't seen anything like it again until the 1980s, when I got Jonathan Palmer to take me round Thruxton, concluded Kevin Cooney.

The RS1600 did not get off to a good start in the reliability stakes, camshaft seizures occuring even on pampered press fleet cars. I think it is fair to say that it is a tough task to keep one running well today. Although a lot more is known now about the engine — forget that original Ford claim to run on two-star, for instance! — and parts are unlikely to dry up in the way they have for the Lotus Twin Cam, keeping the rest of the car tidy, trimmed and original is almost a full time job, if it is used regularly.

However, if you decide that an RS1600 is for you — and there are probably still more competition cars around than those kept for road use — I would certainly encourage that choice. For I can honestly say the RS1600 was one of the most exciting cars given into my care. Even though it was 'owned' alongside a Lotus Seven, the RS1600 loan car was *the* potion to turn blue days into joyful miles. It was also the first public product of the Cosworth-Ford partnership which is now an established tradition and looks set to provide more exciting road cars yet. And for the RS story it was quite an opening act.

RS1600 on the road

I am indebted to Ford AVO Owner's Club and their *Havoc* magazine for allowing me to use William Arnold's account of three years' RS1600 ownership and to Ford RSOC secretary Kevin Shortis, the 40-year-old M25 police patrolman who reported his more recent experience with NEL 637M, a pristine red RS1600.

William Arnold's RS1600 is a diamond white 1974 machine with alloy block and the later, upright rear damper layout. His interesting and enthusiastic comments make clear how much he values TOO 456N.

To me it is one of the best little cars Ford has ever made, possessing a unique charm and character... To own one, though, requires a certain amount of dedication as regards servicing, which can be quite tedious, especially in respect of adjusting the valve clearances.

A Group 2 RS1600 (OOO 96M, a widely used machine that won the Circuit of Ireland for Billy Coleman) and a Granada service 'barge' in front of the mobile classroom used for Ford Rally School activities. In 1975 a day's tuition cost around £25.

The first batch of RS1600 road cars lined up with their 'Potent Mix' stickers for a dealer promotion at Mallory Park in the summer of 1970.

But one cannot afford to skimp here, and this is possibly why some owners have experienced problems. Fortunately, my own example has proved to be very reliable on the whole; the original owner must have thought so, to keep it eight years! He even went touring in Europe with it one year...

One of the criticisms most frequently levelled at RS1600s is that the carburation continually goes out of tune, resulting in poor performance and economy. Yet I have never found mine to require anything more than slight rebalancing of the carburettors at the normal service intervals. I have found the economy of my car to be surprisingly good for an RS1600 at 27mpg normally driven, 31mpg on a long run and 23mpg when really hard pressed, reports Arnold.

At something over 75,000 miles this RS1600 was dismantled for a rebuild because of the oil consumption, its only major previous problems being a burnt-out exhaust valve and a seized needle bearing in the rear of the crankshaft.

Kevin Shortis bought his RS1600 from former racer Nick Whiting's All Car Equipe in May 1986. It had covered 69,000 miles before he sold it in 1987.

The vehicle has one of the full alloy BDA engines and is in the basic original roadgoing trim. I use the car during the summer and I garage it in the winter months, he explained.

The good points: a car that sounds and drives like a car should. The performance surprises many modern car owners. Wherever the car goes some interest is always shown and some good friendships have been born as a result. The bad points: there are none! The only minus is that I will not drive it in the winter months. I do drive it in summer rain, but never over winter salt.

This RS is one in a long line owned by me and I hope also to purchase an RS1800 in the future. . .

4

Escort Mexico

The Escort Mexico, in Mk1 form, was not in fact marketed with an RS label. But that was really only a detail. In every other way, in its design and development, where it was made and sold, and the kind of customers it appealed to, it was so close to the RS-badged Escorts of the FAVO era that the story would be incomplete if it were omitted from these pages. Apart from anything else, it was the pushrod-engined Mexico which provided the bread and butter for FAVO's production line. When the time came for the Mexico to take on the Mk2 body shape, and an overhead-camshaft engine to go with it, FAVO was no more, but the car's status was fully acknowledged for it was advertised as an RS and had an RS-embossed steering wheel.

An important achievement of the Mexico was to bring RS-style motoring to a wider market than its more specialized cousins could. During 1972-75 many more Mexicos were registered in the UK than any other RS product and a substantial percentage of enthusiast club membership totals today are Mexico owners.

The second Mexico, sold between 1976 and 1979 (only eight cars in the last 12 months), was a commercial failure by Ford standards, over-shadowed by the RS2000, but the Ford figures show that it sold best in its last year of manufacture, 1978. Even then its peak was less than half the RS2000 Mk2 sales total for 1978. . .

Mechanically speaking, the first Mexico was the simplest RS and that may well be one of the key reasons that so many survive into the 1980s. Although great stress was laid by Ford at the car's announcement in November 1970 on the link with the pushrod-engined victors of the London-Mexico World Cup Rally that spring, the customers knew that they were getting basically an RS1600 with the pushrod Kent crossflow engine.

Instead of the RS1600's advanced BDA power unit, with its 16 valves and double overhead camshafts, the Mexico employed the engine previously well known for its role in the Cortina GT and 1600E and the Capri 1600GT. Peak power of 86bhp came at 5,500rpm and torque delivery culminated in 92lb/ft at 4,000 revs.

Ancillary details were much the same as in the engine's other applications: compound twin-choke downdraught Weber (32/36 DGV-FA); compression ratio, 9:1; oil-filled, ballast resistor coil to serve the ignition circuit's Motorcraft AG22 spark plugs. The conventional distributor, with its contact breaker, governor weights and manifold vacuum advance system may well be as incomprehensible to today's youth as the modules, podules, sensors and microchips of an RS Sierra are to the older enthusiast!

This inline four, of all-iron construction, had a capacity measured at 1,598cc, based on the usual 80.97mm × 77.62mm bore and stroke. The BDA engine, sharing the same block and crank, was always specified at the top tolerance figure of 1,601cc (80.98mm × 77.72mm) in the catalogues of the period, to allow the RS1600 to race and rally in the 1.6 to 2-litre class, but for the Mexico customer such details were incidental. The 1600GT motor had a proven reputation in road cars and Formula Ford 1600 for toughness and comparative simplicity. Mated to transmission and chassis components that were designed and tested to accommodate the BDA version's 120bhp, the engine held the promise — one amply fulfilled over the years — of performance motoring with affordable running costs.

A slightly smaller diameter clutch plate, of 7.54in diameter, was specified to replace the 8.09in RS1600 unit. The hydraulic system was altered during the production run, the common clutch and brake fluid reservoir of the earlier cars being changed in favour of separate systems.

Other changes resulted from the original Cortina/Escort TC/RS plan of mounting the battery in the boot being abandoned after October 1972. The brake servo was relocated from its original position in the standard Escort battery tray zone to a mounting bracket extended from the front bulkhead. The battery could then be mounted in the engine bay. The spare wheel was moved from its old place bolted to the boot floor and was secured by rubber webbing and wire security hooks in a near-upright position to the left of the boot, slotting into the battery's old abode.

The four-speed gearbox was as for the RS1600, a heritage of the Corsair/Cortina/Escort Twin Cam lineage. For the driver that meant the kind of slick and swift gear changes characteristic of performance Fords in the 1970s, something less easy to achieve with transverse engines and front-wheel drive, although the rear-drive Sierra/Sapphire RS reminds us that the company still knows about gearchange quality, even if it has to be bought from Borg-Warner in the USA.

Ratios remained as for the RS1600: first 2.97:1, second 2.01:1, third 1.40:1, and fourth a direct 1:1. Others might have changed the final drive in recognition of having 86bhp instead of 120bhp, but the Mexico retained the familiar 3.77:1. Nobody complained about the acceleration rate of 10.7 seconds for the 0-60mph sprint, in fact it was above average for a £1,150 performance car in 1970-71. The advantage of that comparatively tall rear axle ratio was that even hard driving failed to pull the parsimonious crossflow much below 30mpg; including testing, *Autocar* returned 27.5mpg overall.

Top speed was quoted by Ford as slightly in excess of 100mph and *Autocar* managed just 99mph. More important were the economy and acceleration, combined with exploitable handling, capable brakes and simple servicing needs. On the latter point the Mexico was particularly undemanding by the standards of the era in which it was

produced. The Ford that was reputably concocted on the back of an envelope during the return flight from those celebrations in Mexico, and was initially built by converting existing RS1600s, required a major service with oil change only at 6,000-mile intervals.

It is simplest to say that the Mexico was identical in its running gear and Type 49 body to the RS1600, but it might be useful to run over some of those details again. An important point is that the RS2000, Mk1 or 2, differed from both the RS1600 and Mexico considerably. Neither the rear brakes, differential ratio nor gearbox were the same, never mind the 2-litre OHC motor, so don't regard these visually similar RS products as necessarily mechanically compatible.

The servo assisted braking of the Mexico was provided by solid front discs measuring 9.62in, with 9.0in × 1.75in drums at the rear, a size familiar to owners of some non-V6 Capris.

Steering was by the Escort Mk1's usual rack-and-pinion, but the FAVO suspension shared only the basic layout of MacPherson struts and a live axle on leaf springs with mainstream production Escorts. Negative camber, to the noticeable extent of 2.2 degrees, was introduced by FAVO's special front crossmember. Springs were unique to the Mexico/RS1600 range, with rates of 100lb/in for the front coils and 97lb/in for the rear multiple leaves. The axle was restrained by the faithful trailing radius arms of Twin Cam heritage, and there were Armstrong hydraulic dampers; gas dampers were one of many options and after-market items that are likely to be found in a secondhand Mexico's specification today.

Strong slotted steel 5.5in × 13in diameter wheels with plain chrome hubcaps and four-stud fixing were standard equipment. Production specification tyres, usually by Goodyear or Dunlop, were 165 SR radials. They were not identified as 70 series aspect ratio in those days before 'low profile' became an in phrase with the performance orientated public.

Although that basic 165 SR 13 fitment served Fords from the Cortina TC through the Escort TC to the RS Mk1 Escorts, note that standard and optional wheel specifications changed frequently. Many Escort competitors followed the expensive factory team route of fitting Minilite magnesium alloy multi-spoke wheels, very strong and light but with a limited life because of progressive embrittlement. The Minilite look became well known and

Simple but effective recipe: 1600GT engine slotted into an Escort shell modified to RS1600 standards to make the Mexico a practical sporting proposition. Broad decal stripes were optionally alternative to the twin coachline style.

PGU 97K, right, is one of the rarest Mexicos alive. Owned by Phillip Elby, pictured, it is one of only three such prototype estates to be built, dating from 1972. The black vinyl roof was original equipment.

Two interiors showing the original dished steering wheel and, far right, the flat-spoke wheel and sports seat. RS and Mexico facia badges and centre console are later additions, not standard equipment.

is now perpetuated by some popular aluminium alloy imitations available in the UK. But the FAVO four-spoke wheel in the standard 5.5in × 13in measurement, announced in January 1971 and available on new cars from March, soon became the most popular optional choice. Designed and engineered by Ford mainstream and FAVO engineering together, these forged alloys were manufactured by GKN Kent Alloys Ltd.

Ford steel wheels are virtually a subject in themselves. I can swiftly think of five types (Cortina and Escort TC, Cortina 1600E, Capri 3-litre, two stages of RS) that will fit RS Escorts and I am sure that is just the beginning. It is worth noting that the first Mexico wheels had rectangular slotted sections next to their safety ledge rims, but later Mexicos and Mk1 RS2000s had circular orifices and an attempt at styled steel 'spokes'. Like all but the eagerly stolen Rostyles of 1600E fame, these Ford-supplied steel wheels proved man enough for competition use in FF1600. RS Escorts also used various standard-size steel wheels in events such as the Mexico road rally challenge and the Tour of Britain.

As with the RS cars, Mexico buyers were offered several packages of additional equipment. July 1971 saw the debut of the Clubman pack at £145.24, that figure swiftly overtaken by a taxation change that left it at £139.06. This Rallye Sport package comprised quadruple quartz iodine fog and long-range lamps from Cibié; a roll-over hoop; fixed-back sports seats made in Britain; a flexible map-reading lamp; Bilstein gas damping front and rear, plus stiffer coil springs that, on the press demonstrator, raised the ride height. Further options on the competition theme included QI bulbs for the headlamps, a sump shield, an oil cooler and the then-fashionable Dunlop SP44 'chunkies' at just £17.30!

In October 1971 the most significant option pack for RS products made its debut. The Custom Pack was still with us in 1988 as an extra equipment option on the Escort RS Turbo, and the manner in which buyers were prepared to spend extra on their RS1600s, Mexicos and RS2000s led Ford to revise their RS marketing approach considerably. That first Custom Pack comprised a sound insulation kit of absorbent panels at known reverberation points (particularly evident on the Mexico at a 4,000rpm motorway cruising speed); thick pile black carpeting instead of rubber mats; cloth trim for improved front seating with matching back seat

squabs. A small centre console, map reading light and electrically heated rear screen were also classified as Custom components.

The price was £108.44 and the Custom Pack was a Mexico option to the end, minus the carpeting when that became standard in October 1972. The Mk1 RS2000 was to feature the key ingredients of the Custom Pack in its basic specification, but Ford accountants relied upon the extensive option list and Race/Rallye packs for extra income, and the Custom Pack was back with a vengeance on the RS2000 Mk2 and has remained a weapon in the Ford RS marketing arsenal ever since.

By December 1974, the official closing month of FAVO, the 86bhp Mexico was priced at £1,854.48. That compared with £2,076.67 for the first RS2000 and £2,528.94 to purchase an RS1600.

By 1975, ordinary Escorts had switched to the Mk2 shell and in due course the Mexico followed suit. Born in January 1976 and killed in September 1978, the second Ford Escort to bear the Mexico logo was more closely identified with the RS mystique and had an overhead-camshaft engine, yet it did not repeat the Mk1's success. There was nothing wrong with the 'Ford Escort RS Mexico' as it was now titled, in fact it was thoroughly agile and a pleasure to drive. However, at £2,443, compared with £2,847 for a contemporary RS2000 which had more of everything that an RS buyer was likely to prefer, the second Mexico struggled for each sale against its big brother.

There was another sales complication: Ford had taken those mechanical elements of the previous Mexico that might appeal in the showroom and wrapped them up in a second-generation Escort Sport (also available as a 1300) for less than £2,000. Thus the new Mexico was squeezed between a cheaper 1.6-litre of sporty appearance and 11bhp less or the RS2000 offering another 15bhp, radical restyling and considerable mid-range punch for just another £403. . .

As for previous generations of rear-drive RS Escorts much of the Mexico's running gear was shared with its more powerful brethren. The 1,593cc engine, at 87.67mm × 66mm, shared neither bore nor stroke with that of the RS2000 but the belt-drive single overhead camshaft unit was of the same Pinto family with the same 9.2:1 compression ratio. Carburation was provided by a

Escort Mk2 in Mexico trim. Garrie Sadler's restored car shows the style of bumpers, spoilers and decals adopted for the second Mexico. Minilite replica wheels are a later addition.

Pinto 1600 engine powered the Mk 2 Mexico, the absence of the production drive-belt cover on this example emphasizing the unit's single overhead camshaft layout. The RS-emblazoned exhaust manifold was the only major engine change.

Four-spoke alloy wheels were optionally available from 1971, their centres displaying the early RS badge. Slotted steel wheels were the alternative style often fitted.

32/36 Weber twin-choke unit, type DGV, slightly different from the RS2000's outwardly similar DGAV.

In the RS tradition the engine was uprated slightly over its normal service power output, for it was usually rated at 88bhp at 5,700rpm for duty in contemporary machinery such as the Capri II 1600S. An extra 7bhp was claimed for the special Mexico exhaust system, and maximum power was therefore reported as 95bhp at 5,750rpm, with torque practically identical to the Capri at 92lb/ft delivered at 4,000rpm.

The second Mexico shared its four-speed gearbox, rack-and-pinion steering, disc/drum braking, 5.5in × 13in steel wheels and many other features with the RS2000. In fact the German-sourced gearbox went back, in RS terms, to the first RS2000. The ratios were: first 3.65:1, second 1.97:1, third 1.37:1, fourth 1:1 and reverse 3.66:1. The transmission was completed by the RS2000's 3.54:1 final drive and 175/70 radials to produce the same 18.6mph per 1,000rpm in top gear. However, the tyre specification was subtly different as Ford were able to use SR speed ratings on the Mexico rather than the RS2000's HR fitment, that variation forming the only significant reflection of the smaller-engined car's lower performance.

The Mk2 Mexico's performance was not measured by the contemporary weekly magazines, but I had one to compare with an RS2000 and an RS1800. The figures obtained on a dampish day using the **Motoring News** fifth-wheel electronic speedometer are reproduced in the appendix and include a 0-60mph time of 11.1sec and a standing-start quarter mile in 17.8sec. A comparison with the results for the Mk1 version obtained by **Autocar** tells us that the first and second generations of Mexicos were broadly similar in performance ability, the Mk1's deficit in horsepower (86bhp against 95bhp) offset by the later car's greater weight, taller gearing and less aerodynamic shape.

Mexico on the road

I found no shortage of people willing to talk about their experience as Mexico Mk1 proprietors. As ever I owe some of my up to date background knowledge to Peter Williams and Martyn Castick of the AVO Owners Club, but in the search for new material, I interviewed 22-year-old Paul Heritage of the Bucks, Berks and Oxon RSOC region.

Paul represents the corps of younger owners now gaining their first taste of performance motoring through the Fords of the 1970s. There were no compromises about the Modena green Mexico he presented for photography. He acquired it privately for £1,500 and decided to *Replace everything I could, and you could say that virtually everything outside the engine has had some work. Even that has got a K&N air filter and Janspeed manifold, but the engine itself was in really good condition for a car that had been around the clock once!*

In spending at least £5,000 on this Mexico, Paul reckoned that the body had swallowed most money. *The panels, such as front wings, upright front sections, bonnet and boot lid came to about £600. Most expensive single item was the boot at more than £90 which puzzled me a bit as the bigger and more complex bonnet was £55. Those new Mexico badges cost £5.80 each.*

Most of the stuff came direct from Ford, ordered through West, at Thame, Oxon.

They are not RS dealers but, as with Prestwoods at Wycombe, they seem to be able to get a surprising amount of RS stuff for the older cars.

Jim Avery sprayed the car and I spent about two days putting the stripes on. They are an exact copy of the real thing from RSR at just over £60...I enquired of a specialist about the originals they have in stock, but they wanted £175 plus VAT! I simply wasn't prepared to pay that kind of money...

Mechanically, Paul has had to replace the rear axle, because it was whining, and the car (known to Paul prior to purchase) has had two differentials in recent years — a fact attributed by his teasing club colleagues to all those traffic light Grand Prix starts!

Most serious running problem in the 25 to 30,000 miles Paul Heritage has covered has been the continual recurrence of split water hoses, particularly to the heater. Paul says: *They're all bought from the dealer but sometimes I've found seven splits and lost all the water...I have checked all the obvious things like thermostat and radiator flow, but we don't seem to be able to get to the bottom of it.*

Paul reports — from the safety of the Goodwood circuit — that this Mexico will pull *just over 6,500 in top. It indicated 122mph in favourable conditions, but any way you look at it, down to an honest 110mph-plus, you can say I'm satisfied with the way it goes. Fuel consumption is good, at least 30mpg on a run, and I like the car as much as ever.*

I don't think it dates at all and I'm looking forward to getting all the correct wheels, tyres and interior bits like the seating and steering wheel to return it to an original look, concluded Paul Heritage proudly.

As to how the second Mexico felt to an owner in the 1980s, I had a fascinating letter from N. Leslie Jones in Newcastle-under-Lyme, Staffs, to confirm that RS owners are not confined to any predetermined or limited age group.

Amongst the understatements from this 77-year-old enthusiast, with 63 years of licensed driving and motorcycling behind him, was this explanation: *The engine is smooth so long as 30mph in top gear is avoided, as it should be. It feels best at 60mph and over. I don't think I have ever exceeded 90mph, unless I have been too busy to look at the speedometer. As I am 77 years old this year I cannot afford to take risks....though I still enjoy motorcycling on fine days.*

His well thought out and beautifully typed letter contained a lot of useful service information. Mr Jones' Mexico was bought new in August 1977 from T. C. Harrison at Newcastle-under-Lyme, receiving the full Ziebart treatment, RS2000 seating, door trim from the same source and a full-length Tudor Webasto sliding roof.

That folding roof has remained waterproof over 10 years and 54,754 miles. Standard exhaust systems lasted to 23,800

miles in 1980 and 46,000 miles in 1985; today the Mexico wears a Falcon stainless steel exhaust.

Other running modifications have included a Kenlowe electric fan (11,000 miles onwards) and the same company's electronic ignition. Leslie Jones commented that these items proved to be excellent, although the substitute ignition did not make any appreciable difference to performance or smoothness throughout the rev-range.

In December 1984, when 44,000 miles were recorded, the electronic ignition was abandoned because the Motorcraft distributor bearings were worn, the Bosch replacement not catering for Kenlowe's rotating magnet system. Spark plugs are changed every 10,000 miles, while the battery made it to March 1984 and 40,683 miles, longevity which Mr Jones attributes to *the regular use of Battoids, obtainable at Halfords.*

Oil changes have been made every 3,000 miles with a new filter at 6,000 and the only serious maintenance problem to be faced was the installation of a new brake master cylinder at 50,967 miles in July 1986. At this juncture automatic brake bleed valves were fitted, which makes brake bleeding a simple matter for one person.

Leslie Jones summarizes his lengthy ownership of the Mk2 Mexico like this: *It has always been satisfying and the close-ratio gearbox is a joy to use. The car has a certain character and feel about it which seems absent with the general run of mass produced cars of today.*

5

Escort RS2000

As a basic idea, the concept of lowering the 2-litre SOHC Cortina power unit into the Escort had proved nearly as popular amongst the specialists as the earlier Escort speciality of inserting the pushrod OHV 1600GT engine. There were probably several hundred such 2-litre Escorts running around by the time the factory turned its attention to the combination. Just as with the 1600GT Mexico the result proved immediately popular.

In contrast with the RS1600, which came about basically to provide Ford with a means of participating successfully in motorsport, and particularly in rallying, the RS2000 was born for directly commercial rather than competition reasons. Hence it foreshadowed the way in which most manufacturers now broaden their model ranges with profitable mass-production performance derivatives.

The need was for an Escort providing higher performance, and perhaps more refinement, than the existing Sport or Mexico versions but without the cost and complexity, both of production and servicing, associated with the RS1600 and its specialized engine. Such a practical performer might well appeal to a wider market than just the fervent enthusiasts drawn to FAVO's earlier products, an idea confirmed by the reaction of a visiting party of RS factory personnel and dealers from Ford of Germany. Stuart Turner had arranged for them to see and try the prototype RS2000 at Brands Hatch and the result was an order worth some £2 million for left-hand-drive cars.

The LHD version was ready for announcement on July 4, 1973: it was not until October 11, 1973 that the first RS2000 was released for RHD sale. In both cases the design and engineering was carried out during 1972 and 1973 by FAVO under the direction of Rod Dyble.

There were less than 20 engineers at Aveley, but it has to be remembered that the might of Ford's mainstream engineering and production facilities provided the basic Escorts on which FAVO worked. The primary building block was the basic two-door Mk1 bodyshell with its modest use of glass and the Type 49 heavy-duty features already described in relating the RS1600 tale. These strengthened bodies were sent down to the FAVO facility from Halewood on Merseyside, usually trimmed, painted and wired. The Arisdale Avenue workforce then united body and mechanical components on those overhead lines.

FAVO engineering chose some simple solutions from the school of practical transplants to graft the big four into an Escort. Most obvious was the deletion of the normal mechanical fan between radiator and engine to gain a few extra inches lengthways. The new, larger radiator was cooled when necessary by a Kenlowe electric fan placed between radiator and front grille.

The engine, with bore and stroke dimensions of 90.82mm × 76.95mm giving a capacity of 1,993cc, and a 9.2:1 compression ratio, was not specifically modified to produce extra power, but the electric fan was worth about 2bhp so Ford quoted 100bhp in place of 98 for the similarly equipped Cortina. Peak torque was 107lb/ft at just 2,750rpm. A new aluminium sump was fitted to adapt the engine to the Escort front cross-member and a central oil pick-up point was fitted as a precaution against oil surge.

Connecting the motor to a wide-ratio gearbox, as used in 2-litre Cortina and Capri models of the period, required a new aluminium bellhousing. Coincidentally this beefy component moved a critical resonance point from 5,400rpm to over 6,000 revs, allowing the RS2000 driver far more peace and quiet than might have been expected from Mexico and RS1600 experience. FAVO had wanted a more civilized product and this bellhousing really assisted in that aim. The four-speed gearbox introduced a different set of ratios from those used previously. Lower gears, compared with the RS1600's in brackets, were: first, 3.65:1 (2.97:1); second, 1.97:1 (2.01:1); third, 1.37:1 (1.40:1). Top gear was direct in both cases, but the RS1600 ran a 3.77:1 final drive to produce 17.8mph per 1,000rpm whilst the RS2000's axle ratio was 3.54:1, giving 18.7mph per 1,000rpm. In practical terms this meant 70mph demanded 3,750rpm, about 250rpm less, in the bigger-engined car.

Some RS2000s today, usually of the later series, have been equipped with Ford five-speed gearboxes from Capri or Sierra stock. Whilst this is a sensible conversion for anyone who spends much of their time on motorways, it is worth pointing out, if originality is of any concern, that Ford five-speed gearboxes did not appear in production until the 1980s. Capris and rear-drive Escorts, RS or otherwise, in factory trim only ever had five forward gears in the 1970s for competition use, and those boxes came from ZF rather than from a Ford plant.

Within the new alloy bellhousing was an 8.5in diameter clutch plate, operated by Ford's traditional cable, rather than the hydraulic conversion that had been a feature of earlier RS and Twin Cam Escorts. The gearchange mechanism was modified from that of the Cortina, with a raised pivot point for the single-rail shift linkage. This simple alteration provided the kind of precise, short-throw gearchange that won road test plaudits and has yet to be equalled, never mind bettered, by current Ford five-speed designs.

FAVO's traditional combination of 5.5J wheel rims and 165 SR 13 tyres was retained, but an increasing percentage of customers took the four-spoke alloy wheel option rather than the steel units. Availability of wider alloy rims, still with 13in diameter, continued to grow during this period and not many machines remain on production steel wheels today.

The usual 9.62in solid front brake discs were employed, with vacuum servo-assistance, but the rear drums were decreased in size to 8in diameter and 1.5in width compared with the RS1600, Escort TC and Mexico dimensions of 9in × 1.75in also found on many Capris. Suspension, of course, was as for other Escorts, with MacPherson struts at the front and a live axle on multi-leaf springs at the rear (single-leaf units were reserved for competition use but could be supplied through the RS parts or X-pack systems). There was one change even during the Mk1 RS2000's life: as for the mainstream Escort, FAVO had to incorporate the vertical rear damper mounting changes of November 1973. Since that initial batch of left-hand-drive RS2000s took up most production until autumn 1973, when the RS2000 was officially released for UK sales, it is unlikely you would find a UK-market RS2000 with the original, inclined, rear dampers, unless you came across one of the XVX 390L-series of registrations applied to the LHD RS2000s used for the press preview of the model in July 1973.

Spring rates had to be changed to accommodate the heavier weight of a 2-litre all-iron engine in the RS2000. Instead of the 1.6-litre car's 100lb/in fronts and 97lb/in rears, 130lb/in fronts and comparatively soft 85lb/in rears were chosen, a selection reflecting a racing rather than rallying influence. These were allied with the usual sturdy front anti-roll bar slotting into the lower track control arms. The stubby back axle location rods, in the style of those developed for the Lotus Cortina and passed on to the Escort Twin Cam and RS1600, appeared again on the RS2000. Neither this RS product nor its brethren picked up the rather spindly rear anti-roll bar cum location linkage that mainstream Escorts and Capris of the mid-1970s period employed.

Neither gas-filled dampers or struts nor alloy wheels were standard but both items were widely specified from the option lists or packs of the period. Usually this meant Bilstein dampers and FAVO four-spoke alloy wheels, the latter made by GKN Kent Alloys Ltd. Initially rim widths were a modest 5.5 or 6J, but later X-pack offerings went up to 7.5in widths.

Cabin finish and fittings for the RS2000 were superior to those offered on the earlier Mexico and RS1600 breed. A flat three-spoke steering wheel, effective in crash testing, was standard. But the old Escort 1300GT six-pack of instruments remained

Simple coachline treatment, a no-cost optional alternative to the broad stripe decals, soon became the most popular wear for RS2000s. The heavy-duty body-shell's flared front wheelarches were shared with other Mk 1 RS Escorts from the FAVO stable.

Two views of the Mk 1 RS2000 interior, with Custom Pack wooden facia trim, the upper from Ford in 1973, the lower a well-preserved car photographed in 1986.

Tight fit! Installing the Cortina/Capri SOHC 2-litre engine in the Escort required some modifications, including the use of an electric fan and a special cast-alloy sump. The bellhousing too was in light alloy.

— matching speedo and tachometer, plus a quartet of smaller dials to cover water temperature, oil pressure, fuel tank contents and battery condition.

Seating was a good deal more comfortable than in some earlier Ford offerings. LHD cars, including the initial UK press demonstrators, went out with large Scheel seats. British testers disliked those, so a similar look in front seats, fully reclining, but much cheaper to produce, from British sources, became the standard RHD fitment. Other internal equipment included loop pile carpet. A laminated screen was standard, and an electrically heated rear screen, halogen headlamps and hazard warning flashers were all production items too.

During a brief sales life, from October 1973 to the last sales in 1975 (following notice of closure of the FAVO factory's production facility in December 1974), the Escort RS2000's list price skipped from £1,441.82 to £2,075.67. In spite of the increase, it fitted naturally into the RS Escort line-up and poached sales from the Mexico and

RS1600, if anything rather too well. In October 1973 the Mexico was below £1,200 and the RS1600 hovered around £1,600: the RS2000's promise of 95% of RS1600 performance with everyday ease of servicing and durability at several hundred pounds less was hard to ignore.

The Custom Pack was no longer needed for the RS2000's updated interior, but there were two other Pack offerings from FAVO for the model. The Race Pack provided a comprehensive roll cage to meet contemporary scrutineering requirements, a fire-protected rear bulkhead, an oil catch tank, two master switches, Bilstein dampers and a four-point racing safety harness. The Rally Pack included the same mandatory competition items (roll cage regulations of the period differed in racing and rallying, racing always requiring a cross brace in the back passenger compartment) plus a map light, sump shield and appropriate Bilsteins. Other popular individual RS2000 options were the ubiquitous Salisbury limited-slip differential, push-button radio, wood

Flat-spoked steering wheel carried one version of the RS monogram, while the six-dial instrument pack was as used in other sporting Mk 1 Escorts.

RS2000 boot opens to reveal the near-vertical spare wheel mounting made possible by positioning the battery in the engine bay, and the carpeting fitted neatly over the fuel tank.

Bootlid badge shows a different style of RS symbol from the oval used on the RS1600.

Definitive study of a standard 1974 Escort RS2000 wearing decals with a darker body colour that reduces considerably the impact of the side stripe. Some RS2000 Mk 1s were assembled after the official closure of FAVO and registered in 1975, but the bulk of production of RHD cars took place in 1974.

trim for facia and glove box, a tidy centre console, metallic paint, a rear fog warning lamp and the aluminium wheels referred to earlier. Incidentally the standard steel wheel, now wearing a fancy multi-spoke pattern, proved durable enough to use when the model competed successfully in Group 1 production races and rallies.

Putting a relatively large and torquey engine in a car weighing just 2,015lb (915kg) was a recipe which gave the RS2000 the kind of mid-range muscularity allowing brisk progress without resorting to unduly high revs. Tyres wreathed in smoke, it would cover 0-60mph in 9 seconds and go on to around 110mph. Because of its cubic capacity advantage, the RS2000 would accelerate from 50 to 70mph in top gear faster than the RS1600: 8.8 seconds versus 9.5 seconds, according to *Autocar.* Fuel consumption of the unstressed power unit with its single twin-choke Weber was invariably better than the 16-valve RS1600: 26.6mpg, again according to *Autocar.*

Although production numbers were small by Ford standards, the Mk1 RS2000 exerted an enormous influence in favour of the continued production of a practical performance Ford. Whereas the RS1600 and the Mexico were, as John Bolster succinctly put it in *Autosport, tremendous fun for playing at boy-racers round a circuit, but rather lacking in refinement for road use,* their high noise levels, body boom and lack of flexibility making them *a bore for duty journeys and unacceptable for long distance touring,* the RS2000 was much more pleasant and usable as everyday transport while not sacrificing much in the way of performance. It gave a broader cross section of the public a chance to enjoy RS motoring without temperament, a concept that has survived to give a new generation affordable fun in the 1980s.

As we have seen, FAVO conceived the RS2000, just like the 1600GT Mexico, to fill a commercial need and use existing Ford components in a new market slot. It was essentially a road-car concept: but the result was a machine of far greater appeal than the complex RS1600 to those in the lower echelons of motorsport too.

Initially it was the fuel crisis which prompted Ford's sporting instincts in the direction of providing a clubman rallying RS2000 with twin sidedraught Weber 45s. Roger Clark was given the job of publicizing its existence and used its 160bhp to scrape home, just, on the 1974 Mintex Seven Dales rally against a field of top British runners with more than 200bhp in their RS1600s. I cannot recall the experiment being repeated by the factory, but the briefest perusal of adverts for second-hand rally cars on offer will show that plenty of people have adapted the idea to suit areas of rather less fierce competition, usually without the expense of reproducing that first car's specification exactly.

More significantly, the factory (egged on by Roger Clark, I suspect) fielded Escort RS2000s instead of 3-litre Capris in the Tour of Britain. This event was restricted to production Group 1 vehicles, rather than being run to the more radical rules of Group 2 which accommodated the lower-production RS1600.

For the 1973 event, sponsored by Avon, the Ford drivers were Roger Clark with Jim Porter and GM refugee Gerry Marshall paired with Paul White, later World Championship Peugeot-Talbot team co-ordinator. The white and blue 2000s wore Dunlop SP4-treaded road tyres and carried the registrations PVX 445M and 446M.

Ford Motorsport in Germany had developed the engine with a pair of downdraught Solex 40/42mm carburettors, WC30 camshaft and twin downpipe exhaust system. Properly assembled at Boreham, these units gave 138bhp. The cars also used the close-ratio Rocket gearbox, a competition replacement for the 2000E type, acceleration-biased 4:1 final drives, Bilstein damping and single-leaf rear springs.

Clark headed Marshall home for a fine debut 1-2 and anyone who saw the pair of them travel the circuits of Britain in flawless sideways formation will recall the event as the stuff of which legends are made. So far as the Group 1 competition RS2000 itself was concerned it took little time for the experts to substitute Weber downdraughts for the Solexes and power outputs escalated even during the car's abbreviated life. It was the privateers who benefited from most of the subsequent development as Ford themselves were using Mk2 Escorts by 1975.

However, the factory did have time to support some other interesting excursions. Tom Walkin-

Popular FAVO extras were big Cibié lamps, front spoiler and alloy wheels. Chrome quarter bumpers were standard wear.

shaw appeared sporadically in the 1975 British Saloon Car Championship with an RS2000 Mk1 in green with dark green decals and FAVO development engineer Allan Wilkinson had some outings in his own car, though neither made a permanent impression on the ruling Triumph Dolomite dynasty.

Of more historic and lasting interest was Tony Pond's 1975 victory on the Avon Motor Tour of Britain in TFR 8, a privately entered and owned Mk1 that was unofficially but substantially assisted by Goodyear and Ford. Most of the advice on construction came from Mick Jones at Boreham, but even then the car had a job to withstand the unnatural loads imposed by the roads of the Eppynt military ranges and to defeat the outstanding opposition, much of it from other RS2000s.

Since then many clubmen have enjoyed the Mk1 RS2000's competitive nature and the Mk2 was also widely used. The enormous choice of equipment that can still be purchased for either version of the RS2000 shows how the appeal of these cars endures.

When the curvaceous Mk1 Escort gave way to the Mk2 version, boxier and with a much bigger glass area, in mainstream production, the RS range also had to change. Fortunately perhaps, the differences were more in outward cladding than in basic engineering, the mechanical underpinnings were not greatly altered, and much of

Roger Clark in the RS2000 during the 1974 Avon Motor Tour of Britain. Broad stripe decals are prominent on a light coloured car, and standard steel wheels were used. Note the low ride height – it's not *that* bumpy on this rare off-tarmac section.

Tour of Britain again: Roger Clark ahead of Gerry Marshall at Cadwell Park on their way to first and second places in 1974. . .

. . .and the same venue a year later with Tony Pond nudging the straw bales in the Norman Reeves-entered car he drove to victory on the 1975 event.

FAVO's earlier work could therefore be applied easily to the new car.

In the case of the Mk2 RS2000, though, the opportunity was taken to distance the car in appearance, not just in mechanical specification, from the ordinary series production versions to a greater degree than with any previous RS model. Just as GM Vauxhall had their Firenza 'droop snoot', enhancing the image of a mass-produced two-door coupe, so Ford decided the boxy Escort should receive a new nose. The styling was drafted at the main Essex R&D centre, but the underbody engineering was carried out at Arisdale Avenue.

I remember the first RS2000 'beak nose' prototype well. I particularly remember us — myself, Mike Smith and Harry Worrall, amongst others — working at Aveley to produce the first runner, doing a cut-and-shut job on a Mk1 Escort registered YOO 470L. Really, we just bent some sheet steel to fit, but still the car went out and did both MIRA and Italian high-speed running. It can't have been any real trouble, because we went on to make the thing; in fact I went over to Saarlouis to help the pre-production build up over there. . .

recalled Allan Wilkinson, well known for his spell as the Ford Boreham engineer during the late 1970s, particularly 1979, the World Championship year for RS1800.

Ford RS engineer Bill Meade remembers they ran heat durability tests in Morocco on RS2000, combining the outing with a chance to test Sears Roebuck tyres against more conventional European products as there was then a financial incentive for competing on the American covers.

With the new RS2000, RS1800 and second generation Mexico established in production specification, that FAVO engineering team was split up during the course of 1975. It was nearly five years before the key elements like Rod Mansfield, Harry Worrall, Mike Smith *et al* drifted back to form Special Vehicle Engineering (SVE) for the 1980s.

The second RS2000 took an entirely different production route from the first. Whereas the Mk1 RS2000 was one of a trio of models assembled at FAVO in Arisdale Avenue (the others were the 1600GT pushrod-engined Mexico and the RS1600) the second version, a far more sophisticated product in terms of equipment and style, but utilizing the same general mechanical specifications, began a significant move in RS production still in effect today.

The pristine RS2000 of Shropshire-based Peter Nixon flaunts its stylish nose, a feature not shared with any other version of the Mk2 Escort.

Streamlined nosecone added to the Mk 2 Escort bodyshell gave the second version of the RS2000 a more clearly distinctive identity than any previous RS type, as well as helping with the aerodynamics. The polyurethane moulding was flexible enough to withstand small accidental impacts without damage. This beautifully maintained car illustrates the strength of ownership loyalty a decade after the model made its debut.

The car was engineered by the Aveley-based British team who had created all the previous RS models, and also employed the product-planning talents of Mike Moreton. Yet production responsibilities, as today, were assigned to Ford of Germany. This does *not* mean that all post-FAVO RS cars were *made* in West Germany, but it does mean that Ford of Germany staff controlled the manufacturing process, initially at the Cologne-Niehl plant, but later at Saarlouis on the Franco-German borders, a site purchased in 1965 and operational from 1968/69 onward. The Mk2 RS2000 was made at Saarlouis. Other RS models might come from Genk, a 441-acre site purchased in 1962, strategically placed beside the Albert Canal in Belgium and managed by Ford of Germany.

The multi-national production policy for high-performance Fords, initiated with the second 2-litre Escort, means that in the 1980s some XR models, notably the XR2 Fiesta, come from Spain, performance Sierras (XR or RS) are produced in Belgium, whilst an XR3i can be made in Britain or West Germany. Administratively speaking, another big decision was the axe for a planned third Capri RS, Capri II RS2800.

RS product planner Mike Moreton recalled: *We*

had a lot on our plates in the aftermath of FAVO's closure. There was approval for a flared wheelarch, 2.8-litre Capri II in RS2800 trim, given at the same time as that for RS2000 Mk2. What with the RS1800 and a second generation of both Mexico and RS2000 to do, and the engineers being gradually split up as FAVO wound down, there was no way we could tackle that RS Capri and it went. Ironically, the first project Rod Mansfield and SVE began to tackle on February 1 1980 was the Capri 2.8 injection. . .

The new RS2000's deformable polyurethane beak added 8.6in to the length of the Mk2 Escort and brought the claimed aerodynamic drag factor down to 0.383Cd, including the effect of a deformable rear spoiler. This compared to 0.45 for the unaltered second Escort body style and 0.43 for the first Escort. Ford themselves claimed a drag reduction figure of 16% compared to the standard versions of the new, boxier Escort of 1975.

How was the new nose, which really did reform after low-speed 'dings', installed? Ford had the front wings cut back just 100mm (3.93in) and flanged to accept the polyurethane component. *To hold it all together we had a steel flange plate from front wing to extension, screwed within, plus a selection of expanding nuts lower down,* recalled

SVE supervisor Harry Worrall in July 1986. Incidentally, Ford knew about this deformable material's useful low-speed accident reformation properties through its use on export Capris designed to meet US Federal regulations.

This soft-nosed Ford wore quadruple Cibié quartz-halogen headlamps (220/120 watt) of $6\frac{1}{8}$in diameter. These were a considerable improvement over any standard production Escort lighting I have assessed — better than the quad lamps offered on the RS Capris as well.

This later RS2000 looked very different from the original, a distinction that extended to the interior, where the facia naturally incorporated the Mk2 Escort's clear black and white single-pane instrument cluster, winner of a Design Council award. Yet the 2-litre engine and four-speed transmission, along with the rest of the running gear, were very much as for the original Escort.

The sturdy, and weighty, single overhead camshaft 1,993cc engine of Pinto ancestry came in several states of tune and is still used today in the Transit van. In 1987 it provided 115bhp with electronically managed fuel injection for the Scorpio and Sierra/Sapphire 2.0i models or about 10 horsepower less with a downdraught twin-choke Weber carburettor.

RS2000 Mk2 details include matt black bumpers, flexible polyurethane rear spoiler added to the boot lid, and silhouette-style logo. This concours example belongs to Steve Rockingham in Oxfordshire.

In combination with the modified nose section, the rear spoiler allowed the RS2000 to slip below the 0.4Cd drag barrier, making it one of the few rear-drive production saloons to achieve such aerodynamic efficiency, unbeaten in the Escort line until the advent of the front-drive cars – and then there wasn't much in it!

RS2000 Mk 2 engine bay. As for the contemporary Mexico, the exhaust manifold was replaced in the cause of extra performance, and it is very hard to tell 1.6 and 2-litre engines apart externally. The second body shape accommodated the Pinto engine without recourse to the electric fan in front of the radiator which had been needed on the Mk 1 car, though many owners subsequently installed such fans.

FAVO four-spoke alloy wheels were a popular RS2000 fitment. This example illustrates the later RS badge as well as the Pirelli CN36 175/70 radial-ply tyre often used on the car.

Then, as now, it came with a standard 9.2:1 compression ratio and single downdraught Weber, but Ford claimed 12bhp more for the second generation RS2000 than for the engine in other contemporary applications. They did not have the benefit of the electric fan this time, but the cast iron exhaust system was not the standard item, and the flow capabilities of its dual downpipes were matched by a larger exhaust pipe bore and absorption silencers designed for a modest horsepower increase, so Ford felt they had done enough to claim 110bhp at 5,500rpm and 121lb/ft of torque at 3,750rpm.

The unaltered gearbox was still of the E-series (Cortina 1600E, Corsair 2000E in years gone by) but was now mated to a two-piece propshaft, whereas the original had a one-piece shaft. Final drive ratio remained at 3.54:1 and the mph per 1,000rpm figure, on a car with standard production wheels and tyres, was just under 19mph. At first, four-spoke alloy wheels (6J × 13 with 175/70 HR tyres) were standard wear for Britain. Alloys became an option as prices escalated, so plenty of cars were sold on the cheaper 5.5 × 13 steel wheels, many subsequently to be fitted with aftermarket alloys, rather than the original four-spoke Ford RS alloys.

The heavy-duty body parts of the Mk2 RS Escorts were fewer than on the earlier shells, comprising only stronger mounting points for front and rear suspension loads — a beefier back crossmember to which the upright telescopic dampers attached, and increased metalwork to reinforce the top strut attachments at the front. Kerb weight was up to a total of 2,057lb (935kg), only 20lb of which was attributable to that extended nose.

The suspension was changed again, though only in detail. I have an unconfirmed suspicion that the original RS2000 did have a spring and damper change during its brief production span, one that owed much to the influence of Tom Walkinshaw, employed in the wake of Gerry Birrell's death.

The low level of noise and the high level of appointment in the cabin were a pleasant surprise after many years of spartan performance cars. The seats were exceptionally effective in providing comfortable location at speed. Instrumentation, shared with the Mk2 Mexico and RS1800, was very clear: for post-1978 models, orange markings replaced black and white.

The second generation RS range (1800 and 2000) shared 130lb/in front spring rates like the first RS2000, and 115lb/in rears, with dampers by Armstrong (front) and Girling (rear) or later by Fichtel and Sachs. As before there was an anti-roll bar at the front, but not at the back: the RS2000's leaf-spring layout was restrained only by the traditional top-mounting axle links.

Front end castor was considerably reduced and the general road feel of the cars was of understeer until provoked by low-gear power to tail slide. One owner commented that the second RS2000 tended to 'skip around at the back' to a greater extent than a standard Mk1.

Rack-and-pinion steering remained, officially geared at 3.5 turns lock-to-lock and as accurate and sensitive a system as you could wish to find, even if the replacement RS parts 'quick rack' made it feel sluggish by comparison.

Detail alterations were made to the braking. The

solid front 9.6in discs and vacuum servo (7in diameter) remained, but the rear brakes returned from the original RS2000's 8in diameter drums to the larger and earlier RS specification, 9in diameter 1.75in wide drums.

Shared RS features in the new era continued inside. On the facia a matching 140mph speedometer and 7,000rpm tachometer flanked three smaller dials: fuel contents, water temperature and oil pressure. The widely-used flat three-spoke sports steering wheel went with either standard seating that included a precise handwheel adjustment for backrest rake, or with any of the RS seat options. A centre console had made it onto the standard equipment list, along with a glove box, intermittent wipe facility, Escort's new three-stalk switchgear, electric windscreen washers and feeble horn. Included in the January 1976 launch price of £2,857 were items previously optional such as a heated rear window, laminated windscreen and matt black paint on the rear panel.

Mike Moreton recalled in the spring of 1986 that *the second RS2000 gained product approval in October 1974, revised to meet a situation where FAVO no longer existed on February 4, 1975. Originally we scheduled to make the first RS2000s of the second series in November 1975, but the problems delayed true production by three months, so it was February 1976 before Saarlouis began volume manufacture.*

The public preview of the RS2000 'beak nose' came at a traditional Ford RS exhibition ground, the annual springtime Geneva motor show. In 1987 it was the Sierra Sapphire RS Cosworth getting the full treatment; in 1975 Geneva was chosen to trumpet the RS2000's attributes.

I am told a small run of 20 prototypes were made in June 1975, some of them ending up at subsequent shows to maintain public interest. The first RHD press cars were also issued in advance of the production date, arriving during the closing months of 1975.

Although weight had increased in the later RS2000, it did seem that Ford had applied sufficient extra power to counter any adverse effect on acceleration, and the sleeker front helped with the maximum speed too: both British weeklies, **Autocar** and **Motor,** got a maximum around 112mph and screeched from 0-60mph in a still respectable 8.5 seconds. Full figures will be found in the appendices, but it is worth commenting that economy was improved in my experience, and it

was rare that I got down to the sub-25mpg figure recorded by **Autocar.**

In September 1978 Ford decided to alter the marketing approach for the RS2000 in Britain. The second Mexico had been a commercial flop and the RS1800 remained a very rare beast. Ford took the Mexico's cheaper interior and installed it with Escort Sport seats in a steel-wheeled RS2000 at £3,901.68. Now they charged £4,415.73 for a version called the Custom RS2000, equipped with 6J × 13 alloy wheels, ex-Capri S Recaro front seats, bronzed glass, remote control for the driver's door mirror, luggage compartment light, centre console, glove box, carpeted boot and extra trim.

The Escort RS2000 was replaced by the front-drive Escorts of September 1980, so far as Ford were concerned. Cars from remaining stock continued to be sold new, and often at a premium, after the model's last appearance in the catalogue, in August 1980, when it was listed at £4,995 for the steel-wheel RS2000 and £5,650 for the Custom model described earlier.

Now there are RS specialists like Mike Young at Ilford offering a choice of second-hand Mk2 RS2000s. The former Superspeed Anglia works driver had four examples on offer in early 1987, for example, priced between £2,995 for a 1978 model with 205/60 tyres and a Janspeed exhaust system to £4,495 for an otherwise original 1980 machine with full length sunroof, nearly new Pirelli CN36s and some 55,000 miles recorded.

In the classifieds that surround Young's weekly **Motoring News** advertisement, you would typically find up to a dozen second generation RS2000s. Prices ranged from £1,950 to £4,895, at the time of writing, but the better examples were all clustered around £3,000 to £3,600, according to year. Significantly, the most expensive privately owned car had been purchased by the previous owner from Young's Ilford establishment.

Some of the machines in **Motoring News** will be competition cars built without the 'beak' and others, like the first generation RS2000s, may have been built up from another Escort base as a conversion. The genuine RS2000s from Saarlouis should have a chassis plate that begins with a G for Germany. Further help on identifying RS models is available from either the RS Owners Club or the FAVO Owners Club listed in the appendices, the latter only catering for pre-1974 types.

Like its predecessor, the Mk2 RS2000, although developed as a road car, found a place in

The Tour of Britain continued to be a successful RS2000 stamping ground. Ari Vatanen, seen above without Peter Bryant on the Mallory Park circuit stage and below in action on a looser surface, dominated the 1976 event.

motorsport too. Ford at Boreham, particularly in the form of their homologation and engines engineering expert John Griffiths, continued to develop the engine's competition potential in the newer body. Again competing in the Group 1 production category, for which more suitable parts could now be homologated with the international sporting authorities in Paris, the net result was a formidable 160 to 165bhp with many key components replaced.

So far as the engine went, a number of outside specialists also began to meet the increasing demand in the late 1970s for more speed for rallying or racing by using the homologated Ford parts assembled in time-honoured 'blueprinted and balanced' manner.

Ford homologated a pair of twin-choke downdraught Weber carburettors to replace those initial Solexes. Equally important were new inlet manifolding, a new air cleaner, enlarged valves (1.75in inlet; 1.5in exhaust) and continuous camshaft development, including a roller-bearing conversion that had the additional benefit of overcoming the high camshaft lobe wear rates suffered by so many Pinto-engined Fords.

From April 1, 1976 Ford homologated the high-ratio steering rack (approximately 2.5 turns lock-to-lock) made familiar in the works RS1600/1800 along with ventilated front disc brakes and the heavyweight 3-litre Capri axle. These joined the closer-ratio Rocket gear set to provide, with the engine kit, an extremely competitive rally car.

I had the chance of assessing just how competitive with my RS2000, LHJ 928P. Equipped with the homologated parts described — the engine assembled by AVJ in Worcestershire — and trailing the *Motoring News* fifth wheel, I covered 0-80mph in 15.41 seconds rather than the standard 23.1 seconds. In action during that year's Tour of Britain the car proved capable of

Many competition RS2000s intended for rallying wore the flat front and quarter bumpers of the Mexico or RS1800. This example is Mike Stuart's Quicks for Ford machine on the Granite City Rally in which it won the Group 1 category. The registration, NOO 895P, first appeared on a beak-nosed RS2000 for HRH Prince Michael of Kent and Nigel Clarkson who finished just outside the top ten on the 1976 Tour of Britain.

Power behind many an RS2000 victory in the Group 1 production category was this version of the SOHC engine with twin down-draught Weber carburettors. Good examples, with the right camshaft and valves, gave over 160bhp in place of the standard output of 110bhp.

outdistancing 3-litre Capris. . . Incidentally, I also tried an RS2000 converted by Oselli of Oxford under much the same conditions and that was slightly slower to 60mph, faster to 80mph, with a completely different sidedraught carburettor 'Clubman' specification, one sorted and used in competition by Bill Gwynne.

As a factory team Ford naturally did not spend over-much of their time on the RS2000 and its category-winning abilities: outright victories with the 16-valve cars were factory meat. However, they had four representatives in the 1976 Tour of Britain: Roger Clark/Jim Porter; Timo Makinen/Henry Liddon; Ari Vatanen/Peter Bryant; and a fourth works-registered car assigned to HRH

Prince Michael of Kent/Nigel Clarkson, but I remember that as prepared by Vospers in Plymouth.

Both Makinen and Clark retired early but Vatanen, who was British Open Rally Champion that year in the Allied Polymer works RS1800, won the event. Nigel Clarkson brought his royal charge home 11th after some excellent racing performances.

The RS2000 went on to provide Group 1 rungs to stardom for Britons such as Malcolm Wilson, who persuaded his example to finish 10th overall on Britain's World Championship qualifier, the Lombard RAC Rally. More powerful RS Escorts won the RAC Rally outright each year from 1972 to 1979. But even in November 1980 Julian Raymond/John Daniels won Group 1 for Ford on the RAC: driving the freshly obsolescent RS2000 which had performed so well for Raymond during that season, they finished 11th overall.

The 'RS2' had also established a reputation for sturdy reliability and easy handling that saw many rally schools employ it in teaching a new generation of would-be winners. Ford themselves used the car at their Rallye Sport schools in the 1970s and others have taken the hint in the 1980s,

whether they have schools in Welsh forests or on converted Midlands airfields.

In 1986 the RS2000 was still winning the majority of British road rally events in the **Motoring News** series. There is still a strong demand for competition parts, promising that it will continue to be campaigned by amateurs into the 1990s. Yet it is as a thoroughly enjoyable and practical 'family sports car' that most will rightly remember this outstanding example of the RS breed.

RS2000 on the road

Finding a clean first-generation RS2000 over a decade after the model ceased production is far from easy. The March 1987 classified adverts in **Motoring News**, for example, provided three genuine FAVO-constructed RS2000s, priced from £1,400 to £2,100. There were plenty of 2-litre Escort specials in the £950-£1,375 bracket, but by far the most numerous RS products on the secondhand market at this stage were the second-generation RS2000, front-drive RS1600i and a scattering of front-drive Escort RS Turbos.

To find out a little more about running such an RS in 1987 I contacted Stuart Adams, who had provided his distinctively registered SOW 146N for photographic purposes. Even though he was but a lad of 22 at the time of the interview, this British Telecom technician had already owned two previous RS2000s, a white and blue decal Mk1 and a black X-pack Mk2, his main problem in motoring life being that his RS-types are so well kept that others steal them. . .sometimes twice!

SOW was bought privately in October 1985 for £3,300 and had recorded over 89,000 miles. Today it has exceeded 102,000 and modifications include Bilsteins, a one-inch chop in spring ride heights all round (145lb/in front, 112lb/in single-leaf rear) and a totally rebuilt engine of 2.1 litres.

I felt I ought to put the performance back to where it belongs, near the top of the stack. It needed a rebore, so it went out to 2.1 litres,

a big-valve cylinder head carries a Burton 40/41 camshaft; there is a 2in bore manifold and exhaust system, plus balanced and lightened components. Using a Weber 38 DGAS carburettor the output is approximately 130bhp at the rear wheels. It revs to over 7,000 and gives about 22mpg.

Aside from camshaft failures twice during engine rebuild, rectified by Rolling Road Auto Tune, this engine and a full Group 1 twin-carburettor unit experienced in his X-pack machine appear to have been very reliable.

On the practical front, Mr Adams has had the stereo stolen and some trim wrecked and he commented that interior parts are becoming increasingly difficult to obtain, especially trim and the original decals. He added that his concours competition record had been achieved despite the lack of a garage.

Another to buy a Mk1 RS2000 with over 85,000 miles on the clock was Steve George, son of Ford RS Owners Club Chairman Geoff George. A 23-year-old Lloyds reinsurance broker, Steve had run the first 10,000 odd miles in his secondhand purchase in standard form, apart from a full-length sunroof and Janspeed exhaust.

However, a 38 DGAS carburettor was bought for £50, operating at its best with the K&N air filtration and inlet manifolding included in the bargain price, plus a Filter King to overcome problems of fuel pressure. Just before a major rebuild, Steve George also installed ventilated front discs, World

Still appealing to the enthusiast, and still capable of being modified and developed, the rugged, simple and effective RS2000 continues to have a role in club motorsport: Norman Collier launches his RS along Madeira Drive during the 1984 running of the annual Brighton Speed Trials.

The open road. Moorland border country and an RS2000 continue to be an agreeable recipe for fine motoring into the 1990s.

Cup front Bilsteins, 145lb/in front coils allied to CD8 rear leaf springs and Group 1 Bilsteins. I think we can take it that the young George used to drive the RS quickly, and his father still recalls the totalization of a subsequent RS!

As the Stardust Silver paintwork had turned decidedly grey at 97,000 miles, Steve treated the car to a respray, engine rebuild and new Ford decalling, applying the new decals with *enough soapy water — it's rather like fixing a large Airfix decal.*

Essex Autotrim of Ilford renovated the seating, the door trims, rear panels and kick panels were painted with upholstery paint and some new wood was acquired to fill in a facia panel without radio. The latter came from Bob Tickner of Rallye Spares, Peterborough, but most other acquisitions came from the spares and accessories section of *Motoring News.*

The engine was dismantled for the head to be modified by Colin Voyce, whilst the bottom end was rebuilt in Essex using Powermax 11:1 pistons, HP/HC oil pump, Vandervell bearings and appropriate balancing and lightening. The head incorporated a Burton BE30 performance camshaft, larger valves, reworked porting and dual-coil springs for the valvegear. Not surprisingly fuel consumption fell to 25mpg, or less, after those extensive modifications.

Like his father, Steve George had a lot of time for the RS2000 and it was followed by a second-generation example. The only real drawbacks expressed by father and son concerned finding a good car at the right money (more difficult every year), the risk of having it stolen — a problem all RS owners seem aware of — and the spongey brakes.

Of the standard and original RS2000 I have nothing but pleasant memories and would also point out the experience of former LAT chief photographer Maurice Selden, responsible for some of the finest rallying pictures you will see. Maurice logged 85,000 miles in a P-registered example, running trouble free until 45,000. At that point the rigours of a life spent covering all kinds of rallies were emphasized by a crying need for new struts, dampers and springs! At 50,000 miles engine overheating was traced to a faulty sensor on the radiator failing to fire up the electric fan, whilst 60,000 miles saw an alternator replaced. No wonder this photographer went on to buy two more RS2000s.

Ford RSOC spares procurement and publicity officer Peter Nixon runs a suave yellow RS2000, MTG 100P, so I thought I'd ask him about his ownership experiences. His RS2000 came from a dealership in May 1976 at a cost of £2,850 with a scant 4,400 miles on the clock. Even in 1987 it had only 16,750 recorded! Equipment includes the black vinyl roof so redolent of the period; Ford-supplied Group 1 engine (vented disc kit awaits fitment); Britax sunroof; Kenlowe fan; Hella horns and an alloy boot bulkhead.

In pristine condition and with minimal mileage the car has needed little attention beyond extensive rust proofing. A stainless steel exhaust has been installed to save the need for frequent replacement.

Mr Nixon sums his RS2000 up as: *Sound and reliable classic motoring without the expense of exotica (or that which fancies itself as such, because the classic car magazines say so!); performance good, fuel economy acceptable. Original Pirellis sold and replaced by standard size Michelin XVS. Some dealers sadly know much less than they ought.*

Young Steve George, who also told me about his Mk1 RS2000, graduated to the Mk2 and had this to write: *The Mk1 had taken eight months searching for a good car at a reasonable price; the Mk2 proved almost as elusive.*

After countless phone calls we found a signal yellow 1980 W-registered Custom version in Chelmsford. Despite the fact that it had been resprayed and had some minor tattiness, this RS2000 has proved extremely sound, especially as they managed to bargain the vendor down to £3,000.

In nine months and 12,000 miles the only trouble was a broken clutch cable. It has now had two new headlamps and bezels and an exhaust clamp. It represents an incredible bargain for a total of £3,200 and could easily be sold for over £3,600, but at the present I can't see a possible replacement....until such time as the Sierra RS Cosworth comes into my price bracket, that is!

Steve George definitely likes his RS2000: *Wherever and whenever I drive her I get out of the car with a smile on my face. It has given me 12,000 miles fast, economical and very safe driving. To say that on a Saturday night I am prepared to drive and abstain from alcoholic beverages proves this adequately.*

The only black cloud is worrying whether the car will still be there when you return. The rate at which they are stolen causes constant anxiety and not a little anger. All the reasonable precautions have been taken but, if someone wants her, they will get her, and that seems a sad indictment of today's society.

6

Escort RS1800

Not for publication before June 10, 1975. Escort RS1800 NOW ON SALE IN BRITAIN. High Performance Escort now available from Ford Rallye Sport Dealers. Production is now well underway of the high performance Escort announced earlier this year. From today two roadgoing versions of Ford's successful rally car will be available from Ford Rallye Sports Dealers throughout Britain.

That was the press release announcing the launch of the RS1800 as a car available, at least nominally, to the man in the street. As the run of the mill Escorts made the transition to the new Mk2 bodyshell it was necessary for the BDA-powered car to be similarly transformed so that Ford could continue its successful rally career with a vehicle looking at least outwardly very much like the models in the high street showrooms.

The two versions of the single-carburettor 16-valve RS1800 for the public were, first, the basic RS1800, with fixed-back bucket seats, at £2,825.15 and second, the 'fully trimmed' Custom RS1800 at £2,990.12. It had been evident for a long time that very few were actually delivered and it has recently become more important to know exactly how many RS1800s were built as road cars, because their fast appreciating value relates closely to their rarity.

In April 1987 Ford decided that they would allow details of most RS production to be published, including sales figures from 1972 onward, and the results can be found in the appendix. Here we are concerned with the RS1800 and it seems (not for the first time) that by keeping mum on the subject Ford may have done themselves an injus-

In Mk2 form the BDA-powered Escort became the RS1800. Black rear spoiler and wide steel wheels were standard wear, the latter often replaced by optional alloys. This Irish-registered car, photographed in 1987, was restored by Colin Beverley.

tice. It was the UK market which took the RS1800, only made in RHD form, and an official company analysis shows that 109 such cars were registered in Britain between 1975 and 1978. I had previously been told that 50 'pilot build' converted Mexicos were the majority of production.

Ford did not have to do much more than publicize the RS1800's existence and run some kind of token production, for they were able to register the car with the international sporting authority as a further development of the RS1600 Escort. This avoided the need to make a fresh batch of 1,000 cars per annum to qualify for Group 2, and the RS1800 was accepted in that grouping from January 1975 onward. As Ford Motorsport homologation expert John Griffiths recalled, the RS1800's acceptance for competition was a two-stage affair. *First we evolved the 1,800cc engine within the Mk1 and got that accepted as a Group 2 competitor. Then, three months later, the international sporting authority accepted all the Mk2 body and ancillaries to give us complete recognition of the RS1800. All the changes that gave us the right to run the RS1800 in international motorsports were incorporated on* the same form as the original RS1600s with all the modifications entailed.*

Griffiths also explained how it came about that the first 'production' batch of RS1800s were converted from the Mk2 version of the Mexico which was launched in January 1976. *I do recall the company building cars for a subsequent FISA inspection. They were constructed by taking flat-front Mexicos, bought as a batch of fleet cars, with Pinto engines. We removed the 1600 and inserted the 1800 BDA. As I remember it, that engine transplant work was carried out at the Pilot plant in Aveley.*

The Pilot plant was another department at the site which had housed FAVO, by then closed for some time, of course. Thus a genuine RS1800 road car from that batch would have a German chassis plate and a reference to a 1600 not an 1800 powerplant! Further to confuse the issue, the Motorsports department at Boreham did build some RS1800s that did duty outside the competitions world, and there have also been published claims of batch production in Halewood and at Saarlouis in West Germany. Since all the Mexicos referred to were made in the German

The RS1800 delivered more mid-range power than the RS1600 and thus felt considerably quicker over crowded British roads. The side stripe was in two-tone blue and the bumpers were black.

plant, it is true to say that the RS1800 was partially a German product, but I have been able to establish definitely that Halewood did not make any original RS1800s.

Inside the square-cut Mk2 Escort shape, the RS1800's BDA engine was basically similar to that of the RS1600, with the alloy cylinder block which had become usual during the earlier car's production run. The typical Cosworth features, the alloy 16-valve cylinder head and twin belt-driven overhead camshafts, remained. Instead of the RS1600's bore and stroke of 80.98mm × 77.72mm, top tolerance figures quoted to give a nominal 1,601cc capacity, the RS1800 had the ordinary Ford 1600 pushrod engine's stroke of 77.62mm allied to a bigger bore of 86.75mm to give a capacity of 1,835cc. The compression ratio was 9:1 and valve sizes remained as for the RS1600. The increase in cubic capacity was offset by a measure of detuning for the roadgoing engine, a new small-port manifold carrying a single twin-choke downdraught Weber 32/36 DGAV carburettor, widely used on regular production Fords, in place of the RS1600's twin sidedraught Webers or Dellortos.

The power output of this revised unit was 115bhp at 6,000rpm, 5bhp and 500rpm down on the initial BDA claim. Maximum torque went up to

120lb/ft at 4,000rpm and proved very useful in typical British motoring. The development of this engine for road use had been the work of Brian Hart, and it had taken into account a revision of Group 2 competition regulations limiting the amount by which the standard capacity could be increased, hence the enlargement from the original 1,601cc, a step taken to allow the continued use of the 2-litre version in rallying.

Assembly of the engines, whether for the small number of road cars or for sale in larger numbers through the Motorsport parts department at Arisdale Avenue, was entrusted to Holbay Racing Engines at Martlesham Heath, Ipswich. Nowadays Holbay manufacture racing and prototype engine components, rather than the complete racing power units as they used to, but the founder and owner Mr Read chuckled at the recollection of the RS1800 job.

You could say we had a few slight problems to overcome in making those units... 'minor development snags,' I think we should say! he explained. For instance our contract called for every tenth engine to be power tested on the brake, rather than the hot test for oil pressure and lack of leakage that we gave each unit produced...But first, we had to get the engine to turn! What happened was simply that the crankshaft throw was too long for free movement within the crankcase, so we had to grind down the webs, and that kind of thing, to get it right again. We also had some minor oil drainage hitches to overcome, but nothing drastic. I remember that we made about eight to ten RS1800 units a week for a considerable period, more than a year. All made from lorry-loads of Ford-supplied parts that were sent back as complete engines on the same lorry.

Holbay were also involved in uprating BDAs for competition use and, although the details are a little vague ten years after the event, it seems that the owners of a very small final batch of roadgoing RS1800s got extremely lucky and were sold cars with an HRE-prefix motor (Holbay Racing Engin-

eering). The specification for such units included a 12-bolt flywheel and a steel crankshaft, rather than the cast iron of a normal Ford bottom end, though the connecting rods remained standard.

In place of the RS1600's hydraulically-actuated 8in diameter clutch, the RS1800 had an 8.5in clutch operated by a cable. The gearbox had been uprated over contemporary Mk2 RS2000 models with competition requirements in mind. Although only the unfortunate Group 2 racers from Zakspeed and Alec Poole's small European Championship team ever had to use the four-speed in anger on a regular basis: factory rallying Fords, both Group 2 and Group 4, used a five-speed ZF, as before.

RS1800 interior was as other contemporary Escorts. This Custom Pack model shows the usual five-dial instrument pack with fuel, oil pressure and water temperature gauges between the 7,000rpm tachometer and speedometer.

Two views of the immaculate engine bay of KIA 9922, a credit to all concerned. The BDA was only slightly less of a tight fit in the Mk 2 shell.

79

Standard steel RS wheel measures 5.5in × 13in, a familiar size on all the rear-drive RS Escorts.

RS1800 logo on the front spoiler is not original but so well done that perhaps it should have been!

The four-speed box used was from Ford of Germany, one that was also fitted to Mustangs with the 2.3-litre Pinto engine as well as being mated to German-market 108bhp 2.3-litre V6 engines. Its ratios were: first 3.36:1, second 1.81:1, third 1.26:1, and fourth 1:1. Final drive ratio in the usual RS/Mexico series axle was 3.54:1, allowing a tolerable 18.6mph per 1,000rpm in top gear. You could, for example, cruise at 70mph using under 3,800 revs.

The two-door unitary steel Escort body was less radically modified for RS products than had been the case for the first Escorts: changes were confined to strengthening for the strut mounting points at the front and a stronger rear cross-member to carry the post-1974 upright damper layout.

The RS1800 shared the same suspension set-up as the other second-generation sporting Escorts, the RS2000 and the Mexico, with 130lb/in front springs and 115lb/in rear. As ever there were MacPherson struts at the front, with single track control arms each side and the anti-roll bar jointed into them. The rear axle was suspended on the usual multi-leaf springs, with telescopic dampers, and located by the familiar short links. Armstrong front dampers and Girling at the rear were fitted as standard, but gas-filled Bilsteins, along with single-leaf rear springs, were available amongst the wide range of popular optional equipment sold through the Motorsport parts department.

The standard wheel and tyre specification for the RS1800 called for steel 5.5 × 13in rims equipped with 175/70 HR radials, Pirelli CN36 tyres being fitted to the original test car I drove. Obviously four-spoke alloys were optionally available, as for other contemporary RS models. These were supplied in widths from 5.5in to 7in, all of 13in diameter. Usually only the 5.5 or 6in rim was fitted beneath unmodified Mk 2 bodywork.

The braking system followed the established high-performance Ford pattern with solid 9.63in front discs and 9.0in diameter 1.75in wide rear drums. Vacuum servo assistance was by Girling.

Interior trim details included the usual Mk 2 Escort RS/Mexico instrument panel. This was an adaptation of the admirably clear series production Mk 2 single-pane cluster, with matching black

and white speedometer and tachometer reading to 120mph and 7,000rpm respectively. Between these lay three smaller dials to indicate oil pressure, water temperature and fuel level in the standard 9-gallon tank.

Standard external trim details included a two-tone blue side stripe and RS1800 badge work on both rear flanks and the bootlid. The Ford performance tradition of front quarter-bumpers was continued, in matt black this time. There were small '1.8' badges, low on the front wings, just above the sidestripe.

Front and rear spoilers were installed. The front was the usual hard plastic extension shared with the Mexico, but the back was in deformable plastics; the original road test car had this colour-coded, but its successor wore a matt black one. Other standard features included 7in diameter halogen headlamps with 110/100 watt bulbs, two-speed wipers with an intermittent setting, electric screen washers and hazard warning flashers.

In addition to the alloy wheels already mentioned as options, the first Ford RS1800 demonstrator of 1975 had a black vinyl roof fitted. You could also get tinted glass, rear fog lamps, opening front quarter-lights, and a remote-control driver's door mirror. Incidentally, the mirrors were in matt black, not colour coded. There was a choice of radios from the Ford option list, but the one I remember had a single speaker in the facia and push buttons.

Standard equipment included: *Extensive sound proofing, loop pile carpets and special competition bucket seats trimmed in black cloth,* according to Ford in June 1975, but for an extra £164.97 the Custom Pack brought: *Fully trimmed doors and rear quarters, reclining front seats fitted with head restraints, a glove pocket and clock, plus a lidded glove box and deep centre console unit, a boot carpet and inertia reel seat belts as standard.* In that form the car cost just a tenner short of £3,000.

The two weekly magazines *Motor* and *Autocar* carried tests of the original Ford Escort RS1800 demonstrator, JJN 981N, in July 1975. Both achieved more than the 112mph Ford claimed for their second 16-valve Escort, *Motor* recording a best of 115.4mph and *Autocar* 114mph. Those speeds are similar to those achieved by the 105bhp Escort XR3i, reflecting the improvements in aerodynamics made in the 1980s. Acceleration was also in advance of the RS1800's era, from rest to 60mph taking 8.7 seconds for *Motor* and an average of 9 seconds for *Autocar.*

On fuel consumption, the two weeklies exactly agreed on 26.5mpg, an excellent figure for a car of this performance in 1975. Government-approved consumption figures were not required at the time, but *Autocar* measured constant-speed figures of 30.8mpg at 70mph and 41.2mpg at 50mph.

All of which helped to show that the RS1800 in roadgoing trim, with the excellent blend of power

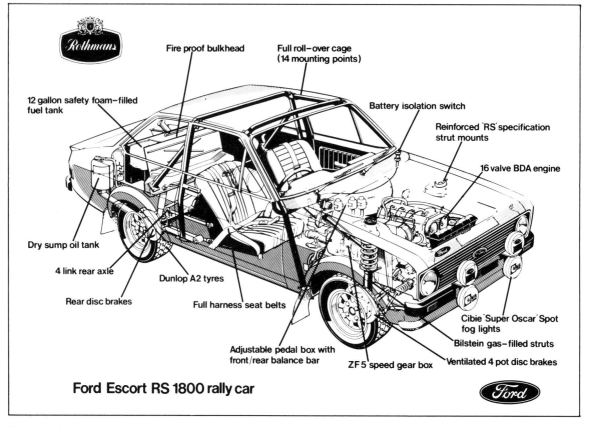

Rothmans

Fire proof bulkhead

Full roll–over cage
(14 mounting points)

12 gallon safety foam–filled
fuel tank

Battery isolation switch

Reinforced 'RS' specification
strut mounts

16 valve BDA engine

Dry sump oil tank

4 link rear axle

Dunlop A2 tyres

Rear disc brakes

Full harness seat belts

Cibie 'Super Oscar' Spot
fog lights

Bilstein gas–filled struts

Adjustable pedal box with
front/rear balance bar

ZF 5 speed gear box

Ventilated 4 pot disc brakes

Ford Escort RS 1800 rally car

Ford

Competitor from inside: press-release cutaway drawing reveals the primary features of the rallying RS1800 that served so many competitors so well. The efforts of Ford at Boreham, David Sutton Cars and numerous privateers continuing well into the 1980s ensured that a lot more rallying RS1800s were built than the road car from which the name and basic layout came.

and economy provided by its single-carburettor 16-valve engine, could probably have been a commercial success many years before manufacturers like Toyota and Honda began to sell cars with similarly advanced power-unit engineering. Instead, it was destined to remain a rarity. It did have a rival in the showroom in the form of the Triumph Dolomite Sprint, the engine of which had 16 valves operated by an ingenious single-camshaft layout, but more relevant was the fact that the RS2000 provided something fairly close to RS1800 performance yet cost significantly less, generally used less fuel and was simpler and cheaper to maintain. The RS1800 existed only to promote Ford's aims in motorsport.

From April 1, 1977, International Group 4 status was granted to Ford for the Escort RS1800 with all the usual competition extras that had been proven in the original RS1600 as well as the Group 2 RS1800. This meant that Ford would have a competitive car under new regulations that

demanded 400-off production in 24 months, this requirement being satisfied on the basis of the enormous number of competition Escorts built to the main outlines of the agreed specification. In other words the works team, together with numerous privateers, made a lot more RS1800s for competition than were ever completed for the showroom!

The typical Group 4 specification, as accepted by FISA and used throughout the remainder of the Escort's ever successful rallying life, included a 2-litre 240-265bhp version of the alloy BDA, with double twin-choke carburettors or fuel injection and dry-sump lubrication, a five-speed ZF gearbox, disc brakes all round, a heavy-duty 'Atlas' rear axle located by quadruple trailing links and a Panhard rod, a roll cage increasingly integrated into the structure of the bodyshell, and wheelarch extensions to suit competition tyres of varying widths.

In this form the RS1800 proved a brilliant rally car, winning Ford the World Championship for

Makes in 1979 and Ari Vatanen the Driver's title in 1981. It suited Ford to concentrate the factory effort on rallying as the regulations for European international touring car races swung towards emphasizing cars which were closer to large-volume production specification under the so-called 'Group 1 ½' rules. The Capri was left to defend the honour of the name in that field, and the RS1800 did not match the racing record of its predecessor.

The German National Championship, though, was run to more radical Group 5 rules, nicknamed the 'Silhouette' formula. Zakspeed used the RS1800 as the basis for a machine to compete successfully with the BMW and Opel opposition and secure first and second places in the 1976 Championship for Hans Heyer and Klaus Ludwig. Their 2-litre cars developed 280bhp with the aid of Lucas fuel injection.

In rallying, on a worldwide scale, the RS1800's reputation was established by results like victory on the 1977 East African Safari, four wins on the tough Acropolis (1977 and 1979-81), a 1-2 in Portugal in 1979, two wins on the 1,000 Lakes in Finland (1977 and 1981) and single wins as far afield as New Zealand, Canada, Brazil and Sweden. The Monte Carlo always eluded the Escort, though Bjorn Waldegard got very close in 1979, finishing second to Darniche's Stratos.

The correctness of the practical, rugged Ford-Cosworth-Escort formula was underlined when the RS1800 took on the might of the Fiat Group's

The outside view. Roger Clark takes the brand new HHJ 700N to its maiden victory on the 1975 Granite City. The car was much better known in red Cossack hairspray colours with Clark's locks featured in a national TV advertising campaign. . .

Above, Timo Makinen accompanied by Henry Liddon completes that historic RAC Rally hat-trick with the first win on the event for the Mk 2-bodied car. Roger Clark was second but would win again in 1977. Below, Ari Vatanen won the Welsh Rally in 1980 and 1981. This is the dusty 1980 event in which he beat Mikkola in another David Sutton RS1800 by just 50 seconds. Dave Richards is the brave co-driver nearest the camera.

competition effort, nearly won the world title in 1977 and then succeeded in 1979 and 1981. Making that formula work were the people at Boreham, ably led from 1972 to date by Peter Ashcroft, a small band compared to their international rivals and occupying modest premises.

A formidable array of highly talented drivers was seen in the RS1800 over the years, continuing the RS1600's dominance of British events and making the Escort name known all over the world, something that became commercially important when the later front-wheel-drive Escort went on sale on both sides of the Atlantic. Roger Clark, at the time of writing still the only Briton to win a World Championship event, won the RAC Rally in both the RS1600 (1972) and the RS1800 (1976). Bjorn Waldegard from Sweden played a major part in the World Championship success. Then there were the Finns: Hannu Mikkola, Ari Vatanen, Timo Makinen, Pentti Airikkala and Kyosti Hamalainen all won World Championship events, often extracting performances from the car that startled even the most seasoned Ford Motorsport staff.

There were some notable Escort drives too from Malcolm Wilson, Russell Brookes, John Taylor

Tidy fuel-injection RS1800 power unit, in this case of 1,800cc capacity rather than the usual 2-litres of the rally cars, belongs to the Group 2 Escort raced by Alec Poole in European Touring Car Championship events. Availability of sufficient power was not a problem, but reliability, using standard components that included the four-speed gearbox, sometimes was.

Malcolm Wilson was the British Ford hero of the late 1970s and early 1980s. He is seen on the 1980 Welsh in the Total-sponsored FEV 1T and aviating to an excellent third overall on the 1981 Manx in the ex-works STW 201R operated by the Rothmans/David Sutton team.

and Billy Coleman. A Mk1 Escort brought Taylor the first European Rallycross Championship, but Martin Schanche from Norway used increasingly powerful Mk2 RS types to take the title in 1978, 1979 and 1981. His '81 car used a turbo BDA from one of Zakspeed's amazing Capri racers.

Just as impressive was the fact that many club drivers could take the basic Escort recipe and go on assembling winning cars into the 1980s. In 1983 the car was still winning national events in Australia, New Zealand, Cyprus, Kenya, Finland and Norway. In club events in the UK only the influx of Group B four-wheel-drive machines in 1987 displaced it and it was winning again in 1989 when the supercars were tamed by handicapping or banned.

We must salute the RS1800 as a rallying legend — in terms of victories for an all-British car it may well never be matched.

Typical Escort RS1800 forest rallying stance as Ari Vatanen takes the slightly weather-beaten Sutton car to second place on the 1980 Scottish, beaten this time by team mate Mikkola.

The RS1800 in tarmac rally trim with extended arches covering wide Minilites and slick tyres. Ari Vatanen and Dave Richards were second on the 1980 Manx, enough to secure the Sedan-sponsored British Open home international championship of that season.

Two production roadgoing RS1800s in the care of one man. ONO 804P was the second Ford press demonstrator and is seen here during its long wait for a production specification power unit rather than the later Group 4 motor which eventually proved too much for the clutch. A set of authentic wheels and tyres would be installed at the same time as the engine. The completed car, KIA 9922, stands by.

RS1800 on the road

Colin Beverley, of Penn, Buckinghamshire, told us all we needed to know about owning an RS1800 in 1987 by showing us over two examples in his care, authentic rarities that shared garage accommodation with his enthusiastic wife's 150bhp 1,700cc Mexico.

Colin is no moneybags: the RS craving was satisfied only by long hours working on Mick Collard's Hot Rod Escorts in the 1970s (including the World Championship season) and subsequently by his current occupation as a heating and ventilating engineer. I did not have to ask him what he did for a living, his air-conditioned garage marked him out from the neighbours. . .

The RS1800 pair inspected were his own car, KIA 9922, and Mick Collard's restoration project, ONO 804P. The latter registration may ring a bell with anyone who has read an RS Escort road test, as it was the number carried by the second of two road RS1800s that the Ford Motor Company registered for press duty.

Colin bought his own RS1800 in June 1986 for £3,600 from Graham Lepley Cars in Derbyshire. First registered in Wales by Ford dealers Davis of Welshpool on February 23, 1977, it was logged in Ireland two days later and used in that country for most of the 41,000 miles registered when Colin bought the car in running, but not immaculate, order.

It has now been comprehensively rebuilt over a nine-month period. By spring 1987, with 49,300 miles indicated, it was gleaming in white, with the authentic decalled livery,

Mr Beverley having bought the last six sets of decals from J. C. Withers.

Colin recalled: *Most of the RS1800s we saw were old and tired rally cars with holes in the floor, but this one was a very fair road car. I was a bit worried by the original log book; it recorded engine and chassis numbers showing a conversion from an Escort Mexico base. Then I checked and found that was just the way many of the cars were built.*

Basically it was a sound RS, but I decided to spray in below the waist line properly. For Mick's car we went the whole hog and had it done during dead time over six months by the local Wycombe Accident Repair concern. For both cars I also found the neighbourhood Ford dealer, not an RS dealer, Prestwood Motors, equally helpful.

Trims are the hardest stuff to find, but you also get the bits and bobs like the door jamb courtesy light switch and those mounting clips for the under-bonnet stay that are tough to get as well. I have deliberately made my car the way I want it in some respects rather than try and get 100% factory originality, but I know what's different and I have tackled ONO as a faithful copy of the road test machine.

My car differs from production in having the polished radiator; that small RS1800 badge on the front spoiler; the vital anti-theft locks and alarm, plus the roof aerial. I get most of my stuff in three ways: **Motoring News** *classified ads, Prestwood, or an exceptionally helpful scrap dealer in the Midlands,* said Colin. He competes in concours on the steel wheels and standard Pirelli CN36 175/70s that I accompanied him on. But there is also a set of Italian-made Carmona Minilite-style alloys that can be used for pleasure with 185/60 Pirelli P6 tyres giving up to date grip.

Mechanically, KIA still runs the ventilated front discs that were fitted in Ireland, but the stopping power is one of the machine's worst features. The engine is contrastingly excellent with far less rattle than when it was new! This BDA also displays *very* strong torque from 3,000 to 6,000rpm, giving sheer speed that puzzles hot-hatchback drivers!

On the engine, Colin reported: *I went to a firm who trade from Northampton as Dick Langford Engineering — they have over 20 years' experience of rebuilding Cosworth DFVs. It's the sort of place where they ask you to have a look round before asking if you want to leave your cylinder head with them. The work space was a treat to look at, and so was the head. I took up a dirty old remmnant and got back something that looked like a brand new casting. As you can see, it runs a treat and, just as they promised, it has never looked like dropping a valve. . .*

The Collard car lacked an engine when I visited, because it had covered most of its miles with its World Championship-winning owner using the full Group 4 unit from an ex-Dessie McCartney rally machine, 111 MN. *Not surprisingly, that tore the centre out of the clutch and it was left in a barn for years before we persuaded Mick to have it restored,* explained Colin.

The original RS1800 engine builders, Holbay, knew Collard well through Hot Rodding and readily agreed to produce a faithful rendition of the original power plant. Just the engine and trim were needed at the time of my visit, but those were the major items — it's always the fiddly little jobs that take the real time in restoration work.

Those two RS1800s are no longer in Colin Beverley's capable hands. Further insight came from another owner who contacted us some time later with his account of another two RS1800s. An authenticated name and address was supplied, but in this case I am respecting an earnest plea for anonymity.

This 49-year-old farmer bought his first RS1800 in 1980, paying £4,500 for a 1978 example with 14,000 miles recorded. Today, this modified machine registers 20,000 miles. Delighted with his 180bhp five-speed RS, our contact paid £4,000 for a 99% original 1977 RS1800 in 1983 to Custom Pack specification. The cheaper second RS1800 had 37,000 miles indicated, and only 3,000 more miles had been added by late July 1987.

Commenting that it is a case of either DIY or 'four-figure sums' to maintain the 16-valve engine, this owner asserts: *A magic car to drive — second only to a Ferrari. The sound recalls the Welsh forests of the 1970s.*

7

Escort RS1600i

The RS1600i was an unexpected showroom success. The car was specifically conceived by Ford of Germany Motorsport engineers to participate in the new competition categories, Group A and Group N, regulations for the latter permitting even fewer deviations from standard specification than the former. It was initially planned that Ford should make just the 5,000 examples needed to meet the annual production requirement for eligibility in international motorsport.

A prototype RS1600i was shown at the Frankfurt show in West Germany in September 1981 and production cars trickled out initially in left-hand-drive form. When the British market began to receive Type Approved supplies in November 1982 Ford were forced to reappraise demand and by January 1983 they were looking at the possibilities of increasing the production run to 8,000, not a bad total considering that the original suggestion had been for just 3,000 special RS1600i Escorts for Britain. In the first four months of UK sales over 700 front-drive RS1600s were sold. The eventual total of cars made, both LHD and RHD, was 8,659.

In Britain the RS1600i was first listed in **Autocar** on October 20, 1982 at £6,700 and last appeared in the same journal on August 20, 1983 at £6,834. Secondhand values remain high in the United Kingdom. In March 1987 examples with Y suffix or A prefix registrations could still fetch over £5,000 with more than 30,000 miles recorded and it took a 44,000-mile example, Y-registered, to drop just £50 under that £5,000 barrier; the most expensive examples were all close to £5,500.

Ford of Germany Motorsport engineers, men like current German Ford competitions boss Lothar Pinske and former BMW employee Otto Stulle, had brought the RS1600i to fruition, ready for marketing by Fritz Boettinger, in an environment very different from that which had greeted the rear-drive RS1600 of 1970, both because European regulations on emission levels were an everyday development worry and because inspection of production numbers for motorsport homologation purposes was heavily policed in a way that British competition managers would have found a calamity a decade previously. Neither the Mini Cooper S nor the Lotus Cortina, nor any of the rear-drive TC/RS Escorts would have existed had homologation procedures been so sternly enforced at such numbers: the 5,000 annual production requirement contrasted with only 1,000 for the popular Group 2, the previous Escort hunting ground, and the progression from RS1600 to 1800 had been regarded simply as evolution, with no stipulation at all about further series production.

Ford Motorsport started work on the project in 1979, the days of Escort front-drive prototypes, and were backed by the main company in their efforts to ally the new CVH engine and Bosch K-Jetronic injection. This widely used system worked on mechanical principles with continuous (*kontinuierlich* in German, thus the K in Jetronic. . .) injection, and had proved so suitable in providing 110 smooth bhp from Volkswagen's widely-imitated Golf GTI. The effective use of injection had to be an essential element in any new sport-orientated Escort.

By April 1981 the practical Motorsport engin-

Seven-spoke RS alloy wheels, unique side stripes with inset model name and Motorsport spoiler set gave the RS1600i a strong visual identity quite distinct from that of the contemporary XR3i.

RS1600i Escorts for the British market came with comprehensive standard equipment including the auxiliary lighting seen on this early 1983 example. The deeper front spoiler continued to be favoured among Escort Mk3 competition drivers for years after the RS1600i's demise and was still in stock at Ford Motorsport in 1987. Note the extensive decalling on the bonnet, with another reminder of the car's identity on the front edge.

eers had finished their task. The LHD version of the RS1600i shown to the German public at that September 1981 Frankfurt motor show was the first new RS to appear since the rear-drive Escort RS2000's debut in 1975. Nobody doubted the aura surrounding the initials RS and Ford, for Escort RS1800s had won the World Championship for Makes in 1979 and that for drivers (Ari Vatanen) in 1981. There was an effective RS parts marketing operation, too, to keep the enthusiast customer happy.

Sales of the RS1600i were initially small, owing to limited production availability in Germany, but by the summer of 1982 output was beginning to gather pace and growing interest was accompanied by favourable Continental press comments. In this context it is important to point out that tests of left-hand-drive cars usually cited the earlier Escort XR3 carburettor model as the base over which improvement was made, whilst British press comment was against the later background of the fuel-injected XR3i which arrived on the UK market at the same time as the RS1600i.

That the RS1600i was not available for so long in RHD was not a problem of the original development team, according to Karl Ludvigsen, motor industry writer and boss of Ford European Motorsports briefly in the early 1980s. *No, it was simply that old problem . . . trying to get the Brits and the Germans to work together!*

As in Germany, delays were also caused by a sheer lack of manpower to tackle paperwork and mandatory tests, British regulations demanding that Bill Meade and his assistants such as Terry Bradley work at Boreham from June 1982 on Type Approval questions that were not finally resolved until November of that year.

Converting the RS1600i for the UK included the installation of a cross-shaft to link a right-hand brake pedal with a left-hand servo. There was also work on radio suppression; a new glovebox to mask transposition of the steering; a four-spoke steering wheel with leather rim to replace the triple-spoke item seen on the Continent; UK-certified seat belt anchorages and a seat crash test.

A lot of Boreham's practical engineering time on the transformation was devoted to the brake system, trying to overcome the inherent sloppiness of the cross-shaft linkage. The conversion (not foreseen by the Germans) made the centre pedal intermittently slack in action, a problem also encountered with some VW-Audi products

imported into Britain at that time, such as the earlier Golf GTIs with mixed disc/drum braking.

The British team also substituted 195/50 Dunlop D4 tyres for the German market Phoenix 190/50. The French, on the other hand, would not take their 1,000 RS1600i Escorts without switching to a 60-series Phoenix to try to achieve a better rough-road ride. National road characteristics, perhaps, play a part in these varying preferences!

The essential elements of the RS1600i remained, though, in any market. Complete with Escort's first fuel injection system and a slightly raised compression ratio (9.9:1 instead of 9.5:1), the CVH engine recorded 115bhp at 6,000rpm. This useful output was matched by a peaky torque maximum of 109lb/ft at 5,250rpm. Equivalent figures for the XR3i were 105bhp at 6,000rpm and 101lb/ft at 4,800rpm. Although 10bhp was a modest enough increase with the car in showroom condition, over 160bhp proved to be available when the RS1600i was prepared, for example, by Richard Longman for Group A racing. Most importantly, this engine had a more suitable cylinder head for competition purposes. It featured mechanical valve actuation rather than hydraulic tappets, opened out cylinder head porting that was matched by an exhaust system increased in diameter to 40mm, and a new camshaft profile that concentrated on obtaining the maximum lift commensurate with passable street manners.

These features were necessary because the Group A regulations of the period did not permit a change in valve lift, an important source of extra power via deeper breathing, so Ford had to provide the best possible figure for competitors. The solid-lifter valve gear permitted higher rpm to be maintained safely and the cylinder port modifications could also provide the basis for extra power in competition trim.

The engine wore a finned aluminium camshaft cover with the words *Ford Motorsport* cast into its face. The four-branch exhaust system looked particularly impressive and it is as well to remember that, when the RS1600i made its Continental debut, Ford owners had not seen the CVH engine fitted with fuel injection, so that was a novelty as well.

The ignition system was new too. Ludvigsen proudly stated: *Those engine electronics were a world first in production fitment, we even beat*

Ford Germany's Motorsport department did a good job in developing the basic changes, including the deletion of hydraulic valve lifters, needed to make the CVH engine an effective basis for a competition unit. This was the first fuel-injected production Escort and used the mechanical Bosch K-Jetronic system. The unique twin-pack AFT ignition system can be seen to the right of the Motorsport-embossed alloy rocker cover.

Gerard Sauer investigated the original RS1600i thoroughly for the magazine *Hot Car* and found the handling untidy. He took the trouble to find out that the car lacked the rear anti-roll bar promised in some brochures and the majority of magazines. A Motorsport rear anti-roll bar kit is available for pre-May 1983 Escorts, part number 9094603. It does not fit models with the revised underbody built after that date, fouling the fuel tank, though a very few owners have installed the bar on later cars by using spacers. Ford's view is that the later cars' suspension is sufficiently improved not to require modification and, since the geometry is totally different, may actually be adversely affected by fitting an anti-roll bar.

Porsche there! And it wasn't easy to get the standards we wanted. Bosch were really too big a company to be responsive, but I believe Stulle did contact Weber-Marelli and I would think that led on to the Sierra RS Cosworth installation they have today.

It was Otto Stulle who found Atlas Fahrzeug Technik (AFT). They came up with a twin-coil, distributorless system with computerized ignition timing that was triggered from the flywheel. Inbuilt in the system for road use was a rev limiter set at 6,500rpm. Although this meant frustration when trying to explore the engine's top-range abilities, the device served to limit the RS1600i's acceleration and so mollify German insurance demands.

Controversy inside Ford was generated by the use of a fuel overrun cut-off system, for company engineers had advised the directors against the adoption of this now-popular fuel saving device (initially only found in association with Bosch injection). Now a Motorsport engineer was telling them they were wrong! One insider told me, *God, was there ever a fight over that, but good old Otto got that, and the AFT system, through somehow!*

In Britain the RS1600i became delayed to the point where the first fuel-injection XR3i caught up with it and both made their debut together on Ford's motor show stand at the NEC in Birmingham in October 1982. Since RS1600i and XR3i prices were only £670 apart in basic form (as with most Escorts you could spend over £1,000 on options) there was press and public confusion over which model should be purchased in the UK, particularly as the operation of the rev limiter on the RS1600i did not allow it to demonstrate a significant performance advantage over the cheaper XR3i.

However the RS1600i was not to be denied commercial success, overcoming not only those initially apathetic reports in Britain but also a lack of outright competition success that was inevitable, given the changes in sporting regulations. Contributing to the car's sales appeal in Britain were the extrovert exterior and sporty interior. Inside there were ASS seats that were smartly cloth trimmed and a sturdy, four-spoke, leather-rim steering wheel that was larger than the original XR3 two-spoke fitment.

Outside there was a nine-stripe *RS1600i*-emblazoned bonnet decal and side stripes continued the *injection RS* message. Spoilers, front and rear, were different to those of the XR3 base

on which the RS1600i was first built, comprising a large front unit balanced by a wraparound rear air dam. No reduction over the XR3's 0.375Cd aerodynamic drag factor was mentioned: about 0.38Cd seems the best it could have recorded, for the rear wheel spats were removed and the car used a fatter wheel and tyre combination — 195/50 tyres on 6J × 15 RS seven-spoke wheels rather than the XR3's 185/60s on 5.5 × 14 rims.

Britain received two sets of auxiliary lights on the front. My 1982-built test car sported an international lighting assortment, with Carello round driving lamps and Hella rectangular fog units mounted in front of the spoiler, and Lucas H4 headlamps.

The ventilated front disc brakes remained those of all 1600 and XR Escorts to date, with the usual 7in rear drums, all operated by that rather cumbersome linkage and vacuum servo assistance. You could find an RS1600i with 8in diameter rear brakes, this aftermarket improvement being offered through RS dealers and recommended by the Motorsport team that developed the RHD version of the car.

Although the usual front-wheel-drive Escort layout of front MacPherson struts and independent rear was retained on the RS1600i, there was the important modification that the anti-roll bar was divorced from front wheel location duties. Instead, short links ran from the track control arms to individual body mountings. The separated anti-roll bar, 26mm in diameter, was mounted on a smart aluminium crossmember. No rear anti-roll bar was fitted although it appeared in publicity material which was faithfully copied by many of the magazines I have studied save the now extinct **Hot Car.** However Motorsport engineers had put together an optional 18mm bar that assisted the handling enormously and you may find that a keen owner has installed such an item, like the larger rear brakes mentioned. The rear anti-roll bar was listed in 1987 by the Ford Motorsport parts operation at Arisdale Avenue under order code 909.4599, but you should note that this bar will not fit cars made after May 1983.

This brings us to some important changes in the RS1600i's production specification that came up in discussing the car with owners, were explained more fully by an RS dealer parts man, Jeff Mann of KT Dartford, and were also reported in the March/April 1987 Ford RS Owners Club magazine.

Originally, RS1600i suspension was based

on uprating the specification of the original carburettor-equipped XR3. Thus the RS included high-quality shock absorbers from Koni, and the front spring platforms were altered to provide a ride height an inch lower than standard. As at the rear, standard XR3 springs were used, but the 26mm front anti-roll bar and location links, plus replacement shock absorber strut inserts, and the lowered front end, resulted in totally altered handling — responsive on smooth roads, but extremely twitchy during faster British B-road motoring.

In May 1983 Ford brought the RS1600i closer to the production specification of other Escorts. There were 10 bodyshell changes accompanied by important suspension modifications and the fitment of a 48-litre fuel tank in association with a repositioned fuel pump. It is because of the enlarged tank and associated changes that the Ford anti-roll bar kit mentioned earlier is not recommended for these later cars. The switch brought the RS1600i — like other Escorts of the period — into line with the Sierra in terms of the front strut top mounts: however the RS model maintained its individuality with Koni damping. The front struts were mounted in revised strut towers and the noticeable rear wheel negative camber of all the original FWD Escorts was eliminated.

When it came to comparing RS and XR Escort performance, differences in gearing as well as in engine specification and rev limits made a direct match perhaps misleading. The five-speed Escort transaxle, a fairly new design at the time, usually had a 0.76:1 fifth gear, but for the RS1600i the German engineers specified a shorter 0.83:1 ratio and then teamed it up with the 3.84:1 final drive ratio of the original four-speed XR3 rather than the ordinary five-speed 1600 Escort's 3.58:1 or the lower 4.29:1 used for the five-speed XR3i. This allowed the RS1600i 20.7mph per 1,000rpm (compared with the four-speed XR3 at 17.89mph per 1,000rpm, the five-speed XR3 at 22.5mph per 1,000rpm, or the XR3i at 20.29mph per 1,000rpm) so that a 100mph cruising speed demanded just under 4,900rpm.

RS1600i performance is detailed along with that of other RS cars in the appendix but it is relevant here to note that it was not measurably very much different from an XR3i though it was a considerable improvement over the original 96bhp XR3 with which its development began.

Another rendition of the RS symbol adorned the alloy wheels, above. For Britain, Dunlop D4s replaced the Phoenix tyres chosen in Germany. Rear anti-roll bar, applicable only to early FWD Escorts, is the lower of the two shown in this complete uprated suspension kit, below.

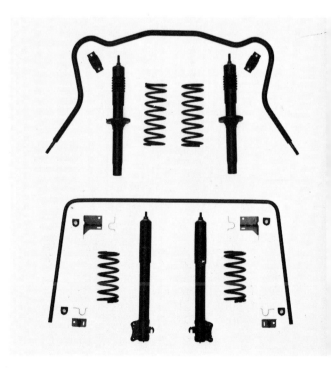

Successful competitors in Group A British Championship saloon car racing in 1983-84 were the RS1600i Escorts prepared by Richard Longman's company at Christchurch in Dorset. With engines producing over 160bhp, driven by Longman and Alan Curnow, the small Fords won their capacity class during both seasons and only narrowly failed to secure the overall championship title for Longman. These photographs are from 1984, including, right, a shot from the Brands Hatch Grand Prix meeting.

Autocar recorded 0-60mph times of 8.7 seconds for the RS against 9.2 for the XR3 and 0-100mph times of 27.9 seconds against nearly 32 seconds. The XR3 would reach 113mph, the RS1600i at least an average 116mph. Naturally when the comparison was made with the 105bhp XR3i, the figures were closer, *Autocar* measuring the same maximum for both, along with similar acceleration times.

Official fuel consumption figures given at the time of the RS1600i's introduction were 28.5mpg for the standard urban cycle, 46.3mpg at a constant 56mph and a modest 35.8mpg whilst slipping along at 3,623rpm in fifth (75mph).

In demand though it proved to be as a road car, the RS1600i was fundamentally intended to provide a suitable basis for competition machinery.

Its most prestigious competition award came with a surprise 1983 presentation in Paris to Stuart Turner. A generous FIA cup was handed over for the most successful car of the season in Group N (that closest to production specification category), almost entirely due to the efforts of Italian privateers. Italy had also provided a moment of World Championship glory for Mauro Pregliasco, who had led the 1983 Sanremo rally Group A competitors in an RS1600i, but transmission trouble ended that attempt to thwart another Alfa Group A victory. Incidentally clutch, gearbox and drive-shaft problems were a constant trial when the car was rallied with more than 145 to 150bhp; on the other hand, the transmission components were no problem in smooth circuit racing even with up to 165bhp on tap.

In Britain, Ford backed two Group A RS1600i Escorts for the Rothmans RAC Open Rally Championship. They were prepared and entered by MCD at Widnes, better known as R-E-D in later seasons. Normally driven by Louise Aitken/Ellen Morgan and Malcolm Wilson/Phil Short, they failed to finish the opening championship round in Yorkshire, but petite and determined Louise scored a fine seventh overall on the mainly tarmac Circuit of Ireland, beaten in Group A only by the evergreen Chris Lord's Mazda RX-7.

It was Malcolm Wilson's turn to take the RS1600i to seventh place on the Welsh international, but still the car wasn't an outright Group A winner as the Per Eklund Toyota in the same category finished fourth. Louise Aitken — later to be seen in R-E-D's turbocharged 'Aunty Sarah' Sierra long before the RS Cosworth existed — flung the RS1600i to tenth in Ulster, second in Group A to that 16-valve Toyota. In the final Championship round, the Manx, neither Escort finished. Though occupied with much development mileage in a new breed of turbo competition Ford, Malcolm Wilson finished 13th overall in the surviving Escort RS1600i on the 1983 Lombard RAC Rally, but it was far from the pace of the

Group A-winning Golf GTI of Kalle Grundel, a factory driver for Ford in 1986-87.

In motor racing the RS1600i had a spell of success in Britain until the privateers realized that a 16-valve rear-drive Toyota was a better way to go . . . maybe Ford should have kept the original RS1600 in production! The factory backed the efforts of Datapost-sponsored West Countrymen Richard Longman and Alan Curnow, Longman winning the class and nearly snatching the overall title in 1983 and 1984. Men like Chris Hodgetts — a success in 1986 with Toyota — also showed the RS1600i's speed in 1985 and it was only the extraordinary run of success recorded by Andrew Rouse (three times a British Champion in three brands of saloon: Alfa, Rover and Ford Sierra XR4Ti) that stood in the way of at least one Escort RS1600i outright Championship win in the 1980s.

Although its competition achievements were limited compared with some of its illustrious forebears, the RS of the front-drive generation could be *the* classic Ford Escort choice of the discerning enthusiast in the 1990s. Or will it be the Turbo RS Escort which captures the imagination of future restorers?

RS1600i on the road

More RS1600i Escort owners wrote more about their ownership experiences of this model than for any other featured in this book, highlighting its popularity, a success endorsed by high resale values four years after production ceased.

Aero industry employee, 49-year-old **Rallye News** editor Peter de Frere owned a Caspian blue RS1600i for three years and commented from Bristol: *When first introduced this model received some criticism from the motoring press, mainly centred on the handling and braking. It was believed that handling would benefit from the addition of a rear anti-roll bar and the brakes from the use of Escort XR3i standard rear drums. These criticisms led a number of owners into modification of their cars. Although Ford did not, to my knowledge, accept these criticisms, some modifications were made on the production line to the brake operating assembly and the rear suspension. This could mean that later cars handle better than earlier versions.*

My car was purchased with full knowledge of these criticisms. However, at no time did I modify the car, or feel the need so to do. The brakes did not inspire confidence, but in fact they worked very well. It was the pedal action which cast doubts on their efficiency. I believe the conversion from left to right-hand

drive and subsequent loss of motion in the transfer shaft was really the problem.

Tyres were a problem both for myself and earlier owners. The early Dunlop D4s could suffer from circumferential cracks in the walls. To be fair, the manufacturers gave good allowances for replacements. I had three new ones, which were perfect. Tyre mileage was very good for most drivers, although the usual few could not make them last 10,000 miles! At 20,000 miles my front tyres were barely half worn, but we did also discover that the ultra low profiles and potholes did not mix, leading to severe dents in the rim between the spokes.

The expensive exhaust system was also prone to cracks around the join with the rear silencer box. Luckily I spotted the early signs and had support brackets welded onto mine, between the pipe and the box. Nevertheless, the system lasted less than two years.

Servicing the car was easy and it used no oil at all between changes, reported Mr de Frere of his 1983 model, purchased from a dealer for a premium £7,750. He ran it for 38,000 miles and found that it always started easily and ran smoothly over the rev range, even when cold. Spark plug life varied, some not making it to his six-month limit. Fuel consumption averaged 33mpg in this careful owner's hands. He concluded: *The five-*

Although fitted with spoilers and auxiliary lamps, the RS1600i lacked the XR3/XR3i-style side mouldings and consequently had a somewhat less cluttered appearance.

speed gearbox was not the happiest I have ever tried and quick changes are not always easy. Second to third gear can be a bit of a lottery at times, and my Turbo is the same. It was only with regret that I made the change but I am very happy with my Turbo replacement. Perhaps one day, I will be able to own one of each...

A 23-year-old joiner from West Lothian in Scotland, Steven Reid bought his RS1600i, first registered in July 1983, for £6,400 in 1986. It had then covered 22,000 miles, and when he wrote to me that had increased to 39,500. His long and extremely instructive letter uncovered some facets of RS1600i ownership I had not appreciated and drew my attention to some important changes in specification during production.

He began with the expected story of the difficulties experienced in finding a good example, for he wanted only the post-July 1983 model. Giving his reasons, Mr Reid comments that the original hard suspension was one factor. Later models, he explained, had *the struts on the front modified, which is apparent with the bonnet up because a disc held by a nut replaces the large rubber and two nuts of the earlier cars. This is a sure way of checking whether your 1600i is a late or early model.*

The fuel tanks and pumps were also altered, later cars having a larger tank, but the real differences lie inside the car as the upholstery is totally different. Early upholstery for seats and door panels was in a crushed finish, whilst the later RS1600i has a smooth finish.

Incidentally, the early model had a dash illumination dimmer, but not the late one. On the early door mirrors the control knob was just a little stub, but the later cars had a large grip. You may have guessed by now that Mr Reid is a very effective concours competitor with an eye for detail. Other little tips he passed on included the note that on early cars the gear knob carried the shift pattern moulded within whilst late models used white lettering, and the steering wheel also followed the trim changes in swopping a

rippled leather finish for a smooth touch in the same hide.

Steven Reid had very little trouble with his RS1600i, although finding a replacement battery box was impossible. He eventually resolved this by fitting a box from a Mk2 RS2000, the only difference being that there is no clip to bolt the earth wire to — apparently only one concours judge has spotted the difference. But it was a job to convince Ford dealerships of the basic differences between XR3i and RS1600i in the engine bay, a subject pretty well publicized over the years...

Commenting that the clutch was replaced at 35,000 miles and that his RS1600i is serviced at 3,000-mile intervals, Steven Reid also added that friends with early RS1600i Escorts all run the Ford rear anti-roll bar kit with great results: *It stops that terrible twitchiness.*

Simon Sage, a 29-year-old accountant from Wolverhampton, acquired his RS1600i as a new car in August 1983 for £7,200 and it has now covered 44,000 miles. Having previously owned a second-generation Mexico and an RS2000 with extensive modifications, Simon observed: *After three years the RS1600i is in better bodywork condition than the RS2000 at the same age.*

As you would expect of a man who ran X-pack suspension and other modifications on his RS2000, Mr Sage had changed his RS1600i extensively. Underneath a KAT body kit it has a rear anti-roll bar added as well as front and rear springs and struts swopped and set up by Turbo Technics in Northampton in association with Andy Dawson. Also, a softer camshaft replaced the standard cam to bring in the torque at lower revs, 3,000rpm rather than 4,000.

He was not satisfied with Ford service (other owners were downright scathing about RS dealerships except for the favoured few already mentioned). *I now use a local garage man who normally services Rolls-Royce and Bentley, but who also handles RS types as he is a fellow enthusiast,* was Simon Sage's significant comment.

8

Escort RS Turbo

European Ford Motorsport boss Stuart Turner's office on the sixth floor at Ford's Warley HQ was the scene in April 1983 of a meeting between representatives of Motorsport, Product Planning (today incorporated under assigned Programme Directors) and Special Vehicle Engineering. The subject was how Motorsport's ambitions could be pursued through new performance products and two RS types resulted, the Sierra RS and the Escort RS Turbo. *Stuart Turner saw the Sierra RS as the racer and the Escort for rallying, simple as that,* said one senior executive who attended this fertile meeting.

Of course solving competition problems is never quite the same once battle is joined. The Escort actually became an excellent Group N and Group A production racer in the UK whilst the Sierra RS Cosworth raced and rallied at World Championship level.

But Turner's view of what was required at the time was the starting point for Ford's first European production car with turbocharging. Not that it was their first production turbo car internationally: I remember driving an earlier Mustang II, equipped with a turbo system for its 2.3-litre Pinto engine, that the company would probably have rather forgotten; later they decided intercooling really was needed and there have been at least three American models with turbo Pinto power including intercooling since then (Merkur XR4Ti, Mustang SVO and Thunderbird).

Ford had some earlier experience of turbocharged Escorts, but all were carburettor-equipped conversions rather than the Bosch fuel-injected production model that SVE would be charged with

developing. Further hard points laid down early in the specification of the first Escort RS Turbo included the use of the highest numerical final drive ratio feasible, for at that time Group A regulations were very restrictive on alternative ratios. What was envisaged as the fastest production Escort yet also had to employ wheelarch extensions as Ford Motorsport wanted to accommodate tyres up to 10in wide on the 8.5in rim widths permitted by the class regulations.

Further Motorsport requirements for the Escort, determined by the homologation requirements of Group A, included the following basics: suspension to accept 180 to 200bhp (Boreham could achieve 230 to 260bhp, but transmitting it durably to the ground was their major problem); Garrett T03 turbocharger for maximum power rather than the more road-suitable T02; the presence of an intercooler; and a limited-slip differential.

The company had most experience of using the Ferguson-patented Viscous Coupling to fulfil the limited-slip function. Works-constructed and works-backed front-drive Fiestas, developing over 250bhp in rallycross and rally test trim, had utilized the VC, as did the later Escorts converted to carburettor turbo trim for rallying. SVE backed the choice of the VC, rather than the mechanical types of LSD which can have an even more dramatic wheel-tugging effect on the steering of a powerful front-drive car. But engineering to produce acceptable road manners even with the fluid action of a VC proved a major development headache and there are those who will tell you Ford failed. When the second-generation Escort Turbo came along

there were important changes in tightened production tolerances that suggested Ford themselves were not satisfied on this front.

Bill Meade, legendary for his practical engineering with Ford Competitions and FAVO, had a track record that encompassed developing the Ford-produced Cortina Lotus Twin Cam and then cramming the same engine into an Escort engine bay, besides his other Boreham competition duties in the 1960s. Bill had initiated an Escort Turbo development exercise in the autumn of 1980. Assisted by Terry Bradley, he took the new front-drive Escort and had a running prototype, using Garrett turbocharging, for senior management assessment in early 1981. The response was enthusiastic, to the extent that Ford's mainstream

engineers also looked at the possibilities of a mass-production Escort turbo, possibly based on the 1.3 CVH.

So by the time of that spring meeting in 1983 Ford had a lot of practical data on the CVH Escort and turbocharging, having persuaded the Garrett T3 to provide between 125 and 140bhp, depending on purpose. Ford Motorsport boosted development feedback by running an Escort Turbo Rally Championship in 1983 and 1984, supplying conversion kits for would-be competitors to fit to their own cars.

The Escort Turbo rally series did not attract enough runners and riders to be deemed a commercial success worthy of continuation, but it did highlight Mark Lovell's talent and led to him

Escort RS Turbo, the first turbocharged production European Ford, at its press debut in the rain in Essex late in 1984.

Colour matching of panels made possible the use of mostly in-house Ford parts, but some additional bits were provided by Marley. Bumpers and rear spoiler were colour-matched XR3/XR3i items, but extended wheelarches were necessary for Group A competition purposes. Black marks on the Millbrook test track are the legacy of repeated brake fade testing.

driving the factory's Escort RS Turbo in 1985. It also provided valuable experience of turbo engine performance under arduous conditions and was a major factor in the presence of an uprated transmission and Viscous Coupling in the final specification of the Escort RS Turbo.

Ford Motorsport, and later SVE, drew considerable assistance from the work of former Garrett AiResearch employee Geoff Kershaw at Turbo Technics in Northampton. He first produced his own carburettor XR3 conversion and Ford later loaned an XR3i on which a T3 was employed and assessed. Kershaw then sold the jigs and tooling to complete such an injection turbo installation to Ford. These items included the all-important engineering of a new exhaust system and mounting points for the turbo unit in front of the engine. Most of that work is visible in the engine bay of the 1984-90 Escort RS Turbo, but it is important to remember that Ford also had to complete their own development work to satisfy both their own standards of durability and external emission control requirements.

Ford Motorsport and Turbo Technics sold their handiwork individually, both for the fully built Escort RS Turbos of either generation and in conversion kit form. Components to turbocharge a carburettor Ford 1600 CVH were available under Ford Motorsport part number 909.6000: this installation was normally rated at 125bhp at 5,800rpm with 130lb/ft of torque. Turbo Technics can boost Ford CVH engines with injection or carburettor to varying specifications offering from 130 to 170bhp (the latter making uprated chassis and brakes a must).

As work progressed, former Weslake engineer and current Ford Boreham homologation expert John Griffiths was loaned to SVE, along with Bill Meade, to work under the overall direction of Escort RS Turbo projects leader Mike Smith.

Despite Ford's earlier work on carburettor-equipped turbocharged engines, it seems there was never any doubt about using fuel injection on the product to be offered to the public. Bosch KE-Jetronic injection was specified, this system being a hybrid version of the famous K system employed on the XR3i and so many other European performance cars. The E denoted electronic control of the cold start period.

A number of detail changes to the CVH engine were necessary for durability and compatibility with the turbo installation. Most obvious was a

reduction in compression from the XR3i's 9.5:1 to 8.3:1, this achieved by eliminating the raised piston crown, which is there primarily to assist emission control. Tapered secondary rings on the replacement pistons yielded extra cylinder bore oil circulation. The gudgeon pins and the main bearings were of an uprated specification when compared to the XR3i. Complex cutout systems limited engine revs progressively in the 6,300 to 6,500rpm band: both fuel and ignition cut-offs were provided, set just 100rpm apart. There was also a master system to limit boost at high underbonnet temperatures and in straightforward over-boost situations. An engine-to-turbocharger oil feed and return system was a necessary addition.

Valve timing was modified by the installation of a 1.3 Escort camshaft sprocket to provide an overall retardation in cam timing. Originally, the CVH head was equipped with Nimonic exhaust valves, but a series of endurance tests, including a 300-hour spell, led to sodium-cooled exhaust valves being specified.

The incorporation of a Bosch-Motorola management system balancing ignition curve against turbo boost and fuelling requirements provided excellent engine manners, even though some of the part-throttle mapping was simply extrapolated from full power data. This point was attended to in the preparation of the second-generation RS Turbo.

There was no sign of such development haste, though, the turbocharged injection Escort driving away from cold faultlessly and earning consistent praise as one of the best turbocharging installations available. Best, that is, in terms of civilization as well as extra power, without sudden surges of turbo boost.

Boost remained restrained to very low levels indeed. According to inlet manifold temperature anything from 0.25bar to 0.55bar (3.5psi to 7.8psi) was the permitted maximum. In British production racing trim for 1986 the official maximum recorded in the car's regulation paperwork was 0.8bar. It is worth checking that even the standard 0.5bar setting is being reached on these models. Any competition specialist in the marque will assist, but Richard Longman at Christchurch, outside Bournemouth, Hants, is extremely familiar with such work.

Complete with the cast nickel-iron high temperature four-branch manifold and stainless-steel

Individual RS identification was extended to the side panels for those who had not already got the message from the alloy wheels, extended arches and front spoiler. Auxiliary lamps were standard.

Dashboard from higher level models in the ordinary production Escort range was retained, complete with red zone on the tachometer to remind the driver of the progressively enforced rev limit. No boost gauge: not until the Sierra RS Cosworth was able to borrow one ready-made from the USA-market Merkur XR4Ti did such a device feature in SVE's designs.

exhaust system (exiting with a 2.4in diameter flourish) the RS Turbo power unit was rated at 132bhp. This occurred at 6,000rpm, with a hefty 133lb/ft of torque present at 3,000rpm which is the reason (together with Motorsport's gearing requirements) why SVE found an uprated transmission assembly necessary. . .

Rod Mansfield, manager of SVE, recalled the

further development of the five-speed XR3i transaxle needed to accommodate Motorsport and mainstream engineering demands for maximum acceleration and road-going durability respectively. *The official torque peak is 3,000rpm, but you would find near enough 133lb/ft spread across a very wide power band indeed.*

Given that we have a Ford test that involves a

stop start procedure, with a cruel tear-away through the gears, plus constant on-off throttle changes, it was obvious we would have to make changes in the transaxle. These tied in exactly with the feedback we were getting from the rally championship.

Basically we went from the XR3i's final drive of 4.29 to a 4.27 by using bigger and stronger transmission teeth, rather than the finer teeth that are usually specified for mass production. I don't think we encountered any noise problem on that score. . . We also found that the championship cars were cracking gearbox casings and suffering bearing failures.

So the casings were stiffened up with bracing webs and the squash-fit Belville washer replaced with carefully sized shims. Personally, I think it was the stiffer casing that gave us double the previous life in subsequent Ford tests.

Related to that transmission work was the fitment of the Viscous Coupling limited-slip differential. Now widely known for its use in four-wheel-drive systems (BMW, Ford and VW are amongst its leading customers), the VC had not been adopted elsewhere in a powerful front-driven road car so its behaviour was, and remained, a problem unique to the Ford Escort RS Turbo. Remember Ford's first independent rear end on a front-drive car, modified considerably over the years but still exercising the minds of performance engineers, and you begin to understand the

development problems that had to be overcome

During development all kinds of VC plate arrangements and fluid viscosity ratings were assessed, but even when they felt they had the right progressive action for public roads the car was twitchy under full acceleration. Incidentally a complete Group A Type AF gearbox assembly, including final drive, clutch, limited-slip differential and gearbox linkage, was available from Ford Motorsport. So were shot-peened final drive gears (4.27:1) and an alternative 140,000 centistokes setting for the limited-slip assembly. (A stokes, by the way, is a unit of kinematic viscosity.)

A persistent Michelin tyre rep talked his company's MXVs (195/50 VR) onto the 15in rims that

Escort hatchback versatility was part of the RS Turbo recipe, with split rear seat backs adding to the number of varied possible arrangements.

The RS Turbo press demonstrator came complete with Custom Pack electric windows. The Recaro seats provided their usual outstandingly good combination of comfort and location for the occupants.

Right, Turbo Technics Escort XR3i with Garrett AiResearch turbocharger, a conversion which provided Ford with further data to add to that obtained from their own carburettor-equipped rallying and roadgoing Escorts. In the production Ford layout, below, the feed from intercooler to manifold runs at an angle across the rocker cover. The turbocharger casing can be seen below the feed pipe joint in front of the engine.

were needed to accommodate the most common competition tyre sizes, and that helped the road car's handling considerably.

For the second-generation RS Turbo approved tyres are Dunlop or Goodyear. It may also help to note on the tyre choice question that the produc-

tion racers tended to use buffed Yokohamas for their 10-lappers in 1986, but BBC DJ Mike Smith and farmer co-driver Lionel Abbott consumed only Dunlop D4s of German origin to win the 1986 Snetterton 24 hours in the Ilford Escort RS Turbo. By contrast Karl Jones in the Richard

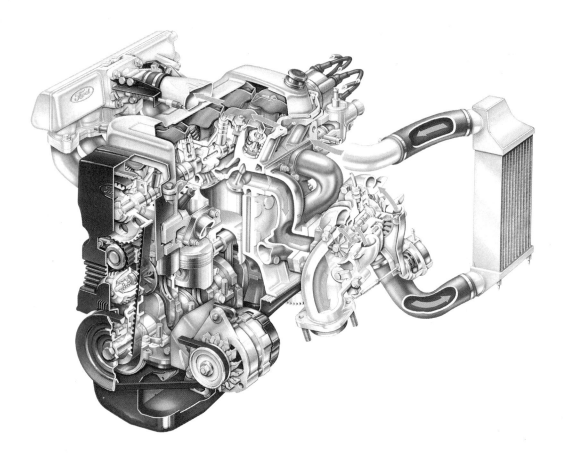

Ford cutaway highlights the pistons used to lower the compression ratio to 8.3:1, the Bosch KE-Jetronic fuel injection system and the small intercooler. The electronically-managed unit was restrained to 132bhp on modest boost and in consequence delivered outstanding flexibility.

Asquith class-winning car of 1987 used BF Goodrich TA-R tyres in the standard sizing and these assisted in providing the best handling Turbo I have driven.

The SVE development team led by Ford's Mike Smith supplied the necessary tie-bar front suspension with a separate anti-roll bar *à la* RS1600i, but the car failed its first frontal impact crash test. The tie bars were then mounted in heavyweight iron castings at the forward, body end of the linkage. It added weight in the nose of the car, just where it is not required in a turbocharged front-drive performer, yet the links worked as well as ever and the next crash test session also proved successful.

Co-operating with that tie-bar front end were many of the suspension components used in the pre-1986 model year XR3i. Springs were the same 98lb/in front and 102lb/in rear, mated to similar Girling gas-filled monotube dampers, but softened

in their bump and rebound settings for the RS Turbo compared with those of the XR3I.

A rear anti-roll bar of just 12mm diameter from the Escort-based Orion range was specified — quite an important fact to note, for this was the first time Ford had fitted the rear anti-roll bar to a production Escort.

Scandalously, SVE were not allowed to change the braking system in the original car. For competition the Group A RS Turbos had four-wheel disc braking from AP with the choice of 290mm/ 11.4in diameter for tarmac rallying and outright racing, or 264mm/10.4in, and in both cases suitable calipers are listed by Ford Motorsport. The hapless road customer was stuck with the discs and drums from a 105bhp XR3i in a 132bhp cousin capable of close to 130mph! Others did not complain as much as I did, though, and the fitment of improved friction materials, plus brake cooling ducts in the front spoiler, were gestures in the right direction. On the second-generation RS Turbo bigger brakes were provided. . .

Cockpit changes were minimal for the production of the first version. British secondhand buyers should remember that the £9,250 launch price of the Escort RS Turbo in 1985 (*a few, literally a handful, were made in December 1984,* said one SVE insider) did *not* include a glass tilt and slide sunroof, electric front window operation, tinted glass and central locking: all those features formed a £470 Custom Pack option.

Capable of exceeding 125mph, the RS Turbo made an exciting road car, though the advantages conferred by carefully located front suspension and the pioneering use of a Viscous Coupling limited-slip differential were partially negated for road-car customers by the retention of standard Escort disc/drum brakes. Second-generation cars lost the front suspension links but gained better braking!

Not just a well-known DJ! Mike Smith drove two Escort RS Turbos in production racing in 1985-86, one of which went on to be used equally effectively by Karl Jones in 1987. Paired with Lionel Abbott, Smith scored the first turbo and front-drive win in the Willhire Snetterton 24-hour race in 1986.

Two Group A competition RS Escorts that met with rather different fortunes in 1985. Left, Richard Longman's Royal Mail Datapost car proved just as capable a racing class winner as its RS1600i predecessor. The Radiopaging machine, right, is the Mark Lovell/Peter David rally car, shatteringly fast on occasion but plagued by unreliability. The best RS Turbo result on the home international rally series came from Bob Stoneman's car, 30th overall and Group N winner on the Isle of Man: the old rear-drive RS1800 was still finishing just in the top ten in the hands of privateers! The Group A racing RS Turbo, though, was successful as soon as its tardy homologation came through. At Silverstone on June 9, 1985, below, Richard Longman wins the class, finishes sixth overall and sets a new lap record at 102.88mph.

Standard interior equipment was recognizably that of the XR3i, including the three-spoke steering wheel, but a pair of excellent Recaro sports front seats were allowed. The Monza fabric trim was familiar enough from the XR3i and the instrumentation remained of that same clear origin, with a 140mph speedometer but not even a boost gauge in sight. For 1985 the Escort had split rear seats, folding as before for maximum hatchback versatility, and these were part of the Turbo cabin too.

Some customers did pay extra to have alternatives to the basic white paint. These were mainly VIPs, such as a Fleet Street press baron who has insisted on black RS Escorts since the 1970s.

Ford did not officially offer an alternative colour. In fact the Escort RS,Turbo was not catalogued in their monthly glossy brochure, a habit the company seems to preserve even for the second Escort RS Turbo and the Sierra RS Cosworth. Only passing references were made to the RS Turbo's existence in their magazine *Ford Cars.* I had to look to the independent motoring magazines to get the closing January 1986 basic list price of £9,583.

The white colour-coded exterior and seven-spoke RS alloy wheels (6 × 15) were extremely

effective. This RS looked very different from its less powerful brethren thanks to an ingenious body kit of hard plastic panels, those parts which were actually new being mostly of Marley Foam origin.

The colour-coded grille was simply a repainted Orion item, and the same colour change process disguised the XR3/3i rear 'tailplane' as well. The wheelarch extensions, necessary for Motorsport's requirements, swept into a deep front spoiler that had the towing eye neatly hidden behind a removable panel in its lower edge. The usual Escort bumpers endured the spray booth too, but those side panel extensions and front spoiler were original products of a division of Marley Tiles that deals with automotive plastics. Their work can also

be seen on the four-door Sierra RS Cosworth, but not the original three-door Cosworth.

No drag factor was quoted; I was unofficially told that the deeper front spoiler had helped preserve the fatter Ford RS Turbo's Cd 'in the same area' as XR3/3i, which means a company-claimed 0.375. That other body-related vital statistic, kerb weight, was predicted at 950kg/2,090lb, split 565kg/1,243lb front and just 385kg/847lb rear. *Motor* recorded 971kg/2,136lb for their test car and ***Autocar*** some 977kg/2,150lb for the machine for which figures are reproduced in the appendix.

The first Escort RS Turbo's performance certainly matched Ford claims, with the top speed

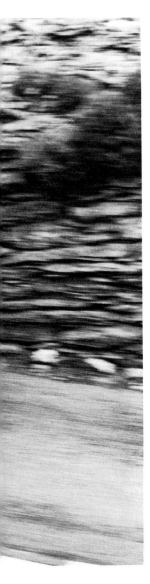

by *Autocar* in March 1987 showed UK sales of the first Escort RS Turbo at 3,990 in 1985; during 1986, the year of transition to the new model, sales were down nearly a thousand. The mockers would love to see the 'XR3 with a turbo' as a flop, but the truth is that this second-generation RS Turbo was actually substantially redeveloped with worthwhile gains in engine security; lower noise levels resulting from revised gearing; and vastly improved braking, with the Girling-Lucas-Ford Stop Control System (SCS) providing an anti-lock facility, as well as bigger discs and drums. In fact virtually every aspect of the car had been improved, so why did it get such a bad press and more than its fair share of moans from the purists?

My feeling is that two factors hit the second RS Turbo hard. Firstly, it lacked more than minor visual differences to distinguish it from the XR3i, which was getting criticized by the specialist press for lack of performance in comparison with a new wave of 'hot hatch' rivals. Secondly, the relative lack of drama in its road manners — both low noise levels at high cruising speeds and the reduction of the odd behaviour associated with the original VC differential — seemingly convinced many that the RS Turbo was *not exciting anymore ... a bit bland ... no fireball.* These and many more such comments were delivered even on first impressions, which is unusual in the UK press.

Autocar made it their cover car in August 1986, but could not hide their disappointment, and that was understandable, given that it weighed nearly 100lb more (2,247lb) and took over 9 seconds to reach 60mph; top speed was down to 124 from 125mph, despite the claimed improvement in

The Escort RS Turbo in second-series form was announced in July 1986 (when the Sierra RS Cosworth also became available). Based on the restyled 1986 Escort line, it was visually closer to the XR3i but extensively re-engineered in many areas. Lucas-Girling SCS anti-lock braking was included in the standard equipment. Side badging was discontinued for the second-generation Turbo, but the colour-matched back spoiler and bootlid script ensured that few failed to identify the £10,000-plus Escort. Mirrors were not colour coded on the early cars provided for press assessment.

often proving beyond their 125mph prophesy. Testing for **Performance Car** around a very windy Millbrook banking the standard wipers hovered above the screen as we recorded a best of 126.76mph and an average around the two-mile bowl of just beyond 122mph. Timed electronically, acceleration from 0-60mph occupied 8.18 seconds, 0-100mph 23.99 seconds and the standing quarter-mile squeaked and wooshed by in 16.21 seconds at an average of 85.1mph. I averaged 24.63mpg in a week full of hard motoring for **Performance Car,** but owners tended to do much better, many recording over 30mpg.

Unofficial figures obtained by a freelance journalist from either the SMMT or Ford and printed

aerodynamics conferred by the reskinned 1986 Escort body.

Did **Autocar** have a duff example? Certainly the 0-60mph time was slow by rival standards, and the magazine attributed this to a *ridiculously long 1.3 seconds* to negotiate the second-to-third gearchange. Jeff Daniels recorded 0-60mph in 8.3 seconds for **Performance Car** with that magazine's sophisticated test equipment. He also registered top-end performance of 125.4mph average and 127.1mph as the best flying quarter-mile in good conditions. That left the new car slightly slower than the original — though not by the large margin implied by the **Autocar** acceleration figures — but the trouble was that it *felt* so languid.

What were the detail differences incorporated in this second-generation RS Turbo? It had, of course, the 1986-style Escort shell with its new, smoother nose, and it was closely based on the XR3i version. Harry Worrall at SVE was the project engineer in charge of redeveloping the Escort Turbo and he reminded me that without the need to support a separate Motorsport homologation application for the new car some competition orientated items could be deleted. Notable among these were the 4.27:1 final drive, the extra wide extensions beyond the standard Escort wheelarches and the need for tie-bar front suspension.

The brakes, complete with the award-winning anti-lock system, were new to the Escort line. At the front they were based on those of the obsolete Sierra XR4i: ventilated discs of 260mm/10.2in diameter and a thickness of 24mm/0.94in. The rear brakes were still drums but up an inch in diameter to 229mm/9in, and 44mm/1.75in wide. I can't say I liked the anti-lock system when I first tried it in 1986, but during the snow in the winter of 1987 its responses seemed far speedier and I welcomed its presence on the car and the surprisingly taut brake pedal action.

The CVH turbocharged engine looked the same as before, but hid many changes. Most significantly, the Bosch-Motorola management system received those part-throttle calibrations, taking the ignition advance into more secure zones and ensuring optimum fuel economy under lighter loads. Programmed as a 'running change' for September 1986 but actually implemented in April 1987 was an additional knock sensor that could cope with any grade of fuel, including super unleaded. It was a so-called 'active' system that

Bonnet vents, side sill extensions and modest wheelarch lips distinguished the RS Turbo from the XR3i. The wheels were different in every key dimension to the XR, though sharing the overall style.

Jeff Daniels heels the RS Turbo over while testing at MIRA for the November 1986 issue of *Performance Car*. The second-generation machine recorded 127.1mph as its best speed, with 0-60mph in 8.3 seconds, better than most testers achieved, but fuel consumption was an unremarkable 25mpg.

modified the ignition curve in relation to combustion within the revised Lean Burn chambers.

'Lean Burn' was the Ford buzzword of the period and reminds us that the company had incorporated all the 1.6-litre CVH's 1986 model year changes in the turbo unit. That meant slight changes in cylinder head porting and combustion chamber shape and an 'improved efficiency' oil pump but how it was improved was not revealed. I suspect it had a lower pressure output because Ford mainstream engineers had looked for ways to reduce friction to uprate the basic 1600 from 79bhp to 90bhp.

Specific SVE changes for the Turbo in 1986 included a one-piece inlet manifold, plus *detail design changes to the air-to-air intercooler for greater efficiency.* More importantly Garrett had served up a new water-cooled centre bearing housing on the T3 turbo unit which should ensure longer bearing life, particularly by avoiding the damaging heat-soak period when a motor is stopped straight after a hard driving session.

External and internal clues distinguishing a Turbo from an XR3i were few. There were modest extensions both on the wheelarches and to emphasize the sill between front and rear wheelarches, plus the Sierra RS-style bonnet vents on either side of the new, smooth Escort bonnet. Also the new-style XR3i rear wing was colour-coded when fitted to a Turbo. Even the previously loved RS wheels had been ditched, and the apparent similarity between XR3i and Turbo wheels in the

Standard 1986 Escort instrumentation for the RS Turbo, retaining a 6,400rpm rev counter redline and providing neither boost nor oil pressure readings.

Alloy wheels of 6J section at 15in diameter carried Dunlop SP Sport D40 195/50 low-profile tyres on the press demonstrators, replacing the Michelin MXVs in the same size used on the previous model.

current generation is a styling trick, because they are an inch different in diameter and are far from the same wheel in terms of offsets. The XR3i continues to use 185/60 HRs mounted upon a 6J × 14in version of the new five-spoke wheel, whilst the RS Turbo has 6 × 15in wheels and 195/50 VR tyres, usually from Dunlop or Goodyear on early examples.

The aerodynamic drag factor for the new car was claimed to have been reduced to 0.36Cd, most of that improvement drawn from an overall 8% drag reduction achieved by Ford for the later Escort shape. Principally the advantages have come from deleting the front grille and smoothing the nose contours, but there is also a vestigial Orion-style lip in the tailgate.

Kerb weight was expected to rise slightly, and quoted as 965kg/2,123lb. The maximum figure (based on options such as the Custom Pack) was 980kg/2,156lb and the **Autocar** example actually weighed 1,021kg/2,247lb ready to test.

To meet some of the criticisms made by press and public of the original RS Turbo's handling, SVE made a series of detail changes the combined effect of which created what felt like a completely new car from the driving seat. The suspension was now far more like that of the XR3i than before, picking up the 1986 changes. These included *moving the front stabilizer bar's mounting points forward, thereby reducing the nose's inclination to lift under hard acceleration and dip when the brakes are applied*, according to Ford.

Ford personnel at the February launch of the new Escort also said of XR3i, *The effect has been to lengthen the anti-roll bar and the steering arms have been dropped. In general, front spring rates have increased and every effort has been made to improve traction as well as high-speed stability.*

The same Pilot Plant engineers confirmed that SVE and mainstream engineering had worked in opposite directions with some slight geometry changes involving the ride height: *SVE originally dropped it 18mm, now it's been raised 10mm!* said one wryly. The company has also introduced a solid, Rose-type joint at the inner end of the track control arms for their version of the XR3i whilst SVE have generally been taking such hard joints out. Another major change is that Fichtel & Sachs dampers, gas-filled twin-tube units, are now used in both the XR3i and RS Turbo.

SVE tackled the new car's suspensions by first replacing the XR3i's 19kNm (106.4lb/in) front springs and 46.5kNm (260.4lb/in) rears with 24kNm (134.4lb/in) fronts and 52kNm (291.2lb/in) rears. That may sound as if there is an enormous disparity in spring rate front to rear, but the effects of the Escort's unique independent rear suspension geometry produce such leverage distortions on the apparent spring rate at the back that I am assured that the figures given represent an *honest attempt to try and equalize out the front to rear rates.*

The Fichtel & Sachs gas dampers from the XR3i effectively soften the car, a feature that has provoked much comment from those who think it should have the firmer ride of the original. I understand the 24mm roll bar was of the same girth, if not with the same outline and mounting points, as has been present since the advent of the XR3i. The rear anti-roll bar of Orion extraction was again fitted at the rear of the Escort RST, but this time the diameter was 16mm.

The handling and the feel provided by the steering changed dramatically — for the better, in my view. The limited-slip differential problems had been tackled with some extra holes drilled in the Viscous Coupling plates and *a general tightening*

up in manufacturing tolerances for the front VC differential. We did not alter the plate thickness or the specified fluid viscosity, but we did find a change in tolerances assisted us in the fight to avoid any fierceness in the differential's action, reported Harry Worrall.

Transaxle changes centred on a tougher, eight-bolt differential unit, its principal components subjected to a shot peening process. It was engineered by mainstream in place of the old six-bolt differential to suit their ordinary Escort 1.6. The Turbo's final drive ratio was now 3.82:1 instead of the old 4.27:1.

According to Ford, top speed increased, benefiting from that reduced drag factor as well as the numerically lower (higher ratio) final drive. Far more important to the driver was the sharply reduced noise level in motorway cruising, 100mph now seeming about as noisy as 85mph had felt in the previous version.

That replacement final drive also helped fuel consumption. Fuel figures released by Ford were 25.9mpg for urban driving, a frugal 42.8mpg at 56mph and a reasonable 34mpg at a constant 75mph.

Neat interior of the later Escort was ergonomically well designed, with unobtrusive but effective electric window controls incorporated in the door pulls, and power adjustment of the door mirrors directed by the knob above the ventilation grille closest to the camera.

July 15, 1986 brought the official Ford announcement that the Escort RS Turbo, still Saarlouis-built, was available again to complement the revised Escort range which had gone on sale in February. Production of the first Turbo had finished on December 20, 1985 (Ford quoted total output as 8,604 examples), but there was not much of a gap in UK Ford showrooms because most dealers had enough of the original models in stock to sell during the intermission. It was about the only time you could get a decent discount deal on an Escort RS Turbo!

The new look demanded a hefty premium. Basic price was £10,028 and the inevitable Custom Pack — comprising the usual sunroof, electric window operation and central locking — added another £572. The standard equipment list in 1986 included tinted glass, radio/stereo cassette player, rear seat belts and those auxiliary driving lamps. The production specification also covered the Lucas-Girling mechanical anti-lock braking system that was a £300-plus option on all other five-speed 1.6-litre Escorts. From late 1987 the Custom Pack items became part of the standard specification.

Ford subsequently admitted that they had supplied their dealers with relatively large stocks of the original Escort RS Turbo to plug the gap between the two versions, and that — plus the factors mentioned earlier, as well as increasing competition in the 'hot hatchback' market — could account for the possibly slower than expected sales recorded at the start of this controversial RS type's career.

RS Turbo on the road

Our first general observations on the Escort RS Turbo as originally launched come from former RS1600i owner Peter de Frere: *I think the RS Turbo is a lazy man's car and that suits me fine! On those rare occasions when I want to go fast (or indeed am allowed to), I simply apply slight pressure to the pedal and off we jolly well go. So the answer is yes, I do like the Turbo and I'm glad I made the change.*

More detailed comment came from a 25-year-old trainee pilot who bought his RST for £9,400 with 14 miles on the clock in August 1985. I am sure it came complete with the Custom Pack, so he bought at a competitive price. No modifications were made by the time he had covered 15,900 miles, save to try to alleviate the worry of theft by fitting a Sparkrite alarm, install his own choice in stereo and provide a sunroof deflector.

His experience of owning an RST was: *Expensive! A great head-turner, but you pay the cost in insurance in group 6A. Theft is always a threat in the back of your mind and I have had one failed attempt caught out by the alarm. Performance and comfort are superb, but the suspension is very rattly at 30-40mph on normal roads. I think all four tyres will require replacing at 18,000 miles, and they are likely to cost £75 each.*

Measured by the tankful, I obtain 32mpg in summer and 29mpg in winter. A typical tankful will cover a mixture of 80 miles motorway, 80 miles A-roads and about the same distance bumper-to-bumper, to and from work. Faults have been minimal, but there were some of a PDI nature to be sorted out at the first service.

Mr I. McNicoll was our high-mileage man, a 34-year-old vet who purchased his RS new in August 1985 for roughly £10,000. The only specific modification made was to fit a dimmer switch to the panel lights to eliminate severe reflections in the windshield.

Obviously an experienced driver (16 years) who would be called out in all weathers, Mr McNicoll felt the Escort RST was: *A great car to own and drive. The handling and roadholding are superb; the acceleration breathtaking. However the brakes are easy to lock and have a tendency to judder when braking from speed.*

I have used Michelin MXV tyres throughout my 46,000 miles and have bills and dates to prove that I get an average 20,000 miles per cover. Over the total mileage I averaged 31mpg, but it's easy to drop below 30mpg if you constantly thrash the car, and similarly tyre life will drop to 15,000 miles.

My RS dealer in Norwich (Spruce) gives me no problems — which is encouraging as this tough customer managed to rack up 29,000 miles within the warranty period,

The 1990 Escort RS Turbo shared a colour-coded version of the later 'droopy' XR3i rear wing and also featured minor badge and interior trim changes. If the experience of owners we talked to is typical, RS Turbos from 1989 onward were more reliable than the earlier second generation cars.

when the clutch required replacement. This RS also required two windscreen washer motors (18,000 and 24,000 miles) and a fuel pump relay at 500 miles.

In addition to his concours RS2000, Steve Rockingham in Oxfordshire ran two of the later shape RS Turbos. The young quantity surveyor, who racks up an annual mileage of 25,000, commented in January 1990: *I have had what can only be described as a chequered relationship with two RS Turbos during the past 15 months.*

The first car was a white F-registered example that I bought in September 1988 for £11,000 on the road from Hartford Motors, Oxford and it was disposed of in August 1989. During the disastrous 11 months and 22,000 miles the problems encountered were numerous. I have not got space for all of them, but the most significant were: three gearbox rebuilds to overcome jamming in fifth gear; four exhaust systems under warranty, finally fixed by a later two-section system to overcome cracking on the downpipe bend (a common problem — thus the work on Fiesta RS Turbo recounted later); replacement engine management system after failure to start; precautionary change of CVH OHC drive belt as valve gear was rattling badly (I have known ordinary Escorts break this component at 25,000 miles); and loss of turbo boost rectified with a new wastegate solenoid. And that account does not bother with some of the door rattles, or tyre wear sufficient to require four new covers at 12,000 miles.

Despite heaving a huge sigh of relief when he sold the car back to Hartfords, Steve Rockingham bought another RST. Much of the reason was the exceptional after sales service provided by this RS dealer. This time it was a G-registered model exchanged in an 'incredibly preferential' deal. Rockingham commented: *The second car has now covered 8,500 miles of trouble-free motoring and is a vast improvement over the first vehicle.* Both RS Turbos averaged 28mpg, the later car run on 98 octane super unleaded which *seems to make the car perform better.*

Mr Rockingham was not impressed with the handling (*somewhat uninspiring*) and he felt — like so many others — that the SCS anti-lock braking makes the pedal feel *very spongy and feels less efficient than a non-SCS XR3i or Orion 1.6i. Having tried Dunlop D40, Goodyear NCTs and Michelin MXV tyres I feel the NCTs have superior handling to the D40s, but the MXVs seem to offer the best compromise between wet and dry handling and certainly wear far more slowly than Goodyear or Dunlop rubber.*

In summary, the earlier nightmare turned into an appreciation for *exceptional mid-range performance as part of a well equipped package. The car was originally chosen in preference to the Golf GTI or a Peugeot 309 GTI and I am now convinced that the Ford offered the optimum in performance and equipment for the money, although the opposition had superior handling. Servicing is remarkably cheap and the only expensive item is the tyre consumption at approximately 14,000 miles a set,* reported Rockingham.

9

Capri RS2600 and RS3100

So far we have discussed only RS Escorts in detail. Over the years they came in every variety from relatively simple rear-drive machines to much more complex turbocharged and fuel-injected front-wheel-drive cars. But there were always those at Ford who argued that the RS factor could successfully be applied elsewhere too. In the case of the Capri, which was, after all, Ford's most overtly sporting production car, the most enthusiastic advocate was Jochen Neerpasch.

A former Porsche works racing driver, Neerpasch managed the German Ford Motorsport department that was established on January 7, 1968 as a Continental counterpart to Ford Competitions at Boreham. The department was housed in two-storey workshops and offices within the Ford Cologne factory at Niehl, on the Rhine, and the staff included Michael Kranefuss, who has subsequently become Ford's World Motorsport chief. Their competition successes with Escort and Taunus models included victory on the 1969 East African Safari using a Weslake-modified V6 engine in the Taunus 20M RS saloon. But what concerns us here is the development of the Capri as a competition car, a story which embraces both high and low moments — such low points that Jochen Neerpasch offered his resignation prior to the 1971 season. It was not accepted, but that the proud and competitive Neerpasch should have felt such a step was necessary indicates the depths to which the Capri's reliability in endurance racing sank. But then came the golden years, with the Capri in dominant form in the 1971 and 1972 European Touring Car Championship seasons.

First German competition moves with the Capri concerned the 2300GT, which appeared on the Lyons-Charbonnières rally as a prototype in March 1969. That model was the first use of the V6 engine from the Taunus saloons in the larger-capacity German Capris. Later this iron-block V6 family — which the production Capri used in every capacity from 2.0 to 2.6 litres — became the base on which the RS2600 was constructed for road and competition use. Later still, drawing on expertise gained during the European Touring Car Championship campaign, the production block was strengthened as a basis for the Federal 2.8 Arizona V6 that was seen in Capris and Mustangs for the USA. Finally, it is worth remembering that the iron-block pushrod OHV 2.8 became the propulsion for a range of European Fords in the 1970s and 1980s, including the Granada 2.8i, Capri injection, Sierra XRs and the Granada/Scorpio line.

That first competition Capri back in March 1969 ran with Weslake engine modifications that boosted it from the standard 108bhp (later in 1969 some 125 horsepower was offered) at 5,100rpm to 170bhp at 6,500 revs. The changes to the 2,293cc (90mm × 60.1mm) V6 included triple Solex downdraught carburettors, and high compression (10:1 instead of 9:1) for the Weslake iron heads, which retained siamese porting, as did the production engines right up until the advent of the 2.9 V6 seen in 1987-specification Granada/Scorpios. However, the competition development of the Capri soon saw far more adventurous schemes than those early efforts with what were basically modified road-registered cars. . .

The 2300GT Capri's debut was marked by a

fourth overall for Dieter Glemser/Klaus Kaiser and the factory were encouraged to keep on rallying the Ford coupe through 1969. The 2300GT motor was constantly uprated, making 192bhp at 7,200rpm with Lucas fuel injection and a 10.5:1 compression ratio for the Tour de France, in which Jean-Francois Piot grasped an encouraging sixth overall against high-quality opposition.

The best 1969 result for the German-entered Capri GTs came on the Tour de Corse, the fast Corsican road event which is now part of the World Championship. A Group 6 prototype Capri 2600GT (2,550cc, 90mm × 66.8mm) for Piot and Jean Todt (Peugeot-Talbot competition boss in the 1990s) finished an outstanding third overall. That 2600GT had some 200 horsepower at its disposal at just 6,000rpm (compared with 125bhp for the street 2600GT).

The Corsican result, plus the unexpected win for Robin Hillyar/Jock Aird in the Safari Taunus, sent the Ford Competitions department up something of a blind alley in 1970, rallying the Capri on the East African Safari *and* tackling the European Touring Car Championship. In both cases, the 2300GT model was deployed, evolving to the point where it had 2,397cc and an official 230bhp on Kugelfischer fuel injection to propel ever-larger front spoilers and wheelarch extensions, with a kerb weight for racing of 940kg/2,016lb.

Back in Britain, the RS Capri plan was being executed. . . A month after Ford managerial approval was granted for the establishment of FAVO in October 1969, agreement to go ahead on the project to build the first RS Capri was received. Bob Howe, the first engineering chief for FAVO, recalled the project's starting point: *Jochen Neerpasch had identified the need for a sporting Capri to support his racing programme. We had already looked at the 3-litre, but the 2,600cc-plus capacity was what Jochen wanted, based on the engines that Ford of Germany had already been using in the sport. We didn't need the fuel injection for the competition department, but we did feel we needed it for usable road power.*

An incidental effect of choosing the RS2600 route was that there was no future in international competitions for the 3-litre Capri with its British V6 engine (a distinct and separate design from the German unit, sharing only the basic 60-degree V layout), though it did continue to appear at club level and in some national events. The 3-litre racing Capris came into their own, though, for the

Cutaway drawing reveals the salient features of the RS2600 in full race trim, with wide, slick-shod alloy wheels and large ventilated disc brakes at each corner. Weslake-developed V6 power unit has Kugelfischer fuel injection, the large, belt-driven injector pump clearly visible in the engine compartment. Live rear axle is suspended on coil springs and located by radius rods: vestigial leaf springs serve only to maintain a tenuous link with the road car's specification and so satisfy the regulations. Sturdy tubular roll cage is integrated into the structure to provide additional stiffness. Large spare wheel, rapid fuel filler and dry-sump oil tank occupy the boot.

Group 1 category of 1974-82, winning both internationally and within Britain.

By December 1969, the first employees of the FAVO engineering department were at work on left-hand-drive Capri RS prototypes, with two important targets of diverse character to aim for. First priority was the manufacture of a flyweight Capri which could be homologated for racing at 900kg/1,980lb, with an engine bigger than 2.6 litres so that it could subsequently be enlarged within the permitted allowance, by increasing the bore size, to something nearer 3 litres. The second target was to have a car to exhibit at the Geneva motor show in March 1970 in order to convince press and public of its existence as a roadgoing model.

The version of the German V6 developed to meet these needs for the RS2600 as offered to the public kept the production 2600GT bore of 90mm with a stroke lengthened by 2.2mm to 69mm to give a standard capacity of 2,637cc. It is worth remembering that the road car had siamese-port iron cylinder heads, not the special alloy heads of Weslake parentage that were allowed under Group 2 regulations for international competition.

The roadgoing engine had a compression ratio of 10:1 (also quoted as 10.5:1 in some company

documentation) — on the high side for the period. The camshaft was that used to boost the production 2300GT Capri's output from 108 to 125bhp. The four-bearing crankshaft was safe to 6,500rpm, but the maximum power output of 150bhp was available at between 5,600 and 5,800rpm, with 165lb/ft of torque at 3,500rpm. Those were the official figures in 1972, anyway, and the specific power output of 56.9bhp per litre was creditable enough by the standards of the time, particularly as the car conformed to prevailing European emission control regulations. For comparison, the 2.8-litre V6s found in much more recent Fords were rated at 150bhp (Sierra XR) or 160bhp (Capri 2.8i).

The racing versions of the RS2600 were aimed at developing more than 100bhp per litre. In full-blooded Group 2 trim they had dry-sump lubrication and an 11.3:1 compression ratio. The stroke was restricted to 69mm, but the bore size was progressively increased and by 1973 it had reached 96mm, giving 2,995cc, and officially quoted power outputs in excess of 320bhp.

The development of the power unit had drawn heavily on the tuning expertise and manufacturing capabilities of Weslake at Rye, in Sussex, their engineers working not only to adapt the Kugel-

Capri characters: Jochen Neerpasch, above right, the first Cologne competition manager, is chatting to Martin Braungart, responsible for all competition engineering outside the engine bay. Both later went to BMW, leaving Michael Kranefuss, below (in 1972 headgear!), to face their onslaught in 1973. Kranefuss later became Ford's worldwide Motorsport boss.

The first RS2600s had no bumpers, but subsequent cars had quarter bumpers in front and a full-width blade at the rear, chrome at first, black later. While quadruple headlamps and contrasting bonnet colour made the front view very distinctive, the rear was closer to other Capris, with the decal stripe carrying injection and RS lettering as the principal identification.

Only the first 'plastikbombe' competition cars had the light-weight glassfibre doors with sliding plastic windows, below.

fischer fuel-injection system to the V6, but also evolving ever more powerful competition engines, which came complete with those alloy cylinder heads and 8,000rpm limits.

Incidentally, Weslake are still very much in business. In 1983, the original company ceased trading, but Weslake Developments Ltd, under the managerial care of former Weslake technical manager Brian Lovell, carries out research into many aspects of engine behaviour, both petrol and diesel, from new premises in Rye. They were not involved in motorsports when I talked to them in 1987, and none of the key Capri components remained. However, they had decided that their

expanding engine research facility and its 32 employees were capable of tackling competition again; it seemed possible that they would return to working on engines for motorsport at some future date.

Kugelfischer was the leading brand of competition injection in Germany, as well as being used on road cars by manufacturers as diverse as BMW, Peugeot and Lancia, and the company has since been absorbed within the Stuttgart-based Robert Bosch GmbH.

While the evolution of the RS Capri proceeded rapidly, the public saw the GT versions still competing in 1970 — a brace of second places were the best European Championship racing results, their power and durability being disappointing. The first display example of the RS2600 did make it to Switzerland for its debut on March 12, 1970 at the Geneva show, but only because a well-connected FAVO employee chartered a special plane to get it there!

Just over a month later, the first of 50 light-weight Capri RS2600s, minus the injection system but complete with the all-important long-throw crankshaft, were built on the line at the Cologne-Niehl plant. Those original lightweights were illegal for sale in Germany on a number of counts. Weight-saving was the major concern in their specification and to get down to a figure that defied most subsequent works Capris a number of drastic measures were applied.

Those first RS2600s had no bumpers. They were removed in the cause of the racing diet and the displaced front flashers incorporated beneath a then-unique quadruple round headlamp system. The British engineers bought in number-plate lamps from Halfords to provide rear plate illumination on either side. Usually the Capri's blade rear bumper carried the number-plate light. The cars also had no heater (FAVO employed an electrically heated rear screen to overcome the lack of demisting), no carpets, Perspex sliding panels for the side windows and thinner glass wherever possible. Other significant points were the use of Minilite magnesium-alloy wheels and fixed-back bucket seats. Even single-coat paint was applied to the machines that would be weighed by the international sporting authority — the last gram counted, so undercoat was out!

Glassfibre panels replaced doors, bonnet and boot. They were made by the BBS company, who later became best known for their racing and road wheels. Ford Cologne development engineer Martin Braungart had then just established a partnership in the company that today occupies him full time. Then, BBS were just learning about body panels and the Ford quality inspectors were not amused. . . Early Capri RS2600s were usually painted silver, the works livery in 1970 and early 1971. Official Ford managerial approval of the RS2600 body modifications came in July 1970. There was an aerodynamic spoiler blade beneath the nose, and sheet metal changes to the front panelwork, originally intended for export Capris to American Federal requirements, allowed the installation of Cibié Biode headlamps.

By August 1970, FAVO had engineering approval of the running gear. That encompassed the injection engine, single-leaf rear springs and a redrilled front cross-member to relocate the lower track control arms outward, introducing negative camber angles. Bilstein gas damping for the front strut inserts and rear telescopics was an integral part of the RS2600 recipe.

The first production fuel-injection RS2600 Capris clambered from the Cologne factory on September 14, 1970. They were in immediate trouble! The front wings had to be attacked to make clearance for fat tyres on lowered suspension. With all the legal features installed, instead of the parts that had led to the original lightweight car being dubbed *Plastikbombe,* the RS2600 for general sale weighed 1,060kg. Those 2600s dis-

RS2600 of 1973-74, with four-spoke alloy wheels and clean duo-tone lines. Added to these later cars were the bonnet-top injection logo and ornate rear quarter-panel decal.

RS2600 interior changed as the mainstream Capri was altered, but always had better-than-standard seating and a sporty steering wheel. The dished wheel was widely used on earlier FAVO cars, and is seen in a car with comfortable cord seats, whilst the flat wheel is in front of the facia design introduced in autumn 1972.

Kugelfischer fuel injection and neat cast alloy plenum chamber are evidence of Weslake's work on the road car's 2.6-litre engine, but it lacks the alloy cylinder heads which were strictly reserved for the Group 2 competition version. An honest 150bhp was delivered by the all-iron V6, enough for 125mph.

tributed in the big selling years of 1972 and 1973 were more like 1,080kg, or 180kg heavier than the first flyweights!

While racing RS Capris all took a leaf out of the successful Escort RS competition book and employed ZF five-speed gearboxes, the production road cars only ever had four speeds. There were two types of box used in the 2600's produc-

tion run. The first had gearing based on Ford Germany's Taunus line. It contained the following ratios: first 3.65:1; second, 1.97:1; third, 1.37:1; fourth, 1:1. From September 1973, a second ratio set, shared by the 3-litre Capris of the period, featured a 3.16:1 first gear, 1.94:1 second, 1.41:1 third and the usual direct fourth.

Originally, the clutch was modified to accept

hydraulic operation, but later examples with Capri 3-litre transmission should have cable operation. Initially, the axle ratio was that of the first 3-litre Capris (3.22:1) but it later moved on with the British V6 to a 3.09:1 ratio. A limited-slip differential was a widely sold option, but not part of the standard specification.

Suspension was initially based on whatever racing parts (such as the single-leaf rear springs) FAVO could find on the shelf, but as the car became a commercial success more civilization for road use was desirable, so spring rates and ride heights were progressively modified and the settings of the Bilstein dampers were softened off considerably during the production run. Basic principles were, of course, typical Ford rear-drive with MacPherson-strut front suspension utilizing a single track control arm each side jointed into the forward anti-roll bar.

Those single-leaf springs at the back had been developed for competition Escorts and Capris and they were combined on the roadgoing Capri RS with the usual Capri/Mustang staggered damper layout on either side of the rear axle to assist location, along with short radius links. What minimal rear axle travel the Capri did allow was cut down in the RS versions, thus carrying heavy passengers in the back could be uncomfortable for them and the nervous driver!

In October 1971, a number of important running changes were made to the RS2600 as it became more of a mass-production catalogue model and less a racing parts-bin special. The suspension was unchanged in layout, but the ride height was raised from its original underbelly-bruising level and the springs were swopped from competition to road ratings that were later adopted for the RS3100 too. Externally, the original Richard Grant alloy wheels were rejected in favour of FAVO four-spoke alloys in the same 6J × 13 dimensions. The radial-ply tyres remained the same 185/70 HR size, and most cars were supplied on Pirelli CN36 tyres.

Bumpers, chromium ones, were also fitted in this autumn 1971 refit. At the front, these were the traditional Ford performance items, the quarter-width type, but at the rear, a full-width unit was installed. Later in the run, these bumpers became matt black, just like those of many other mid-1970s Fords.

Inside the new alloy wheels were important changes to the brakes. Originally, the RS2600 was

The 1971 racing team line up with drivers, left to right: Dieter Glemser; Alex Soler Roig; John Fitzpatrick; Francois Mazet; Jochen Mass; and Helmut Marko.

sold with solid front discs and big back drums, as seen in the British 3-litre Capri and Germany's 2600GT. Harry Worrall, project engineer at FAVO and SVE, recalled: *The new wheels gave us an opportunity to adopt the Cortina 3-litre disc brake conversion we had been engineering. This was based on a unique ventilated front disc, unique hub and an ordinary M16J disc caliper, for the new Granada of the period.*

The RS2600 was ahead of many contemporary rivals in offering an improved interior, too. There was an initial combination of ribbed cord seat trim and a dished Springalex three-spoke steering wheel. Then the front seats, with adjustable backrests, were slightly revamped with less intrusive headrests; the basic design and manufacture was still by Scheel. The later seats sported a smoother cord finish and were complemented by the flat sports steering wheel that was widely used in other Fords, performance or otherwise, in later years.

RS Capri instrumentation was the same as on other V6 LHD Capris. That meant a matching 7,000rpm tachometer (red warning band from 6,000 onward) and 220km/h speedometer, plus four minor dials measuring volts, oil pressure, water temperature and fuel tank contents.

The RS Capri's rump wore distinctive twin oval exhaust pipes — and that was the view drivers of a good many other cars were most likely to see. The factory stated that the RS2600 Capri was able to romp from 0-60mph in 8.2 seconds and reach

124mph. In 1971, I was privileged to accompany John Fitzpatrick in an original lightweight silver RS2600 that covered a measured quarter-mile on the Silverstone Club straight in less than 15.5 seconds and ran from 0-60mph in less than 7.5 seconds. I have also been able to secure accurate fifth-wheel performance figures for the production RS2600, quoted in the appendix. I must thank *Road & Track* editor John Dinkel for allowing us this opportunity to see what Ford's first European fuel-injection car was capable of. Yes, I have seen German acceleration figures for the RS2600 before, but they do not exactly align with our mph measurements, 0-100km/h always taking disproportionately longer than 0-60mph, mainly because 'Sod's Law' always seems to dictate an extra gear change. The figures make satisfying reading, exceptionally close to the factory claims, putting some flesh on those bald statistics.

The RS2600 was marketed in many European LHD markets, becoming a familiar sight in Belgium, France and Austria, as well as Germany, and 3,479 examples were sold according to former FAVO employees. It inspired the development of the RHD RS3100 and ceased production in 1973, along with the rest of the 'Mk1' Capri range. The hot-selling two-door Capri — the millionth car was an RS2600, made 4½ years after the model's debut — was replaced by the Capri II hatchback in February 1974.

To my knowledge, only three RS2600 Capris were converted to RHD for British use: Walter Hayes had a full production model in blue and white corporate livery, as did Stuart Turner, and I inherited Mr Hayes' earlier mongrel 2600GT/RS2600, a carburettor-equipped car uprated by Weslake and finished in Boss Mustang yellow, complete with rear window slats and a vinyl roof. 'My' car was passed on to Formula 3/3000 team owner Murray Taylor when I left *Motoring News* and *Motor Sport* to go and work for Ford at FAVO in September 1972.

The only recent owner of an RS2600 road car I have been able to contact in Britain is former Ford RS Owners Club secretary Jacques le Clainche. The only racing RS2600 I am aware of in the UK is awaiting restoration by Tom Walkinshaw Racing who purchased it in 1989 from Jeremy Nightingale. This Capri was the ex-works Frami Racing machine which appeared with Kent cigarettes sponsorship in the hands of Gerry Birrell on a number of outings in 1972. I hope that there are other 2600s in Britain and look forward to hearing about them, for at present the Australians seem to have more of this machinery than us Poms!

So much for the RS2600 as a road car. It had been conceived to form the basis for a competition machine, and as the first examples went on sale to the public Ford's motorsport departments began a process of Anglo-German co-operation to fulfill that intention.

The relevant paperwork for homologation was stamped from October 1, 1970, allowing Ford the right to compete in Group 2 (1,000 units annual production) with a number of specified options. Ford assembled roughly 20 of the first lightweight RS Capris for inspection: five made it under 900kg, with only 880kg recorded. The rest averaged 900kg, with the heaviest on 920kg. Even the lightest of the production cars which followed were positively obese at 940kg. . .

The V6 engine was first prepared for competition in 2.7-litre form, but initial trials went poorly. By November 1970 Jochen Neerpasch had called on Stuart Turner for help, with the result that Peter Ashcroft, at that time senior engine builder at Boreham, now Competition Manager, was sent to the Cologne department to offer practical assistance.

Mr Ashcroft found a dismal selection of wet-sump V6s with non-standard 'ventilation' holes all over the place, each marking the abrupt departure of yet another damaged component. First priorities were to strengthen the moving parts — crankshaft, connecting rods, pistons — by upgrading their materials. Ford engineers also set about enhancing the prospects of lubricant reaching afflicted areas at high cornering speeds by adopting dry-sump lubrication. These basic competition strategies were well established in the works Escorts, but a V6 posed special problems of dynamic balance that were only resolved when Peter Ashcroft telephoned Keith Duckworth of Cosworth Engineering for some 'back-to-basics' advice.

Another fundamental change was to increase the rigidity with which the cylinder block encased all these higher-revving components. Filling a sample block with Plasticine, Peter Ashcroft was able to demonstrate how the block should be cast. Not only was that a successful exercise for racing, but the basic lessons were also utilized to provide a rigid block for the later Ford 2.8-litre V6 production engines.

Ford Cologne competition centre, above left, with the 1972 cars in preparation. First European Championship success for the works RS2600s was a 1-2 at the Salzburgring in 1971; Helmut Marko's silver and light blue second place car, above right, leads its predecessor, a 1970-model 2300GT. Below: an evocative shot of the field streaming through the first corner at the start of the Spa 24-hour race in July 1971. The Glemser/Soler Roig RS2600 is pursued by Camaro, AMG Mercedes, Ford Cologne RS1600, Steinmetz Opel, Alpina BMW CS, striped Broadspeed RS1600 and the rest. Ford won at an average of over 113mph.

The ultimate road Capris in convoy on the open road: Tour de France, September 1971. This RS2600, on German tax-free export number plates, is that of Dieter Glemser and Klaus Kaiser, which retired, but the car in the background, crewed by Jean Francois Piot and Jim Porter, won its class and was seventh overall against top class sports and sports-racing opposition.

Complete with steel caps for the four crankshaft bearings and a new crank from Weslake attached to a lighter flywheel, the RS2600 unit was ready for further competition modification. Brand new cylinder heads in aluminium alloy sported larger valves and a compression ratio that varied over the years from 10.5:1 for 24-hour racing to 11.3:1 for shorter events in 1973. A range of competition camshafts worked in alliance with the mechanical Kugelfischer fuel injection to provide performance at up to 7,500rpm, and the RS Capris ventured into the 1971 European Touring Car season with approximately 260bhp on tap.

The engine capacity grew over the years, but the stroke — restricted under Group 2 regulations — remained at a stubby 69mm. Initially, the RS2600 raced with a 94mm bore, giving 2,873cc, instead of the production 90mm. During that opening season it went out to 95mm and 2,940cc.

Finally, equipped with additional underbonnet cooling and moved well back against the bulkhead in pursuit of balanced handling, the toughened block was scraped out to 95.8mm and some 2,995cc for 1973. By then it sported huge 48.2mm inlet valves, 38mm exhausts and a regular 11:1 compression ratio. That gave an official 320bhp at 7,600rpm, getting on for triple the roadgoing output, and some 239lb/ft of torque at 5,500rpm. In that last season the Ford drivers were told to use no more than 7,800-8,000rpm.

By the standards of 1971 saloon car racing, the Capri was an extremely sophisticated competitor, one that opened the eyes of BMW and others to the principle of constructing a competition car dressed as a saloon, rather than converting a road car for racing.

Ford also employed the best in driving talent over the three seasons they campaigned the Capri RS2600. Mainstays were Dieter Glemser, John Fitzpatrick, Helmut Marko, Jochen Mass and Hans Joachim Stuck, plus Scotland's Gerry Birrell. The headlines were made by Jackie Stewart, most regular and successful of a number of Grand Prix drivers employed, plus Jody Scheckter, Emerson Fittipaldi, John Surtees, Graham Hill and Francois Cevert.

You had only to look at the Capri's replacement wings, cuddling over racing slicks 10 inches wide at the front and 11.5 inches at the rear, to know this was a very special Ford indeed. It had the same suspension layout as a road car — MacPherson strut front, live axle rear — but every component was replaced by a purpose-built racing item. Thus it was no surprise to find also that the rear leaf springs were dummies in plastic, the real work being done by coil springs above the axle line. These elongated rear struts with concentric coils and massive Bilstein alloy-cased dampers fed their incoming loads into increasingly sophisticated rollover cages. These welded tubular structures gradually evolved to the point where they took over the bulk of the bodyshell's stress-bearing duties.

Naturally, all four wheels were disc-braked, massive units being needed to restrain a vehicle capable of 158mph early on and closer to 170mph in its final form. Acceleration from 0-100km/h (62mph) was measured by **Auto Motor und Sport** in 4.6sec, and 0-200km/h (124mph) in 14.3sec. At that point the Capris sported 295bhp for the 1972 season.

Although the works Capris were not successful on their debut at Monza in March 1971, they soon settled into a pattern of race-winning durability. The first win came in April and it was a 1-2-3 for Dieter Glemser, Helmut Marko and Alex Soler-Roig in the Austrian qualifying round of the European Touring Car Championship at the Salzburgring. After that, nothing seemed able to challenge the Capris. The 1971 season saw them go on to win before huge crowds at Czechoslovakia's fabulous Brno street circuit, and on the old 14-mile Nurburgring in Germany.

The engine durability bugs had been completely conquered, as evidenced by Dieter Glemser/Alex Soler-Roig's 113.5mph *average* for 24 hours on the Spa-Francorchamps road circuit in July 1971. They didn't win in Holland (BMW got a look in there), but a 1-2 at the Circuit Paul Ricard in France provided compensation. The 1971 European drivers' title went to Dieter Glemser. Capris also won that year's German national title for Jochen Mass, and the same driver racked up enough results in the 1971 South African Springbok series to gain Ford the manufacturers' cup.

The 1972 season was even better for Ford fans. Now proven, the blue and white RS wonders overwhelmed any sign of opposition in all but one round of that year's European Touring Car Championship. Unfortunately, that one was *the* Championship round to win for a German-based team: Nurburgring. It also highlighted the fact that Jochen Neerpasch and the talented engineer Martin Braungart had departed for BMW in Munich, a move that would bring BMW into major league motorsport again by 1973.

Nevertheless, 1972 was a year to savour. Titles won by Capri RS2600 drivers encompassed an astonishing variety. Jochen Mass won the European Championship, Stuck the German, and Claude Bourgoignie the Belgian. Most astonishing of all was Timo Makinen winning the Finnish ice racing title in an RS2600 loaned by Boreham, complete with non-standard rectangular headlamps. In the 24-hour race at Spa the works-prepared Fords had perhaps their finest success, with a 1-2-3 led by Hans Stuck and Jochen Mass at

Familiar RS2600 racer in Britain in 1972 was this blue 'Wiggins Teape Pacemaker', prepared by Ted Grace and driven by the late Brian Muir. He and John Miles took the car abroad for its greatest victory ahead of the works Capris at Paul Ricard that season.

an average of 116.4mph for the day and night racing, over 3mph faster than in the previous year.

These were all saloon car events, and it is surprising today to recall that the Capri RS could also happily compete in the long-distance sports car races of the day, finishing seventh and eighth in the prestigious Nurburgring 1,000kms, and 10th and 11th overall in the Le Mans 24 hours.

At first the arrival of BMW Motorsport GmbH in 1973 did not seem to threaten the end of the Capri RS2600's racing world. The well-developed RS held on to second at Monza and showed excellent qualifying speed. The works Capri showed well, too, in a classic non-championship battle between Jochen Mass and Niki Lauda (BMW) at Spa and improved to sixth overall in the Nurburgring 1,000kms. The races at the Salzburgring and at Mantorp Park in Sweden saw the Capri winning again.

But in July 1973 BMW's employment of Martin Braungart was amply rewarded. The BMWs sprouted the infamous Batmobile wing kits, developed by the former Ford employee and

homologated just at the right time to prevent a Ford reply, even if one could have been argued through an obstructive British hierarchy. The lap times posted by the BMW CSL coupes dropped to the point where Ford RS Capri drivers knew they were in for a thrashing.

As the BMWs settled into reliability, with power outputs from their inline 3.5-litre engines climbing beyond 350bhp, Ford's RS Capri was simply outpaced. Some of the drivers responded magnificently, notably Jochen Mass, who could wrestle a Capri round to equal BMW lap times, wings or no wings. However, the long-distance winning was over until Ford could deploy the next RS Capri . . . RS3100.

On September 25, 1973 a Ford Product Strategy Committee gave its approval for the long-awaited right-hand-drive Capri RS. What became available to British customers was something of a hastily-concocted homologation special rather than the developed road car that the RS2600 represented in its final form, but it was a significant step forward for the British-market Capri. Especially praise-

For its last season, 1973, the RS2600's V6 engine in racing form, with alloy heads and bored out to 2.9 litres, was credited with 320bhp, progressive development having nearly tripled the output of the roadgoing unit.

Rarity: not many RS2600s, press fleet cars or otherwise, visited Britain, never mind calling at Cosworth in St James Mill Road, Northampton. In evidence are the quarter bumpers and the subsequently widely imitated front spoiler.

Broadspeed RS2600 racer backed by Lindrick Finance appeared in Britain and Belgium, regularly driven by Dave Matthews until its demise at the 1973 British GP meeting, and was one of two built by Ralph Broad's team at Southam, the other, with RHD, being driven by Andy Rouse.

The 1973 racing Capri featured the squared-off wide-arch look that would become popular for road cars in the 1980s. John Fitzpatrick waves a wheel during the Silverstone Tourist Trophy.

worthy were its outstanding stability, the extra performance provided by nearly 150bhp, increased braking power and better handling.

Mike Moreton, the product planner at FAVO, outlined the basis of the RS3100 project. The instructions were: *To produce a limited-volume Capri RS derivative at Halewood during November/December. The car will be designated in sales literature, but not badged, as Capri RS3100 and will be sold through Rallye Sport dealers only. The vehicle is to be based on the Capri 3-litre GT, but with an engine over-bored to 3.1 litres, a front air dam and rear spoiler, with suspension, brakes and alloy road wheels carried over from the AVO Capri RS2600.*

The 3-litre Capri's Essex V6 engine had bore and stroke dimensions of 93.76mm × 72.42mm to give 2,993cc and the capacity enlargement was needed to qualify the Capri in the over-3-litre racing class. It was achieved by a maximum service overbore (always referred to as '60 thou' — 60 thousandths of an inch) which left the official cubic capacity as 3,091cc: 95.19mm bore with the stroke unchanged at 72.42mm.

The competition version of the RS3100 to be run by Ford in Cologne would carry a massive 3.4-litre Ford Cosworth 100mm × 72.42mm 'big bore' version of the Essex V6, a 400bhp-plus package of which more later.

Ford at Boreham had built half-a-dozen road-going RS3100s by November 1973, and these duly appeared at strategic points around the route of the RAC Rally whilst the homologation inspection proceeded for approval to compete internationally in 1974. Production at Halewood, possibly of an initial 50 RS3100s, began, according to the records of RS3100 registrar Dennis Sellars, with NHK 281M (chassis number BBECNDO7322), a vehicle actually registered on November 2, 1973. The production process continued into 1974 despite the advent of the Capri II.

The Boreham-built RS3100s all looked slightly different, some lacking the quadruple Capri 3000GXL headlamps (a cheap alternative to the RS2600's original Cibiés), and one that I borrowed to cover that year's RAC Rally had 165 burbling horsepower. This was achieved with a replacement higher-lift camshaft and specially-fabricated dual exhaust system, but the production RS3100s (mostly constructed in the early months of 1974) lacked such power-boosting modifications.

Utilizing standard 3-litre Capri ancillaries, including the Weber 38 EGAS twin-choke carburettor, the 3.1-litre V6 was rated at 148bhp at 5,000rpm and 187lb/ft of torque at 3,000rpm. This compared with 138bhp and 174lb/ft at the same revs for the standard production 3.0 V6.

Ford felt they could claim some 10% extra on the power figures because the inlet manifolding and porting had been polished, along with the exhaust ports; compression, camshaft and exhaust manifolding were left as for the 3-litre of the period. Although the changes to the engine were slight, Ford did use their nostalgic blue rocker covers to signal that this was no ordinary 3-litre.

Speed and stability were improved by employing the RS2600's simple blade under-bumper front air dam. A unique black rear spoiler served a critical competition purpose in holding the back wheels on the tarmac at the racing model's quoted 180mph-plus velocities. For public-road customers, the improvement in motorway crosswind stability was most noticeable — and the spoiler was a useful parking guide, too.

The front and rear spoiler combination, plus the use of lowered RS2600-style suspension, provided a MIRA-measured wind-tunnel drag factor of 0.375. That is the best figure I have on record for the original Capri outline and an excellent achievement, for the first Ford to benefit from extensive use of wind-tunnel time, the front-drive Escort of September 1980, did little more than match that figure, even in XR3 guise.

Capri RS2600 influence continued with the redrilled front cross-member to provide some negative camber at the front wheels. Also employed from the later RS2600 Capris were the 6 × 13in FAVO four-spoke alloy wheels and the 185/70 radials, usually provided by Goodyear or Pirelli.

When FAVO in Britain started work on the RS3100, the suspension was softer than that first offered on the RS2600, but still with a stiffish 142lb/in front spring rate and 112lb/in rear. A 1-inch chop in ride height meant that even the modified rear bumpstop rubbers (one section was removed in an effort to find extra clearance) came into abrupt and immediate contact when back seat passengers were carried.

The rear suspension featured the later production anti-roll bar-cum-axle linkage that mainstream 3-litre Capris used, rather than the RS2600's initial set-up with short axle radius links. Single-leaf springs remained a common feature between RS2600 and 3100. Bilstein gas damping was used, but the damper settings were coded 'director's' and aimed at comfort, as distinct from the first RS2600's competition-orientated suspension, a system so low that spoiler-to-ground clearance checks had to be carried out on the engineer's local driveways during development.

Also borrowed from the RS2600 were the 9.75in vented front discs. The improved servo assistance that the British V6 Capri deployed had been introduced during the RS2600's production run. A pair of 9.0in × 2.25in back drums came as part of the 3-litre base on which the RS3100 was built, as did the 3.09:1 axle ratio that can be found even in the last Capri 2.8s.

Production Capri RS3100 showroom features at the debut asking price of £2,450 did not include the 14in diameter three-spoke RS steering wheel, but did offer a modified version of the decals used on the RS2600 of the period. Ford just removed the RS2600 and injection references! Such decals have become impossible for the concours competitor to obtain from new stock, so have to be made up using the originals for patterns. The traditional quarter-bumpers were preserved for the front of the RS3100. As with the 2600, both chrome and matt-black examples were owned and photographed by Ford: the catalogue specification was matt-black. I am told Escort 1100 Mk2 Popular bolts can be used to replace any absent originals.

Capri RS3100 performance? There are fifth-wheel figures from *Motor* in the appendix. An average result from weekly and monthly magazines in the UK was a maximum of 124mph, 0-60mph in the 7-second bracket and around 22mpg overall.

Only two officially badged RS Capris made it into production, but there were quite a few other attempts to bring RS and Capri together over the years that followed the RS3100's brief production run. Some of the following, like the Escort Mexicos, were sold only by RS dealers. Some were conceived by German Motorsport personnel and then only sold through RS outlets. Some were proposed as RS products, but never quite achieved anything more than limited Ford mainstream approval, with some sections of the normal

The Capri RS3100 road car had many visual affinities to the RS2600, but was built only in RHD form. Ducktail rear spoiler was vital to enable the car's racing cousins to use all their power. Stripe decals were adapted from late RS2600, with lettering deleted. The overbored V6 nestled beneath a single Weber twin-choke carburettor, and was rated at 148bhp, just 10bhp more than the standard 3-litre unit. Interior of this example sports a three-spoke RS steering wheel, but the two-spoke production item was often used, as were those ribbed seats and 3-litre Capri GT furnishings.

warranty absent in deference to radically increased engine power.

The closure of Ford Advanced Vehicle Operations was a protracted affair. Various departments stayed operational into 1975, notably engineering. The parts operation stayed on this site until 1989 when it moved to join the main Motorsport operation at Boreham. So Aveley stayed busy despite the closure of the production line in 1974 and the consequent dispersal of the majority of the workforce of 200 or so.

Product planner Mike Moreton prepared a plan in 1975 to produce a fuel-injected 2.8-litre RS Capri that should have reached the production lines along with the Escort RS2000. Management approval was given for this project, but the car was never made, owing to the time-consuming business of putting the RS2000 into production in a mainstream facility, rather than at the FAVO plant for which it had originally been conceived.

However, prototype RS2800 Capri IIs were constructed, with help from Thomas Ammerschlager in Ford Germany's Motorsport department, and such cars were subsequently demonstrated to the press in Capri III trim. At the time it was said that it was not worth the cost of development and crash testing to combine the 2.8 with the Capri hatchback shell, but sales buoyancy in Britain eventually changed all that and the 2.8 injection appeared, going on to achieve a very high ratio of profitable sales.

There is some logic in owners of Capri 2.8 Injection, Special or 280 versions feeling they have a genuine RS car, but the project lacked any intention on the part of the factory to use it in competition. It was, though, a product of many of the same engineers who were at FAVO. Men who conceived the RS2600/3100 went to work on the 2.8 Injection, the first car handled by the Special Vehicle Engineering group.

That the resulting vehicle did not carry an RS badge was simply a marketing decision. For the 2.8i was as thoroughly modified from a production base as many RS types have been. In fact, a former engineering chief at FAVO told me: *When I drove an injection Capri for the first time, I thought it was the perfect development of the RS2600 series. Suspension, brakes, engine, all felt like developed versions of that first RS Capri.*

A similar lack of competition intention was the reason why the Ford of Germany/Zakspeed Capri turbo did not become an official RS product, despite being sold by RS dealers and developed by Motorsport personnel. The Zakspeed-Ford alliance had already produced a breed of phenomenally successful 1.4 and 1.7-litre turbo Capri racers based on Cosworth BDA technology, but aside from Zakspeed's work in its production and engineering, the Capri 2.8 Turbo sold by RS dealers in Germany in 1981-82 had few features in common with the turbocharged, 16-valve racing cars. Just 200 of these 134mph road cars were made by the Zakspeed-Ford co-operation, though a run of 300 to 400 was originally envisaged. Ford of Europe Vice President Karl Ludvigsen did have one brought over to Britain. All were LHD and their carburettor-equipped 2.8-litre V6s were given only a modest boost of 0.38 bar by a KKK turbo at first. For later production, a Garrett AiResearch turbine was adopted, when boost was apparently increased to nearly 0.5 bar. With the higher boost figure these special Capris gave 188bhp at 5,500rpm and at least 200lb/ft of torque was on tap at a highish 4,500 revs.

Externally they were the wildest Capris ever to be offered by a Ford dealership. They had a very large rear wing in the style of the 16-valve racers, high and wide. The popular X-pack/RS body kit inflated the wheelarches over alloy wheels 6.5 or 7.5in wide. The front spoiler was the largest German authorities would allow, and it was usually removed when transporting new vehicles! The price, at the close of production in September 1982, was just under £8,900 without options.

There have also been turbo Capris on sale through Ford dealerships in Britain that might well have achieved RS status, for SVE were very interested and co-operative in their formative stages. First was the Tickford Capri 2.8T, based on the 2.8i with a Japanese IHI turbo conversion giving 205bhp. This package, of which less than 90 had been made when I checked in 1986, included disc brakes for the back axle and comprehensive body modifications, its price creeping up from something over £15,000 closer to £20,000 for the final batch in 1986-87.

The second Ford-approved Capri Turbo was an engine conversion only (with optional braking and handling improvements) from Turbo Technics, prices starting at £1,400 without VAT.

Back in 1974, the RS3100 Capri, with its 100mph cruising capabilities and 3.1-litre flexibility, was priced in the same £2,500 sector of the market as BMW's 2002 saloon, Alfa Romeo's 2000 GTV Bertone coupe and the 3.5-litre MGB

The Capri RS3100 was created to race, but its appearances were limited by the fuel crisis of the 1973-74 winter. Here the two works team cars of Rolf Stommelen (right) and Toine Hezemans storm the 1974 Eifelrennen, Stommelen leading a 1-2 finish.

V8 GT. In fact the RS3100 was not a commercial success, but that was not the car's fault. It simply arrived at the wrong moment both in Ford terms (they were preoccupied with launching Capri II) and during that traumatic fuel crisis when many British garages rationed petrol and prices per gallon rocketed. Only in the 1980s has appreciation of the model's worth begun to spread. We can estimate that 150, or perhaps less, original examples remain in use.

Additionally, some RS3100 clones have been constructed, based on 3-litre Capris of the period. Fine, if that is what you are paying for, or what you wish to construct. Not so good if your intention is to own a genuine original example: buyer beware!

Development of the racing Capri RS3100 was shared between Cosworth Engineering at Northampton and Ford Motorsport in Cologne. Responsible for the engine work at Cosworth was Michael Hall, whilst the Ford engineer on the Capri that would surround that uprated V6 was Thomas Ammerschlager, who has also worked with NSU and Audi and at the time of writing was the BMW Motorsport executive engineer with responsibility for the M3. Development driving and

a little race mileage came from the Dutchman Toine Hezemans, who had been 1973 European Touring Car Champion with BMW.

The Cosworth-Ford GAA engine developed in 1973 for the car retained the four-bearing 60-degree V6 iron Essex block to conform with Group 2 regulations, but everything else was new. The cylinder heads, cast in LM25 aluminium alloy, contained four valves per cylinder, in the well-established Cosworth manner, operated by four overhead camshafts driven by toothed belts. The steel crankshaft and all the other moving parts were to Cosworth racing specification. A nicely-engineered dry-sump pan, again in light alloy, enclosed the bottom end. Lucas mechanical fuel injection was used.

The production V6 stroke dimension of 72.4mm was combined with a bore size enlarged to 100mm to give the racing engine a capacity of 3,412.5cc, and the compression ratio was 12:1. With a safe maximum of 9,000rpm, it developed peak power at 8,500rpm and initial trials produced just over 400bhp. Further development was limited until Ford were able to ensure the co-operation of the foundry at Dagenham in

Forceful appearance of the Group 2 racing Capri is displayed by the works RS3100 of Glemser and Hezemans at the Nurburgring in 1974. Delayed by axle repairs, they finished second to the winning Zakspeed Escort.

100 GAA engines in order to satisfy the Group 2 homologation requirements, but the cutback in racing activities in 1974, which was one result of the fuel crisis, meant that few of them were used in racing Capris. Some found their way into Formula 5000 single-seaters and thence into a variety of specials. Development continued, too, with Cosworth-approved builders such as Swindon Racing Engines extracting over 136bhp per litre from the unit in the 1980s. That meant around 465bhp for a rear-wheel-drive Mk3 Escort special I tried in 1985. Torque delivery felt rather more impressive and spread wider throughout the rev range than the figures would suggest, and the engine had an attractive six-cylinder note and surprising smoothness in operation.

First trials of the racing RS3100 were held with the old 12-valve Weslake-Ford installed and a rear-mounted radiator. However, this had obvious disadvantages in close combat, so side radiators were deployed. As ever, Thomas Ammerschlager spent time on wind-tunnel testing to discover the optimum front spoiler and wheelarch arrangements, the RS Capri emerging with a blanked-off grille and the side rads to produce over 170mph on the 415bhp that was initially available.

Handling was assisted by the rear spoiler that came as part of the RS3100 package, but weight was up considerably and a lot of it was just where racing saloons loathe avoirdupois: in their noses! The old Weslake weighed 360lb, versus 385lb for the new motor, and so the RS3100 raced at 2,315lb/1,050kg, rather than the sub-1,000kg kerb weights of the 1973 Capri RS racers. Hence the need to shift all movable mass rearward, including radiators for oil and water.

Although suspension layout remained as for the racing RS2600, spring rates continued to climb as Ford fought to contain the roll angles that developed as their coupe got faster, heavier and more powerful. BBS centre-lock alloy wheels grew to 16in diameter and carried 10.8in and 13.8in wide Dunlop slick tyres. Also improved were the disc brakes: four ventilated ATE units, 11.9in/302mm front and 11.5in/292mm rear, powered by an electro-hydraulic pump that was later developed for production cars such as BMWs.

No British testers measured the performance of these new wave Capri RS racers, but *Auto Motor und Sport* in Germany recorded 0-100km/h (0-62mph) in 4.2 seconds and 0-200km/h (0-124mph) in 13.1 seconds. Not that much of a

providing a few selected cylinder blocks with the durability to withstand racing conditions.

Stronger blocks were completed after a few initial upsets of the 'well ventilated engine' variety and 440bhp at 8,500rpm, plus 280lb/ft of torque at 7,000rpm were quoted later in the RS3100's racing career. At first, the specific power output corresponded to 121.6bhp per litre compared to the 108.5 of the last Weslake 12-valve V6s (that is at a generous 325bhp for the latter), but during 1974 Cosworth were certainly supplying units giving over 129bhp per litre.

Cosworth had to make enough parts for a run of

Perhaps the greatest duel of the 1970s Ford versus BMW battles: the fourth round of the German Championship at the Norisring in June 1975, where Jochen Mass (RS3100) repeatedly swopped the lead with Hans Joachim Stuck (BMW CSL). The Capri driver won and set fastest lap, but that year's title went to the Zakspeed RS1800 of Hans Heyer.

Works Ford team pit stop at the 1974 Nurburgring 6 hours, directed by Thomas Ammerschlager, in spectacles to the right, to be found in 1987 overseeing the engineering of BMW's successful M3 racer.

gain over the RS2600 on paper, but lap times were considerably reduced thanks to the extra pulling power and the stability conferred by the back wing and other 1974 aerodynamics. To demonstrate the point, the 1972 works Capri RS2600 lapped the ultra quick 4.2-mile Hockenheimring in 2min 24.7sec (104.9mph average). The lap time two years later in a parallel practice session was 2min 15.4sec (112.09mph).

The works RS3100s made their first appearance in April 1974 for both German and European Championships. In the European series at Salzburgring there were two RS3100s against a single works BMW CSL (which also featured an injection 24-valve six, but in-line). The faster Capri was that of Toine Hezemans/Dieter Glemser (1min 17.44sec versus the pole position BMW's 1min 17.14sec) and the other was crewed by Niki

Lauda/Jochen Mass. The Capris led, but both broke their engines.

Just four days later, the Capris wreaked vengeance before their home crowd at the Nurburgring, finishing 1-2, but opposition from BMW was patchy in that year's home series. In fact the German series was a bit of a Ford benefit, for Dieter Glemser won the outright German national title for the Zakspeed Escort RS1600 and the over 3-litre class was headed 1-2 by Klaus Ludwig and Rolf Stommelen in the corporate blue and white RS3100s.

The first European Championship win for the factory Ford Capri RS3100 was recorded on August 11, 1974 at Zandvoort. A pair of works Capris faced the SCA Freight Chevrolet Camaro of Aussies Frank Gardner/Brian Muir and Jochen Mass/Rolf Stommelen were the winners.

The works RS3100s also won their next engagement, at Jarama in Spain, when Hezemans/Heyer with Klaus Ludwig ensured that the Zakspeed Escort won Ford's first title as a manufacturer in the European series since the days of the Lotus Cortinas. Drivers' titles were easier than beating the small class manufacturers to an overall Makes award...Finally, in 1974, the works went to South Africa again and finished fifth overall in the 9-hour sports car race at Kyalami, Mass and Hezemans winning the saloon car class.

Ford Cologne did manage to race the RS3100 into 1975, but only German and South African events were tackled as a factory team, and then subsidiary sponsorship was needed. Ford were not really gaining anything by racing the obsolete two-door body. In the European series BMW were absent, too. The legendary confrontation between

Capri RS and BMW CSL for premier league European honours last occured in July 1974, when neither six-cylinder car won: a Zakspeed Escort took that Nurburgring result after a dramatic race.

In German Championship racing, the BMW-versus-Ford fight continued into 1975, but sporadically. The 1975 works Capri RS3100, now with Kugelfischer injection adopted during a South African winter sojourn, began with a win on June 29 at the televized Norisring meeting for Jochen Mass after a battle with Hans Stuck's BMW.

Klaus Ludwig showed well at Kassel-Calden in August, setting fastest training and race laps in the works Capri to lead the opening 13 laps, but finally finished ninth after a collision with the winning BMW. Later that month the good Klaus won an international German round at Hockenheim, the Capri now capable of lapping in 2min 12.5sec (114.5mph,) so lap speeds were still going up even if the RS3100 was obsolete by factory standards.

As the season closed at Hockenheim in September, Ludwig clinched another victory, but did not lap quite so quickly as in August. Was this the last outright win for a works-run Capri? Mmm, Ford followers could debate the merits of that statement: the RS3100 was entered by Team *General Anzeiger,* a Bonn newspaper.

However, the important point was that the works RS3100 beat a strong field of Porsches and BMWs to finish second overall in the points totals for the 1975 *Deutsche Rennsport Meisterschaft,* beaten, by just eight points, by the Hans Heyer Zakspeed Escort RS. It was Zakspeed's third successive German Championship year with the Escort.

The last record I had of the works running their Capri RS3100 was for the Wynns 1,000km in South Africa on November 1, 1975, when Jochen Mass and Klaus Ludwig retired. However, information from Australia in 1987 indicated that Derek Bell and Jody Scheckter also competed in that South African Capri finale. A fire in practice, and a lost wheel, did not prevent them finishing fifth overall behind 'pure' sports cars.

The Bell/Scheckter Capri was the ex-Cologne RS3100 that Australian-domiciled saloon car folk hero Allan Moffat had secured. He ran it in 1975 against highly modified local V8s with some

Cosworth-Ford GAA engine, with four valves per cylinder and twin camshafts on each bank, was an impressive sight with its shining Lucas fuel injection intake stacks. Minimum target output of 400bhp was exceeded on the first test-bed run.

success and returned it to the tracks in 1976 when his Chevrolet Monza hit eligibility problems. Thus the Capri RS3100, still in Ford colours but with additional Pan Am airline backing, was the car which ensured that the 1976 Australian Sport Sedan Championship was won by Allan Moffat.

Even that is not the end of the ex-works RS3100 saga. For 1985, former Ford dealer Vince Woodman paired up with current dealer Jonathan Buncombe and they won eight out of eight national Shell Thundersaloon qualifying rounds in Vince's RHD ex-Broadspeed RS3100. That car was prepared by Dave Cook in York, one of many successful Capris engineered over the years by this gentleman and his close-knit band of helpers, and it was propelled by 465bhp from Swindon Racings's updated version of the 3.4-litre V6.

Some old racing saloons just get better by the season . . . and more valuable. A 1989 Brooks auction at Motorfair realized over £50,000 for the ex-works Allan Moffat RS3100 returning from Australia. A spare endurance-specification Cosworth V6 for the car was sold separately to former two and four-wheel World Champion, John Surtees.

Capri RS that might have been: Tom Walkinshaw, the man behind the TWR Rover and Jaguar winners in the 1980s, seen here back in 1975 outside the admin building at Boreham leaning on a Capri II with flared arches and rear spoiler which could have become the RS2800, five years before the 2.8 injection model appeared, had the need to produce the RS2000 for a larger potential market not taken precedence.

Capri RS on the road

The only British owner we have been able to contact was 38-year-old teacher and Ford RSOC official, Jacques le Clainche. Now living in Peterborough, Jacques was an ideal candidate for RS2600 ownership, having swopped an RS3100 for the 2600 as a private exchange in June 1986.

As he reported somewhat wryly: *I do have a lot of information about spares for RS Capri cars...I have to, as I was always looking for parts for my RS3100 — and now for my 2600!*

His RS2600 arrived with the equivalent of 25,000 miles registered and Jacques covered just over 1,800 miles before entrusting the restoration of standard specification bodywork (it came with extended wheelarches) to Unit 5 in Brimington, Chesterfield. The car was being restored when this was written and the owner was beginning to get to grips with costs such as £50 for engine gaskets from Germany and £75 per wing.

Aside from my own driving impressions, later in the book, I do know of one contracted racer, Frank Mazet, who exceeded 50,000 miles quite happily in his RS2600, re-registered in Monaco, before the factory doctors descended upon it.

If you feel as though only an RS2600 will do as your RS, then the only realistic way I can see of getting any sort of choice is to try and find one in Germany, France or Belgium. Prices naturally vary sharply with fluctuations in the exchange rate. However, it seems certain that the RS2600 is more highly valued in Germany than we value the 3100 in the UK, for the car originally cost about £1,800 to £2,000 in 1971, whereas the example I found in March 1987, far from standard, was £5,500 in round figures. Then you have got to import personally, paying import duties on the way...so it is unlikely we'll see even the keenest RS seekers duplicating Jacques le Clainche's purchase in significant numbers.

Response from RS3100 Capri owners was excellent, but before I detail some of their experiences I must thank Dennis Sellars, RS3100 registrar of the AVO Owners Club, who provided much of the detail information that has helped me keep in touch with the realities of owning such a Capri in the 1980s. As of summer 1986, Mr Sellars kept track of 103 club-registered RS3100 Capris, whilst 17 Capri RS3100 owners had registered with Ford RSOC in Britain.

My thanks also to Australians Tom Chaplin and Norman 'Norm' Walls for their extensive contributions. As a result of their work it is possible to estimate that total RS3100 production was closer to 250 than the 200 to 225 I had previously accepted as accurate.

Australia was particularly relevant to these calculations as 14 RS3100s are now registered with the Australian Ford RS Owners Club, of which Tom Chaplin is the secretary, based in Narara. Official records suggest that 50 RS3100s went to Australia, but some sources say that only 25 actually made it down under: if the latter is true a tremendous percentage have survived that rigorous decade of motoring! Incidentally the Australians have also had two examples of the factory team RS Capri racers, a 1972 RS2600 in full works colours at a museum in Perth, and the ex-Allan Moffat RS3100 which came back to Britain in 1989.

First, the more typical British owners such as M. J. Parkinson of Winsford in Cheshire have their say. Mr Parkinson bought his 1974 RS3100 privately for £3,000 in July 1984, when it had covered 40,000 miles. By the spring of 1987 it had registered 48,245 miles and had continued to supply the great enjoyment that this 33-year-old HGV fitter expected from previous ownership of a Mexico and an RS2000.

Mr Parkinson reported exemplary reliability, but the car was a very special find. He explained: *A Janspeed exhaust system was fitted by the previous owner, but the car is otherwise completely original. It has not been restored in any way, but the body panels are original, and in immaculate condition. This is mostly due to the fact that the previous owner stored this Capri for four years. In over 2½ years ownership I have had no trouble with it, part from renewing the exhaust manifolds. These I obtained from Withers of Winsford, who stock most parts for RS cars.*

A more problematic approach was chosen by AVO Owners Club member Tony Llyn-Jones, who restored a shabby RS3100, now registered AGU 209N. It was the subject of an informative article in their club magazine, **Havoc**, quoted here with permission from club secretary Peter Williams.

Mr Llyn-Jones started with the advantage of a 'spare' 1974 Capri GXL of the same colour as the RS3100 to be restored. He confirmed that the negative camber front suspension means the wheels do foul the standard front wings on even the slightest amount of steering lock. As Fords were out of stock of flared RS Capri wings, Tony went to Withers of Winsford and purchased a pair. Tony Whiting in Plumstead fitted the wings, resprayed it all, and did a marvellous job, as confirmed by subsequent show outings.

Tony spent one year and 10,000 miles with this RS, but not without one major incident: *I slipped into third and floored the throttle. Not a lot happened, except that the engine note immediately took to imitating a demented sewing machine! Accompanied by prodigious quantities of smoke from under the bonnet, we slowly limped home on considerably less than the full quota of cylinders.*

The engine malfunction was a blown head gasket, but since the oversize 3.1-litre unit was well past its best, it was entrusted to Auriga Racing Engines in Swanley, Kent, for a comprehensive rebuild. The famed constructors of Formula Ford engines balanced

Ducktail line-up: there were more RS3100s at Stanford Hall for this Ford AVO Owners Club annual celebration than have been seen in one place since the original homologation!

the bottom end components, gas-flowed the cylinder heads and installed a Kent V63 fast road cam. The required oversize pistons came from Powermax.

Commenting that the engine now seemed *more like a V8 than a six*, Tony Llyn-Jones was delighted. Unfortunately the feeling was short-lived, for scarcely had the engine been run-in when the fibre timing wheel decided to shed all its teeth. This problem, not uncommon on the Ford Essex V6 (usually at higher mileages than average), cost three bent valves and deposited much debris in the sump.

Auriga met the cost of the rebuild and Llyn-Jones again became a regular RS Capri driver with a Sebring Red machine worthy of its classic show dates. Before he sold it to return to Mexico motoring, Tony Llyn-Jones made some very pertinent comments on owning this model. He liked *the turbine-like power delivery and immense torque* and found that *the spoilers really do keep the car straight and quite indifferent to side winds.* He found the handling *perfectly acceptable and adequate...despite the big V6 up front.*

A more critical note after that year's experience was: *Fuel consumption can obviously be a problem. I think the best I ever saw was 28mpg, obtained with considerable restraint, dropping to about 18 for fast cross-country driving, with an average probably about 21-22mpg.*

The braking scored a lukewarm *adequate, yet never gave cause for concern, provided you were prepared to shove on the pedal hard enough. The ride is certainly choppy with the standard Bilstein set-up, but not uncomfortably so.* Mr Llyn-Jones felt the Capri was probably more comfortable than a similarly equipped Escort over the bumps, because of the longer wheelbase, and put forward the idea that: *A good variable-rate power steering system would greatly enhance the car's handling and make the initial understeer less of a problem.*

In the wake of recent accidents that have destroyed some outstanding examples of the RS3100, I heartily endorse Tony Llyn-Jones'

warning about driving this Capri (or any of the V6 breed): *The RS3100 is a car that needs, indeed in wet or damp weather demands, to be treated with respect. Even under ideal conditions it can be something of a handful for the unwary.*

Finally we came to the well-known concours Capri RS3100 of Norman Walls, which has been winning awards spread over eight UK shows since 1984. This machine is probably the finest advertisement for the RS3100's durability, for it was never a glass-case preservation item, experiencing Australia's rough roads before the owner brought it back to England.

Forklift engineer Walls (42) bought the 1974 RS3100 in Australia, with 29,000 miles recorded, in August 1977. Still going strong after 88,500 miles, this remarkable RS3100 has an American-manufactured sunroof and a ZF limited-slip differential. Because of Australian conditions — which can reduce a 10,000-mile Rover to driving like a 100,000-mile car in my experience — Norman made some further sensible changes. These included a stainless steel dual-pipe exhaust tucked up and away from outback ripples, and German Scheel 501S seating in fabric *à la* Capri RS2600. These were vital, replacing Ford's standard vinyl finish which became positively adhesive at 46 degrees centigrade!

These and the provision of four seat belts with head-restraints in line with Australian regulations are understandable. I'm not sure if Norman exhibits the Capri RS on Simmons spun alloy wheels and Pirelli P6 low profiles on their 14in diameters, a combination acquired with the understandable aim of increasing grip. If Norman is winning with those in place, the concours judges he has met are a lot more loveable and understanding than yours truly!

Complete with extra Australian-market RS3100 decalling, Norman's RS Capri has had two engine rebuilds but the main parts (bores and crank) are still virtually original sizes. He feels synthetic oils such as Castrol R synthetic and Mobil 1 helped in this respect.

10

Sierra RS Cosworth - 1

The first Ford to carry the name Cosworth (though by no means the first to benefit from Cosworth know-how, as we have seen) went into production on June 17, 1986. The Sierra RS Cosworth project began at the same meeting of Motorsport, SVE and Product Planning personnel, in April 1983, that had commissioned the Escort RS Turbo, and when it reached fruition, this, Ford's fourth sporting Sierra derivative, proved to be a sensational performer.

The first hot Sierra had been the V6 2.8-litre XR4i of 1983, with its 'biplane' rear wing and idiosyncratic three-door six-light version of the basic Sierra shell. The similarly styled XR4Ti Merkur, with a turbocharged 2.3-litre four-cylinder engine, was an American market special not offered for general sale in Europe, although it did appear on European race tracks to some effect. The four-wheel-drive Sierra XR4 × 4 of 1985, V6-powered again, was as restrained in its styling as the XR4i had been bold and earned respect for its effective transmission engineering.

True to the RS tradition, the fourth variation on the theme had strong competition connections. Stuart Turner, Director of Motorsports, Ford of Europe, recalled how the RS Sierra germinated, and how Ford almost accidentally stumbled across the perfect engine to power it:

Really the idea of a race Sierra was low priority on our Motorsport shopping list. Then Walter Hayes and I spectated at a British GP meeting in which we watched Rovers trample all over everything. Naturally we said to each other that it would be nice to see Fords out there winning again, but we didn't have the specific Cosworth idea in mind.

Then I had the job of showing our senior American management, Jim Capalongo and Ed Blanch, around Cosworth Engineering in Northampton during the summer of 1983. The highlight of our visit was to look at the Grand Prix DFY engines that were then on stream. However, we walked past a 16-valve Sierra motor that Cosworth had put together privately. Who better to do the kind of production engine we needed for a racing Sierra?

SVE were given the commission to develop an RS Sierra that the public would buy in large enough numbers to justify production of the 5,000 cars a year required for eligibility in the Group A international competition category, and that would provide the basis for an effective saloon car racer to take Ford successfully back into the fray where they could expect stiff opposition from traditional adversaries, BMW.

As with the first Escort RS Turbo, SVE borrowed engineer John Griffiths from Motorsport at Boreham to oversee progress on the power unit, this time in liaison with Cosworth, who signed a three-year contract with Ford to provide not only an initial 5,000 engines in that first year, but also up to 5,000 units per year for another two years.

It transpired that people in the production engineering departments at Ford did know about the existence of the Cosworth engine, but were not particularly keen at that time to see it installed in a mass-production car. Looking back, John Griffiths said, *Ford had not really been interested in the 16-valve cylinder head for the iron-block Pinto four-cylinder. They did not see it as something to slot into a Granada or Sierra, but we could see the basis for a Group A competitor with the addition of turbocharging.*

The decision to use a turbo was crucial, because Ford Motorsport knew that the car would have to have 200bhp in roadgoing form if they were to achieve the 300 to 325bhp needed for racing, as Group A regulations set very strict limits to permissible modifications. Many people had got into the habit of regarding four-valve heads and turbocharging as alternative, mutually exclusive routes to high performance, at least for road cars. *Cosworth were a bit puzzled that we should want to turbocharge their 16-valver. 'Overkill', they said, 'you don't need it with our 16-valves',* reported Griffiths. Cosworth's reluctance was understandable for, apart from all their earlier achievements, they had just successfully completed a non-turbo 16-valve cylinder-head programme for a manufacturer with a considerable reputation for very high standards, Mercedes-Benz. Turbocharging could so easily spoil the instant throttle response, economy and durability of such a power unit.

The emergence of BMW's sporting 3-series derivative, the M3, with 200bhp from a fuel-injected 16-valve 2.3-litre engine, shows what is possible with a non-turbo road car. Significantly, though, when I asked BMW engineers what they would do to improve that power unit, the prompt if unofficial answer was *put a turbocharger on it!*

The point is that a turbocharger opens up the potential for as much power as considerations of reliability will allow the engineers to use for touring car races of anything between 3 and 24 hours' duration. Even in 1985, SVE had envisaged a second-generation Sierra RS with a 400bhp capability, but that plan would only begin to reach fruition through the endeavours of the Motorsport department in 1987.

By June 1984, the first redeveloped Ford-Cosworth powerplants were available in turbo trim, ready to power the first two prototype RS Sierras. Key Cosworth personnel on the project included Mike Hall, Paul Fricker and liason engineering executive John Dickens.

That first pair of RS prototypes looked like XR4i 'biplanes', for it was a subsequent Ford management decision to drop the XR4i-style body in favour of the plain three-door Sierra shell with two side windows, previously a rarity in Britain because it had been marketed only briefly in RHD form.

The Ford Sierra RS Cosworth arrived on the British market in the summer of 1986 offering performance into the supercar league – some 145mph and acceleration comparable, for example, with a Porsche 944 Turbo – for less than £16,000. It introduced some newcomers to motoring over 140mph, and a surprising number of Porsche and Ferrari owners decided to have one in the stable too. It was a new and powerful proof of the commercial and technical strength of the Ford/RS combination.

That tailplane gathered on-lookers everywhere when the motoring press were introduced to the car in Spain in December 1985. The old cliché about 'this is the view other drivers will see' had a particular relevance in this case: C235 HVW returned to Britain to serve as the official British Racing and Sports Car Club pace car. If you passed this vehicle in 1987 you were in Big Trouble!

In developing their 16-valve cylinder head for the 2-litre T88 Pinto engine, Cosworth followed the pattern established with the BDA and chose a toothed belt drive for the twin overhead camshafts. The belts were from Uniroyal, made of rubber reinforced by glassfibre, and also turned the short internal shaft that drove the oil pump and distributor through a skew gear. Drive belt pulleys on the crankshaft and camshaft came from the CVH Escort/Fiesta motor, which also uses belt drive.

Five bearings were provided for the camshafts which operated the valves via inverted bucket tappets with hydraulic lash adjustment to reduce noise and service maintenance. The inlet valves

Pre-production LHD Sierra RS Cosworth prepared for its public debut at the Frankfurt show, September 1985. Body modifications and high tail wing completely changed the Sierra appearance, and a new style of RS multispoke alloy wheel completed the effect.

were of 35mm diameter and the sodium-cooled exhaust valves 31mm.

The classic pentroof Cosworth combustion chambers, with a central spark plug location, gave an 8:1 compression ratio. This comparatively low compression, suitable for turbocharging, caused problems in creating the right combustion conditions for legal exhaust emissions and acceptable fuel economy.

Mahle forged pistons were installed, and to reduce piston temperatures, the diesel engine ploy of spraying oil on the undersides of the crowns from the lower ends of the cylinder bores was employed. Enhanced strength came from heat-treated steel forgings for the connecting rods and a similar material for the crankshaft. The bore and stroke dimensions were those of a normal production Sierra, Capri or Granada 2.0, 90.82mm × 76.95mm, to give a capacity of 1,993cc.

Boost was quoted as 0.65bar/9.25psi when I gathered the pre-production details at SVE, but Cosworth and Ford subsequently settled on 0.55bar/8psi. On the subject of boost characteristics, Ford and Cosworth had this interesting explanation to make:

To generate as much low-speed torque as possible, the turbocharger characteristics are set to reach high levels as quickly as possible. To control maximum boost below the present limit of 8psi, the wastegate opens to dump excess pressure according to a calibration stored in the ECU (Electronic Control Unit). The wastegate actuator is therefore controlled by a solenoid-operated modulator valve which generates a series of boost curves, according to the speed and load conditions. It provides a very progressive governing at the top end, which is followed by incremental fuel cut-off to each injector in turn. Fuel is also cut off on the over-run to improve economy and emissions.

Poised and ready to disappear very rapidly into the distance, this new breed of RS had drivers revelling in the open road as never before.

This, believe it or not, was the model that provided the basic shell for the RS. The three-door Sierra was only briefly marketed in Britain: note that the side window arrangement is quite different from that of the 'six-light' XR4i and Merkur XR4Ti.

That gives some idea of the way in which Ford and Cosworth had capitalized on the rapid advances in electronic engine management technology to iron out the undesirable characteristics of some earlier, cruder turbocharger installations. It is also

clear that they had long left behind the days when the rev limiter was an abrupt ignition cutout: on an insensitively driven BDA that could sometimes do more damage than it prevented!

Various power output figures for the engine have been quoted, a subject worth investigating further. The unit is now rated at 204bhp (DIN) at 6,000rpm, with a torque of 278Nm, the equivalent of 203lb/ft, at 4,500rpm: but you will find anything from 201 to 205bhp quoted in past Ford literature and consequent journalism. Some journalists also told me that the half-dozen long-term loan cars used to acquaint the press with the machine were in the 235 to 237bhp 'top tolerance' tune from Cosworth. Since this would represent a healthy boost over the standard production figure, I asked Rod Mansfield at SVE to comment. Rod told me categorically, *Those 230-horsepower ratings are nonsense. The highest we have seen from a production specification RS Cosworth is 218bhp and the press ones gave 204 to 210bhp in our experience; good, but not extraordinary.*

The outstanding characteristic of the turbo Ford-Cosworth was its broad power band. It was the fact that it proved so docile that was to make a car like its successor, the four-door, seem possible to senior Ford management, who had previously been sceptical of the capability of SVE and Cosworth to produce so much power in a civilized form. Quite unlike earlier turbos, it produced at least 80% of its maximum torque (equivalent to 163lb/ft) all the way from 2,300rpm to 6,500rpm. On the road, these qualities translated into supremely usable performance. Figures like the 50-70mph acceleration times of under 6 seconds in fourth gear or just over 7 seconds in fifth give an inkling of the effect — all from just 2 litres.

Grand tourer: the Sierra RS Cosworth combined the capability for ferocious performance with a level of civilization which made long-distance motoring an attractive prospect, and it was tractable and docile enough for the high street too. Additions to the mass-production bodyshell served sound engineering functions (unlike some body kits) as well as being styled to create a strong visual impact.

Dramatic outward aspect and turbocharged 16-valve power were complemented by the rest of the mechanical specification including four-wheel disc brakes with an anti-lock system as standard and a Viscous Coupling limited-slip differential.

Author's aero test: pre-production Sierra RS ambled along European motorways at 130mph and 22-23mpg. Front-end styling changes included a central air intake and a ducted spoiler to match the German Phoenix arch and sill extensions.

Vital to the production of that prodigious power output (102.4bhp per litre) was the Garrett AiResearch T03 turbocharger, with a water-cooled casing. The turbo was mounted on a nickel-iron exhaust manifold casting, merging from four branches into twin downpipes. Under the car it swept into one pipe to emerge as a large-bore tailpipe. Keeping power-unit temperatures under control were a large radiator, an oil/water heat exchanger sandwiched between the block and the oil filter, and an air-to-air intercooler of modest dimensions between the turbo and the inlet manifold.

A Weber-Marelli ignition, multi-point fuel injection and engine management system was chosen. Why Weber-Marelli? *Mainly because Keith Duckworth was working with them in Formula 1,* revealed Rod Mansfield. *In fact we had chosen to go with Bosch, but the engineers were excited by the opportunity to try the new Weber-Marelli layout and so I removed my original objections to Keith's request.*

Extracting high performance from comparatively large four-cylinder engines often produces severe mid-range vibrations and resonances. Cosworth and Ford did run into some problems with critical harshness periods. Engineers at Southampton University provided assistance in the form of friction dampers fitted to the inlet and exhaust manifolding. These suppressed the harshness period around 4,000rpm considerably in the production cars: some of the late pre-production RS Cosworths were undeniably noisy in the 4,000 to 4,500 band, and you could still never describe progress as exactly peaceful in this part of the engine's range.

The RS Sierra created considerable controversy both within Ford and outside over the appearance of its high-wing rump, but such a design really was necessary to turn the lift generated by the production saloon body shape at the high speeds of which the car was capable into the downforce needed to ensure stability and maximize roadholding. Measurements taken in the Ford Cologne wind tunnel revealed that the RS wing generated a downforce of 164 Newtons — something like 37lb in layman's terms — at 200km/h (124mph), contrasted with 513 Newtons, about 115lb, of *lift* generated at the rear of a Sierra with a simple bootlid spoiler.

SVE aerodynamic specialist Gordon Prout explained: *That downforce figure was the reason we had such a high wing on the RS Cossie, and it had to be in that position. Any lower and its effect was nullified, any higher and the drag figure went up to an extraordinary degree. We would have loved to extend the wing rearward for even better figures, but the law prevents protrusion beyond the bodywork. Besides, the expense of an extended bumper puts that approach out of the question.*

Rod Mansfield described how the eventual form of the wing had been arrived at: *We started aero work in July 1984 and went through 92 separate layouts at the Motor Industry Research Association (MIRA) wind tunnel. The result looked pretty horrible in card and alloy mock-ups, but it removed the high forces of lift we were getting at the rear end.*

Naturally, the styling aces were horrified when they saw our pop-riveted abortion, which then included Formula 1-style end plates for the rear wing! Patrick le Quement and Uwe Bahnsen's men really kept faith with our needs, and the shape you see today is a very much more elegant solution than ours. . .

Handling of the Cosworth RS initially attracted some comment for its darting habits on the press launch, but the 1986 cars were considerably tamed by a reduction in steering sensitivity. Developmental running changes of this and other aspects of the car continued into production.

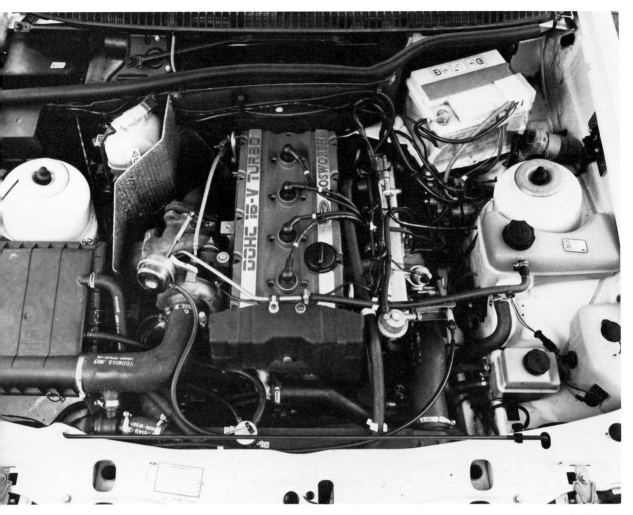

The turbocharged 16-valve twin cam power unit was a tightish fit and the installation needed some careful planning. The multiple electronic sensors and fuses were accessible, though: I know, I had to change most of them during the 1987 Willhire 24 hours before we found the particular 20A charmer that had failed. . .

In 1987, a drag factor of 0.345Cd was revealed for the production RS Cosworth, which is extemely creditable in the trade-off with increased high-speed stability that had been generated. The Group A racers, of course, benefited from the rear wing, but the original plan to block the nose with sheet alloy was vetoed, leaving the front with a slight lift figure, albeit less even than that of the XR4 × 4, a difference detectable to the driver on the road or (preferably!) track.

A pre-production batch of 15 Sierra RS Cosworths, 10 RHD and five LHD, was constructed in December 1985 for press assessment, all finished in Diamond White paint. Unlike the Escort RS Turbo, though, other colours were available when the car went into production. But they all came with the distinctive RS look created by the rear wing and a Phoenix body kit in polyurethane which comprised wheelarch extensions (necessary to cover racing tyre widths), sill extensions and a completely reprofiled nose, the under-bumper area also including the air scoops that saloon car racers find vital. A small flexible rubber extension increases effective spoiler depth and absorbs pavement parking with equanimity. Initially, SVE had the bright idea of making these flexible extensions of differing front end depths to help the saloon car racing effort, but a replacement spoiler was specified for the competition machine anyway, as one of the changes forming the permitted 'evolution' process.

The steel bonnet wore twin plastic vents and a

grille had been let into the plastic panel section between the headlamps. The overall visual effect was a very different Sierra, one that looked particularly effective in black, but was also widely chosen in a Moonstone metallic grey, as well as the original white.

Below the seductive racetrack-inspired style there were two worrying areas, steering and gearbox, which required work between the press debut in December 1985 and the commencement of production in June 1986.

The gearbox problem was simply one of production quality, but it delayed Ford putting the car on the production line at Genk in Belgium by nearly half a year over the original plan. There was nothing wrong with the design or shift quality of the Borg-Warner five-speed box. It had already been proven in American models, and in fact it shared its first four ratios — 2.95:1, 1.94:1, 1.34:1 and 1:1 — with the turbo Mustang built by SVE's transatlantic counterpart, SVO (Special Vehicle Operations). However, fifth gear for the Sierra RS was an 0.80:1 overdrive, rather than the American 0.73:1. The trouble was detected only when half a dozen pre-production Sierra RS types were put through endurance trials at the Lommel test track in Belgium at sustained speeds around 130mph. All the gearboxes gave trouble, and there were

failures within 100km (62 miles), including seizures. Ironically, Ford had been studying the durability of the turbocharger installation and head gasket design, not the transmission, when these failures occurred, but a change in specification of the gearbox bearings helped equip them for sustained high speeds not encountered in the USA with its blanket 55mph limit. The box remained part of the 1986 specification through-out production, but after those early failures they were built specially for the Sierra RS on a separate Borg-Warner line.

Some of the journalists who tried the car at the press launch in Spain complained of an over-light and twitchy quality in the steering, so efforts were made to modify the feel, as Rod Mansfield explained:

We looked at many alternatives after press criticism of over-sensitive steering in Spain, but concentrated on two primary answers. Most important is that we have decided to go away from the use of solid plastic inner pivot bushes for the track control arms in our strut front suspension. You saw this first on SVE's Sierra 4 × 4 Wagon and the decision was taken to also apply the same philosophy, using softer rubber inner mounting bushes, on our 4 × 4 Granadas and Sierra XRs, as well as the Sierra RS.

Garrett AiResearch T03B turbo-charger and attendant wastegate controls were installed on the opposite side of the engine from the Weber-Marelli electronically managed fuel injection. There were three belts to see and a fourth, the cam drive, hidden under that plastic front cover.

Cutaway drawings by Terry Collins take us inside the 204bhp motor and its ancillaries, below left, as well as revealing the mechanical layout of the production Sierra RS Cosworth, left, and a Group A rally version, below. Modifications to be spotted on the competition car include twin rear springs, a secondary coil being fitted round the damper; enlarged, cross-drilled brake discs; a comprehensive roll cage that extends to the top mounts of the front MacPherson struts; replacement front and rear anti-roll bars; new rear trailing arm linkages; new front hubs and suspension arms; Recaro seats with full harness — and, of course, a battery of long-range lamps.

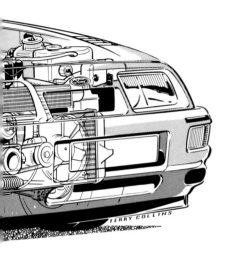

The RS interior was not radically different from that of other Sierras, though Recaro seats were provided for this sports model, and the turbocharger's presence was acknowledged by a small boost gauge, top left of the 7,000rpm tachometer, which SVE were able to borrow from the American XR4Ti.

Secondly, we altered three of the primary settings with our Cam Gears-TRW power steering. The quick action of the rack-and-pinion remains, just 2.6 turns lock-to-lock, but the inputs relayed to the driver are not so nervous.

The Sierra RS also incorporated other basic front-end modifications. A new cast-iron hub carrier installed at the bottom of the MacPherson struts raised the front roll centre by 92mm to 143mm (over 3.5 inches increase). This had been demanded by Motorsport to suit competition handling requirements, but was to be abandoned in the subsequent four-door RS. Marked negative camber, 1 degree 15 minutes front and 1 degree 48 minutes rear, was another feature of this Ford's suspension layout.

Another handling-related detail came to light when SVE discovered that cars were coming off the production line with the front suspension on the bottom limit of castor settings, all within a fine tolerance of 15 minutes. *This spoke well of production techniques, but gave us a problem in yet further increased steering sensitivity,* confessed Rod Mansfield.

I gather, unofficially, that a different length of front anti-roll bar was made available to pull the castor back from the planned 1.5-2.0 degrees to a production 0.5-1.0 degrees because the Genk production people were worried about the front wheel striking the extended wheelarch. This certainly contributed to the light feel of production cars in a straight line. It seems that a replacement front anti-roll bar to the original specification was made available to German customers who swore hard enough at their dealers! The original, longer, roll bar is now available as a retro-fitment with full service approval in Germany.

Both front and rear suspension featured anti-roll bars, a hefty 28mm diameter in front and 14mm at the rear. The front dampers were gas-filled twin-tube units from Fichtel & Sachs, assisting in providing a fine ride for a sports saloon. The independent trailing-arm rear end of the RS Sierra, with uniball joints replacing standard rubber bushes, and with gas-filled monotube dampers from Fichtel and Sachs, also utilized much of the Sierra XR4 × 4's layout. Some features, such as the viscous coupling 190mm differential unit and the 273mm diameter solid back disc brakes, are also shared with the Granada/Scorpio line. The front discs were generous in dimension, being of 283mm diameter

and 24mm thickness, and four-piston front calipers were fitted.

For the road Cosworths, anti-lock braking was standard from the start, as on the Granada/Scorpio. The Teves (ATE) system employed an electric pump for hydraulic pressure, sensors at all four wheels, and two microprocessors. The two processors constantly compared data in failsafe checks and two lights in the main instrument display indicated a full operating check as soon as the ignition key was turned.

German-developed and produced D40 Dunlop tyres of 205/50-series ultra-low profile were installed on Rial-manufactured alloy rims that look like BBS products. Similar wheels are now available on the aftermarket. The wheels measure 15in in diameter, with a 7in rim section, the diameter allowing large brakes to be installed and a wide selection of competition rubber to be installed. Those road tyres were reckoned not to be the ultimate in grip, but quiet and with forgiving manners in a wide variety of conditions, by those in the know. Apparently the original development of this cover was to meet Porsche's demands, and its exceptional ride qualities for a low-profile tyre may well have been vital in its selection for the Sierra RS. Group A rules allow a 2in increase or decrease in diameter over the 15in figure, so the Eggenberger Motorsport factory racers were engineered to use either 16 or 17in diameter wheels.

In addition to the impressive mechanical specification of the Sierra RS Cosworth, the standard equipment list had plenty of showroom appeal when it was launched on July 15, 1986 at a price of £15,950. Details included: Ford-trimmed Recaro front seats; rear seat belts; leather-rim XR3i-style steering wheel; tinted glass (laminated front screen, of course); tilting and sliding glass sunroof; electric front window and mirror operation; central locking; and a four-speaker stereo radio/cassette player.

By the time *Autocar* published a full test of the RS Cosworth, in August 1986, nominated rivals included a £20,000 BMW and a near-£22,000 for the Cosworth-assisted Mercedes 2.3-16, so expectations were high. The Sierra RS also lined up commercially against competition such as the 200bhp Rover V8 Vitesse (£17,029) and the 16-valve turbocharged SAAB 9000 (£15,995), but had the advantage of extra speed with competitive economy.

The car's maximum speed of 240km/h,

equivalent to 149.8mph, had been observed by the German TUV authority at the Ford test track at Lommel. Ford computers predicted 0-60mph in 6.47 seconds. Fuel consumption, assessed according to the British government standards, was quoted as 22.8mpg for the urban cycle, 38.2mpg at a constant 56mph and 30.1mpg at a constant 75mph.

Figures recorded by the **Autocar** testers included a top speed of 145mph, a 0-60mph time of 6.2 seconds and 0-100mph in 16.1 seconds. **Performance Car** took a pre-production Sierra RS down to the Mugello circuit in Italy where, in spite of some interference from gradients, they timed a number of 0-60mph runs at an average 6.75 seconds with a best figure, as Ford predicted, right in the 6.4 seconds bracket. 0-100mph averaged less than 20 seconds.

The journey to Italy and back, in convoy with the 130mph BMW 325i, provided the opportunity for a fuel consumption check over 2,000 miles, and the car averaged over 23mpg. The best tankful gave more than 25mpg and even the test track session only reduced the figure to 17.6mpg. By the standards of 140mph machinery, this RS was positively frugal.

Sierra RS Cosworth production began at 96 per week from June 17, 1986 and climbed to 300 units, pursuing Group A homologation as fast as possible. Ford received approval for competition in Groups A and N with effect from January 1, 1987, and survived an independently audited check of production numbers initiated by a motorsport rival. At least 500 of the pre-facelift 1986 bodies were kept aside for the pre-planned evolution version that would be used in competition at a later date. *Not the cheapest way of doing things, but by far the most convenient,* in the words of one Motorsport executive.

The car began to appear in competition even before homologation into Group A was granted. Ford and Securicor got together to organize the Securicor Sierra Challenge, a rally series which ran within some British national championship events in 1986. The series winner was Welsh borderer Phil Collins. With co-driver Roger Freeman he

Seven of the ten cars used for the Spanish press launch were subsequently assigned to the 1986 Securicor Sierra Challenge rally series. Motorsport Manager Peter Ashcroft, left, and former Ford Marketing Director Bill Camplisson, next to him, line up with drivers Dougie Watson-Clark, John Weatherley, winner Phil Collins, Trevor Smith, Chris Mellors, Rob Stoneman and Kenny McInstry. The Collins car is in the foreground. Collins continued rallying RS Sierras, with some international placings, before concentrating on preparation: he built the Toyota GT-Four that secured the 1989 British Open Championship for David Llewellin.

Fated: the car prepared for Stig Blomqvist and Bruno Berglund to use on the 1987 East African Safari had no chance of repeating the RS1800's win in the hands of Bjorn Waldegard ten years earlier – it was damaged too badly to compete before it got to scrutineering! The Boreham team had a difficult opening half to the 1987 World Championship season.

1986 Securicor Sierra Challenge winner Phil Collins on his way to a ten-second class win on the Lindisfarne Rally, based outside Newcastle. In the five-round series, Collins in the 300bhp car backed by Ford dealers Brooklyn scored three wins and two third places.

won three of five qualifying rounds and also recorded an outstanding third overall against the highly developed Group B and special cars that faced him on the Isle of Man for the Manx Stages in May.

The Sierras taking part in that 1986 Securicor series mostly abided by a gentleman's agreement which limited maximum power from the Cosworth engine to no more than 300bhp, but they were still extremely rapid (0-60mph in 5.1 seconds) and clearly indicated the car's further competition potential.

When I visited Ford at Boreham in the winter of 1986-87 to see how the factory were progressing with the Sierras for international competition, it was immediately obvious that while the Securicor cars had been a useful test of the kind of maximum power outputs agreed for 1987 World Championship rallying, the homologated cars would be different in many important details. Skimming through the homologation forms quickly made it clear that the engineers, John Wheeler and John Griffiths, under Peter Ashcroft's overall direction, had somehow found time, in spite of the enormous work load on the RS200 project during the preceding year, to develop an impressive collection of suspension, braking and chassis modifications for both the XR4 × 4 and the Sierra RS Cosworth.

For racing and rallying, an enormous variety of braking equipment would be available with disc diameters from 315mm to 285mm, mostly cross-drilled as well as radially ventilated. As for the suspension and vital hub components, some of it derived from lessons learnt with the RS200, while the front disc brake and MacPherson assemblies used in Group A, along with the larger rear discs and hubs, dated back to development carried out by Ford Germany Motorsport for the Merkur XR4Ti, which was campaigned by Andy Rouse in the 1985-86 British Championship and then used in the 1987 German national series.

The division of competition duties originally envisaged for Ford's two turbo cars had already been upended by the Escort RS Turbo's emergence as a circuit racer, and the RS Sierra was clearly going to play an important part in rallying in addition to the saloon car racing role for which it had been conceived. As the 1987 season opened, Boreham's intention seemed to be to run either the RS or the XR4 × 4 according to whether sheer performance on tarmac or four-wheel-drive traction on rougher surfaces was likely to be most in

demand. The first international outing for the works RS was the Monte Carlo Rally, where snow spoiled the chances of Kalle Grundel and Terry Harryman, though they did manage fastest time on one stage.

Ford declined to send a works team to Portugal, abstaining for safety reasons (the company is twitchier than any European or Japanese rival on this subject, perhaps because of the American influence). But Mike Little prepared an RS, reportedly with 295bhp and weighing around 1,200kg, for Carlos Sainz. The Michelin-shod machine in Marlboro colours was able to show the pace-setting Lancias and Mazdas the way around the opening stage at Estoril, setting a time a clear 8 seconds faster than its closest rival and suggesting that the lack of four-wheel drive was less of a handicap than some of the pundits thought.

Other non-factory teams and some privateers were beginning to discover the car's rallying potential. In France, the combination of smooth gravel and tarmac stages in national championship events suited it well. The Lyons-Charbonnières rally has always been a good event for Ford, right back to the Capri's formative years as a competition car, and in 1987 it produced a marvellous result with the Group A Sierra RS Cosworth of Rigollet/Bathelot first and the Group N car of Rouget/Bounours third.

On the World Championship scene, though, the factory and factory-backed Sierra Cosworth efforts were plagued with problems in the opening months of 1987, to the point where the complete programme was re-examined in May. On the Safari, the team had suffered the elimination of Blomqvist's car even before the start, and their Corsican outing ended just two stages into the event! In Corsica, the cars run by Mike Little for Carlos Sainz/Antonio Soto and by R-E-D for Didier Auriol/Bernard Occelli got into the World Championship points with seventh and eighth places, respectively.

If the works team were to get the best out of the potent Sierra a new plan was required. The major decision was taken to concentrate on the RS rather than continue to divide their effort between the Cosworth-powered car and the XR4 × 4.

Meanwhile, Easter 1987 brought a fine first outright victory for the RS Cosworth on Britain's home international series as Jimmy McRae took his fifth win on the Circuit of Ireland after a magnificent event-long scrap with David

Jimmy McRae had always driven GM cars at amazing speed on the Circuit of Ireland, but in 1987 Ford were able to benefit from his availability. His works-registered RS prepared by R-E-D at Widnes is seen here on its way to a notable victory, one success against the season-long challenge provided by David Llewellin's non-turbo four-wheel drive Audi Coupe. McRae went on to win the British Open Championship, and Sierra RS Cosworth drivers also secured the titles in Belgium, France and Spain.

Llewellin's non-turbo Audi Coupe quattro. McRae's RS was a works-registered Cosworth (D541 UVW) run by R-E-D and far from fully sorted, a promise of things to come.

The Sierra RS Cosworth's racing programme was the responsibility of the German Motorsport department, and Lothar Pinske chose the Swiss-based German-speaking Eggenberger team to run the cars. These masters of the immaculate touring car had prepared winning Group A BMWs and Volvos in previous seasons, and the black Texaco Fords for 1987 looked every bit as good.

Gleaming purposefully, they were presented for Steve Soper, Klaus Ludwig, Klaus Niedzwiedz, and Pierre Dieudonne to drive at the opening World Touring Car Championship qualifier, at Monza in March 1987. Unfortunately, they did not even start this troubled event, in which the leading six BMW M3s were disqualified!

The authorities and Eggenberger-Ford could not agree on the technical regulations, for the works Sierras were presented with Bosch Motronic engine management rather than the production Weber-Marelli system. Andy Rouse did get a start in his Zytec-managed Sierra, presumably on the basis that this was a rework of the production item rather than a complete brand and type substitution. Andy grabbed the pole position in the red RS he was scheduled to share with Belgian star Thierry Tassin, but it went out with a head gasket failure before a dozen laps had elapsed.

The Eggenberger cars were certainly well prepared, with a theoretical top speed of 320km/h (199mph)! At Bathurst in 1987 one was timed at 275km/h (171mph). The engine had a 91.2mm bore in place of the standard 90.8mm, the stroke remaining at 76.95mm: that is 2,010cc by my calculations.

It seems pretty certain compression was reduced from 8:1 to 7.5:1, but boost went up enormously over the production 8psi. Eggenberger drivers were allowed to dial a maximum of 1.5bar/21.3psi and a minimum of 1.3bar/18.5psi, which was said to provide horsepower readings from 385 to 350bhp; *average* peak power was quoted as 365bhp at 6,400rpm. Peak torque had moved from the production figure of 203lb/ft at 4,500rpm to 323lb/ft at 4,800rpm. Racing weight for the Eggenbergers was quoted at only 1,035kg/2,277lb. A five-speed Getrag gearbox, previously used on the XR4Ti, was employed.

Incidentally, the XR4Ti racer had performed nobly in British and German Championship racing, Rouse securing the 1985 British title with this German-developed American-market car, but it could only be a stand-in until the Sierra Cosworth appeared as it developed at least 25bhp less and weighed 335kg/738lb more. *It makes most V8s look lightweight,* said one racer.

The Sierra RS Cosworth racers for the European Touring Car Championship were entrusted to the Swiss-based Eggenberger team. By June 1987 when the series moved to Zolder in Belgium they had got into their stride, scoring a convincing 1-2. The car of Klaus Ludwig and Thierry Boutsen, seen opposite on a precise, apex-clipping line, finished second. Right, the Sierras in line-ahead keeping five of the numerous BMW M3 squad at bay: in second place here is the winning car which was shared by Klaus Niedzwiedz, Steve Soper and Pierre Dieudonne, the latter being officially credited with fastest lap.

Away from international events, the rate at which privateers purchased the Sierra RS ensured that the results started looking good within months. For instance, in March 1987 British disc jockey Mike Smith won the opening two rounds of the Monroe British Championship with a 260bhp Group N RS, and the model was obviously set to dominate at least the sprint race results of 1987 UK production (Group N) races in the Monroe and Uniroyal series.

At the first round of the 1987 Uniroyal series the previously all-conquering Mitsubishi Starion finished sixth, following four RS Cosworths and Karl Jones in one of two ex-Mike Smith Escort RSTs. At least, that was the result 'on the road': you soon learn that post-race scrutineering, protests and subsequent appeals may well alter the final, final result, never mind noting who won the attendant pugilistic displays. . .

Eggenberger, meanwhile, looked good as soon as they had put Monza behind them and were only robbed of victory by over-zealous officials in the second round of the European series, at Estoril in Portugal, finishing second and third. Later results in the series included a 1-2 at Zolder in Belgium.

In the concurrent World Touring Car Championship competition, it was July 1987 before the black and red Fords won a race outright, that victory going to Klaus Ludwig/Klaus Niedzwiedz at the new Nurburgring. The series, destined to run for only one season, was marred somewhat by eligibility squabbles, but Ford emerged with the manufacturers' title at least, after races as far afield as Bathurst and Fuji. Helping the Eggenburger team to that success in the latter part of the season was one of two further, divergent developments of the Sierra RS theme.

It had always been part of the Sierra RS Cosworth plan that extra power for competition could be summoned via the evolution homologation process. With that in mind, Ford laid down an extra 500 bodyshells of the original 1986 outline to provide for later construction of an RS Cosworth that would offer extra speed, stability and alternative chassis settings, all arrived at according to the company's competitive requirements in the light of experience with the first RS Cosworth. Company sports and SVE personnel were all aware that a larger turbocharger could release over 400bhp for racing purposes, Rod Mansfield confirming such thinking, along with the expectation of further aerodynamic improvements, during December 1985.

In complete contrast, the Sapphire-bodied development of the RS Cosworth theme was entirely aimed at the road car market. At the 1986 preview in a Geneva hotel of a vehicle still under development, Ford chiefs (including Ford of Europe Chairman, Ken Whipple) told me that there would be no upper production limit. Their confirmation that the target market was formed by West Germany's BMW 3-series, Audi 80/90 and Mercedes 190 underlined how impressed Ford management had been with the comparatively civilized blend of speed and refinement preferred in the first Cosworth RS.

The competition orientated evolution version of the Sierra RS was named RS500 in a similar manner to RS200, the figure signifying the number to be made to qualify for international competition. Due to the upheavals in 1986 World Championship rallying there was no chance Ford could produce an evolution Sierra for rallying (a move specifically banned by the Paris authorities) but for Group A racing, production of a further 500 cars, with significant modifications, was allowed. The RS500 came first, arriving for public announcement on July 22, 1987 and on the race tracks by August 1, 1987, whereas the four-door RS Cosworth was only sneak previewed in 1987 with a press launch scheduled for January 1988 and sales of RHD cars commencing a couple of months later.

As Ford staff admitted, the process of putting 500 completed Sierra RS Cosworths on one side was not the cheapest way of going about the motorsport homologation process, but it was the quickest and least disruptive to factory output. The potential snag to the scheme for road customers was the amount of time completed cars were stored and the sometimes rough handling suffered during transportation. This led to extra rectification work when Aston Martin Tickford Ltd began the strip down and re-assembly process at their Bedworth factory in June 1987.

However, the end result had quite a pedigree, involving Cosworth and Aston Martin Tickford as well as the original conception by Ford Motorsport. The RS500's creation owed a particular debt to the input of Ford Germany's Lothar Pinske, and then it was overseen to production by Boreham personnel including Mike Moreton and John Griffiths. That meant the establishment of five production lines and four work stations to hand-assemble the car at Tickford. Type approval and durability engineering was also from Aston Martin Tickford, while Cosworth assembled and bench-tested engines at Wellingborough.

The price of such parentage? Some £19,950, or £15,175 less than the similarly speedy Porsche 944 Turbo. Contemporary price competitors included Nissan's 300 Turbo ZX (£20,875), SAAB's front drive 9000 Turbo 16 (£18,995) the Mercedes-Cosworth 2.3/16 (£25,540) and the LHD-only BMW M3 at £23,550.

Ford and their cohorts had co-operated to produce the ultimate RS Sierra three-door, a roadgoing car rated at 224bhp with a 153mph capability, a machine that charged from 0-60mph in a claimed 6.2 seconds, yet reportedly returned 33mpg at 56mph. Urban fuel consumption? Did anyone care if it did 20.6mpg in ECE 15 trials, or 24.5mpg at a constant 75mph — drivers of early examples simply spoke rapturously of the enhanced speed and stability.

Before and after: the unconverted Cosworths, above, await Tickford's ministrations in the Bedworth compound, this batch all in black. Right, a sprinkling of the 52 RS500s that were finished in white join the other completed cars awaiting the Ford transporters to move them out to the dealers.

Inside the Aston Martin Tickford plant at Bedworth. Closest to the camera is the final work station, whilst the farther cars are entering the strip and rebuild process. Rectification and sub-assembly areas are out of the picture to the right.

In addition to considerable assistance from John Griffiths, the company's competition homologation expert, Mike Moreton of Ford Motorsport outlined the early history of the RS500 project for me: *In the autumn of 1986, it must have been September, we at Ford were talking about the year, and what had befallen the RS200 — and what would be needed for Group A in 1987. The decision was taken to build the extra 500 RS Cosworths, cars we could have simply sold in a straight extension of the original run, such was the demand.*

I am indebted to Tickford Managing Director John Thurston and Manufacturing Manager Brian Tennant for the wealth of background detail that I was allowed to collect during a visit in late July 1987 to see the RS500s being assembled. We travelled to and fro in one of the last Tickford turbocharged Capris, courtesy of PR consultant Graham Butterworth — another era altogether was the Capri, a fact emphasized by the contrast of its squared-off flares against the dramatic array of rounded RS500 Sierras in the factory yard.

Aston Martin Tickford became independent from the Aston Martin car company in 1984 and is wholly owned by CH Industrials (hence, Tickford were not involved in the Ford takeover of Aston Martin Cars). In a tidy full circle it was CH Industrials' original foothold in the motor business, the Bedworth site once occupied by the Coventry Car Hood & Seating Company, that housed the RS500 work. Bedworth has also played limited-production assembly line to the first 250 Jaguar Cabriolets, the Tickford Capri (the last of 100 was

made in July 1987) and the Rover V8-engined version of the Sherpa van.

John Thurston explained how the RS500 contract, worth more than half a million to Tickford, had come about. *Ford came to us with the basic format of the car in autumn 1986, but were not specific about details.*

Why did Ford pick Tickford? *Our Bedworth facility is tailor-made for small runs of special vehicles,* said Thurston. *We had dealt with Ford previously, having been assigned responsibility for turning the rally RS200 into a road car, but that was a 13-month project. In the RS500's case the first prototypes were delivered just before Christmas 1986, but the availability of Cosworth production engines in the spring of 1987 dictated the timing for the whole programme.*

Our responsibilities extended well beyond just assembling cars. We were assigned all engineering drawings to package the revised engine, plus all the support engineering that would be needed to durability prove and validate the vehicle (particularly in respect of Europe Emissions standard 1504). Our brief was to produce a thoroughly good car at the end. To do that we became involved in supplementary work on the Weber-Marelli injection and ignition management system and far more durability testing than originally envisaged — we ended up completing 30,000 miles at high speed. That was in separate chunks, rather than in one long session; plus thousands over pavé, it added up to much the same thing as Ford's own endurance tests for brand new products.

Comparison of the induction side of the original Cosworth Sierra engine, above, with an RS500 unit on the bench at Bedworth, below, shows up clearly the revised plenum chamber and secondary injection rail. Other details of the Weber-Marelli system are unchanged. Note the alloy engine mounting arm.

The 30mm extension lip added to the standard Cosworth wing is clearly visible on this RS500, one of the Moonstone-painted cars, which has not yet had the extra lower spoiler fitted.

The stripped Cosworth Sierra starts to assume its new RS500 identity as the uprated engine with its additional injector equipment is lowered into place.

The first batch of cars were black, as were 392 of the 500 total. Here, the production sequence has been upset in the cause of photography, the dual-winged machine closest to the camera apparently at the end of production while its compatriots in line have yet to receive their first stage spoiler set – look a little harder and you'll see an assembly area full of wingless RS500s! Parts supply problems meant construction sometimes had to take place out of sequence. Nice picture though. . .

Dramatic rear view. Central pylon and wrap-around lower extension demanded a notch in the lower spoiler and an electric aerial override switch respectively. To have found even more downforce for competition, Ford would have had to extend the back bumper to allow legally for a further rearward extension of the wing, something that was deemed too radical and expensive.

John Griffiths (left) and Mike Moreton of Ford Motorsport salute their Tickford colleagues on the other side of the final RS500, including Manufacturing Manager Brian Tennant (centre, right). The first prototypes arrived on December 23, 1986; the first ten training-production cars were constructed in June 1987, and the bulk were made between July 7 and July 30, the final FISA inspection date, the 44-strong team working all hours and then some. This unregistered RS500 clearly displays the front-end air ducting modifications and the lower addition to the front spoiler.

One key point was to check that the car ran coolly despite a number of tight fits in the engine bay and the bigger turbo, and I'm glad to say it passed with flying colours. A four-cylinder engine has considerable movement within the engine bay and another task in this connection was to make sure that nothing chafed, explained the Tickford Managing Director. An underbonnet look immediately shows that all stray lines were secured, and that the heat shielding arrangements differed substantially from the first Cosworth RS.

It quickly became an item of folklore that all RS500s were painted black, but it wasn't true, though that colour did predominate. It was just that the black cars were the ones seen in the publicity pictures. Altogether, 392 black RS500s were built, plus 52 in Moonstone Blue and 52 in white. To complete the 500, there were four white prototypes constructed using the expertise of Tickford's engineering base at Milton Keynes; D115 VEV was one of that series retained at Bedworth when I called.

How was the roadgoing RS500 changed from the original Sierra RS Cosworth? The bulk of the work centred on the engine bay and would provide the basis on which the works-assisted Eggenberger and Andy Rouse Engineering racing teams could comfortably employ over 500bhp. Most noticeable were the bigger capacity Garrett AiResearch T31/T04 hybrid turbocharger, a second fuel injection rail, and a large intercooler stretching across the rear of the enlarged water radiator, instead of the small one mounted above the original Cosworth RS rad. A lot of other less obvious changes made

The 224bhp power unit installed, left, with the replacement heat shielding visible around the new, bigger turbocharger, and the extra pipework for the secondary injector system. The grilles replacing the lower auxiliary lamps, next to the flashers, can also be seen.

RS500 front end, opposite, with the central cutout in the upper edge of the bumper and the other enlarged air intakes: compare with the original front end illustrated earlier. The lowline air splitter underneath was more effective in balancing rear downforce than the flexible spoiler extension of the first RS Cosworths, although more damage-prone and less practical.

this car a better road proposition, as well as a competition certainty.

The Cosworth YDB four-cylinder engine retained its 1,993cc (90.82 × 76.95mm) dimensions and 8:1 compression, but the cylinder block was now a reinforced version of the one used for the familiar 2-litre...*For the RS500 the block has been strengthened to withstand considerably higher loadings by reducing the size of the sand cores used in the casting...This gives the cylinders a thicker wall section and increases support to the top and bottom decks,* said Ford in July 1987.

Having ensured a good foundation for four times the power the Pinto unit originally yielded, Cosworth installed the 1988 specification 16-valve head which featured a three-bolt thermostat housing instead of the earlier two-bolt design. Valve sizes for the road car, inlet at 35mm diameter and exhaust at 31mm, remained as before, but Ford revealed, *The diameter of the air induction path has been enlarged from 56mm to 65mm.*

That induction tract bonus meant plenty of intake porting space to pass on the increased boost capacity of the racing engine, but the road car ran at the normal level, *10psi or so,* in one

engineer's words. The same source added that the extra power claimed for the RS500, up almost 10% from 204 to 224bhp at the same 6,000rpm peak, came primarily from the effect of that larger intercooler which had the capacity to reduce the temperature of the boosted air by a further 15°C, to around 45°C, increasing its density and hence the engine's efficiency. Maximum torque was minimally affected, quoted as 206lb/ft instead of 203. The official company figures left peak torque at 4,500rpm, but three engineering sources I spoke with agreed it wasn't quite like that: *The peak is up another 500 revs, because of the bigger turbo's characteristics. You'll also find that maximum power stretches from 6,000 to 6,250rpm.*

On the subject of production turbocharger boost, the level of which is controlled by the integral wastegate which opens to dump excess pressure, a Ford Motorsport insider told me, *Standard Cosworth RS boost is usually 0.7bar but the company does warrant up to 0.9bar.* The lower value, 0.7bar, is very close to the 10psi figure mentioned earlier (though rather more than the 8psi talked about at the time of the original Sierra RS Cosworth launch); 0.9bar is almost exactly

13psi. The inference was that the latter figure was more suitable for production (Group N) competition purposes. In British club racing an air restrictor (first of 27mm, then 26mm) was placed in the intercooler to injection feed pipe to control power, with boost of up to 1.6bar/22.77psi employed to release 285-296bhp. Please do not think I recommend such practices for quick road cars, for engine life was naturally foreshortened dramatically in this way by teams who promptly complained about the cost of it all! However, from personal experience I can say that 0.9bar is a perfectly feasible figure for 24-hour racing durability with a sensational turn of speed for a production car.

Like the induction passages, the fuel injection system of the RS500 was modified to suit the racer's requirements. A new plenum chamber was fitted to accommodate four secondary injectors that would spray into the intake trumpets when activated. All RS500s had to have the secondary fuel rail, electrical harness and extra pipework, in order to comply with competition homologation rules, but the second set of injectors was purely for racing use and required substitution of a specially calibrated electronic control unit (ECU). Apart from being unnecessary on a road car, that increased fuel flow potential would pose expensive problems for the emission control engineer — to say nothing of warranty headaches with up to 400bhp on tap! So the rest of the system remained in production trim like the later 204bhp engines, as far as roadgoing RS500s were concerned, with the usual Marelli electronic management of Weber injection equipment.

There were some minor changes in the exhaust and turbo mountings to accommodate the bigger puffer, but the basic layout was as before, with upswept four-into-two manifolding in nickel-iron. The turbocharger itself may have been bigger but retained a water-cooled casing and similar lubrication and wastegate arrangements. Internally, the engine had pistons to a new specification, fully skirted and with three compression and oil-control rings. Other important engine changes included new water and oil pumps, the latter with the same rotor but a new housing providing a double feed to increase flow for the rigours of competition.

Looking over the RS500 engine on the workbench, some of the new bracketry that Tickford

173

designed and made to complete the assembly was apparent, particularly a dropped alternator mounting to ease installation. The alternator itself was dubbed 'heavy duty' by Ford and was actually transferred from the original standard Cosworth engines in the examples I saw built at Bedworth.

Some important changes for durability, initiated by Ford and Cosworth during the run of the earlier car, were inherited by the RS500. An example was a cooling system modification to circulate water through the pump even when the thermostat was closed, aimed at reducing the risk of damage from using high power too soon after a cold start. Like the three-bolt thermostat housing, these features would subsequently apply to the engine of the four-door version as well.

Other basic elements of the Ford-Cosworth 2-litre engine that might be worth recalling because they were part of the original hatchback, then the RS500, and the subsequent Sapphire-style RS, included a gravity-cast alloy sump with a sandwich water/oil cooler between the block face and filter housing. Also part of the production specification were forged steel connecting rods, and a five-bearing crankshaft, also of forged steel. The steel crankshaft is the first I can recall in a mass-production Ford: OK, some RS1800s and the RS200 had steel crankshafts, but production of those was counted in hundreds, not the thousands of the Sierra RS series.

Body changes for the RS500 were not extensive, but modifications at the rear yielded, Ford said, *over 100kg* (220lb, nearly 2cwt) *of aerodynamic load*, and were balanced by a small, hard plastic splitter extension to the front spoiler, which itself was a modified design incorporating considerable cooling-biased changes.

At the back there was a 30mm/1.18in 'Gurney Flap' spoiler lip added to the production high wing: like the majority of Sierra RS body additions, it came from Phoenix in Germany. Beneath, modified with a small central cutout to accommodate the RS Sierra's central pylon, was an RS parts tailgate spoiler in black. This looked like the standard item from a Sierra 2.0iS, but I am assured they differed.

At the front the changes didn't look much on a registered vehicle, but a lot of subtle work saw more air admitted and the drag factor suffering. Ford talked about 0.345Cd in their press material in place of the original car's 0.34, but company sources spoke of a 0.015 rise in Cd, placing the RS500 closer to 0.36Cd, unfashionably high in 1987. Remember, a Capri RS3100 emerged from MIRA way back in 1973 credited with a 0.37 rating.

Look at the front moulding from the bumper line downward and you see a central indentation beneath the usual RS cutout that lies between the headlamps. Below the bumper line, and partially masked by a UK registration plate, are far wider air entry slots. These are augmented by the removal of the spot lamps in favour of a wire-grilled fresh air entry on either side, so five gains in fresh air supply were made possible by these modest looking changes: cunning, these Ford Motorsport men!

In fact the most cunning step of all was underneath the floor. A simple steel U-bracket and bolt holes allowed homologation of an alternative trailing arm mounting position for the rear suspension, one at least two inches forward of the original bolt holes. Again the road cars were not set up to utilize the alteration, but it gave freedom for much improved circuit racing characteristics. Taken in conjunction with the homologated alternative suspension arms allowed in Group A, the result would be a transformed competition chassis.

As ever, the homologation aspect dominated the RS500's final specification and the changes listed were joined only at a late stage prior to production by cosmetic touches, front and side badges, plus single side stripes, to complete the £19,950 package on offer to the public. Left untouched were the usual four-wheel disc brakes with Alfred Teves ABS, the previous late run suspension settings and many other primary features such as the power steering and interior trim. Perhaps surprising, because it would have been so easy to do (but would naturally have further worsened the aerodynamic drag factor), was the omission of wider wheels. There is no doubt in my mind that the 205/50 tyre specification is far from generous for such a powerful rear drive car, but the 7J × 15in alloys remained, along with VR Dunlop D40s on the cars I saw at Tickford.

There are three buildings at the Bedworth site and a lot of secure, wire-netted storage space, but every external passageway and car park spot was filled with RS500s when I called in July 1987, three days before the last homologation inspection. At the time of my visit the cars had already been inspected (as is routine today) by a rival manufacturer's representative. The gentleman chosen could not have known more about Ford as

Rear view, above, shows that there were less subtle changes at the back of the RS500: a secondary lower spoiler from the RS stores and a lip on the upper wing increased that effect hard to find on a production car, rear downforce, and so uprated the high-speed cornering potential with the race track in mind. Top view, above right, shows that standard Cosworth features such as the bonnet vents and glass sunroof were not altered.

The RS500 came very comprehensively equipped, but wider wheels and tyres might well be on the shopping list of the owner anxious to stay on the road and out of the scenery while using all that performance potential.

Two generations of performance car, both springing from Ford and Tickford co-operation. This picture, from July 27, 1987, was taken as the last of 100 Tickford turbocharged Capris was being completed. Alongside Tickford's last Capri demonstrator is one of 52 white production RS500s, its front air splitter stowed in the boot for transportation, whilst the tailplane on the left belongs to one of the four RS500 prototypes from December 1986, Essex-registered D115 VEV.

a competitor: he was Thomas Ammerschlager, recently designer-engineer behind BMW's M3, who had been the Ford Cologne engineer in charge of the Capri RS2600 and RS3100 programmes after Martin Braungart's departure for BMW.

To build an RS500 from a Sierra Cosworth 3-door base involved five distinct stages, for I am including the task of completely removing wax hardened by months of storage, which proved exceptionally laborious!

De-waxed, the RS Cosworth entered one of five parallel lines staffed by 44 men, a minority of them permanent Tickford employees. The first tasks centred on stripping off the rear spoiler and refitting the double blade system with its extension lip on the upper wing. Some refinements were necessary, including a small cutout in the leading edge of the lower spoiler to clear the central pylon and an electrical override to make sure the rear radio aerial was retracted whenever the hatchback was opened, owing to the risk of a tangle with the extended sides of the lower spoiler. An anti-rust solution was also applied where, it had been found, water could dribble in from underneath that lower spoiler and it's fair to say that some light surface rust was evident on the completed Cosworths after storage.

At the front of the car, this preliminary stage saw the stripping continue with the front spoiler

removed and the engine mounting bolts released prior to the next work station. The removed front spoiler went to a side sub-assembly area where its spot lights were removed and a new Phoenix moulding substituted with the enlarged bumper cut-out, enlarged front slots and grilles over the space formerly occupied by the spot lights. An extra grille was also fitted behind the RS500's central bumper air intake.

Incidentally, the front spoiler extension was not factory fitted, being stored in the boot for the dealership to fit after the perils of transportation were over: it was easy enough to hook one off in a parking manoeuvre, never mind the loading ramps of a two-tier transporter. . .

Work station 2 craned the 204bhp Cosworth motor out, whence it was wheeled away to a second sub-assembly area. With denuded front end, the car ascended upon dual workshop ramps for installation of two new rear suspension extension brackets and holes that would legitimize remounting the trailing suspension arm about two inches further forward in competition. Such bolt holes were like the secondary injectors: intended purely for competition, *not* road use.

The engine sub-assembly area usually made the original motors give up items like their alternators and clutches before packing them off for return to Ford. The replacement Cosworth-built unit was hot-tested and checked for correct oil level,

The specification of the RS500 was devised to give the racing teams the basis they needed to stay in contention in Group A competition, and the first win for this second-phase Sierra racer in the World Championship series came at Brno in August 1987. These two racing interiors, photographed at the Silverstone Tourist Trophy meeting in September, are those of one of the LHD Ford and Texaco financed Eggenberger cars and the RHD machine of Andy Rouse,

arriving complete with items like the big turbo and secondary injector rail in place.

As already observed, Tickford had fabricated their own, dropped, alternator mounting plate for easier installation of the RS500-equipped motor, and this is of particular importance to future collectors. For behind this plate was a blank

ground onto the block, ready to accept a GG-prefixed RS500 serial number.

Work station 3 saw the RS500 begin to take shape, the Cosworth replacement engine bolted up to the usual Borg-Warner box. The gearbox remained in place throughout the transplant operation, but was eased on its mountings, ready to accept the incoming engine with minimal fuss. Other major components came into view to surround the installed 224bhp unit, including the enlarged intercooler, whilst the exhaust mani-folding (modified internally to constrict rather than increase flow) mated to the rest of the standard Cosworth RS plumbing. Underbonnet finishing touches at this stage included the secure retention, usually by clips or loops, of any stray cables or lines and the mass of electronic leads.

Station 4 was primarily about two stages of quality control, applied to 95% finished motor cars. Ford had entrusted Tickford with all the quality control procedures and I was impressed with their enthusiastic implementation of such duties — I doubt if Ford accountants felt so warmly about the piles of returned components, including clutches! There was no doubt in my mind that Tickford did their best, with each production line squad spending eight hours per car, and that a genuinely improved product was the result. In fact the whole process reminded me of a small-scale FAVO, with its attention to rectification and paint-work standards. A pity that the Bedworth factory

RS500 racing features include two rear suspension layouts (yes, both homologated for Group A!). Left is the Eggenberger entry with a fabricated link, and the coil spring wrapped around the Bilstein, while the Andy Rouse Engineering car, right, uses a production-based pressed steel trailing arm, with the spring in its usual place, hidden behind the disc, and a fabricated bracket including an anti-roll bar mounting aft of the axle line. Other Eggenberger details are the massive four-piston caliper and wheelarch-mounted air jacking ram, below, and a side-exit exhaust worthy of around 500bhp, right. Eggenberger and Rouse cars lapped within split seconds of each other at the 1987 TT meeting and dominated the fight for fastest qualifying time.

was not a patch on that late lamented purpose-built Aveley site.

A late Ford managerial decision saw the RS500 name selected, so among the last work station's tasks was the application of two side stripes, further identification decals and the bootlid message *Sierra RS500 Cosworth*.

An eight-mile road test session followed the successful passage of each completed car through the first stage of quality control. Following a fixed route, each RS500 went through a second inspection. Failure at either stage put the car into quarantine for subsequent remedial action in a far corner of the assembly hall, all cars thus afflicted being identified by large windscreen warnings. Discussing screen signs reminds me that at least one wag followed the usual screen sticker *Made in Belgium* with *Repaired in Britain*!

Andy Rouse was 'Mr Racing Cosworth Sierra' in Britain. Rouse, a former Broadspeed mechanic and 1972 Mexico Champion, is seen below acknowledging the crowd's applause after beating the works Eggenberger machine of Steve Soper in a thrilling Brands Hatch encounter, July 1988, and right, on the podium at Silverstone in April 1989 after his first win of that season's British Touring Car Championship series in which only one man, Robb Gravett, ever managed to beat him.

In motorsport, circuit racing was the arena for which the RS500 was destined, such limited-production 'evolution' cars having been banned from rallying by the sweeping changes in international regulations which accompanied the banning of the Group B supercars. And there was no doubt what an effective racing machine it proved to be. From its debut in August 1987 through to the early 1990s, the RS500 was the overwhelming track winner among Group A racing saloons. *Perhaps it was too effective,* ruminated Stuart Turner, Ford's European Motorsport supremo, in March 1990; *it almost killed off the World Championship for saloons on its own, it was so quick.*

In 1987, the single year of that Championship, as we have seen, the Eggenberger Sierras secured the manufacturers' title for Ford, while rivals BMW were rewarded with the drivers' title for Roberto Ravaglia. The RS500 started setting the pace from its first race at Brno in Czechoslovakia and, when unfettered, it was never matched for outright lap speeds in the 1987–89 period.

To find out how the RS500 performed in its intended race-track role, I was lucky to grab five minutes with Steve Soper at the Silverstone Tourist trophy. That was in early September, 1987, and the RS500 version was more than fulfilling its promise, pulling an astonishing 1m

35.78s lap for Soper's pole position in the Texaco-Eggenberger Ford. This versus times beyond 1m 40s for the BMW M3s that had pushed the previous Sierras so hard, often outqualifying them in earlier Championship rounds.

I asked Steve to explain to us mortals how the RS500 felt in comparison to the earlier version for circuit use. He grinned and quipped: *Any idiot can feel the extra horsepower* (rival teams estimated a racing figure for the RS500 of 480bhp!) *But the feeling for the driver is also of a proper racing car.*

The engine now wants to go another 1,000rpm and the aerodynamics make it a very stable car, especially at the fast tracks. In fact, here at Silverstone, it's so fast that it's pushing into an understeer problem that is not easy to solve because of that back wing set-up's strong downforce over the rear wheels balanced only by the splitter at the front.

Success, however, eluded Soper at Silverstone; he had driven away from the field to lead by a minute, a convincing enough demonstration of his and the car's superiority, when the differential failed.

I referred earlier to the RS500 as the fastest Group A car around 'when unfettered' because in the national German Championship the organ-

The RS500 was the ultimate racing saloon of the late 1980s and won both championships and individual prestige races all over the world. The works-backed Texaco Eggenberger team, left, won the last European Championship of Marques in 1988. Privateer RS500s were also fearsome 500bhp racing machines, exemplified by the Rouse-built Labatts car of Laurence Bristow, right, at Oulton Park in 1989.

izers progressively clipped its power output in an attempt to keep other marques competitive. They did this by increasing restrictions on air admission to the oversize RS500 Garrett, in addition to their usual weight handicaps. Even when it was pegged down to 360bhp the RS500 was a formidable adversary for the Mercedes 190 2.5-16s and BMW M3s with 320–330bhp that Germany wanted to see with a chance of winning.

In 1988 Klaus Ludwig confounded all the opposition taking a Grab-prepared and entered Ford RS500 to outright Championship honours. Klaus then quit for a miserable 1989 with Mercedes in Germany's hothouse home international series. By then we had almost become acclimatized to seeing Steve Soper in a BMW M3, Steve leaving Eggenberger Ford when the European Touring car series was abolished after the 1988 season.

That final year of European Championship racing saw BMW scoop the honours with Roberto Ravaglia again, but the headline battles were mainly fought amongst RS500s. There was a considerable upset of form when the Eggenberger car came to Britain for Steve Soper to challenge Andy Rouse (Andy on his way to another British class title), for Rouse beat Soper in some of the closest and most exciting Brands Hatch laps I have ever witnessed. Rouse went on to beat not only the Eggenberger equipe, but also the fastest-lap combination at the 1988 Tourist Trophy, the visiting RS500 of Australian racers Dick Johnson and John Bowe.

With no 1989 European title to fight for, the RS500 works cars of Eggenberger were deprived of their principal hunting ground, yet the German-speaking Swiss team still came up with a most significant victory for the fastest Ford saloon. In late July the heavyweights of saloon car racing assembled in Belgium for the annual 24-hour race at Spa. Ford scored their first win since the days of the Capri and robbed BMW of what had begun to look like an undisputed right to reign in saloon car racing's toughest event, also beating a GT-class Porsche 944 into the bargain. The Eggenberger cars, now dressed in Bastos livery, finished first and third, former TWR ace Win Percy joining Gianfranco Brancatelli and German F1 hope Bernd Schneider in a crushing 8-lap victory at an average 86.96mph.

The 1989 racing season was tougher on Ford in Germany, but Klaus Niedzwiedz grabbed four victories and enough leading positions to take the RS500 into second place in the *Deutsche Tourenwagen Meisterschaft*. For reasons that I do not fully understand — mainly a feeling of being picked on as the only turbo car in the series, I suspect — Ford competition manager Lothar Pinske and European Motorsport director Stuart Turner agreed on withdrawing from Europe's most prestigious saloon car racing series for 1990. Maybe it had something to do with the priority given to World Championship rallying for 1990/91, but it was sad not to see the RS500 — even handicapped — out in front against opposition that included not just 1989 champions

BMW but also 1990 favourites Mercedes (now managed by Jochen Neerpasch of Cologne Capri and BMW Motorsport fame), Opel, and Audi's fabulous-sounding V8.

In Britain and Australia the RS500 had no problems in dominating outright and class results between 1987–1989, but there was scattered opposition that looked most serious in Australia. The Fords (including the spectacle of former GM Holden star Peter Brock in 'a four-letter car!') did not have too much trouble with the opposition from TWR Special Vehicle Operation Holden V8s. But Nissan did have the right elements in place, first with the comparatively square-rigged Skyline GTR-S (a force in Britain and Europe, out of Milton Keynes and the Howard Marsden operation, until the Japanese axed it at the close of 1988) and then with an aerodynamic GTR that really was 'the business'. Nissan technology included four-wheel drive and four-wheel steer, plus a turbocharged twin-cam six. This only became a reality in the 1990 season, and was not offered for sale in Europe: nevertheless some British production racing was planned to challenge the Cosworth monopoly and it looked an Australian and Japanese certainty at least to give the RS500 the competition it had been lacking.

In Britain the situation for the premier Championship was confused by the introduction of a 2-litre, normally aspirated, class. Fed up with Ford domination, the RACSMA and its consultants had imposed a new category, this despite the fact that it was BMW and Vauxhall who won the 1988 and 1989 national titles. However those wins had been on points and nothing had won a race outright but a Ford for as long as TV could remember, so the RS500 was served with notice that it would be outlawed in 1991, but allowed to run alongside the 2-litres in 1990.

Away from the regulation makers, Britain enjoyed some good racing amongst the RS500 men. The leading protagonists in 1989 were the perennial Andy Rouse and 1988 Production Saloon Car Champion Robb Gravett. There was no love lost between the two and the title went into legal dispute over the winter (Rouse was declared a winner once more: two class titles in a row for Ford, 1988 and 1989), but the racing was good, and we should not ignore the front-running speed of Tim Harvey (1987 Class A Champion in a Rover V8) in the Labbatts Rouse Sierra either.

In rallying, Ford were restricted to using the original three-door Cosworth or the later four-door, without evolution modifications, and they did not have the best of chances in the World Championship in 1987, '88 and '89, years which saw Lancia riding high and Toyota challenging strongly. There was that solitary win in Corsica in 1988, backed up by a third on the same year's 1,000 Lakes, both astonishing achievements for the French crew of Didier Auriol/Bernard Occelli and their Boreham-built 'Cossie', but in general the World class rallying record reflected both the handicap of two-wheel drive and a lack of top-line Ford involvement during the works team's 1979–86 layoff.

The 1987 and 1988 World Championship season saw an apparent lack of conviction on Ford's part: sometimes they used the XR4 x 4 (and were fined for a non-homologated fuel-injection system on its V6 engine in 1987) and they were generally half-hearted about spending money on a two-wheel drive 'tarmac or forest racer'.

The ultimate disgrace came on the 1989 RAC Rally. After a season of World class events with Fords a rare sight in the top ten (never mind the top three), they were nowhere to be seen in the top ten on the Lombard RAC! British pride, and the honour of first two-wheel drive car home, went to Malcolm Wilson, tenth in a GM Vauxhall/Opel Astra/Kadett which thrashed a horde of Sierra Cosworths. No wonder Ford hired Wilson for 1990 on a two-year contract. . .

British Open Championship events produced better results, but again it was on tarmac that the abilities of Jimmy McRae and the Cosworth were able to tip the balance and win the 1987 and 1988 titles. In 1989 the Andrews Heat for Hire cars ran well, especially that of leading contender Russell Brookes who got within one point of the title, but were pipped by the solitary Toyota GT-Four of David Llewellin/Phil Short for the home international Championship.

In National Championship terms it was a much more competitive car, winning both rally and race titles from Australia to Finland, Switzerland to Portugal, and in most other European nations too. No doubt, then, that the Sierra RS Cosworth had been an enormous success, yet a new impetus was needed for top-level rallying and to sustain a position in the market-place, and it was with the next volume-production development, the Sapphire four-door car, that the brightest hopes now lay.

Appreciating asset: immaculate and original three-door Sierra RS Cosworths of the first generation can only become more valuable after their short production run. Production figures record 5,545 examples made, all in the 1986 calendar year, including the 500 which were put aside and uprated to RS500 specification during the following year.

Sierra RS Cosworth on the road

Oddly enough, only when it came to surveying the owners of Sierra RS Cosworths did we fail to get an immediate response. But there were journalists running long-term test cars who were able to help, and there was certainly no conspiracy of silence on the part of Special Vehicle Engineering: I am indebted to them for practical answers to some of the points raised by the pressmen's experience. I have been able to keep an eye on the progress of *Performance Car* editor Jesse Crosse's long-term loan machine.

Jesse filed his first report with the comment that reverse was difficult to engage and that brake judder was becoming a problem. By the time of his third piece, which appeared in April 1987, it was apparent that there were some more severe service problems. At 7,600 miles the manifold-mounted MAP sensor failed and at 8,280 miles the Electronic Control Unit (ECU) also ceased functioning.

I was offered no inside comment on the ECU problem — which owner Hew Dundas also suffered on his Cosworth, as the magazine's correspondence revealed — but the MAP (Manifold Absolute Pressure) sensor breakdown was no surprise to anyone at

SVE, and was usually related to the ECU shutdown.

A Ford engineer told me: *Good old Weber Marelli told us there'd be a 100% failure rate on this sensor, due to its vertical mounting and the risk of condensate interrupting its operations. However, that priceless piece of information did not arrive with us until after production started! The trouble was that it did not trigger a 'get you home' mode in the ECU, but (usually) a total command cessation, so the car stopped.*

SVE repositioned the MAP sensor horizontally, rather than vertically, on the inlet manifold to avoid condensation fallout interrupting play. They also advised me that brake judder had been tackled by a specification change to Ferodo F3432 pads for the front discs, tighter tolerances on the ex-Scorpio hub bearing races and a significant increase in clamp torque figures.

The next problem on the service list was that of head gasket failure, a subject that was well publicized by the 900 LHD models recalled in Germany. It was not a common failure in Britain — unofficial figures point to just over 40 cases in Germany, under 10 in Britain — but we heard rather too much about head gaskets from the production racing fraternity. Racing teams spread their hands in despair at the frequent failures in the early season, yet they were achieving more than 55 extra horsepower from standard components, so my sympathies were with Ford (unless it happened to me, of course!).

When Ford were assessing a separate, pre-production gearbox problem (the faulty boxes did not enter service, as explained in the car's development story) they ran a 130mph durability test at Lommel and discovered that the water was getting blown out of the engine at sustained high speed.

At first the answer appeared to be in redesigning engine ancillaries including the overflow water bottle and piping, plus work on turbo hot spots and cylinder head water flow rates. Such measures were quickly adopted, but the gaskets still failed, so Ford went to Cosworth for remedial action. The answer was a lot more comprehensive than changing gasket material.

Rod Mansfield, SVE boss, told me: *We found that some cars used for shopping suffered the problem, which was traced to temperature differences and the lack of expansion/contraction ability between head and block. A completely new cylinder head bolt design involving tapered bolts was employed, along with extra meat in the Coopers gasket to accommodate different heat expansion rates, the new gasket being capable of expanding to fill any gaps.*

Such changes were introduced when an extended durability trial revealed that the revised engine arrangements promoted gasket life from 6-10 hours to a stunning 100 hours. The new head bolt and gasket arrangements were introduced in mid-1986, when more than 4,000 Cosworth RS engines had been completed.

A rather more minor problem that had been tackled during Cosworth RS production was the spillage of power steering fluid. This occured on some pre-production models during their Spanish workout and when journalists pounded round the Millbrook banking in search of maximum velocity. Ford tried to recreate the problem and found the Millbrook test, at high speed with steering loads constantly applied, was the worst possible combination, producing very high fluid temperatures. Nevertheless a new cap was introduced and fitted when German customers went along to have the new head sealing arrangements.

It would be a pity, though, to let this catalogue of problems rectified obscure the true nature of the car. The Sierra RS Cosworth's combination of performance in large measure with uncompromised hatchback practicality clearly impressed those who tried it. Despite some reservations about the way the car darted about on less than perfect road surfaces, Jesse Crosse was obviously won over by the car's character: *It is already clear to everybody,* he said, *that this is a modern classic.* After over 12,000 miles, he observed: *The Sierra Supercar still stuns. It still leaves any driver breathless however often driven, and it is still exciting to get into every morning, whatever the weather.*

One of the few privately-owned Cosworths that I was able to monitor belonged to Buckinghamshire-based property developer Grahame Bryant, vying for his affections in a stable that included two Ferrari Boxers, an Aston Martin Volante and many more, including the racing Morgan V8 that has taken him to many club racing victories.

Grahame bought his black RS in the spring of 1987 and it had travelled 5,000 miles when we spoke. Despite the exalted company the car keeps, he was very positive about its virtues: *It's never missed a beat and it's unbelievably fast over cross-country roads. Others have knocked the road-holding, but I find it superb.*

It's also good at motorway travel and extremely comfortable, but you do have to avoid that boomy period around 4,000 revs. You can do that by simply going a bit faster!

The car was up for sale when I called — because he fancied buying an RS500.

11

Sierra RS Cosworth – 2

Back in early April, 1987, almost four months before I visited Bedworth to see how the RS500 came into being, I had been again to Ford's R&D headquarters at Dunton in Essex to hear about the development of the next Sierra Cosworth derivative, the Sapphire-bodied four-door version. That was the one on which no upper production limit had been set, and it constituted Ford's most ambitious sally yet into BMW territory. It would be September of that year before I was able to drive the car, due to be joined that month by 70 pre-production examples, and late November was the scheduled date for the start of series production at the Belgian plant.

What a difference a bodyshell makes! The RS version of the Sierra Sapphire drew primarily on the 1985-86 three-door hatchback Sierra RS Cosworth for its mechanical make-up, yet a very different product had emerged, one that emphasized the kind of high level of equipment and refined performance required in the 1980s and 90s — a far cry from the rubber mats and plastic seats of the Mexico in an earlier decade.

I had been slightly surprised at the performance development of three-door rather than four-door Sierra, because the booted Sapphire saloon looked like a better basis for a rallying Ford than the hatchback, the body being inherently more rigid. Part of the reason for this essential difference lies in the fact that a hatchback carves a literal hole in body strength, though engineers tell me that the difference in torsional strength is not significant enough to alter suspension settings. It is also worth remembering that the Sapphire benefited from further design and development in the light of previous Sierra experience.

Both Sierras and Sapphires in mainstream production were modified in 1987 in the light of computer-guided finite analysis of body strength. *The body side rails and seat crossmember have been redesigned to provide improved vertical and torsional bending modes,* reported Ford, further asserting at the February 1987 launch of the revised Sierra and debutant Sapphire that: *This has resulted in increased levels of body stiffness and strength which improves the body integrity.* (That's Ford-ese for 'The original was a bit floppy and we've fixed it!'—JW).

In action, the new Sapphire did feel notably rigid over the test roads used for the press launch of the ordinary versions in Cyprus and the claim that it provided improved suppression of vibration from rotating masses and road inputs was totally justified in my opinion. Even in 2-litre, 105 bhp Pinto-powered form it was less boomily audible than before.

Other improvements to the range in 1987 included the polystyrene acoustic filling of the front screen pillars and subtle styling changes, such as the extended bonnet and 15mm taller side glass, all shared by Sierra and Sapphire. Aside from the boot, the Sapphire also had a unique hidden drip rail in its notchback outline and aerodynamic strakes incorporated in the back pillars to match those installed as a modification for crosswind stability in the Sierra hatchback.

Thus Ford SVE engineers were able to start from a basic body that was a genuine advance over the original Sierra of October 1982 to February 1987. In April 1987 Rod Mansfield recalled, *We always had the Sapphire in mind for the RS treatment, but it was progressed from the start as a*

From the early prototype days of the four-door Sierra RS project, this SVE workhorse has no rear spoiler and uses the hatchback's alloy wheels. Ford styled their own replacement equipment in both cases, and also changed the mainstream production specification on which the new RS would be based from the sports 2.0iS to the Ghia version of the Sapphire.

C866 NVW

Front view of the early prototype displays triangular bonnet vents, later narrowed and finally deleted altogether, and a front bumper and spoiler assembly adapted from that of the three-door car. The under-bumper lamps were later relocated in a higher and slightly less vulnerable position.

The four-door Sierra RS Cosworth takes shape: here, the road wheels and body are in substantially their final, production form, but the smaller bonnet vents remain.

car free from any need to carry Motorsport features. Motorsport had the Escort and Sierra RS types, with an evolution of the 1986 Sierra (now RS500), to take care of their needs.

However, it was that first RS Cosworth which made the Sapphire possible. It was just so good in rather unexpected ways! I don't think anyone believed that we could produce a 150mph Sierra that was so docile and comfortable in city use. 'Anyone' included many senior mainstream Ford engineers, who were extremely generous in their appreciation of SVE's handiwork.

Clive Ennos, Director of Product Engineering, summarized this attitude perfectly at the 1987 launch of the Sapphire when he said: *Anyone who has driven a Sierra Cosworth must get a considerable level of enjoyment from just the sheer joy of*

driving that vehicle. It handles so well and it is so tractable. . . You can take it through the middle of Knightsbridge and it will be tractable and comfortable. You don't feel like having to go to the osteopath the minute you have arrived!

That viewpoint meant that SVE were credited by their colleagues with having proved a major point, making an RS development of the Sapphire far more credible. *The confidence created by our pre-production RS Cosworths around the time of the Spanish press launch* (December 1985) *led to a very positive attitude within the company, and that made our operation, as a small unit within the main company, notably easier,* said the SVE manager.

Paperwork for the four-door RS car began to flow from April 8, 1986, much of it the result of a

Product Committee Meeting, with SVE's contacts channelled through Nigel Bunter. Primary points were outlined in those documents as follows:

The 1988 model year Sierra Cosworth four-door is based on the Sierra Ghia four-door and is for all EAO Markets except Sweden, Switzerland and Austria — a restriction caused by ECE 15.04 emission level.

The following lists the major features that are different from the Sierra Ghia four-door and not basically carryover from the 1986½ Sierra Cosworth:

*Unique body colour polyurethane front bumper/air dam, rear deck lid spoiler and rocker panel extensions.

*Unique body colour front grille.

*Unique badging, nomenclature 'Sierra RS Cosworth'.

*Three body colours — white, Mercury and Crystal blue.

*Unique 7J × 15 alloy wheel with 205/50 VR 15 tyre.

The following lists major features that are basically carryover from 1986½ Sierra Cosworth, but modified where required to improve durability, performance, to accommodate package changes, or pick up mainstream modifications:

*Cosworth Engineering YBB engine with 16-valve DOHC head and Garrett AiResearch T3 turbocharger, based on the Ford T88 block.

*Weber Marelli multipoint fuel injection and electronic management system.

*Radiator with twin electric fans and air-to-air turbo intercooler.

*Borg Warner T5 transmission with uprated 240mm clutch and uprated two-piece propshaft.

*Rear axle assembly with 3.65:1 final drive ratio, 190mm-diameter Viscous Coupling differential and uprated axle shafts with VL107 CV joints.

*Brakes, 283mm-diameter front vented discs with four piston Teves calipers; 273mm solid rear discs with DE1 (Scorpio) calipers, system operated by Teves ABS.

*Suspension basically carryover 1986½ Cosworth Sierra, with revised rear roll bar and mountings and revised setting springs, roll bars and shock absorbers.

*Instrument cluster with 270km/h/170mph speedometer, tachometer without red sector and engine management warning light.

Sapphire-based RS Cosworth in pre-production trim in September 1987, having finally lost the bonnet vents altogether. 'Unnecessary' said the engineers, and the marketing men seemed unmoved by the loss of a little bit of RS identity established by the earlier Sierra RS and the second Escort RS Turbo.

The question of nomenclature was the subject of later marketing discussions, with a decision coming late in 1987 to drop the RS designation for LHD markets, leaving just the Cosworth connection to denote extra performance. RS badging would be retained for Britain, but, initially at least, it was the intention that the Sapphire tag, already becoming established to identify the four-door bread-and-butter versions, would not officially apply to the car in Cosworth-powered form.

Approval for work to commence was effective from April 1986 and would lead to the construction of eight LHD and RHD prototypes prior to the September 1987 pilot run of 70 production specification four-door Cosworths. The first prototype was running by August 1986 and lacked a rear spoiler, development of which item demanded some additional time in the Ford Germany wind tunnel.

The first alliance of the 204bhp power train and the Sapphire body was actually concocted around an example with 2.0i trim level rather than the planned Ghia specification, but there was also a prototype built in spring 1986 around the hatchback to give management an idea of what was to come and to conduct some trials of aspects unrelated to body type.

That rather tatty Sierra hack went to the Belgian Lommel test track for comparative assessment against the Audi 90, Mercedes 190E and 3-series BMW competition which Ford expected to meet. *It is actually quite hard to find direct comparisons with the Sapphire Cosworth,* commented one SVE engineer shrewdly. *If you do it on a price basis, then they haven't got the performance of our car . . . if you base a back-to-back on performance, then the competition is way beyond our price bracket.* That is actually a classic example of finding an open niche in today's crowded performance car world.

In principle, the blend of 1986 Sierra RS running gear and the 1987 Sapphire shell sounded simple, but important engineering changes influenced the engine and suspension and require explanation.

Theoretically, I would say that all RS Sapphires share an identical engine specification, but in practice that may not be the case down to the last detail because development continued while production of engines began in advance of cars. Cosworth's capacity to build such engines (all based on the Ford Pinto T88 block, not the thickwall RS500-only type) was limited to some 2,000 units annually. This meant the continued production of engines after the cessation of 1986 Sierra RS production, a process that carried on even whilst the RS500 was being assembled, in an effort to stockpile motors prior to four-door RS production beginning. Motors removed from cars about to become RS500s went back to Cosworth for the purpose of eventually supplying the new model.

A new piston design was introduced for 1987 engines. An offset gudgeon pin allows much closer tolerances and an end to the 'dieselling' noise which could accompany a cold start. Another refinement was the switch from spacer washers on the turbo damper to a more durable single coil spring that retained its grip on the damping of turbo vibrations.

All four-door RS units should include the engine durability modifications made to the later 1986 Sierras, including yield head bolts, new Cooper gasket, revised sensor position and cooling system changes. No official changes in power rating were made, but my understanding was that 204bhp was a commendably conservative figure, which falls in line with Rod Mansfield's earlier comments about a 204 to 218bhp span for the press fleet three-door cars.

The most substantial engineering effort was devoted to the suspension, work that continued even when I drove that September pre-production Sapphire, although they were then only fine-tuning low-speed ride. The fundamental change was to drop the raised roll centre and associated special steering knuckle of the original Cosworth Sierra and return to something close to the standard figure. Also fundamental to the new car's lack of twitchiness under braking was a reversion to the original castor angle specification, using the first stabilizer bar design.

As to the damper, spring and anti-roll bar choices selected for the newcomer, in the light of extensive testing to suit a new clientele, I am indebted to Harry Worrall at SVE for letting me have the following data table:

	1988	1986
Front spring rate (kg/Nm)	21	19
Rear spring rate (kg/Nm)	51	47
Front anti-roll bar dia. (mm)	28	28
Rear anti-roll bar dia. (mm)	16	14

At first sight, little change in characteristics might

be expected from these slight alterations, but SVE achieved their objective of combining firm control with minimal sacrifices to the RS tradition of vivid handling capabilities. The key factors were increased spring rates in alliance with softer settings for the dampers, which remained of Fichtel and Sachs twin-tube design. It is worth remembering that the anti-roll bars were different to the original production Sierras. At the front this was for the castor and braking weave reasons explained earlier. At the back a new anti-roll bar attachment was needed because of the 1987 model year changes to all Sierra and Sapphire trailing arm suspension, now mounted on a replacement tubular subframe.

Aerodynamic studies of the 1986 Sierra RS three-door had taken place between December 18 and 20, 1985, and revealed a drag factor of 0.34Cd. Once the Sapphire body had received an enlarged rear spoiler instead of the original skimpy unit, April 28 to 30, 1986, was devoted to studying the RS version at the company's wind tunnel at Merkenich.

Using exactly comparable body loads and sus-pension rakes the four-door car returned a figure of 0.33Cd. What pleased the Ford aerodynamicists particularly was that they had managed virtually the same drag factor and rear-end lift as the Mercedes 190 2.3/16, with a reduction in front-end lift and an improvement in yaw figures over that prestigious rival which shared a Cosworth connection under the bonnet.

Such aerodynamic values were obtained with the front, rear and side body extensions you see on the production cars, plus the twin bonnet vents that were deleted late in the 1987 development schedule. Quite why this recognizable RS feature from the earlier Sierra and second Escort Turbo was deleted after all the tooling was expensively completed is not clear, but I do know that SVE had found that the vents were not necessary on the four-door RS and that the marketing people were unflustered by their loss.

Certainly the Sapphire-style RS had already developed its own identity. Much of this could be traced to the Marley body panels. They gave the same frontal look as the 1986 car but, as Rod Mansfield pointed out, *We couldn't get away with*

The clean shape performed well in the wind tunnel, recording a slight drop in Cd values over the hatchback, and exhibiting better crosswind stability than some prestigious rivals, once the rear spoiler had been reprofiled.

The car in pre-production trim with fully-developed rear spoiler. The 1986 Sierra body kit would not match the later Sapphire shell, though the parentage is obvious around the nose section. Extra panels for the new model came from the automotive division of the well known British tiling makers, Marley, who had provided parts for the Escort Turbo.

Interior was drawn primarily from the Sapphire Ghia base on which this RS derivative was built. That meant the inclusion of the car diagram warning light display and the Ford four-speaker sound system. The speedometer was recalibrated to 170mph but SVE deliberately chose not to retain the boost gauge of the earlier car as inappropriate to the intended market sector.

Rim width and the use of Dunlop D40 rubber remained as before, but the wheels were brand new in style — and owners were quickly to discover that they didn't like cleaning them!

The most restrained high performance Ford yet, in terms of style: the speed with docility of the first Sierra RS Cosworth was the inspiration for this entry into a new market niche for Ford performance derivatives. Production figures from the Genk plant in Belgium record 13,839 examples of this model made up to the end of 1989, and there were a few more in 1990 before they switched to its 4 x 4 descendant — in round figures, 14,000 cars, almost three times as many as the earlier three-door model.

fitting 1986 Sierra body kit panels on the Sapphire. They had just changed the sheet metal too much for that to be practical.

Those Ford-designed alloy wheels were totally different to anything else the company produced, RS or otherwise, but they wore the same dimensions, offsets and D40 Dunlop 205/50 VR 15 tyres on the 1987 car I tried as had always been fitted to the 1986 Cosworth.

Predicted performance was litttle different from that of the 1986 Sierra RS, for a 0.01 reduction in drag factor and a small increase in kerb weight were not expected to have a major effect. Pre-production data from August 1987 suggested that Ford would claim 0-60mph in 6.1 seconds, 0-100km/h (0-62mph) in 6.5 seconds and a maximum speed of 150mph (241km/h). It was anticipated that 30-50mph in fourth and fifth gears would take 6.5 and 11 seconds respectively. For comparison, **Autocar** recorded 6.2 and 10 seconds with the 1986 three-door car.

In fact the **Autocar & Motor** road test of the new car in February 1988 recorded 0–60mph in a sizzling 5.8 seconds, but the maximum speed was predictably closer to 140mph at 142mph. Fuel consumption averaged 20.3mpg and Britain's leading weekly magazine concluded that it was a *budget supercar with saloon practicality*. Overall the Sapphire Cosworth bore the benefits of experience with the earlier car and was a much better product for those lessons. As with all the RS models, including the RS500, my own driving impressions are in Chapter 16: suffice it here to say that I found important gains in refinement with no loss of the original Cosworth's sparkle.

But accomplished though it was, this first four-door RS was only a precursor of more exciting things to come. When Ford decided to commit millions to challenging Lancia and the Japanese in World Championship rallying in the 1990s, the by-product was the third Cosworth RS road car, one that set a new benchmark for sporting four-wheel drive. It immediately replaced its rear-drive predecessor to begin a new phase in the RS story.

UK buyers had already taken more than a million Sierras — a relatively few three-doors, many five-doors and an increasing number of Sapphire four-doors — when this was written in 1990. Amongst that million were just 8,000 RS Cosworths of all types, and there was a distinct feeling that the new 4 x 4 'Ford Sierra Sapphire RS Cosworth' (to give it the full UK title) had to be the best yet. German specification 'Sierra Cosworth' cars (they do not use *RS* or *Sapphire* badges on LHD production) confirmed that view when presented for press appraisal in Spain during February 1990: 31 examples were provided, soon reduced to 30 when the Italian contingent got to work!

Factors that made the newcomer the 'best yet' included civilized noise levels and the promise of enhanced durability for both body and engine, as well as an obvious power and torque bonus. Plus of course 4WD traction, with the unequal power split already proven in the XR4 x 4, to take Ford back into top-level rallying with a sporting chance of winning, something that simple rear-drive denied on all but one occasion.

The RS Cosworth 4 x 4 combined stability with abundant speed (up to a claimed 150mph; 0–60mph in a quoted 6.6 seconds) and was also engineered to deliver the same 220bhp and

214lb/ft with or without twin catalytic converters, engines so equipped having an appropriate green shade applied to the cast alloy cam cover with its *DOHC 16-V TURBO Ford COSWORTH* legend. Otherwise it remained in the original red (though, as we shall see, the engine underneath was subtly but comprehensively reworked).

During a tough two days in the foothills of the aptly named Sierra de Montseny on that Spanish launch trip, the latest in the Cosworth breed, shod exclusively with a new Bridgestone tyre, demonstrated such astonishing road capabilities that it invited frequent and favourable comparison with the major contenders from Toyota, Audi and Lancia. In other words Ford had a world-class car on offer, and even the basic price just £5 shy of £25,000 did nothing to dim the enthusiasm of the press reaction in the run up to the sales debut scheduled for April 1990.

Following in the wake of the charismatic three-door Sierra RS and RS500 types, the four-door Sapphire RS had struggled for the kind of premium-price public recognition that those first hatchbacks had gained largely from their motorsport successes. True, the Sapphire RS had victories in production saloon racing and numerous rally outings for private teams like Evans Halshaw (Chris Lord, Jeremy Easson). But public imagination was not fired on the scale it had been by the original car, and sales of 2,700 examples in 1989 — many at discounts off the last UK list price of £21,300 — created no urgent commercial reason, just as there was no compelling motorsport reason, for continuing the two-wheel drive Sapphire RS. So the last rear-drive RS car passed into history almost without an obituary.

Once again SVE were assigned to the task of developing a new RS model, the 4 x 4 in road trim picking up on specialist knowledge that Ray Diggins and his group had garnered from the Sierra XR4 x 4s and Granada/Scorpio counterparts, with V6 2.8 and later 2.9-litre power, which they had created using Ferguson transmission patents and Viscous Coupling limited-slip differentials. Ford Motorsport personnel kept a watchful eye for any modifications useful for competition that could be incorporated at modest extra cost. SVE was then ten years old and had tackled 16 special projects for the mainstream company, ranging from the Capri 2.8i to air-conditioned Escorts. (Their 17th was the 1990 Fiesta RS Turbo, and that 130bhp package, which sought, among other things, to answer the criticisms levelled at the performance and steering of the XR2i, forms the subject of our next chapter.)

SVE engineers — between six and twelve in number at different points in the project — under Ray Diggins began work in 1988. All but two pre-production cars were built on the production line in order to simulate manufacturing problems from the start and rigorous standards were set. Radically revised engines (*80 to 90% of all components are modified or new*, said SVE manager Rod Mansfield) had to survive the normal Ford 300-hour cycles of dyno testing. 'Real world' test sessions in temperatures over 30 degrees C at the Nardo speed bowl in Southern Italy and below freezing in Finland were completed.

Although the engine looked much the same as before, a DOHC turbo Cosworth conversion of the old Pinto 2-litre unit, it is actually simplest to list what was carried over unchanged: 35mm inlet and 31mm sodium-filled exhaust valves and their springs; heat treated steel connecting rods and caps; gudgeon pins; timing pulley and belt; front oil seal housing and main bearings. Compression remained as before and so did cubic capacity at

SVE prototype of the 4 x 4 in the summer of 1989 exhibited the bonnet vents rejected for its rear-drive predecessor and harked back to the original Sierra Cosworth in the alloy wheel design.

Cutaway of the RS 4 x 4 reveals the alliance of Cosworth engine with all-wheel-drive hardware developed from the XR4 x 4 layout, delivering two thirds of the available power to the rear wheels. Front final drive (without LSD) was accommodated in the redesigned sump. Apart from the obvious traction advantage, big improvements over the earlier rear-drive model in durability and refinement were achieved and there was a modest 16bhp power bonus.

1,993cc (90.82mm x 76.95mm) despite the installation of so many new parts, including the iron block.

The biggest engine changes were to the cylinder head and block castings, both stiffened in a noise reduction and muscle building programme. We were told that the block represented, *RS500 knowledge but our usual production process. The head is strengthened whilst also enhancing its resistance to thermal distortion.* The block was summarized as of RS500 casting thickness but utilizing the original core plug sizing. A new head gasket was specified and knock sensing incorporated on the rearward (fourth) cylinder.

Complementing those basic changes came a new cast sump pan to accommodate 4WD, replacement oil and water pumps to serve revised water and oil distribution systems, new camshaft profiles and 8:1 compression ratio Mahle pistons with rings designed to improve oil consumption. The water pump was driven by twin vee-belts from the crankshaft nose and was equipped with an improved impeller design to increase flow throughout a new bypass system, which also improved heater output. I suspect the latter factor mattered little, but the concern over durability on

the coolant front was fundamental evidence that this aspect had been the original design's Achilles heel, particularly vulnerable in rally use.

There was some RS500 lore designed into the fuelling rail of the stiffened alloy inlet manifold, plus fine changes that made a T3 turbo a TO3B in official brochures. TO3B turbocharger modifications encompassed a lead seal to protect the wastegate against unwarranted intrusions, plus turbo case profile changes to smooth the arrival of low-rpm boost. Water cooling of the casing remained, but the intercooler (a pretty puny item on 204bhp engines) was enlarged. The larger intercooler was credited with greatly improved efficiency (78%). Maximum boost was set at the usual 0.55bar/8psi.

Motorcraft's first platinum-tip plugs were deployed (*we have to find more spark than they need in F1*, reported one engineer) and synthetic oils only were specified, Mobil 1 the current favourite.

Other basic engine moves showed Ford were determined to tackle a variety of objectives. They included a revised profile for the flywheel to permit easier fitting of Motorsport clutches and to improve cooling. There was also another

Motorsport programme to apply in the engine bay that would increase on-event readiness. Sincere pleas were made to keep silent on this secondary service-orientated modification, *too sensitive for print at present*, in the spring of 1990. As the car may not have made its debut by the time this second edition appears, silence will be maintained. Suffice it to say that Ford were not about to let Lancia get away with a controversial advantage.

The biggest saviour for the ears of the Cosworth road-car driver was the change in exhaust, which no longer needed a turbo damper as *outputs beyond 500bhp are not expected*, said one insider with a straight face. Turbo casing revision and replacement exhaust manifolding all aimed to ease low-speed amiability, at outputs below 300bhp, but don't let anyone tell you this was in anyway a soft, non-competitive engine.

The main objective was durable, quieter power. It was not the escalation from 204 to 220bhp at

Externally little had changed, but the 4 x 4 RS delivered speed and stability that begged comparison with the best in the world. During the Spanish press launch, its prowess was thoroughly tested on loose surfaces like this, as well as on tight tarmac corners and motorways, and won enthusiastic approval from all sides. Similar underbonnet appearance to earlier models concealed many detail revisions. Catalytic convertor version (green camshaft cover) and non cat (traditional red) shared the same 220bhp output, only the peak torque rpm differed. Either unit was rev-limted at 6,800 with a final cutout at 7,000rpm.

Back in Britain, the RS badge was restored. Blacked-out tail lights were one of the few identification points when the fourth generation 'Cossie' entered the showrooms in April 1990. At £24,995 the Ford Sierra Sapphire RS Cosworth 4 x 4 offered a 146mph top speed and 0-60mph acceleration at 6.6s only fractionally slower than its rear-drive ancestors. Other figures reveal that a complete exhaust system was over £700, front brake pads were nearly £70 and the rear bumper would cost £355 to replace!

an unchanged 6,000rpm peak (6,250rpm with cat), or the gain from 203lb/ft to 214lb/ft, 1,000rpm earlier, that mattered most to Ford and Cosworth. Their concerns were an improved warranty record and continued potential for competition, this time with the accent on accessible rallying power in the 300bhp zone rather than any 500bhp racing ambitions. My competition sources told me that Ford expected no less than 450Nm torque in Group A World Championship trim, a massive 331lb/ft unlikely to

be accompanied by less than 340 to 350bhp.

On public roads, SVE knew 4 x 4 drive-train losses and a production weight gain of 70kg would absorb much of the 7.9% power and 5.5% torque increases, so no significant performance bonus was to be expected. When *Autocar & Motor* came to put a 4 x 4 through their test procedure they recorded 0–60mph in 6.6 seconds, exactly matching Ford's claim, and a maximum slightly down at 146mph. Full details are in the Appendix. (Comparable figures for the rear-drive Sapphire

The rear-drive Sapphire RS became an increasingly popular choice for production racing in 1989-90. This is Simon Weston, of Falklands fame, enjoying his first race in the Evans Halshaw RS at Thruxton, October 1989.

RS were 5.8 seconds and 142mph, and for the original Sierra RS, 6.2 seconds and 149mph — in layman's terms, not much in it.) What the slightly academic figures conceal is the big advantage conferred by four-wheel drive on anything other than a smooth, dry test-track surface.

Ford SVE project leader Ray Diggins explained to me some of the extensive changes made to the Sierra during development of the 4 x 4 in terms of the contradictory objectives which had to be met: *We had to incorporate 4WD, make a worthwhile car for motorsport purposes and yet remember this was still a family car that we had to sell alongside the rest of the revised Sierra range. The engine had to meet 83 US emissions standards with catalytic converters, yet offer increased power and torque. Finally it had to do all this and be a more civilized, quieter and more durable car to drive and own.*

The family car aspect ruled out the most radical body modifications that Ford Motorsport had in mind, but a tremendous amount of detailing had gone into the four-door body. Diggins reported: *There is a stronger mounting point for the rear dampers, and bracketry to tie between the rear cross-member and the turrets. The inner wings are thicker than a standard Sierra and the complete body takes slightly longer to build than usual, so the modifications are restricted only to Cosworth Sierra 4 x 4*

The benefits from a stronger C-pillar are associated with use of composite glues to stitch things together, whilst the front bulkhead and inner wings have detail strengthening that you cannot see at a casual glance, but which helps complete the integrity of the body in road and special stage use, when it will be equipped with an integrated roll cage of course. Those with longer RS memories will remember that Mk1 rear-drive Escorts of the RS persuasion used a Type 49 shell that also featured basic strengthening.

Having controlled the action of the body upon the suspension — particularly at the back where competitors will know the earlier RS types displayed extensive flexing — the road car suspension was overhauled. Because the body was so much stiffer one at first thinks the SVE engineers thought *to hell with the low-speed ride, let's just keep this baby on the road.* Positive camber angles were visible evidence that 4 x 4 characteristics had arrived, but the Sapphire RS front and rear spring rates were retained. These were reported as 21kNm front, 51kNm rear, a lot stiffer at the back than all but the hardest progression offered in the back of the variable rate XR4 x 4, along with gas damping. Anti-roll bars

Evans Halshaw also backed the efforts of 21-year-old Robbie Head, here on his way to win the Group N class and finish fifth overall on the 1990 Granite City national rally. Youth and Sapphire RS performance seemed a formidable alliance.

were stiffened up 2mm front and rear — this brought the front anti-roll bar thickness up to a sturdy 30mm/1.18in and the rear to 18mm/0.7in — and, Nurburgring *Nordschliefe* aside, it proved hard to induce any sign of front-end floppiness over crests.

Credit for this Cosworth's almost uncanny adhesion is shared between effective four-wheel drive, revised suspension and the replacement of Dunlop D40 tyres by a Bridgestone identified as ER90. We are told this was uniquely developed for SVE; other sources whisper that the Japanese started from the basis of the fabled RE71. Either way, it is an ace tyre in this application, offering minimal squeal and eye-rolling grip.

The 4 x 4 aspect, manufactured by the GKN-

The Viscous Couplings are set up quite 'loose' in the road car and do not interfere with the standard fitment of electronic Teves ABS braking. Rival manufacturers say the VCs are too slack to contribute more than a showroom presence, but few customers or journalists seem to have any complaints about traction with the Ford 4 x 4 system. All seem positively delighted by entertaining handling resulting from a distinct rearward power bias. Regular tail-slides are not part of normal road motoring, even under duress, but over sandy surfaces or on slippery tarmac the 'Cossie' 4 x 4 power-slides with controllable composure.

The centre differential is housed in an aluminium alloy transfer box which replaces the

Colin McRae and Derek Ringer rang up a little bit of RS history, their rear-drive car winning the Cartel Rally in the British home international series in February 1990. This was a first for the Sapphire shape at this level and McRae was the youngest winner in the category.

ZF partnership at Viscodrive under agreement with Ferguson and Ford, remained fundamentally the same as for the previous SVE applications mentioned earlier. That meant a power split roughly in thirds, 34% front and 66% rear. This is achieved by epicyclic gears without the intervention of the Viscous Couplings incorporated in the central and rear axle differentials. In the Sierra 4 x 4 layout, XR or RS type, the VCs are used simply for limited-slip differentials, unlike in some converted front-drive systems such as the VW syncro Golf. There, a VC is used to apportion torque to the rear wheels when, and only when, the front wheels begin to run out of traction. A limited-slip front differential is fitted only to the Group A rally car, not for the road car or for Group N.

standard MT75 gearbox extension housing. Other SVE-developed components abound, most derived from the XR4 x 4 programme of 1983–85. The front drive comes via a multiple-row chain from the centre differential. Then a short propeller shaft runs to the front differential, offset to the right and housed in the special cast alloy sump pan. An extension shaft in a support bearing passes through the sump to the left so that both front drive shafts, fitted with constant velocity joints at either end, are of equal length, helping to reduce any tendency to torque steer.

Accommodating the new front-drive facility is a very important cast aluminium alloy cross-member that replaces the standard Sierra pressed steel structure. On the front suspension revisions, Ford reported that *new nodular cast iron front wheel*

knuckles support large preset bearings for forged steel wheel spindles fitted with 94-tooth rotors for the ABS sensors. This means there is a good chance the original wheel bearing problems will also have been eliminated.

Drive to the back wheels is as before, with a Viscous Coupling limited-slip rear diff. Extra weight of the 4 x 4 system is put at 50kg, 45kg of that added to the front wheels, giving a total of 1,280kg/2,822lb.

Braking is provided by a quartet of vented discs of just under 11in diameter, easily adequate for most situations. However, it has proved a weak point in the Group N rally car, so really energetic road travellers might need to look at alternative friction materials and fluids for harsh use. The electronic ABS from Alfred Teves remains in touch with varying road surfaces, and the system keeps the pedal toward the top of its travel without the disconcerting increases in movement that the original RS hatchbacks exhibited over bumps at speed.

In reviewing the extensive mechanical changes it is easy to overlook just how well equipped a 1990 road performer had to be. Now that electronic anti-lock braking, central locking, electric window winders and mirror adjustment, plus an elaborate stereo sound system, were taken for granted, Ford had to provide yet more equipment as part of the showroom deal. As ever, Continental markets did not demand exactly the same standards, though there was little significant difference: LHD models lacked the power-operated rear windows; there was no lumbar adjustment for the front passenger seat; and halogen headlamps lacked the mandatory UK dim/dip sidelight setting. The only options in either market were metallic paint, air conditioning (not offered with a Cosworth engine previously) and leather upholstery.

Taking a look at the exterior first, the most obvious performance items were those fancy (and hard to clean) 7J x 15in alloys, used on the previous RS Sapphire, a design that also inspired an echo in smaller sizings for later-run Escort XR3i and Cabriolet. Tyre size — test cars were all shod with the excellent ER90 Bridgestone — was 205/50 VR 15.

The body was little changed over the first four-door Sapphire RS, but note the blacked-out rear lamp lenses of the 1990 Sierra. Other RS body details included the colour coded body kit (poly-

Above: inside and outside Boreham in March 1990. The RS 4 x 4 programme takes shape, with a Group A car outside showing the new livery and the redecoration of the Motorsport centre, while inside, G95 CHK is a Group N car in preparation. The workshops are the least changed aspect of the site. Testing prior to the planned homologation in August 1990 took place in many countries: seen left is a Group N car in Wales.

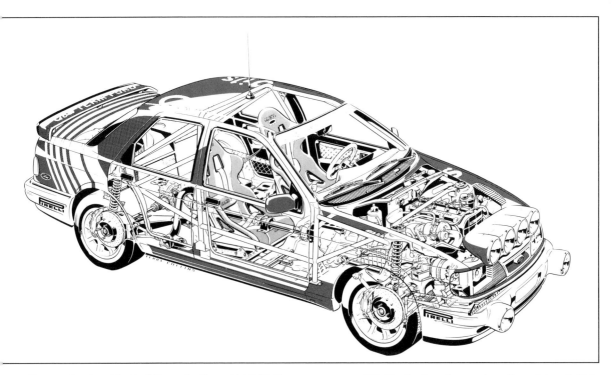

Cutaway drawing of the 4 x 4 Group A rally car highlights the enormous cross-drilled brake discs, the complex roll cage integrated into the structure of the shell and the rear suspension layout with combined coil spring and telescopic damper units.

urethane front spoiler/bumper assembly with auxiliary lamps, and raised rear spoiler) and a return of the bonnet vents that had been deleted at a late stage in the development of its rear-drive predecessor. It is worth looking to see that the slight spoiler extension lip is still in place up front and that tinted glass is installed all round, as per standard 1990 specification.

The door locks of these later models should provide a slight security bonus over the original *welcome, come on over and steal me* variety. An anti-theft alarm was standard. The sound equipment was based on the premium 2007 Ford radio/cassette unit with 4 x 14W amplifiers and speakers; the aerial was incorporated in the heated back screen. The filler cap was specified as a locking item beneath a flap and you should expect a tilt-and-slide manual glass sunroof with slatted and mobile blind unless it is demonstrably a car built using a Ford Motorsport competition bodyshell (or it is a fake Cosworth!).

Internally, the level of trim harked back to the Ghia line with that now dated graphic display to warn of: door open; boot ajar; frost; or bulb failures. The trademark of effective Recaro seats remained, plus a 60/40 split for the back seats to

remind of its hatchback origins and please those searching for extra internal storage. The handy three-spoke Cosworth steering wheel continued, in black, a unit safe and strong enough for the most demanding sports use. New for 1990 was the provision of steering column adjustment. The MT75 gearbox change pattern had one quirk, a gearlever collar that lifted before you could shift into reverse, which is opposite fifth and closest to a RHD pilot.

The Japanese had taught Ford to provide internal boot and fuel filler flap releases even on RS models and there was both lumbar and height adjustment for the driver's Recaro in all markets. Another Japanese touch was the overhead console with map reading lamps and a multifunction LCD digital clock. The German prestige industry (notably Porsche and BMW) had taught Ford to provide a torch key.

Before the advent of the 4 x 4, the Sapphire RS had proven an effective Group N/showroom racing and rallying device. Most publicized win in Britain was outright victory in the June 1989 Willhire Snetterton 25 hours, a fine result for **Fast Lane** deputy editor Mark Hales and Slim Borgudd (remember the Swede in trucks and the

201

ATS Formula 1 car?) because they had to fight for an extra hour over the normal 24 in honour of sponsor Willhire's 25th anniversary, and because opposition from the three-door Sierra RS of Kieth Odor and Barry Williams was fierce throughout the hot day and night.

Hales also used the Sapphire RS to score five outright wins during the 1989 season in both the Uniroyal and Firestone production racing series: he collected the Uniroyal title with the benefit of 11 other victories scored in the more familiar three-door RS.

That was in production racing trim — more restricted even than Group N because of road tyre rules and enforced low boost — but in Group A racing there was not the same enthusiasm for the four-door. Until 1990 nobody was brave enough to eschew the considerable homologation advantages of the RS500 (for which there was no equivalent Sapphire RS) in racing Group A guise, so the Sapphire's circuit outings remained confined to the 1989 Tour of Britain and the Uniroyal/Firestone production categories.

Things looked set to change in 1990, for Andy Rouse Engineering had constructed a 2-litre class Sapphire RS for the British Championship, but that potential 280bhp (no turbo) machine had not tested, never mind raced, when this was written.

On the rally front things were different, with leading teams knowing that Ford support and development would all be directed toward the 4 x 4 RS in 1990/91 and some being bright enough to get in on the act as soon as possible, rather than hanging onto their rear-drive hatchbacks. Still their efforts were primarily confined to Group N until 1990 when Jimmy McRae's son Colin, paired by Derek Ringer, snatched outright victory on the opening National Championship round (the Cartel International). Driving an otherwise conventional Sierra RS in the 1,168kg Group A Sapphire RS body, the 22-year-old had the honour of notching up the first British home international win for the Sapphire in rear-drive form. On the same event Gwyndaf Evans conducted a 265bhp Group N equivalent to sixth overall and easy class victory, so the Sapphire's British forest potential had been proven long before the 4 x 4 could be homologated.

Ford lifted the curtain on their rallying plans for the Sierra on the occasion of the Spanish press launch for the Cosworth RS 4 x 4 road car, but we had to wait about a month before experiencing the real Group A and Group N rally machines at the Ford Motorsport HQ, Boreham. Then, we were allowed to ride in and drive competition versions of cars that had still not yet quite reached the showrooms for public sale. Also evident and suggesting a new impetus in Ford rallying was the smart new 1990 paint job in corporate blue and white applied to Boreham, where the Motorsport parts department had joined the competition base the previous year.

Biggest threat to the programme had been industrial action by the British electricians having a knock-on production effect at Genk, Belgium. This unrest could have prevented production of the necessary 5,000 Cosworths needed for homologation on August 1, 1990, and the planned international debut in that month's 1,000 Lakes Rally in Finland.

As at February 1990, Ford Motorsport at Boreham had constructed three 4 x 4 Group A test cars, the original February 1989 machine being a converted three-door hatchback. A show car on Cologne plates was at the press launch, badged *Cosworth 4 x 4* and constructed by Gordon Spooner. At Boreham in March were two Group A cars, and a brand new Group N machine which had that weekend been given its debut by Gwyndaf Evans.

The current test and chassis programme is controlled by Philip Dunabin at Boreham, but the 4 x 4 RS Cosworths were originally engineered by Ford Motorsport under the direction of senior engineer John Wheeler. That former Porsche employee, who had also been much involved with the RS200, is now on secondment to SVE working on an Escort 4 x 4 for production and competition, a much-rumoured project that was formally approved in June 1990 and displayed to the press, including the author, at that month's static technical launch of the new Escorts due in the autumn. Finished in red, this biplane Ford, with white-faced gauges, looked like a worthy opponent for Lancia, with running gear from a 4 x 4 Cosworth in the shorter-than-Sierra wheelbase of an Escort-shape shell.

Significant, but unspecified, reductions in stage mileage times are reported on loose and tarmac surfaces by Ford sources for the Sapphire 4 x 4 RS. They quoted Stig Blomqvist, Russell Brookes, Malcolm Wilson and Franco Cunico. Test venues included the Welsh forests, Monte Carlo and the scrublands of Boreham, with Portugal, Acropolis

Car and driver: Malcolm Wilson and the Sierra Sapphire RS Cosworth 4 x 4 are Ford's bright hopes for a return to winning form in top level rallying. Wilson's aim is to be able to put his name in the record books as the first British winner of a World Championship rally since Roger Clark and the Escort RS1800 era.

and East African Safari proving sessions scheduled for 1990 appraisal prior to a full-scale assault in 1991.

So far the Ford 4 x 4 has shown a modest 65kg weight gain in competition trim over the two-wheel drive three-door and has manifested no unconquerable disadvantages. *It is a little bigger and heavier than the rallying ideal,* reported one engineer, but the cars shown to the media at Boreham were part of a programme designed to realize 1,150kg, *not bad for such a lot of extra hardware, but not down to the homologated class minimum of 1,100kg.* Our engineering contact added; *The aerodynamics at high speed need some further work compared to the three-door, but we are genuinely pleased with the car which is better not just on the loose but also for tarmac. The 4WD element gives the tyres a much easier time apportioning 299.9bhp and some extra torque per wheel. It will show particularly well when it has to tackle the long stages with variable weather conditions on events like Corsica.*

On March 25,1990 Bardolet and Ferrer took the Marlboro-liveried Mike Taylor Developments Sierra RS Cosworth 4 x 4 to its first outright

victory, on the Alicante Rally in Spain. Run in non-homologated Group A engine trim (40mm restrictor) with a Group N rolling chassis, it defeated a 280bhp Citroen special and outlasted the official Volkswagen Group A G60 Golf 4 x 4 (which retired on the first stage).

There was no room for complacency, however. The Group N Boreham prototype for Gwyndaf Evans/Howard Davies also made its first appearance on the same weekend's York National. Whilst Steve Bannister was proving that the RS1800 (Ethel . . . EHY 390W) could still win national events outright, the works Ford went OTL within three stages. That was the result of punctures and a bent strut, but when the car was sorted a fastest stage time was unofficially accrued and the machine was in speedy health again for its press debut at Boreham a few days later (see Chapter 16). While there would certainly be no easy victories for Ford in world-class rallying against the likes of Lancia and Toyota, teams with a lot of four-wheel-drive experience already under their belts, the Sierra RS Cosworth 4 x 4 looked a promising starting-point.

At 7.45am on July 12, 1990, at Genk in

Belgium, the 5,000th Ford Sierra Cosworth was completed, thus putting the car on course for international homologation in Group A and N. Now only objections from rival manufacturers could prevent Ford from giving the RS 4 x 4 its World Championship debut on the 1,000 Lakes as envisaged in their schedule.

Ford Motorsport's ability to toy creatively with a homologation form has not abated over the years. As the rallying plans for the new car gradually emerged, it was revealed that the RS 4 x 4 in Group A form would have three design features in particular which were intended to give it a distinct competitive advantage. Two concerned the transmission: seven forward gears would be provided and overall ratio changes would be possible by altering the primary gearbox train, far less time-consuming than swapping two final drives. The third item was a two-bolt turbo location that should also help to slash service times. Most of the original engineering thought came from John Wheeler, but the quick-release turbo idea had already been used by Lancia on the 1990 Delta integrale.

The gearbox was particularly clever, incorporating a separately-listed 'crawler' first gear plus six additional ratios. This transmission, a product of co-operation between Ford and FF Developments, had low inertia loads as a design criterion, clutchless changes becoming routine (with plans for Ferrari F1-style semi-automatic operation as a possibility in 1992).

While these developments will help to give the RS 4 x 4 the best possible chance of success in the ultra-competitive world of international rallying, it is worth noting that Ford Motorsport's longer-term planning for the 1990s shows ever-increasing commitment to its Escort-shape successor, first shown to the press in road car form at Dunton. In July 1990 a Blenheim ball for the new Escort was chosen as the occasion to unveil a prediction of the 1992 Escort RS rally car — an emotive moment for all those who had lived through the RS Escort's supremacy in rallying to see it die with the cancellation of the RS1700T.

We were told that such early previews of the RS 4 x 4 rolling chassis with an Escort outline meant that there would be too much loss of public face for the company to cancel this one. For once in my life, I earnestly pray that the public relations soothsayers are proven absolutely right . . .

Sapphire RS Cosworth on the road

When this book was first published the four-door RS had only just gone on sale, so there was no owner experience to report. For this second edition we can remedy that with comment from two sources, a private owner, who had earlier bought the three-door version in both original and RS500 guise, and an enterprising journalist. The 4 x 4 was not even in the showroom when this went to press — time alone will tell if that machine in private hands will live up to its very considerable promise . . .

Steve Smith is a 36-year-old company director who has owned all the rear-drive Cosworths. He bought the four-door RS in August 1988 for £20,000 from a dealer and it had 36,000 miles recorded by the time of our survey. What did he think of the Sapphire variant? *My first reaction was that the car was much smoother and easier to drive at low revs, and that I could also see out of the rear window! It was nice to have four doors (great for the kids) but I was not so pleased at the lack of a rear wiper...this car needs one.*

I still get a thrill every time I drive a Cosworth and look forward to dry roads when I am going to work, when the full potential can sometimes be fulfilled. Driven in the wet I enjoy the Sapphire, but when you want to push it does not handle so well; without the big rear spoiler the Sapphire RS is more nervous than before. It is the worst car on earth for snow driving!

I found the car to be very reliable, the biggest problems were with the burglar alarm, which was no fault of Ford. I used a set of tyres in 20,000 miles, the power steering belt broke at 36,000 and I hated cleaning the wheels.

After owning the Sierra Cosworth and the RS500, the Sapphire looks tame by

Good omen? First outright win for the 4 x 4 was recorded in March 1990, before the model was on public sale, by Mia Bardolet and Jose Maria Ferrer in the Alicante Rally, part of the Spanish gravel championship for which homologation is not required. The car was a mixture of Group A and N specifications.

*comparison. The advantage is that the police have not stopped me on average once per month, as they did with the three-door... The only problem now, is what to buy next? I don't think a 4 x 4 Cosworth will be as much fun...*concluded Steve Smith.

Interestingly, our other Sapphire RS driver, **Motoring News** Executive Editor and Grand Prix reporter David Tremayne ('DJT'), was also reluctant to exchange traditional rear-drive handling for a possibly less exciting 4 x 4. Like a good many Cosworths, David's had its already high performance potential enlivened still further: instead of simply changing the engine management chip, he had gone for the Weber UK conversion kit which is rated at 265bhp. When **Motoring News** tested the result independently it moved 0–60mph firmly below 6 seconds and had the capability of genuinely exceeding 150mph. The only problem attributable to the conversion was a pressurized turbo hose blowing off its clips about 600 miles after the conversion was completed, so David advises, *make sure all hose clips are properly secured before you take it away from the converters.*

Tremayne moved into the Ford after long term usage of a Jaguar XJ and a BMW 528i (old shape) and took delivery of the editorial Ford RS from October 1988 as a new car, not the usual used press demonstrator you find loaned to so many journalists.

The machine has now covered 29,000 miles and has had the Weber modifications running for over 10,000 of that total. According to this editor with a young family, *the four doors and central locking are practical and you do not pay too heavily considering the fun that's available at the wheel. The rear Dunlops lasted 23,000 miles and I still have the original fronts in use. I get 18–20mpg around town (he drives into the City of London regularly) and up to 26mpg on a run.*

How did this globe trotter feel about the Ford in his life? *Mega, it's been absolutely great. Touch wood, the reliability has been good — its using a bit of water at 29,000 and the radiator cap has just been replaced — but I really have enjoyed it. Of course it's not built like a BMW, it's a bit shaky and jolts along the road, but I don't mind that for so much pleasure, and I actually enjoy the noise of the engine. Just like to hear something working for a living...*

The only things I don't like are the gearchange — it quite often baulks first and reverse, especially when cold — and I don't like cleaning those stupid wheels! I suppose the engine could have a little less turbo lag off the lights, but it is better than most other turbos I have tried, so that's not a serious gripe.

As has unfortunately been the case quite often in these RS interviews, the customer was not thrilled with his Ford dealer.

12

Fiesta RS Turbo

It had long been rumoured that Ford would extend the Cosworth treatment to all models in the range, but for 1990 at least the Fiesta high performance version came as an RS and was the responsibility of Special Vehicle Engineering. As has become Ford practice, Britain was served by the RS badge (*Fiesta RS Turbo*) whilst the LHD markets of countries such as Italy, Spain, France and Germany were offered a car simply badged *Fiesta Turbo*. The emissions certification under ECE 1504 reflected the cost-conscious limited-production span of this model (estimated at two years and no more than 20,000 examples) and ensured no catalytic convertor model was offered. Porsche at Weissach were approached to engineer a catalytic convertor alternative to meet US 83 emission levels, but they needed nine months further development time that was not available at that stage. Cost again, as well as concern over handling quirks, ruled out the type of Viscous Coupling limited-slip differential seen in the Escort RS Turbo.

This emphatically was not a simple marriage between Escort Turbo mechanicals and the XR2i version of the new-shape Fiesta first seen publicly in 1989. Coded 'BE13 Turbo' internally, with development managed by Harry Worrall, the quickest Fiesta could not have accommodated a simple engine implant; as it was they had to scrape for every tenth of an inch installation space using a smaller (T2) turbo than that of the Escort. The other basic development imposition was the XR2i itself. This was the first time that SVE had come to grips with a project based on a car not in itself on the production lines when development

began, and nobody could gauge public reaction to the model. When the press, notably **Car** magazine, gave it a thumbs down, Dunton-based director of product engineering, Clive Ennos, was forced to pledge that the turbo Fiesta would be *aimed more at the keen enthusiast*, and that meant a substantial change of course during chassis development. (In fact, journalists notwithstanding, the XR2i was to prove commercially successful, with 10,000 examples ordered before launch and the projection that it would account for 20% of all new Fiesta sales.)

Certainly SVE produced a fast small Ford in the turbocharged variant, for similar power to an Escort Turbo in a smaller body provided 127mph in Ford homologation testing and a 0–60mph time average of 7.7 seconds. Respectably tall gearing by small-car standards also allowed this Fiesta to cruise at 100mph and little more than 4,500rpm in fifth. There were also slight, but measurable, improvements over the Escort RS Turbo in fuel consumption. That for the Fiesta RS was reported at: 26.4 Urban mpg; 34.5mpg at 75mph; and a parsimonious 45mpg at 56mph.

Please remember I wrote this some months before the first car went down the Spanish production lines at Valencia, repeated slippages in the programme delaying its appearance from late 1989 to June 1990. This means that the company could change some of the minor details in the interim, and here I would mention the rear wing, the hub decoration of the triple spoke wheels and exterior trim as most vulnerable in this respect. What follows is an exact description of development supported by experience in three

SVE pre-production cars, all developed from the Fiesta XR2i base. Production specification is outlined in the Appendix.

SVE was positively humming in the months leading up to production of the turbocharged Fiesta, employing 51 personnel under the overall management of Rod Mansfield. Three primary car development programmes were under way: Harry Worrall oversaw the Fiesta described here; Ray Diggins looked after all 4 x 4, body and electrical matters and the acclaimed Sierra Cosworth 4 x 4; whilst John Wheeler took on the Motorsport Escort, more about that in a moment.

There were some intriguing changes in responsibilities assigned to the area, for Ford acquisitions Aston Martin Lagonda and AC Cars had an official liaison point through Tony Batchelor and it was expected that the same would apply to newly Ford-owned Jaguar. From an RS viewpoint the most heartening aspect of the three project teams was a full-blooded competition and production Escort 4 x 4. This programme, coded 'Motorsport CE14', was blanked out in organizational charts supplied to the author, but subsequent research revealed its presence under the leadership of engineer John Wheeler on loan from Boreham. He listed RS1700T, RS200 and competition variants of the Sierra RS Cosworth to his credit by 1990 and was also assigned the chassis engineering aces.

Mick Kelly reported to John Wheeler and there were seven of his staff who bore the brunt of the changeable chassis on the Fiesta Turbo programme. They included familiar names like Fiesta racer Colin Stancombe, Gordon Prout, and John Hitchens. But the complete Fiesta project was the responsibility of that separate Worrall team. Their major concern was the significantly revised CVH engine and Andy Dealtry was given the job of making sure the EEC IV-managed CVH with its own turbocharger layout was squeezed into reliable operation. Far more difficult was the task of electronically mapping EEC IV to suit this turbocharged application, work that was split between Trevor Simpson and The Sorcerer, alias Neville Jackson.

Into the 1990s with the Ford RS line, past, present and near future. The Fiesta RS Turbo is next to the still veiled Escort RS Cosworth planned for road and competition use about two years from the photo date. Among the SVE personnel are Rod Mansfield, second from right on the front row, with secretary Irene Bourne, extreme right, and engineer and Fiesta racer Colin Stancombe at the centre of the front row. The bearded master of 4 x 4 performance motoring, Ray Diggins, has his feet on the second row line, second from left.

Fortunately there were no headaches about producing enough power, or the potential for extra motorsport power, and all the prototypes ran close to the modest 130bhp level that was anticipated in production on a peak boost figure of 0.55bar.

Harry Worrall's tidy mind was deployed to trace the outline of the Fiesta development schedule for me. He explained: *We officially began to appraise the car for production from September 29, 1987, but before and after that date we did practical work on the engine installation, which was a tricky task. Our primary concern was that neither the engine position nor sheet metal could be altered. It was quite obvious that we could not physically insert the T3 Garrett AiResearch turbocharger unit, but we were quite pleased about that because the T2 enables us to have far better mid-range response than the bigger unit of the Escort could allow.*

TUV official tests dated 29/6/89 at Ford Cologne revealed that the torque spread of the revised CVH truly was phenomenal. The realization of 180Nm (132lb/ft) at just 2,400rpm compared well with internal tests of Escort Turbo that revealed 177Nm (130lb/ft) on 2,750rpm, but that was not the point: from 2,400 to 5,100 revs there is not a torque curve at all, it just seems to stay absolutely flat around that peak value!

In the summer of 1989, prototype SV504 (top) rests at Dunton on the original three-spoke alloy wheels with 'cross-drilled disc' centres. Note the lack of bonnet vents which were added primarily for RS marketing identity. Prototype SV510 (G413 XNO) had a busy life, appearing in company press handout pictures between bouts of development mileage. Here it has just tackled the gales of February 1990 with capable poise. The drilled effect of the wheels has been toned down, but this large spoiler unfortunately failed to make initial production after last-minute quality problems. Rear view emphasizes the rectangular tailpipe and the wide-track stance of the 185/55 Uniroyals. Badges are as at UK launch: LHD models lost the RS designation.

The Fiesta RS is pronounced fit for its world premier in April 1990. Photograph taken at Dunton for Ford press material is of the same car that I borrowed to record driving impressions, so it has the 'wrong' rear spoiler and the rear wheels are still dimpled as a legacy of the drilled look which dealers apparently loved but press men loathed.

Bonnet vents did no harm to the air flow in the crowded turbocharged engine bay and helped visually distinguish the faster Fiesta from its cheaper brethren.

Peak power was measured on this occasion by an EEC 80/1269 method on 95 octane (ROZ) unleaded fuel and this meant that the Escort was quoted at marginally less than its usual 132bhp, reported at 127.6bhp on the usual 5,750rpm. The equivalent Fiesta Turbo unit realised another horsepower at 128.6bhp, generated a little lower down the scale: 5,500rpm.

The hardware behind the statistics was based on an Escort Turbo short engine assembly — iron block, crankshaft and 8.2:1 compression pistons. The SOHC alloy cylinder head came from the XR2i — itself a developed CVH engine coded EFI for Electronic Fuel Injection — and the camshaft came from the same source. However an Escort camshaft pulley and valve timing (advanced 3 degrees 50 minutes) was employed to emphasize low speed torque.

Ancillary changes covered the alternator brackets and cast-iron exhaust manifold, the latter extending into a replacement three-box system of 55mm/2.2in bore. The aluminized system has a stainless steel tailpipe of distinctive TV-screen shape. This generous pipe diameter was supported on three standard hanging positions but used a spring-loaded joint between the downpipe and exhaust, a trick Ford SVE had learned from GM which will hopefully contribute (together with internal durability tests for the manifolding) to an absence of warranty and service claims. Frankly, the company record on exhaust manifolds (and

occasionally tailpipes) for performance Fords, especially the two marks of Escort Turbo, has been awful.

Other ancillary engine work encompassed a one-way valve and restrictor to maintain adequate crankcase depression under boost conditions. The T2 turbocharger itself did have a number of development failures and it is worth knowing that the compressor and turbine housing were unique to the small Ford whilst the water-cooled central casing and rotating components had been used in many other applications. SVE felt they had identified six key problem areas to tackle and were pleased that Garrett in Skelmersdale had managed to package up the unit to fit in such tight confines, at the cost of some machining. Harry Worrall recalled: *It was so tight that we seemed to have no space for an exhaust flange. The fix*

Useful features inherited from the basic Fiesta included a wheelbase longer than that of the first front-drive Escort and simple but effective torsion-beam rear suspension. Sill and bumper extensions were shared with the XR2i version. Wheels, modified front suspension and cleverly packaged turbo installation were unique to the RS.

for that was one long stud and a short bolt, but we had two or three trial goes at the installation, juggling inlet and outlet positions, swinging them though their axes to find a solution that integrated the turbo and the exhaust manifold. Initially the wastegate piston ended up too close to the radiator, so we had to accept a cranked operating arm.

External changes included an oil feed to the turbo routed across the camshaft cover, the oil drain system incorporating a flexible hose section for durability reasons. A new air intake system was also devised to suit the move of the air intercooler to a site alongside the water radiator, rather than the original forward position. The alloy feed trunk from the intercooler to the throttle body of the Bosch KE-Jetronic injection system shared a family look with that of the Escort Turbo but the profile and mountings were unique. A minor change was to uprate the fuel pump, now capable of flowing 88 litres per hour.

Some basic components associated with the EEC IV engine management system were taken from the Sierra Cosworth, including the boost control module, 2bar/28psi MAP sensor and wastegate solenoid valve. Otherwise the electronic ignition and other sensors and actuators were suitable reprogrammed EFI and EEC IV items from the XR2i. The Hitachi digital idle-speed control system was also planned for transfer from the XR2i to the RS Turbo, but the XR2i itself had not yet acquired this as a running change at the time of writing.

Back at the body, it was important to understand that the first three of nine SVE prototypes had to be built from Fiesta 1.6S cars (from April 1988), and even these were not full production vehicles. When this was written a further five prototypes had been constructed upon the XR2i base (which itself suffered from repeated engine-linked delays making production behind schedule; the first SVE example was running from June 1988) and one was based on a pre-production (4P) XR2i. A pair of these prototypes underwent standard Ford tests such as 16,000 high speed kilometres and the 40,000kms

(24,855 miles) Passenger Car Durability cycle at Lommel, plus, in September 1988, hot climate testing in Arizona. Cold climate testing was completed in Finland during January 1989 without major drama, but the SVE engineers were now convinced that they could delete the Viscous Coupling LSD from their planning when using the modified suspension that is described later.

The American session highlighted that the intercooler was simply not up to the task at high ambient temperatures when placed in front of the main water radiator. Harry Worrall recalled: *Our aim was then to improve the performance of the carryover Escort intercooler whilst retaining the efficiency of the radiator at a smaller size. Otherwise we could start to run into pre-ignition problems. What we have now is not dissimilar to the Behr intercooler of the Sierra Cosworth.*

The water radiator is based on that of an Escort Turbo, but with reduced core width to accommodate the intercooler. It is served by a 150-Watt electric cooling fan that lies ahead of the radiator (shades of the first RS2000). A replacement head gasket of asbestos-free construction was successfully introduced and ran with the usual Escort Turbo compression of 8.2:1 without trouble.

Here it is relevant to note that standard engine test-bed procedures included twin 600-hour sessions at Cologne and a 180-hour session. The latter was held in the early days and immediately highlighted the difficulty of correctly calibrating the turbocharged unit, with severe detonation problems encountered. I understand unofficially that the XR2i was delayed by similar engine management difficulties which could culminate in number three piston melting. The EEC IV system was recalibrated once more, a far more difficult task in our emission conscious world because you can no longer simply douse such lean-running problems with an excessively rich mixture. Much development time was also spent calibrating EEC IV for two entirely different idle control systems, the carryover Weber analogue manifold sensor and a later digital substitute from Hitachi, the latter envisaged as a running change in production.

An obvious step like moving the radiator would have meant cutting sheet metal and that was *verboten* as the standard XR2i shell had to be used but there was a little leeway allowed so that the production vehicle has the upper surface and reinforcement of the front bumper cut away to clear the electric cooling fan; the grille bar of the standard product is also deleted to improve cooling. The only other basic body change was on more cosmetic lines, because SVE went back to bonnet louvres like those of an Escort Turbo: this was to identify the model primarily because Ford could meet their cooling test standards without the louvres. Externally the blue inlays of the XR2i were likely to be replaced with a fashionable green and there were the alternative badges for different markets as already explained. Exterior colours

were listed as: Diamond white; Radiant red; Mercury grey; and black.

Internal furniture carried some references to the original intention to tie the Benetton name and the performance Fiesta together, Benetton Ascot trim being listed for the seats and door sides. More functionally efficient were the traditional front Recaro sports seats and some grey leather touches for the steering wheel and gearlever. Instrumentation was segmented in the XR2i manner and similarly calibrated, except for a 150mph/240km/h speedometer; the tachometer redline remained at 6,500rpm and there was small EFI symbol to remind one of the source of the instruments.

One insider recalled that they spent an exorbitant amount of time trying to get the chunky-look, macho steering-wheel design favoured by the Ford studios, only to find it was — *too damn thick to use! I literally could not get my hands around it* . . . They settled on a basic unit that was within 0.5mm of the Cosworth diameter that everyone seems to like. It is sourced through Dalphi in Spain and shares some of its metal frame with the one used in the 1991 model-year Escorts. Note that a subtle *turbo* logo is part of the central moulding, emphasizing that the RS identity is kept only for Britain and its chain of RS dealerships.

The major point of discussion about the body as we went to press centred on the rear wing, above the hatchback window, for two types had been used on the turbocharged Fiesta: an XR2i item with cosmetic cut-out section, and a much

The cockpit of this RS was identified simply by a *turbo* legend on the leather-rimmed steering wheel. Instrumentation was as for the XR2i except for a 150mph speedometer. Recaro seats were another welcome feature setting the RS apart from lesser Fiestas.

larger unit, tried in development and submitted for design approval in September 1989, which in production would be a blow-moulding by Caltex. Both had been assessed in the wind tunnel and produced the following figures . . .

	Cd	Front lift	Rear lift
XR2i	0.354	92 Newtons	345 Newtons
Turbo	0.363	88 Newtons	zero

In other words, the larger alternative, which attached by standard mountings and was smartly colour-coded in pre-production examples — though they still failed to meet Ford quality standards — increased drag minimally whilst cutting rear-end lift. This was more significant than it may sound, for in August 1989 I had driven two prototypes with the XR2i back spoiler at Lommel and criticized their high-speed stability on a section of the banking where a gap in the trees allowed a good real-world side pressure change. Others reported the same phenomenon, yet when I drove a later car with the alternative spoiler in gale-force winds in Britain it was as safe as a small car can be in conditions that are turning over panel-vans on the exposed sections of the A12.

Unfortunately it looked as though production deadlines would defeat the 'big wing' concept when this was written, but that August 1989 assessment by myself and other outsiders did deflect the company from offering a cheap and nasty drilled disc look to the alloy wheels. These were gradually blocked out and simplified to the point where I expect them to reach the

showrooms without even the vestigial dimples that my later car displayed.

The chassis engineering contained a lot of better news. Mick Kelly detailed a development schedule that had to accommodate the whims of journalistic comment and shifting management requirements by beginning with the tyres. *We had agreements with four companies to develop a 185/55 VR-14 sizing and expect to supply from a choice of Uniroyal 240/55, Pirelli P600, Dunlop D8 and Michelin MXV.* Uniroyal proved to be the pacesetters on this occasion and were initially approved, but expect to find all four types fitted according to the market served. Tyre testing was extensive and made wide use of Goodyear facilities at Mireval, near Montpelier in France as well as the wet weather facilities of both Goodyear and Pirelli, the latter judged superb by Kelly. Michelin developed three or four compounds and then allowed assessment at the old GP circuit of Clermont Ferrand. Mick Kelly said: *We were surprised how far we had come with the car, just in this aspect, especially regarding wet weather behaviour and overall traction. It was absolutely transformed.*

As with the tyres, the wheels reflect the realities of multinational supply and were sourced from both Germany and Spain. In either case the size was 14in x 5.5in. The style of the wheels was subject to three or four alterations during 1989/90, black paint and machining operations gradually obliterating the original cross-drilled disc look around the wheel hub.

The XR2i wheel bearings were of most

Simple, neat Fiesta styling was given an added note of purposefulness by the deep front apron with auxiliary lamps and the wide wheels of the RS version. The sunroof was standard equipment.

Side view reveals the reduced ride height of the rear suspension and the small rear spoiler adopted for production. These early production cars wore Pirelli P600 tyres rather than the Uniroyals evident on the prototypes.

engineering concern, as they did experience low mileage (under 6,000 miles) failures, requiring extensive consultation and evaluation with suppliers SKF and mainstream Ford engineering. Mainstream's chassis engineering knew a lot about higher front wheel-bearing loads in particular because the loads being generated were similar to those of a Fiesta diesel, and they also talked SVE through a number of changes that had been made on later production Fiestas.

The suspension and steering now amounts to some pretty straightforward combinations with some replacement components applied to the steering rack and ball joints. First the springs and dampers. The front springs are as for XR2i (21KNm) whilst the rears are uprated from XR2i at 19kNm to 23kNm. SVE initiated twin-tube gas damper trials with an AP division in Spain, but a Ford decision based on earlier warranty experience barred this development and SVE were forced to start all over again with Armstrong at York. The Armstrong twin tube units ended up with rating described as +20% when compared with the XR2i at the front rebound setting and similar to the XR2i at the rear. The compression action at the front was slackened off. In my opinion the ride was one of the strongest attractions of the pre-production car, excellent by class standards and good enough to cope with pavé at 50 to 65mph, but the production car was inexplicably harsher.

The familiar pattern of testing at Lommel and on public roads led to some important ride height decisions and the Turbo now sat 12mm/0.47in lower at the back than an XR2i, but remained the same at the front. The XR2i also supplied the front 16mm anti-roll bar, but the fitment of any anti-roll bar to the rear was *a revelation*, as Mick Kelly put it. They settled on a 20mm rear bar giving some elements of the faster turn-in that they had been looking for, but the constant goading to get on terms with the Peugeot 205 GTI (then a five-year-old design) prompted development of a system with *a bit of front-end bite* in Mick Kelly's words.

Target one was the steering, which the journalists and keener company engineers all thought was just too cumbersome at 4.2 turns lock-to-lock. A replacement rack, geared at 3.75 turns, was presented to management in May 1989 and approved, but at the time it was associated with XR2i geometry. Another alternative was variable-ratio steering, under evaluation by the company at that period, but the chance to join in such a programme slipped by and the straightforward TRW Cam Gears high-ratio rack was installed, this despite doubts about raising steering effort (exactly the internal attitude that led to the slow rack of the new Fiesta). When the XR2i failed to attract rapturous applause for its handling and steering, the British arm of Ford knew it had to do something more for any RS-badged version. Initially (August 1989 assessment), they went for a castor change from the XR2i's 1.7 degrees to 0.8 degrees, but criticism over straight-line stability and increasing press hostility to XR2i took them on to more extensive alterations.

A new lower A-arm for the front strut suspension was now permitted by the previously unenthusiastic Purchase department with the object of *putting some camber and castor weight into the steering. A new forged ball joint pushed out the arm 10mm, and there is also a rearward bias of another 10mm,* reported Kelly, who estimated: *We have ¾ degree more of negative camber and around -1 degree castor. I do not think the negative camber was particularly worthwhile, perhaps it gave us a bit on the turn-in quality, but the castor changes were important.* At the wheel, the chassis changes compared with the XR2i are pronounced and do result in more of a Peugeot-style 'painted on tarmac' steering quality that has been missing in front-drive Fords since the wriggling Escort RS Turbo.

Both transmission and braking are essentially volume-production items. The five-speed transaxle comes from Escort Turbo parentage and boasts the same final drive (3.82:1) without the VC differential action that many SVE engineers (especially on the chassis side) disliked anyway for its behaviour over crests. The XR2i braking system is cheered a little by the adoption of Sapphire Cosworth proven Ferodo F3432 materials. The only severe controversy was over the company requirement that the Ford/Lucas/Girling SCS (Stop Control System) be installed.

In company assessments there was a strong body of SVE opinion that disliked the slack and slow action of this anti-lock system under the kind of pressure that the faster Fiesta encourages. Some employees described the system as *unsaleable.* The practical result was that it went from a standard fitment — as featured on Escort RS Turbo — to the status of an option. My advice

This RS took Ford right into the closely contested 'hot hatchback' market — given the praise heaped on the Peugeot 205GTI, perhaps 'into the lion's den' is not inappropriate. A maximum speed of 130mph and acceleration to 60mph in 7.7 seconds (Ford figures), allied to handling that benefited from much development work, made it a worthy competitor.

would be don't bother. It *is* possible to lock a wheel (the one failing the system should defeat) and the reason for that errant behaviour is not irresponsible driving or an SCS defect. Anti-lock braking was the biggest single motoring safety advance since the seat belt and it was bold of Ford and their associates to back an affordable alternative to the very competent but expensive Teves ABS fitted to Sierra Cosworths (and BMWs and Audis). I just do not think it provided the intended benefits on either 1986–90 Escorts or 1989 onward Fiestas. The harder you drive, the worse the system is, and anyone who has used it on a race track will know its failings are not confined to the occasional public road hiccup or increased stopping distances.

The RS Fiesta was not priced when this was written, being anticipated to make its public debut on the Ford stand at the Turin Motor Show. In Britain the turbocharged Fiesta was obviously going to have to slide between the March 1990

tag of £10,445 for an XR2i without alloys and the £13,465 Escort RS Turbo (due for replacement before the close of 1990). A further clue was the prevailing £10,290 and £11,790 costs of the 1.6 and 1.9 Peugeot GTI hatches, recalling that the 1.6 had been the 'target' vehicle that accompanied the Fiesta RS throughout the majority of its handling development sorties. Around £12,000 was my guess, but you will be able to see how close I was by the time this reaches your hands. (*£11,950: close enough!* Ed.)

At that guesstimated cost I thought the considerable extra development work and the driving pleasure (see Chapter 16) was a bonus over what had been achieved with the Escort RST and much more competitive with international opposition. The CVH engine was still hoarse over 5,000 rpm, but replacement of that unit was the high priority within Ford that curtailed the anticipated production life of this unique extension to the RS range.

13

The BDA story

A recurrent theme in the story of the RS cars has been the use of Cosworth-developed engines, based on mass-production Ford designs but with new cylinder heads featuring the distinctive pent roof, four-valve combustion chamber layout. Cosworth Engineering Ltd, formed in 1958 by former Lotus employees Mike Costin and Keith Duckworth, concentrated from the outset on tuning Ford engines and quickly established a considerable reputation for road and more particularly competition power units, many of them used in the earlier Lotus cars.

The three companies, Ford, Cosworth and Lotus, were linked in other ways which are relevant to the RS story. Ford and Lotus became commercially involved together in the Lotus Cortina project, the twin-cam conversion of the Cortina engine in that case being a Lotus rather than a Cosworth design. That car, and the Twin Cam Escort which succeeded it, can be seen as the first germ of the RS idea, predating the RS designation but setting the theme of specialist-modified production cars for competition and sporting road use.

The first public agreement linking Ford and Cosworth was the contract in March 1966 for the development and production of what became the DFV Formula 1 engine which was initially supplied to Lotus on an exclusive basis, scored its first Grand Prix wins behind Jim Clark in 1967 and went on to dominate the formula right through to the early 1980s.

As a preliminary stage in the development of the DFV, an engine based on the Ford Cortina block and suitable for international Formula 2 racing was to be developed. Keith Duckworth was no stranger to overhead-camshaft conversions on Ford blocks, having already produced his own single-cam SCA engine for Formula 2 as well as working on the further development of the Lotus twin-cam design, but the FVA, as it was to be known, was the first chance to try the four-valves-per-cylinder idea. A 1.5-litre prototype, based on the pre-crossflow Cortina block, as envisaged in the contract, was built during 1966 and proved the viability of the design.

For series production, the FVA switched to the later, slightly taller 116E crossflow cylinder block. Its 85.6mm bore (retained for the DFV design) and 69mm stroke gave a capacity of 1,598cc to take full advantage of the contemporary 1.6-litre limit for Formula 2. It was a pure racing engine, with dry-sump lubrication and gear-driven camshafts, and it proved very successful, dominating the Formula 2 Championship from 1967 to 1971. A long-stroke 1,790cc version, the FVC, was produced for sports-car racing (it won the European 2-litre Championship twice) and there was an experimental 1,975cc variant, the FVD.

Ford's next commission to Cosworth was for an engine that they could use in various forms of production car competition and for the limited number of special road cars that would be needed to further those competition aims. The result was the BDA, power unit for the RS1600 and many subsequent RS machines, principally the work of Cosworth's Mike Hall during 1967-68. Similarly based on the 116E cast-iron block (though a special alloy block soon came along, as we have seen), it shared the FVA's 16-valve twin-cam

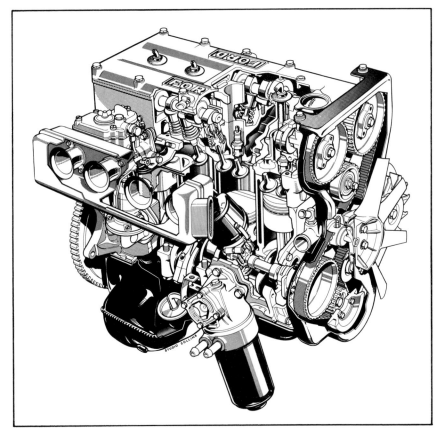

Cutaway drawing of the BDA engine in 1970 form illustrates the twin, belt-driven overhead camshafts operating four valves per cylinder in the Cosworth alloy head. The Kent series pushrod OHV engine supplied the iron cylinder block, and the side camshaft which remained, though now driven by the toothed belt rather than the original chain, to operate the oil pump, distributor and fuel pump. Later BDAs adopted an aluminium alloy block originally developed by Brian Hart.

Underside of the cylinder head shows the essential principle of the Cosworth-Ford family of engines, the four valves in each hemispherical combustion chamber and the central spark plug location. This example is from the Zakspeed turbo Capri of July 1978: roadgoing engines had smaller valves than this out and out racing unit.

layout. Changes to make it suitable for roadgoing use included the adoption of a toothed-belt camshaft drive, a relatively new technique in the 1960s. An ordinary wet-sump lubrication system sufficed for road cars.

Over the years since it first appeared in those Capris in Cyprus in 1968 the BDA has fulfilled its purpose admirably. It has given Ford countless competition successes and it proved to be an excellent road car engine. It may well have had considerable influence further afield as well: the extent to which it can be regarded as having fathered the current crop of 16-valve four-cylinder engines is hard to assess, as no company wants to acknowledge its often unofficial technical debt to another. So far as competition specialists are concerned, I have found that all the leading names have been warm in their appreciation of Cosworth's capabilities. That loyalty is as strong in West Germany — from Zakspeed to Daimler-Benz — as it is amongst Britons such as Brian Hart, or the relevant sections of Ford.

Just as Cosworth — and Lotus — began on a small scale, modifying Ford products to suit special purposes, so a new generation of specialists have taken Cosworth's work and developed it in particular directions of their own, and the BDA has turned up in almost every form of motorsport. While we have already followed its main line of evolution through the RS1600 and RS1800 stories, it is worth reviewing the engines that sprung from the BDA, for they often appeared in cars that thoroughly deserved the RS appellation, even if it was not always attached to their flanks.

In 1970 the BDA begat the 1.7-litre BDB, with an enlarged cylinder bore for competition, a development aimed initially at satisfying the Ford factory's RS1600 rallying ambitions. Built by Cosworth, it was rated at 200bhp and safe to 8,250rpm. Subsequently the BDB found popularity as a kit of parts that could be assembled by specialists or car owners. I am told Cosworth themselves only ever assembled one such unit, the rest were sold in component form.

Also in 1970 came the racing BDC. Again it measured 1,700cc, but it was designed to work with Lucas fuel injection at up to 9,000rpm and it provided 230 reliable horsepower in many famous racing RS1600 Escorts. Perhaps the best known example was the 1971 British Championship season Broadspeed 'RS1700' for John Fitzpatrick, a car for which performance figures are provided in the appendix.

In 1971 the BDD derivative, of 1600cc, was produced for the single-seater Formula Atlantic. Again it was widely sold in kit form and power was quoted as 200bhp, at 8,750rpm as the likely limit, with a full racing car exhaust system and dry-sump installation.

The 1972 BDE and BDF reflected changes in Formula 2, for the regulations now allowed engines of 2 litres in place of 1.6. The BDE had an 85.6mm bore for 1,790cc, whilst the F was bored to 88.9mm and measured 1,927cc. The BDE was rated at 245bhp and 9,000rpm, the larger BDF at 270bhp and 9,250rpm. Although these were conceived as formula car engines, you do occasionally find them popping up in special saloon categories and the like. Cosworth's personnel frankly admitted what a piece of mechanical improvisation the BDF was, for it had liners brazed into the production Ford block which the regulations demanded...others did even nastier things. But it did give them a winning season in 1972, with Mike 'the bike' Hailwood taking the Matchbox Surtees to the European Formula 2 title.

One of the best known BDA descendants appeared in 1973, the 1,975cc BDG. Based on the Brian Hart-designed aluminium alloy cylinder block first seen in 1972, the bore and stroke were 90.0mm × 77.0mm. The BDG was initially rated at 275bhp with a 9,250rpm capability. By 1978 Cosworth had confirmed a solid 280bhp, still at 9,250rpm, with 175lb/ft of torque at 7,000rpm, these figures achieved with a 12:1 compression ratio. Again built for Formula 2, the BDG also appeared in a number of Ford RS Escorts, most notably the 1976/77 Zakspeed German Championship Group 5 racers, overbored to 90.3mm to give 1,995cc.

The BDG did not succeed in continuing Cosworth-Ford's winning record in Formula 2 for 1973. Instead, BMW had their revenge with the debut of their legendary M12 16-valve four. Key Bavarian engineers do privately acknowledge their debt in changing over to the classic Cowsworth combustion chamber layout for their own powerplants after years of frustration with alternative quad-valve layouts.

The BDH of 1973 was based on the Ford Kent crossflow iron block again. It was a demon short-stroke screamer of 1,300cc (81mm × 63mm) and was fitted in an RS Escort that existed only in Group 2, the RS1300. Initially the engine had teething problems, but it was quickly sorted to provide 190bhp at 10,000rpm. During the '73 season drivers such as Vince Woodman and Peter Hanson had their RS1300s running to regular class wins in the British and Belgian Championships.

There were even smaller capacity BDAs yet. The 1-litre cousin was tried in the Escort for racing, but the car was really too big to take on the class-winning Hillman Imp. Then there was the 1,098cc

BDJ of 1974, but it was not familiar in England, being sold for Formula C races in the USA. Two other American-market specials were the 1981 BDP, a strong seller for Midget racing, using methanol fuels, and the BDU, its offroad cousin, both of 1,975cc.

I understand from Cosworth that the popular BDT designation is really an unofficial tag, for Ford were actually responsible for the bulk of these conversions, the T suffix indicating that a turbo-charger was added to the basic 16-valve design. Cosworth did have a hand in casting some of the major components, but the overall direction of the BDT programme — initiated for the RS1700T rear-drive rally car of 1981 — was decided by Ford Boreham personnel.

Thus, to explain the BDT we need to explain an RS that might have been, the RS1700T, developed as a rally car but aborted in March 1983. I am aware of only two potential RS models

Gleaming display engine, cut-away to reveal its construction, is a BDA in 1970 production trim. Note the separated exhaust manifold downpipes, Weber side-draught carburettors, and the use of an alternator, a feature some early Mexicos lacked.

that were worked on but did not make the showroom: the fuel-injection Capri II RS2800 and the Escort RS1700T.

Certainly, the RS1700T got closest to production and cost the most! It grew from a Boreham-built Fiesta equipped with a longitudinal front engine and rear drive in June 1979, but I am told that the first designs and discussions for such a car dated back to 1977. Following two separate cancellations the Fiesta programme was abandoned in favour of a front-engine rear-drive Escort. By September 1980 the first XR3 bodies were being taken in for radical modification, the first steps on a trail that would lead to approximately 12 such RS1700 prototypes being built before the programme was officially axed on March 15, 1983. Cost? At least £1.43 million in production preparations, but my unofficial sources spoke of more than twice that figure.

Although I have lumped these prototypes together as RS1700s, it is important to note that this designation covered machines for road and rally use of vastly differing specifications. To my knowledge a few cars lacked turbocharging, the most photographed being P7, built in April 1981 and registered WVW 101W. It carried a 2.4-litre Hart 420R engine (Brian's own design, not a BDA, though the DOHC 16-valve principle was retained) for comparison with P10 which was BDT-powered. The latter car was registered WVW 100W and took part in the Portuguese tests in April 1982 in which Ari Vatanen severely damaged P7.

For our purposes in tracing the developing BDT's progress I was lucky enough to obtain the proposed homologation form for the RS1700T in road and competition trim. The road car was intended to retail at between £25,000 and £30,000, depending what profit Ford insisted upon making (£23,000 was the ex-factory figure in 1982), and its engine would have been of 1777.5cc from a bore and stroke of 85.4mm × 77.62mm. For competition use in Group B a bore of 85.57mm was planned, giving an actual capacity of 1,786cc but a nominal figure of just under 2.5 litres when multiplied by the equivalency factor of 1.4 applied to turbocharged cars in international competition. To qualify for Group B, 200 cars would have to be constructed, with so-called 'evolution' changes allowed on the strength of a further 20 modified examples.

Both road and competition versions of this special Escort were to share the basic design features of a turbocharged and intercooled 16-valve powerplant at the front driving the rear wheels through a transaxle that housed five forward ratios supplied by Hewland. Also assessed and expected to be utilized was the Ferguson-patented Viscous Coupling device, acting as a limited-slip differential. The VC is now well known for both rally and road use, but it is worth emphasizing that Ford were among the pioneers in exploiting the system, the people at Boreham first adopting the VC for front-drive competition Fiestas in the late 1970s.

For the RS1700T in showroom trim the BDT engine was planned to provide 200bhp. Ford estimated that this would provide the road car with up to 140mph and acceleration from rest to 60mph in 6.5 seconds. The competition version of the BDT in its first Escort form was rated at 320 to 350bhp with an allowable 9,000rpm. Both road and rally versions of the engine had competition specification components such as a steel crank-shaft included. It was reckoned, quite plausibly, that the RS1700T factory rally car would scamper

from rest to 60mph in 4.2 seconds and manage about 3 miles to every gallon of fuel on competitive stages.

I admit to being a complete RS1700T fan. I saw the car on its public debut at the August 1981 preview of a revised Ford Granada in Belgium and thought it looked terrific in a purposeful way that has never been quite duplicated, despite the efforts of so many body kit manufacturers. I did not drive one, but saw some of the prototypes gathered together a couple of weeks before the axe fell in 1983. The white cars with their aggressive stance certainly looked worthy of the praise heaped on them by such talented drivers as Malcolm Wilson, Markku Alen (he very nearly left Lancia for a second stint at Ford after some test times at a Welsh venue better than the World Championship-winning 037 could manage), Pentti Airikkala and others. Make no mistake, the RS1700T was a very promising competition car, but slowness in tackling the problem of producing the minimum 200 examples cost it any chance of appearing and winning before the four-wheel-drive turbo supercars began to commandeer the bulk of rally honours.

Thus the RS1700T almost brought the BDT to the production lines. JQF Engineering, outside Towcester, had built 21 such engines and there were all the parts needed to support a 200-off run for Group B. By the time the next car to use the engine, the RS200, appeared, Ford at Boreham had specified a bore of 86mm, rather than the two

The Escort RS1700T Group B rally car project was ready for unveiling in 1981 when circumstances led to its abandonment. Though based on the front-wheel-drive Escort shell, it had a longitudinally-mounted front engine driving the rear wheels through a rear-mounted transaxle. Its BDT power unit was a turbocharged development of the BDA and subsequently found a home in the RS200.

85mm alternatives given for the RS1700T. With an unchanged 77.62mm stroke, using the same high quality reciprocating components originally specified, the capacity was 1,803cc. Multiplied by the turbo factor, this gave 2,524cc and meant that the car moved up a class to the under 3-litre division compared with the RS1700T's intended 2½-litre classification. Ford Motorsport estimated that the RS200's realistic competition weight was going to be in the 1,050-1,060kg region. Going up a class entitled them to use wider wheels and tyres and also opened up the possibility of class wins because many of their turbo competitiors were in the smaller category.

The final step in the BDT development programme at Boreham was a 2.1-litre evolution version for the RS200. Coded BDT-E by Ford, this was never used by the Group B works rally cars, but did make its public debut, when Martin Schanche used the ex-works RS200 to contest the British Rallycross GP in December 1986.

Measuring 2,137cc, the BDT-E was the work of Brian Hart rather than Cosworth and was rated at 506bhp at 7,500rpm with 1.5bar/21psi boost and over 400lb/ft of torque at 5,500rpm. A further increase in boost (1.6bar/23psi) and replacement camshaft profiles suited for racing gave a reported 580bhp at 7,700rpm and 460lb/ft of torque. For

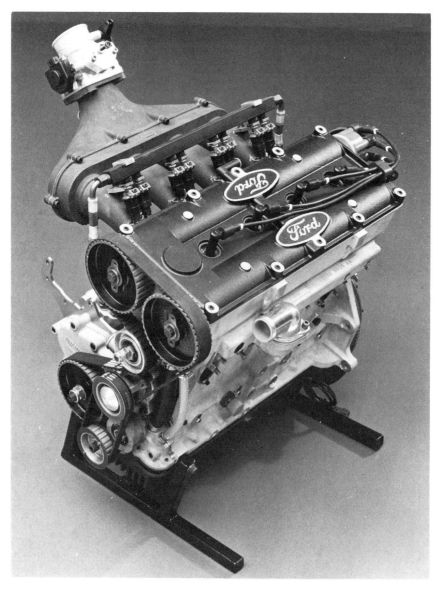

The engine for the proposed evolution version of the RS200 was the Ford Cosworth BDT-E, seen here looking very neat and purposeful but without its turbocharger. Fully developed by 1986, it had a capacity of 2,137cc and, according to application, up to 580bhp. Such power units were used in RS200s for rallycross and the Pike's Peak hillclimb, as well as a Tiga Group C2 endurance racer which was tenth at Le Mans in 1987.

Turbo BDA power, with outputs of up to 575bhp reported, was part of the recipe for success in the Gartrac rallycross Escorts, along with the X/Trac 4WD system and the skills of drivers Martin Schanche and John Welch. This is the car with which Welch won the 1986 British championship.

comparison purposes note that Blomqvist's RS200 in the 1986 RAC Rally was rated at 450bhp on 1.6bar boost and 8,000rpm; maximum torque was recorded as 361lb/ft at 5,500rpm. So the BDT-E, racing unit or otherwise, offered some very useful extra power at lower rpm. And it still fitted in the 3-litre class as its capacity multiplied up to 2,992cc by the turbo equivalency factor.

Another successful turbocharged development of the BDA was that undertaken by Zakspeed for racing in Germany. Again it was far from a Cosworth project, but it has a worthy part in the RS-BDA tale for Zakspeed's work began with Cosworth components when they raced the RS1600 and 1800. Their first turbo BDA for the Escort had the capacity reduced to 1,427cc (80mm × 71mm bore and stroke) and, equipped with a KKK K26 turbocharger, produced 370bhp. Gradual development — and a switch to the Capri body shape, much of it replicated in Kevlar 49 — gave them 460bhp at 9,000rpm by 1979.

Zakspeed and consultant engineers such as Schrick then went a step further, producing 1,746cc from Ford's iron block with a bore and stroke of 87.4mm × 72.75mm. Equipped with the larger KKK K27 turbo huffing at 1.5bar, this motor was credited with 560bhp at 9,000rpm in 1980. Development continued for the Capri and for a subsequent Mustang turbo that raced in the USA, both ultimately credited with some 600bhp.

On occasion the aluminium BDT cylinder block was employed as the Capri in Zakspeed trim raced amongst sports cars in Germany.

There was another twist to the Ford-BDA-Zakspeed alliance that was rather less official and even less to do with Cosworth. These were the rallycross Zakspeed turbo units that were installed in the Gartrac 4WD Escorts of men such as 1984 European Champion Martin Schanche and 1986 British Champion John Welch. These engines typically measured 1,860cc from a bore and stroke of 86.4mm × 77.62mm. Running with a 7.3:1 compression ratio and 1.5bar boost from a Garrett AiResearch TO4B turbocharger more usually found on truck engines, 575bhp was reported at 8,500rpm. Maximum torque was expected to be the equivalent of 294lb/ft from 5,500 to 7,600rpm. By late 1986 John Welch was also using a 2.1-litre development of the Zakspeed engine, such was the pace of rallycross competition.

Even that is by no means the whole story: the BDA family of engines have been utilized for World Championship sports car racing — Roy Baker's efforts in the C2 category in 1986 were centred on BDTs loaned by Ford — and for many other categories. I hope this has provided at least an idea of the versatility exhibited by the basic BDA configuration, and its relevance to RS Fords, whether they officially existed or not!

14

RS200

On a dark evening in the winter of 1986-87, I went with Bob Howe, who had at one time been in charge of product planning at FAVO and was then acting as a consultant on the RS200 programme, to the large hangar beside the test track at Boreham that temporarily housed the RS200 sales operation.

As Bob struggled with the padlock on the hangar door in half a gale, I sat inside RS200 number 122 listening to its engine, an uprated unit giving 315bhp, grunting away at a steady 1,100rpm idle and reflected on the fact that this latest form of the classic Cosworth BDA design, quite tractable enough for road use, produced over 174bhp per litre. About ten years earlier I had driven Timo Makinen's 2-litre RS1800, prepared for tarmac rallying, and had been amazed that its engine would tick over at all, for its output of 125bhp per litre seemed then like the ultimate in competition tuning. By 1986 the equivalent full-house RS200, just about drivable on the road for link sections between rally stages, provided 450bhp from 1,803cc . . . or a fraction under 250bhp per litre. Ten years of very fair progress!

Inside the hangar I was confronted with another side of the story. A podium, wall posters and audio visual equipment had been installed to turn this bleak shed into a passable showroom, evidence of the Ford Motor Company's sheer persistence in the attempt to secure some revenue from the RS200 project. Sweeping changes in the world of rallying, introduced almost overnight by the sport's international governing body, had removed the principal reason for the car's existence.

There were five RS200s in the entrance area and three more in the central 'indoctrination chamber'. The latter trio showed exactly what choices were on offer to the prospective customer at a basic price of £49,950. I was reminded that each car should have earned something like £60,000 for the company to recoup its investment, suggesting that around £12 million had been spent. . .

The RS200 was a very different proposition from any of the RS cars that had preceded it, far more radical and advanced in almost every aspect. To begin with, it was not based on a mass-production Ford bodyshell but had its own unique monocoque structure in composite materials. The rest of the specification was equally sophisticated: turbocharged, mid-engined, four-wheel drive with three Viscous Couplings, glassfibre bodywork styled by Ghia to Ford's requirements, vented disc brakes on all four wheels, unique eight-spoke alloy wheels with 8in rims and, on the road cars, one of the earliest applications of the Pirelli P700 low-profile tyre, size 225/50 VR 16.

As at December 17, 1986, Ford Motorsport's inventory listed 28 RS200s in production rallying specification and 46 cannibalized for spares available through the Motorsport parts operation at Aveley. Immediately available were a further 120 RS200s, 57 RHD cars and 63 LHD, in roadgoing trim. That makes 194 of the original 200, the first six having been constructed primarily at Boreham before the Reliant production programme began at Shenstone. By January 1987 it was known that at least 20 cars had been sold from that hangar with the help of sales talk, videos and exciting demonstration runs, and another five were sold in all but the balance of cash outstanding.

What options were there for those customers?

They had the basic choice between a car trimmed to roadgoing specification and one, easily identified by the battery of auxiliary lamps in a front pod, that lent itself more to conversion for competition. Instant identification points of a car intended for road use included cabin trim with red seats, and the absence of the secondary shift lever for the 2/4WD facility, retained on the rally specification cars.

Cars intended for the competition fraternity had harder spring and damper rates, hard neoprene bushes, a 25mm greater ride height, and black seats — *Show the grubbiness of rally drivers less,* said one experienced rally engineer! Both types featured an engine cover box that coincidentally damped cabin noise to a very acceptable level (by competition Group B standards) though it was actually intended as an interference shield for the sophisticated EEC-IV electronic engine management system.

Over and above the £49,950 basic price, Ford were coolly offering an upmarket version of the well known Custom Pack for a mere £5,750. The work was carried out by the coachbuilders Stratton, at Wilmslow in Cheshire, and included the fitting of black leather seats, retrimmed door panels, thick carpeting and a choice of paint colours apart from the Ford white which was otherwise standard wear for RS200s. At Boreham I saw cars in red, blue and black, all gleaming beneath those showroom lights with the kind of curvaceous sparkle that damages bank accounts memorably.

Another option for the RS200 customer who felt that £50,000 was not enough was increased engine power. The package fitted to the car which I sampled during that evening cost just £952 for an extra 65bhp over the standard figure of 250bhp. By 1987 standards 65 horsepower for under £1,000 was good value, and it was achieved by a number of simple changes to an engine of great potential: a replacement turbocharger housing of increased capacity; boost up from 0.75bar to 1bar; a replacement silencer for extra exhaust gas flow; and a new chip for the EEC-IV 'brain'. In 20 year's time, doubtless people will be arguing the originality of their leather trimmed, 315bhp RS200s with concours judges who have only seen pictures of the standard interior and read the power output figures of 200 to 250bhp in various descriptions issued by the company before the car finally appeared.

By February 2, 1989, the last RS200 had been sold by Ford, the UK list price having increased to £52,950 in 1988. The road cars were often converted by Tickford and could feature many individual touches like special colours, leather trim, Recaro seats and radios. Of 145 cars that were eventually designated for sale, 52 went to the UK, 27 to the USA, 20 to Canada, 14 to Japan, and there were single-figure sales to 12 more countries from Finland to Monaco. Some of those cars were destined for private collections where they would be carefully protected and not actually sullied by contact with the road! In 1990 the value to collectors seemed firmly established over £100,000, with advertised tags averaging £130,000 to £160,000.

But how did Ford come to be involved with this exotic piece of machinery anyway, and what were the steps in its development? Its purpose was to provide Ford with a competitive car for international rallying. In the early 1980s a new breed of rally supercar was emerging. Audi had demonstrated the effectiveness of four-wheel drive in no uncertain terms, and the Lancia 037 had shown what could be done with a purpose-built mid-engined rally car rather than an adapted production model. The next logical step was to combine the two elements, and Austin Rover, Lancia, Peugeot and others had sophisticated mid-engined four-wheel-drive vehicles on the drawing board. This was the wave that had overtaken the RS1700T before it could reach maturity, and the RS200 was Ford's answer to it.

The numerical part of the car's designation was a reference to the requirement for the production of 200 examples for acceptance in Group B, the international category in which it would have to operate, and that requirement influenced almost every aspect of its specification during the gestation period between 1983 and 1985. Homologation in Group B, with the necessary 200 cars built and inspected, was achieved — not without some traumatic setbacks — on February 1, 1986.

The principal instigator of the RS200 project was Stuart Turner, who had some very firm beliefs about safety in rallying and the idiocy of the technical regulations which allowed a batch of 20 lighter and more powerful cars, the so-called 'evolution' version, to be made after the construction of the basic 200. Turner's influence ensured that the RS200 followed a different development

While rival manufacturers opted to keep a tenuous link with production hatchback silhouettes for their mid-engined four-wheel-drive Group B rally cars, Ford chose the high style route for the RS200, with the Sierra windscreen and upper door profiles as the only predetermined body design features. The result, developed by Ghia from spare-time sketches by Ford designers, was a neat, powerful, purposeful shape of great character. A lot of technology was packed into an overall length of just 157.5in/4,000mm, with nowhere for the turbo intercooler to fit except the obvious place, above the cockpit roof.

path to its rivals from Audi, Lancia and Peugeot. Ford did not initially produce a super-powerful ultra-light evolution version of the car — the aim was to make it competitive in its basic form. Apart from the safety consideration, this would mean that Ford could offer a front-runner for sale to private entrants. There were subsequent plans for a later evolution RS but events overtook them. . .

Stuart's principles also pushed the RS200 into the lengthy and costly business of Type Approval, whereas machinery such as the Austin Rover MG Metro 6R4 bypassed such requirements, with their attendant costly crash testing, by dint of being sold only in 'kit form' to competition users rather than being offered as completed road cars. This approach to developing the RS200, ensuring that

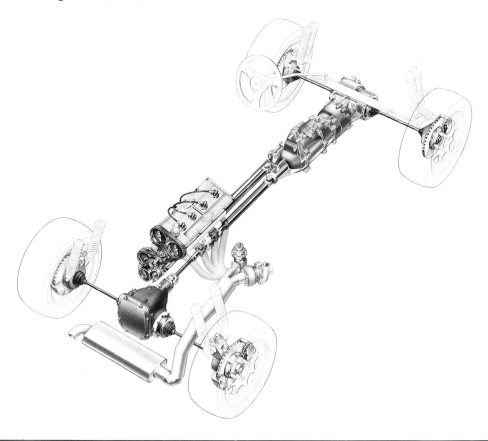

Cutaway drawings show the disposition of the RS200's major mechanical features, including the mid-mounted Cosworth-Ford BDT 16-valve engine, the Garrett TO3/4 turbocharger, ventilated disc brakes for all four wheels and two coil spring and damper units at each corner. Basic to the vehicle's concept was the transmission layout, with transfer gears from engine to primary prop shaft, front-mounted transaxle housing the five-speed gearbox as well as the centre and front differentials, and a second prop shaft driving the rear differential.

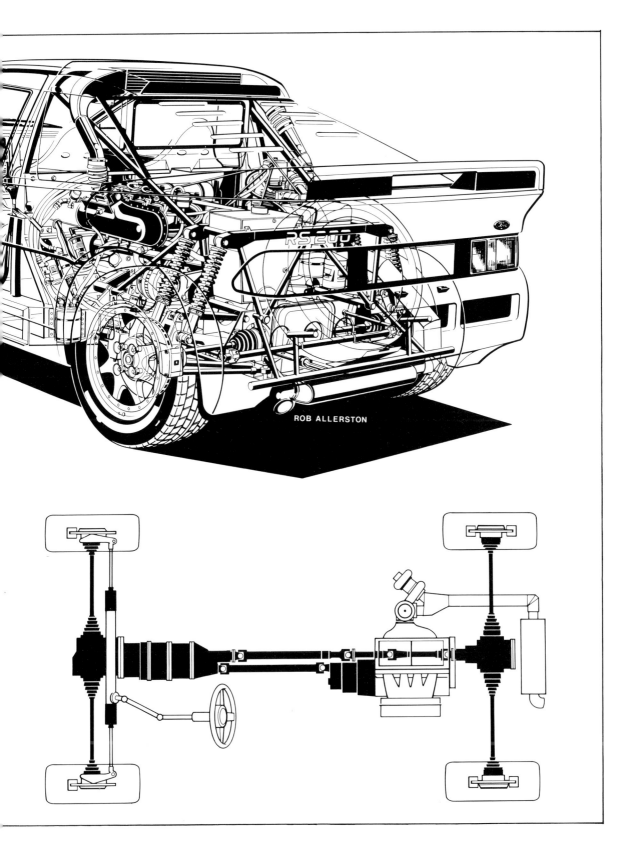

ROB ALLERSTON

Key characters in the RS200 story included the perceptive Stuart Turner, left, drafted back into Motorsport to lay down the guidelines for the project, and the experienced and very talented Stig Blomqvist, right, 1984 World Rally Champion.

it was legally qualified to sell as a road car across most of Europe, did mean that Ford had some hope of achieving the near-£50,000 price by offering the civilized performance levels expected by road car customers, although those customers would probably be conscious of the strong competition link and not just shopping for a Porsche 911 or Ferrari 328 alternative.

In March 1983 the hardworked Boreham team, who had seen their promising Escort RS1700T offspring die after years of development work and 12 prototypes, were naturally stunned. Boreham was, in the words of one employee, *in limbo from April through to about June of 1983. Bill Meade was working on the Turbo Escorts still, and there was more interest in exploring Group A at Peter Ashcroft's instigation. But really it was a time of indecision whilst possibilities were examined for our future — a bit unnerving after so many years hard labour on one central project. . .*

Stuart Turner was then working as head of Public Affairs for Ford of Britain, but he had been Competitions Manager back in the 1970s and maintained a close interest in the sport. *I was saddened to see that the rally Escort RS programme was obviously not happening. I would see Peter Ashcroft from time to time, and I knew him and some of the others well enough to know that things were not going well.*

Early in 1983, Walter Hayes rang over some Public Affairs thing. Walter, being Walter, also casually asked what I thought of the current Motorsport programme. I can remember saying that it 'made me edgy', which was about the most diplomatic thing I could think of to say!

Tell us how you see things, came the immediate reply from the highest-ranked Briton within the Ford Motor Company. Turner's creative mind could not resist the challenge. *I put together two or three sheets on what I thought should happen. It* went on to senior management...

By February 1983 former Motorsport boss Karl Ludvigsen was on his way out of the British HQ. Jim Capalongo, briefly seconded from America as President, Ford of Europe, asked Turner if he was interested in going back to Motorsport.

Not much, though I love motorsports, came the blunt answer. However, Stuart did offer to look again at the question of what Motorsport should be doing and this time, he recalled, *I turned around a Mk2 paper with a sketch of a possible sports car, one quickly drawn up by a stylist from Dunton.* The resulting illustrated brief was presented to Capalongo.

That second motorsport document recommended the death of the Escort RS1700T rally car, and also the C100 endurance racer that had been Ludvigsen's inspiration. It met with immediate approval, and Turner was put in charge of the Motorsport department to implement his plan. He was convinced that the replacement Ford works rally car should be a purpose-built competition machine, not an adaption of an existing production model, and was quite clear about his reasons.

My first priority was a safe car, second a winning car, third an ageless car which would be easier to sell over a long period, worldwide. In my view the paramount safety objective was as easy (or difficult, being realistic!) in a purpose-built competition machine as in a converted production car.

From that point on I knew that performance and the lack of obsolescence, caused by necessary changes in what is available to the general public, would be better served by a unique car.

I looked around at what was winning. No doubt about Audi on loose surfaces with their four-wheel drive, but the success of the Lancia 037 (which won the 1983 World Championship) left me with the feeling that at least the provision for two-wheel drive on tarmac might be a sensible precaution.

One other factor was a strong reminder from the days of the Escort RS1700T project. There was a fine ready-made Ford-Cosworth BDT engine, developed for road and rally use. Some were already built at JQF in Towcester. If, and only if, it suited the faster development of a competitive car, I was prepared to recommend that we use that powerplant. It was not to be a basic part of the design as in 'you must include. . .' but it was certainly a strong recommendation in my mind.

Basically I took my thoughts and put them out to tender with the most talented designers I could find. Nothing came of it in the end, but the most fascinating evening of my motorsport career came with Brabham's Gordon Murray. Brian Hart and I went over there to 'sit at the feet of the master' and listened to Gordon's philosophy of how the car should be. I think we both recognized we were in the presence of a genius, but neither of us felt too confident about selling Ford on a rally car that

Following a rather premature unveiling at the time of the Turin Motor Show, when journalists visited the Ghia studio on November 12, 1984, the prototype RS200s were seen regularly at shows and sporting events around Europe. This car awaits the Frankfurt show in September 1985: specifications at this time spoke of a road version with 230bhp rather than the eventual figure of 250bhp.

233

Testing, testing, always bloomin' testing! That's how it must have felt to the works team at Boreham – even the carefully controlled release of publicity pictures like these showed how the seasons flew by as a production home was found and components supply assured to get the building of those 200 cars under way. Much of the mileage was conducted by Malcolm Wilson, clearly seen in action over Boreham's stony infield, left, but the snowy shot, below, has former Cooper 500 driver Peter Ashcroft away from the managerial desk and back behind the (LHD) steering wheel.

amounted to a Formula 1 racer with mudguards!

One of the people Turner consulted was former BRM designer Tony Southgate, and in the end it was his ideas on chassis design, amalgamated with the vehicle concept and running gear devised by John Wheeler, who had worked on the RS1700T, which formed the starting point for the vehicle. During that summer it was licked into a more tangible shape, so that by September 1983 the project could be presented for official approval. Then the real work of detail development could begin, an exciting prospect for those involved. Obtaining official approval would be Stuart Turner's toughest confrontation in over 25 years of top level motorsport. He explained, *From March to September we were really looking at concepts. There was nothing built. For example, we decided we wanted to get Ghia in Turin involved. It seemed logical if we were to produce a unique two-seater of advanced specification that Ford's own advanced stylists might have something special to contribute.*

We put one creative brake on them. We decided to use some Sierra centre-section technology around the cockpit. Items like Sierra's doors and taillights were part of the original plan, and I wanted the Sierra windscreen in place. It saved the cost of a new screen and I thought the combination of that and the doors would stop them

raking it back too far! I didn't want a spaceship, just a screen my drivers could see through.

The brief went to the top at Ghia, Filippo Sapino working off the basis of our rough ideas (penned in his free time by Tony Catagnani who has since left the company), *and we had some other detail help from the Dunton stylists, including our interior experts.*

I was on holiday in Italy about the time that 50 Ghia drawings were available to bring back to the UK. This I did, but we didn't like any of them very much! I thought we were actually picking which design to go for. In fact they were all kick-about ideas!. Anyway, we talked to some friends in the Dunton design centre, showed them what we'd got and asked them to come up with an interpretation of what we wanted.

Then, Mike Moreton, later to be RS200 project manager, got to take the package back to Ghia. Apparently they had to be let down from the roof! They were not amused. . . However, it had the effect of getting them to pull out all the stops, maximum adrenalin. The result was pretty much the design you see today.

Some of the details, like the provision of 'ears' on the cabin roof for extra supplies of cooling air, or the detailing of the back spoiler section, were the result of initial testing once a prototype had been built, but the basic shape remained as Ghia

rendered it, from the starting point of the Dunton sketches, that second time around.

John Wheeler had meanwhile established his engineering priorities, with the transmission layout as a fundamental element of the concept. It was important to have the main driveline running down the centre-line of the car, giving the advantage of long, equal-length halfshafts front and rear, essential for keeping constant-velocity joint angles within reasonable limits in spite of the requirement for very long suspension travel. Avoiding an offset front or rear final drive also removed the need for the associated transfer chain drive found in many 4WD designs and so helped to keep the system simple, rugged and free of excessive friction losses. A primary transfer drive, incorporated in the clutch bellhousing, would allow the engine to be slightly offset to accommodate the transmission and would also provide a ready and rapid means of

In Sardinia in the spring of 1985 the motoring press had an initial chance to ride and drive in two of the original prototypes, including number P4 seen here in action on the gravel-surfaced 'stage' used for the occasion. The cars were deeply impressive, despite yowling transmissions, but the pace of production would not allow Group B recognition until 1986.

changing the overall gearing without having to interfere with both front and rear final drive assemblies.

The practicalities of keeping a rally car running in the field also had to be taken into consideration, as he explained: *Something I learned at Ford was the need for a car that could perform anywhere with minimal service back-up: Portugal, Africa, Sweden, whatever the conditions. This philosophy was left over from the Escort days, and it was extremely important in conceiving RS200, but I must confess I did rethink some basics on the servicing access side, after the first car was built. Thereafter the concept changed only in detail, not fundamentals.*

For instance, although there has been a lot of press comment about breaking transmissions, the components themselves have never broken: inferior parts in the gear linkages did! And when there was trouble, design features like Aeroquip pipe lines with snap connectors and the basic layout meant that transmission components could be changed rapidly.

The RS200 was not like the original Audis, where a gearbox change meant you were effectively out of time on an event. Our boys started off around 15 minutes for a box, and worked down to 9 minutes with 9-12 minutes becoming the norm. It never did break gears, propeller or halfshafts, or even crown wheel and pinion sets, and that's important to the team, and to me as their designer, emphasized Wheeler.

The result was totally different to the opposition it faced and as advanced as any design in the world. The alloy block BDT motor, now measuring 1,803cc on an 86mm bore, instead of 85.4mm, retained its traditional 77.62mm stroke. It was installed in the mid position, longitudinally rather than the transverse location used for the Peugeot 205 T16. Both Ford and Peugeot had turbocharged four-cylinder units, as did many of their opponents. Exceptions were Audi's front-mounted inline turbo five and MG's non-turbocharged V6.

The Ford-Cosworth turbo engine was mounted with its camshaft drive at the rear, and the power was taken to a front-mounted transaxle via a short propeller shaft. The magnesium-cased transaxle with its five-speed internals was adapted from that developed for the RS1700T, as John Wheeler explained. *We had looked at the RS1700T with four-wheel drive as a possible longer-term option,*

RS200 interiors, pristine in the studio, right, or rather more cluttered in real life, below, reveal a lot of dials, switches and levers to master! The secondary gearlever was to shift out of 4WD and was fitted to cars intended for competition but omitted from the production road version.

Engine bay, with the clearly visible roof-mounted intercooler feeding the Ford-Bosch electronic injection system of the BDT motor. This 1985 prototype photographed in Sardinia has twin Bilstein dampers but only one coil spring for each rear wheel.

but the real point about using this transaxle, with all its gears made by Hewland, was that we had quite a lot of experience with it in the RS1700T, albeit mounted at the rear. It had been a new experience for me, designing a road gearbox with synchromesh and a straight-cut box for competition, but it all seemed to work well in either application. Its use would obviously cut both development costs and time for RS200, just as the use of that BDT engine technology was helpful.

In addition to the gearbox and the differential for the front final drive, the transaxle housed a second differential, with epicyclic gears, controlling the torque bias between front and rear drive in the four-wheel-drive system. The torque split chosen for the road cars was 37% front, 63% rear. Alternatively, the centre differential could be locked, effectively splitting the power equally between front and rear, the locking mechanism being controlled by a three-position lever which could also be used to disengage a dog clutch in the front-drive components and leave the car with rear-wheel drive only. The locked centre diff mode was intended for use only on very slippery surfaces.

A look at the cutaway drawing of the car shows how the rear drive was provided by a second, longer, propshaft running north-south along the central tunnel, through a support bearing adjacent to the engine-mounted clutch, straight back to the rear differential in its magnesium alloy casing.

All three differentials, the two in the front transaxle and the one in the rear final drive, were provided with limited-slip effect by Ferguson Viscous Couplings, making the RS200 one of the few top rallying competitors to stay faithful to the principle of utilizing a trio of VC units. At Audi, Lancia and Peugeot all sorts of other differential types were assessed, Audi in particular favouring the Torsen Gleason unit that is now a production item as the centre diff of an increasing number of their quattro derivatives.

As John Wheeler pointed out: *Again we had experience from the RS1700T that was relevant.*

The VC was by far the best unit we tried, and it was also effective in the front-drive competition Fiestas. We did not have four-wheel-drive competition experience at the time, but it seemed logical to me that, having proved its effectiveness front and rear, the VC's characteristics would also be suitable in a central differential.

The basic structure of the car was to be a monocoque, making use of both metal and composite materials, and the removable body panels would be in plastics reinforced with glass-fibre or some of the other synthetic materials increasingly found in competition cars. The aim was for the weight distribution, front to rear, to be as nearly as possible equal, and in the event the engineers were able to achieve a balance of 49% front, 51% rear.

Independent suspension by wide-based wish-

The Sardinian car again, showing details of the Garrett turbo installation. Note the 'schnorkel' intake for the air filter. These development prototypes were converted to approximate the road car specification, with the correct Pirelli P700 tyres and eight-spoke alloy wheels, and the boost turned down to provide the 240-250bhp expected in production form.

bones was to be fitted all round, with twin dampers and the provision for twin coil springs at each corner, taking into account the need for a successful rally car to be very fast over very rough surfaces. When the RS200s come to compete on the Acropolis Rally in Greece their speed on that event's notoriously destructive tracks was truly an eye-opener for the opposition, and pleasant confirmation of the wisdom of that twin-damper suspension approach. There were those who wondered about the complexity and weight compared to the Lancia 037, which had twin dampers and a single spring each side at the rear with conventional single damper and spring front units. In action, Ford proved that the RS200 had set new standards in high-speed, rough-road ride quality, controllability and traction. As John Wheeler graphically put it, *We prevented any rear-end pogo stick effect over large bumps.*

Fairly conventional competition practice was reflected in some of the other details, including rack-and-pinion steering, using modified Sierra components, with a rapid 2.3 turns lock-to-lock. There were cast alloy suspension uprights, and big ventilated disc brakes for each wheel. Even the road version had discs measuring 285mm — or more than 11in — in diameter and 25mm thick. To accommodate the largest possible brakes, the RS200 was specified from the start with 16in diameter wheels.

That then was the plan, drawn up in considerable detail. The next step was to get approval for the actual construction of the car.

It was the worst meeting of the whole programme, and one of the toughest in my life, said Stuart Turner candidly, recalling the Ford management meeting of September 1983 to decide the future of the amalgam of mechanical and styling concepts that had become RS200. *We came within 5% of not getting that programme.*

Luckily, I had literally had a job headhunting agency after me the previous day. I just thought 'Stuff it! If they don't want to do this properly I'll just go'. It made me perform more aggressively in the presentation, which was in front of Bob Lutz, at our Grafton Street offices.

Bob Lutz was at that time Executive Vice-President, Ford International Automotive Operations, having previously been Chairman, Ford of Europe, a post to which he returned in 1984.

Naturally Mr Lutz was pretty wary of committing Ford to another major World Championship

project so soon after the cancellation of the previous RS1700T. Mike Kranefuss spoke for many when he expressed real concern about our participation, in the light of spectator safety. This was once the hurdle of actually getting permission to go ahead with RS200 had apparently been jumped — and this was back in 1983, don't forget, before the recent tragedies,* explained Turner in 1987. Ironically, in view of later events, safety considerations were kept very much in mind during the car's development. *Right from the start Ford executives were concerned over that aspect, particularly senior management from Dearborn. So there was never any question but that the RS200 would be developed with safety unusually high up its list of competitive attributes.*

The outcome of that September meeting was the decision by Ford senior management to permit the construction of a single prototype. *So we rushed off up to John Thompson's fabrication business, TC Prototypes/AFT, in Northampton,* recalled Mr Turner, *and in five months his efforts, coupled with ours at Boreham, had produced a drivable car for a further presentation on March 9, 1984, at Balderton Street,* which is the site of the Ford Import Export dealership.

Again Bob Lutz was present, but this time Marketing were able to do a nice job with some presentation panels around the place, the car looked super and we had proved that we could actually make something extremely good. No promises or bull, just get on with it. To top a constructive occasion the atmosphere between John Wheeler and Bob Lutz was obviously good, Lutz asking extremely perceptive questions and John pleased to answer fully.

Construction of that solo prototype had been 'a bit of a rush', by all accounts. John Wheeler appreciated the breathing space which followed, permitting him to think again about an important practical aspect of the RS200 concept. *It was the serviceability really,* he explained: *I just had to attend more thoroughly to the access and durability of key components to ensure the mechanics had the best possible chance of keeping it going under rally circumstances. That's when I set myself targets like 10 minutes for a gearbox change, and so on.*

Some six prototypes were subsequently constructed, (five new, one the original). They divided into two for road car development by Ford Motorsport personnel, two for National Type

RS200s on the line at Reliant's factory at Shenstone, above. The local workforce and drafted Ford Motorsport personnel spent much of 1985 and early 1986 labouring to produce and finish all but the initial prototypes. Below are a proportion of the cars gathered at Shenstone prior to their homologation inspection by the international sporting authority.

Pre-homologation competition debut for the RS200 came on September 7, 1985, when Malcolm Wilson and Nigel Harris won the Marlboro Lindisfarne Rally, a British National Championship qualifier. A lucky victory, perhaps, over Tony Pond's MG Metro 6R4, but no less welcome!

Approval certification, including one for crash testing, and two to be used to determine the best rallying specification.

The concern with safety mentioned already found expression in Ford's commitment to the Type Approval crash test procedure being enacted to the letter for the RS200. A costly crash test programme was carried out by David Orchard, at Aston Martin Tickford, and Bob Howe, by now acting as a consultant on many aspects of the project. Tickford engineers at Milton Keynes were assigned responsibility not just for Type Approval conformity, but also for further development of the RS200 for public sale, working in association with the few Ford Motorsport personnel who were available for engineering liaison duties.

With the prototypes built and testing under way, and with any conflicts that there might have been within such a group of talented individuals resolved, Stuart Turner was able to go to Bob Lutz in December 1984 with a costed programme

showing what the price would be, if Ford went back to World Championship rallying with the RS200. Plenty of price predictions had been made before, but Ford Motorsport now had a very good idea of what they were letting themselves in for.

Also Ford had now rediscovered Reliant in Shenstone as potential contractors to build the cars, having initially contacted them with a view to making the RS1700T in that project's later stages. Ford had looked at most of the UK specialists, including their old allies Lotus, but the sheer available space at Reliant and the cost of utilizing it were decisive factors, along with the availability of skilled local labour and the accessibility of many specialist parts suppliers from this Midland base. *The big Shenstone factory could have been made for what we wanted. Really it was like having FAVO back. There was a skilled workforce to hand, as required, and 80% of the components could be sourced from a radius of under 50 miles,* said Stuart Turner.

The Swedish Rally in February 1986 was the RS200's first international competition appearance. Kalle Grundel and Benny Melander finished third and set Ford hopes up for the remainder of the season, but this was to be the car's best performance in an abbreviated World Championship programme.

In December 1984, Bob Lutz signed the necessary documents to permit the construction of a further 194 RS200s, all that would be needed to follow Turner's avowed intent of putting Ford back on the world class rally map without a special 20-off batch of evolution wonders.

Most of the key points in the development of the BDT turbocharged powerplant have been described already, but there were some interesting installation details in the RS200 application.

The alloy four-cylinder engine had to be mounted with great attention to detail in order to suit John Wheeler's unique transmission system. That meant a location 152mm/5.98in offset to the left of the vehicle's centreline, tilted forward 1.5 degrees. The motor was also slant-mounted at an angle of 23 degrees to the right, the DOHC head leaning over toward the centre. A large-bore exhaust swept across the car to meet with a Garrett T04 turbocharger installation, then led out to the transverse silencer and tailpipe.

The 1,803cc unit was not entirely troublefree in its new home. Test-bed trials showed that its original cast-iron exhaust manifolding was becoming too hot in a mid-engine position, so that was changed, as was the turbocharger specification, which ended up as a compromise between two sizes of Garrett, the T03 and the larger T04. The final unit was designated T03/4, and used on both road and rally cars. A fabricated tubular stainless steel exhaust manifold with a four-into-one layout was employed.

Compared with the Escort RS1700T specification there was a new inlet system to suit that 23-degree slant, and a brand new butterfly housing for the Ford electronic injection with EEC-IV management which was fitted to the road cars. *We carried on using Motronic for competition, simply because we had got further with that programme, to a point where the system was giving us complete reliability under arduous competition conditions, and there was not time to develop the Ford EEC-*

IV unit for that purpose. Now it's got some Formula 1 experience behind it, that situation may alter, explained John Wheeler in 1986.

Other engine modifications needed for the new installation involved the dry-sump system, the water pump and the fuel pumps, and the person at Boreham responsible for the changes, Graham Dale-Jones, had a busy time working with JQF on the engines they had already built for the RS1700T, adapting them to suit the RS200.

In November 1984 the specification sheets showed the T04 turbo unit blowing at 0.8bar/11.4psi with an 8.2:1 compression ratio to give 240bhp at 6,000rpm, although Ford also quoted 230bhp in early press releases. Maximum torque was quoted as 280Nm/206lb/ft at 4,500rpm. By March 1985 the company was talking of 248bhp at 6,500rpm from much the same layout, and when I drove the RS200 for two glorious days for *Motoring News* in December, 1986 it had become 250bhp, also at 6,500rpm for the road car. Engine

capacity in successive Ford documentation goes: 1,800cc, 1,804cc, 1,803cc! Going back to the bore and stroke figures, the calculated answer is 1,803cc. . .

For rallying, boost went up to 1.2bar/17psi and the compression down to 7.8:1 and this released 380bhp at unquoted rpm. In 1986 John Wheeler told us: *All 200 of the RS200 road engines were hot-tested at JQF in Towcester and all had the pukka equipment inside that was suitable for competition: steel crankshaft, strong rods, etc.* It is worth noting too that completed RS200s were being delivered to customers via JQF in early 1987.

The Brian Hart association meant that we could have seen the most spectacular Ford-Cosworth BDA series engine of all time, had external events not killed the evolution version of the RS200. That engine, which would have been part of a homologation application in October 1986, measured 2,137cc. Even with the 1.8-litre BDT,

Without winning a single round of the British home international rally series, Mark Lovell and Roger Freeman (who replaced Peter Davis as Lovell's co-driver early in the season) took the 1986 Shell Oils RAC Open Rally Championship title by consistent good placings, defeating old hands Russell Brookes (Opel Manta 400) and Jimmy McRae (MG Metro 6R4).

Production RS200s finally arrived for road testing in the winter of 1986. By that time the switch in international rallying from the Group B supercars to Group A for 1987 had been confirmed, and so Ford put a lot more effort into civilizing the car for sale at a whisker under £50,000. This is the road specification, without provision for extra lighting at the front.

project were first, to get the basic 200 cars built and start competing; second, to develop the design to the full for works team and national club competition use; third, to consider the specification of an evolution version in the light of the lessons learnt; and fourth, (as always!) to avoid unnecessary expenditure.

Ford predicted that competition versions would be used by Ford works drivers towards the end of the 1985 international rally season. In fact they missed the anticipated Group B debut dates several times, including the November 1985 Lombard RAC Rally, an event on which the Metro 6R4 and Lancia Delta S4 not only made their international debuts, but also filled the top three placings.

Eight cars in all were completed prior to line production beginning at Shenstone, and one of them went out and won a British national rally for which international homologation was not required. It was Malcolm Wilson, who had been responsible for much of the test mileage on RS1700T and RS200, who scored this psychologically important win, flinging B55 CHK to

Boreham produced 420bhp with ever-increasing boost pressure (up to 1.5bar in the heat of competition) but the BDT-E version would have given 506bhp at 7,500rpm on 1.5bar/21.3psi boost, plus 401lb/ft of torque at 5,500 revs.

November 12, 1984 saw the international press gathered for the Turin motor show in Northern Italy, and Stuart Turner decided this was the proper point at which to announce the RS200 formally. *We'd had years of whispers and rumours about what we were doing, whether RS1700T or RS200, and I felt it was time we said something definite. Besides, displaying the car at the home of Ghia and in a show famous for styling exhibits had an appealing logic. You can argue we did it too early and that I underestimated the difficulties of getting the four prototypes then built to the stage of production cars, but I don't really feel we had anything to apologize for. It was little over a year since we got the go-ahead.*

The working priorities for those involved in the

victory on the Marlboro Lindisfarne Rally on September 7, 1985 with regular co-driver Nigel Harris. Tragically, Harris died in an African light plane crash in September 1987 with Henry Liddon, former co-driver to Timo Makinen.

Unfortunately that debut victory could not alter the fact that getting an all-new car with many hi-tech features into limited production was a task of considerable complexity. Excluding the engine and transmission sub-assemblies, RS200 construction involved something like 2,000 parts of which about 850 were completely new and so had to be engineered for production and procured from suppliers. It was not until early December 1985 that Reliant at Shenstone could begin to build cars off the line. Up to that point all eight RS200s, including the still healthy original, had been handbuilt, cars seven and eight being assembled at Shenstone as pre-production exercises with help from Ford Motorsport personnel.

Thereafter, the process began to gather speed. Mike Moreton of Ford Motorsport, assisted by Mike Goddard and others, had the unenviable task of managing the overall programme for the production cars. At a press conference, in one of Reliant's empty Shenstone production halls, on January 14, 1986, Stuart Turner announced: *We completed 60 cars for counting on the 13th of this month.* On January 30, 1986 they had their long-awaited homologation, effective from February 1, marking the manufacture of 200 cars, the total including those six prototypes and two pre-production models.

The first couple of European Championship events in Portugal and Belgium did not bring the newly homologated RS200 immediate glory, with retirements in both cases — an XR4 × 4 won the Boucles de Spa in Belgium! During the third weekend of February it was time for Boreham to contest their first World Championship rally as a factory team since 1979.

The event was the Swedish Rally, and Swedes Stig Blomqvist/Bruno Berglund and Kalle Grundel/Benny Melander drove a pair of 420bhp RS200s which made the start, weighing 1,178 and 1,144kg, after some last minutes panics, including a missing sheet from the homologation papers. Following extensive pre-event training for mechanics and team managers around dummy stages laid out at Boreham, the company competition department put on a fair show for their long-delayed return to top class rallying. After 1,056 miles Grundel and co-driver Benny Melander finished a fine third overall, 6min 16sec behind the winning Peugeot.

Blomqvist retired after 11 stages whilst third, with a broken engine, according to Ford sources. Both Blomqvist and Grundel had run in the top six stage times during their participation and the 1986 season looked set to see Ford back amongst the front-runners — especially as Peter Ashcroft had gone on record to say that Ford would, after all, build an evolution RS200 for homologation in October.

As it turned out, though, the RS200s never did achieve a better placing on a World Championship event than on that first outing! Sheer bad luck seemed to haunt their efforts during 1986. In early March they went to Portugal. The two cars which had run in Sweden, now lightened over 60lb by the use of a Kevlar sumpguard in place of the Dural alloy one, were backed up by a brand new car for Joaquim Santos and Miguel Olivera, this one rated at 350bhp rather than the factory's 420bhp and lacking the latest in gearbox specifications.

In the event such technicalities mattered little. Portuguese hero Santos was confronted with a wall of spectators on the first stage and spun into the dense crowd, injuring 30 and killing three. The event did carry on, but Ford management withdrew the Blomqvist and Grundel RS200s promptly, so missing the bizarre scenes when the other top level drivers also walked out, the organizers continuing the rally without them. . .

The bad luck continued, and Kalle Grundel could not escape that RS200 spectre. On the Circuit of Ireland over Easter his RS flipped a teenage spectator into the air, the boy apparently deafened by the helicopter hovering above him. Fortunately that incident did not have fatal results, but it made Ford executives *very* edgy about rally safety. Fears that were to prove all too prophetic. . .

In May 1986 came the deaths of Henri Toivonen and Sergio Cresto when their Lancia Delta S4 crashed in Corsica. Coming on top of the multiple spectator deaths on the Portuguese World Championship round, and other incidents, including the suspension of rallies in Ireland following further spectator injuries, this tragedy precipitated a crisis in rallying. Naturally the public associated many of rallying's ills with the awesome power of the Group B supercars, for 400 to 550bhp was routine by this stage.

In fact it could be argued that Group B was not

Production roadgoing front end with radiator duct and suspension cross-brace exhibited by RS200 number 010. This vehicle lacked the luggage box fitted to later cars.

Rear end of the 1986 road test car, showing the engine cover which damped out electrical interference and suppressed noise levels to quite bearable proportions for motorway travel. Body panel fit and finish was generally good.

necessarily more dangerous than earlier categories, owing to the superior roadholding and braking capabilities of the purpose-built competition car. But the evidence looked bad, there was a strong public awareness of the dangers, and something had to be done.

The international authority in Paris, FISA, the Federation Internationale du Sport Automobile, reacted swiftly, issuing stringent regulation changes to shorten 1986 events and effectively ban the fastest Group B cars in 1987. For 1987 the World series would be devoted to Group A cars, of which at least 5,000 a year had to be made, which is why Ford switched to the XR4 × 4 and Sierra RS Cosworth.

That total change in international rallying regulations meant that the heart was taken out of the RS200 programme. No evolution models were to be allowed and the car would not be a permitted runner in 1987. Following an expenditure in excess of £10 million and countless man-hours from those inside and outside Ford, it was poor reward. Yet rival manufacturers like Peugeot, Lancia and Austin Rover were equally scarred. Audi, who really began the turbocharged, four-

247

wheel-drive approach, retired on safety grounds in mid-1986; Peugeot took FISA to court; Austin Rover sold off £40,000 Metros for less than half price — *everyone was affected by the traumatic events of 1986.*

For Ford it was time to reappraise the RS200 in both road and rally forms. July 8, 1986 saw a London press conference at which Stuart Turner announced Ford's plans to continue to compete in the World Rally Championship in 1987, using both the Sierra XR4 × 4 and the Sierra RS Cosworth. *Once it was clear that we could not expect to run the RS200 in 1987, I set about reducing our investment,* said Turner, the trained accountant.

Of the 200 cars built, he first thought 120 should be offered for sale, most in a refined road form because they could not expect the same number of rally customers as originally anticipated. Others, as mentioned earlier, were set aside for cannibalization to provide spare parts. All the cars to be offered for sale were stripped down and begun again — in fact some already had been, either for competition purposes, or because the cars built for FISA inspection were not developed runners.

Homologation inspection merely ensures that the manufacturer has assembled all the right bits, in the right numbers, as outlined on his homologation application. The cars can be *literally thrown together* in the words of one insider, for most customers would be rebuilding them for competition anyway.

Ford Motorsport contested only one other World Championship event with the RS200 in 1986, the Acropolis Rally, and that was both a high and a low point in the car's competition career. Both Blomqvist and Grundel took turns at leading the rally, Blomqvist for only one stage before he went off. Both set fastest stage times, Grundel twice, but then he too was forced to retire after 17 of the 46 stages. It was really a service problem which sidelined him, an emergency two-man crew proving unable to tackle sheared wheel studs in the available time.

Without a doubt the Acropolis was our most competitive event, said Peter Ashcroft. *Kalle was leading at the time and two of the wheel nuts simply seized on the studs and broke them. It needed a hub but they went OTL by just a minute.* John Wheeler added: *They really made a great sight running 1-2, but within two stages we had*

nothing. John was not immodest enough to add that many onlookers saw the vindication of his twin-damper RS200 suspension system on this event, even Lancia being unable to stay with the Fords over such rough surfaces. Quite a chassis!

Outside the World Championship, in pursuit of International European titles, the RS200 was right in the old Escort league (better, for a debut season) and conquered the British, Dutch and Belgian series. Mark Lovell was the UK Open Championship victor in very difficult circumstances, for Ford's Motorsport management were not then convinced about non-Scandinavian front runners. Apparently nobody at Ford was convinced that Lovell was doing the best possible job, so they swopped co-driver Peter Davis for the amusing and experienced Roger Freeman in mid-season.

It must be said that Mark's results got better. Over six championship rounds, he opened his account with a fifth and a fourth in Yorkshire and Ireland alongside Davis. For the Welsh, in May, Freeman arrived and the first of two third places was recorded. Excellent second overall placings on the Scottish and Ulster ensured that Lovell/ Freeman became a permanent partnership, and made them Championship victors, without winning an event.

For what it's worth, I thought Mark Lovell did an outstanding job against a horde of Metros and many more experienced competitors. His biggest problem was David Llewellin, an even younger charger for the Metro hit squad. For David won two events outright and showed Mikkola the pace on another. . . Yet Ford had a title to promote at the end of the season.

The last rallying appearance of the works RS200s occurred on the Lombard RAC Rally of Great Britain in November, but it was inconclusive. From a quartet of Fords, the factory cars of Blomqvist and Grundel and the Mike Little Preparations and Mike Taylor Developments machines of Mark Lovell/Mike Freeman and Stig Andervang/Dave West, only Grundel's survived, to finish well down the field. According to Peter Ashcroft, Blomqvist's RS200 had been seeping water into the exhaust 36 hours before the event. *By Harrogate people were talking about us and the clouds of steam from Stig's car. We just kept saying it can't be the head gasket having carried out all the usual checks. In fact Stig's RS was stopped by a tiny bit of metallic debris that stripped the scavenge oil pump belt drive. . . It probably would have lasted to the end, but the cylinder head was later found to be porous!*

That was not quite the final factory RS200 appearance in competition, for Stig Blomqvist and Martin Schanche both contested the Bettega Memorial rallysprint in Italy about a month later (December 14) with cars from Boreham. The ex-Blomqvist RAC Rally car, the machine tested by *Autocar* for which figures appear in the appendix, went on to 1987 as Schanche's rallycrosser.

Ford finally said goodbye to the Shenstone factory on May 30, 1986, the last handful of RS200s having been completed in February, leaving Bill Meade and company working at Boreham on the problems of noise, vibration and harshness as they affected the RS200 in its road car role. They also paid particular attention to the problem of on-board fires, which had occurred in Greece on the factory cars during practice.

Of more importance than expected, in view of its largely roadgoing role in the future, was the RS200's detail appearance. The Diamond White panels were exceptionally well finished and of heavier weight than was ideal for competition, opening to reveal the accessible engine bay at the rear and the secrets of the front suspension beneath the scooped bonnet panel. The standard specification did call for a front luggage box and tool kit, and while the press demonstrator of December 1986 lacked this feature and was justly criticized, customers' cars did have it supplied.

The RS200 was not all glassfibre externally. The roof panel and upper door openings were fabricated in a composite of glass, carbon and aramid fibres, and the doors had certainly moved on from their cut-down Sierra origins, remade in glassfibre and, again, aramid fibres.

The bodywork had a drag factor of 0.40Cd and cleverly achieved downforce figures at just 75mph — a rarity in road cars as you could see by the enormous spoilers needed for the evolution Peugeot T16 and Audi Sport S1 of 1985-86. It was hard to attribute the coachwork to any one source, for there were inputs from Ford Design at Dunton and Ghia, with body engineering from hillclimb competition car constructors Mike Pilbeam Racing Enterprises in Lincolnshire, as well as Reliant and Aston Martin Tickford.

It was interesting to find that the FISA inspectors had to view a slightly different body style to the one originally approved. Later development changes had put cooling ducts for the rear brakes in the shape of two 'ears' on the roofline and there was flexible skirting for competition use, along with plastic windows.

None of those items, strictly speaking, belongs on the Type Approved road cars and technically they had to be removed for such customers. Incidentally the car was designed to be quickly adaptable to LHD or RHD steering in production, and although 90% of the first batch I saw were LHD, the mix overall was about evenly split between LHD and RHD.

The monocoque construction contained many different materials besides the central Ciba-Geigy 5052 aluminium honeycomb. The central tunnel had strips of carbon and aramid fibres. The floor section and outer sill panels were bonded with steel outer skins for maximum protection, the complete monocoque being bonded with Redux 410 and riveted. Box-section front and rear extensions, plus the roll cage built into every RS200, were in high grade steel. Fuel capacity of 25.4 gallons was split into two aluminium tanks behind the seats, within the bulkhead, one of 16.2 gallons, the other 9.2 gallons.

The cockpit was as neat as the stubby exterior. Sparco competition seating in red or black was complemented by a red leather-rim version of the Escort XR3i steering wheel. Most of the facia was in neat grey plastics and there were proper ventilation grilles, plus carpeting on the road models.

A generously dimensioned VDO Porsche 911-style 10,000rpm tachometer headed the instrumentation, but I was only allowed to use 7,000 in the two road cars I have tested. A 140mph speedo was provided and six minor dials monitored items from oil pressure and temperature to battery condition and boost pressure. There were no less than eight central rocker switches and normal inertia reel seat belts were fitted, rather than a competition harness.

The suspension was notably neatly fabricated, including provision for ride height adjustment and different mounting points for tarmac or forest stages, already drilled and ready for use.

The mixture of forged steel box and oval section suspension arms were crafted by VW Engineering. Suspension uprights and hubs came from JQF. The eight shock absorbers were all gas-filled Bilsteins and springs were colour-coded according to the rates required for street or sport operation: white for the road, red for rallying.

Transmission components were based on Hewland gear sets and Ferguson patents. Kent Castings technology was responsible for the magnesium alloy transmission casings.

The complete car, with its 99.6in wheelbase, weighed 2,607lb, distributed 1,204lb front and 1,403lb rear in the final road specification. The large disc brakes were by AP, without servo assistance, and the four-piston calipers were laid out with the priority on easy conversion to full competition specification.

I don't suppose Ford will build another wonder like the RS200. It represented the ultimate in technical development and potential since the demise of GT40. If only there had been more time to prove its World Championship worth. Meanwhile, it is certainly the RS no self-respecting — and rich — Ford collector can ignore!

RS200 rally record

Date	Country	Event	Driver	Result
Pre-homologation:				
Sept 7, 1985	UK	Lindisfarne	M. Wilson	1st overall
Jan 8, 1986	Norway	Norway Rally	S. Blomqvist	2nd overall
After homologation in Group B–1986:				
Feb 1	Portugal	Sopete	J. Santos	retired–gearbox
Feb 8/9	Belgium	Boucles de Spa	R. Droogmans	retired–brakes
Feb 8/9	UK	Gwynedd	M. Lovell	retired–suspension
Feb 14/16	Sweden	Swedish	K. Grundel	3rd overall
			S. Blomqvist	retired–engine
Feb 22/23	UK	National Breakdown	M. Lovell	5th overall
			A. Zanini	retired–fuel tanks
March 4/8	Portugal	Rally of Portugal	S. Blomqvist	withdrawn
			K. Grundel	withdrawn
			J. Santos	crashed–withdrawn
March 8/9	Belgium	Rally of Ardennes	R. Droogmans	1st overall
March 14/15	Switzerland	Jurasiennes Rally	M. Surer	retired–motronic
March 21/23	Spain	Costa Blanca	A. Zanini	retired–gearbox
March 22	Portugal	Centro Rally	J. Santos	1st overall
March 28/31	Ireland	Circuit of Ireland	M. Lovell	4th overall
			K. Grundel	retired–puncture
April 12/13	Holland	Tulip Rally	S. Andervang	1st overall
April 12/13	Switzerland	—	C. Jacquillard	4th overall
April 19	Portugal	Oporto Rally	J. Santos	crashed
April 26	Holland	Hellendoorn	S. Andervang	1st overall
April 26	Spain	Sierra Morena	A. Zanini	2nd overall
May 2/5	UK	Welsh	M. Lovell	3rd overall
			S. Blomqvist	retired–suspension
May 3	Portugal	Rota do Sol	J. Santos	1st overall
May 9/12	Belgium	Haspengouw	R. Droogmans	1st overall
May 15/18	Sweden	South Swedish	S. Blomqvist	1st overall
			S. Andervang	2nd overall

Date	Country	Event	Driver	Result
May 23/24	Portugal	Volta Portugal	J. Santos	retired–electrical
May 30/June 1	Spain	Llanes Asturias	A. Zanini	4th overall
May 30/June 1	Germany	Hessen Rally	M. Surer	crashed
May 30/June 1	Belgium	Wallonie	R. Droogmans	1st overall
June 3/6	Greece	Acropolis	K. Grundel	OTL
			S. Blomqvist	off road
June 7	UK	Scottish	M. Lovell	2nd overall
June 20/21	Portugal	San Miguel	J. Santos	retired–engine
June 28/29	Spain	Santa Cruz	A. Zanini	1st overall
June 28/29	Belgium	24 hours	R. Droogmans	1st overall
July 5/6	Spain	El Corte Ingles	A. Zanini	2nd overall
July 26	Germany	Hunsruck	S. Andervang	2nd overall
Aug 1/2	Portugal	Madeira	J. Santos	9th overall
Aug 8	UK	Ulster	M. Lovell	2nd overall
Aug 16	Holland	Limburgia	S. Andervang	1st overall
Aug 30	Belgium	Bianchi	R. Droogmans	1st overall
			S. Andervang	4th overall
Sept 13	UK	Manx	M. Lovell	3rd overall
Sept 20	Denmark	Monroe	S. Andervang	1st overall
Sept 20	Belgium	Loop van Flanders	R. Droogmans	1st overall
Sept 20	Spain	Asturias	A. Zanini	3rd overall
Sept 27	Portugal	Alto Tamega	J. Santos	1st overall
Oct 4	Belgium	Grensland	S. Andervang	1st overall
			R. Droogmans	2nd overall
Oct 11	UK	Audi National	S. Blomqvist	1st overall
			K. Grundel	3rd overall
			M. Lovell	crashed
Oct 11/12	Spain	San Froilan	A. Zanini	2nd overall
Oct 22/26	India	Himalayan	S. Andervang	retired–radiator
Oct 24/25	Spain	Cataluna	A. Zanini	retired–engine
Oct 24/26	Switzerland	Rally du Valais	R. Droogmans	1st overall
Nov 1/2	Portugal	Algarve	J. Santos	1st overall
Nov 8	Belgium	Condroz	R. Droogmans	retired–chassis
Nov 15	Spain	Valeo	A. Zanini	crashed
Nov 16	UK	RAC	S. Andervang	retired–chassis
			M. Lovell	retired–engine
			S. Blomqvist	retired–engine
			K. Grundel	5th overall
Dec 14	Italy	Bettega Memorial	S. Blomqvist	4th overall
			M. Schanche	6th overall

1986 season analysis
Total number of starts, 67. Wins, 19 (28.4%); top three, 32 (47.8%): finishes, 41 (61.2%).

Championships won: Stig Andervang, West Euro Cup; Stig Andervang, Dutch Open Rally Championship; Mark Lovell, British Open Rally Championship; R. Droogmans, Belgian Open Rally Championship.
Also: A. Zanini, fourth overall, Spanish Championship; J. Santos, fifth overall, Portugese Championship.

15

RS parts

Making RS cars, specialized in nature and to some extent set apart from the bulk of Ford's mass-production output, inevitably created the need for some way of supplying spare parts for them.The involvement with motorsport, in particular, meant that it was not just a matter of routine service items to keep the cars running: there was also a lively demand to be met for all the modifications, adaptations and improvements associated both with the competition programme and with the enthusiast road car market. To find out how Ford dealt with the logistics of supplying RS parts, I went to see Charles Mead, who was running what in 1987 was called Ford Motorsport, a 15-strong department devoted to competition rather than cosmetic supplies. Charles, his staff and their trusty Wang computer operated literally acres of Ford storage space full of reminders of RS cars of all ages. The department was then housed at the Aveley site where Ford Advanced Vehicle Operations had been, but in 1989 it moved back to its spiritual home at Boreham, newly redecorated in the corporate white and blue. Charles Mead continued as manager into 1990, his team looking after half a million individual parts grouped into 4,500 Wang-listed choices.

How did such a specialist organization come into being within a large corporation? Mead recalled: *Ford and performance parts for Britain really began from back-door sales to competitors at Ford Competitions on Boreham airfield in the 1960s. Eric Bristow was in charge and Barry Reynolds was 'the boy'.*

(Barry Reynolds was Motorsport press officer in 1990 and the World Rally Championship 4 × 4 material in this book came with his enthusiastic co-operation.)

At first such sales were little more than unofficial

assistance for promising privateers wanting the latest works knowledge in the Cortina era, but Ford soon recognized the demand. By the late 1960s there was a glossy parts booklet of 'Plus Performance' components. Even in 1965 you could buy an uprated second gear cluster for the Cortina at £12. Also available for the same model was an uprated suspension unit at £3 10s, or there was a sump guard at £12, an alternative differential and many other items for the car that was Ford's race and rally winner at that period.

When FAVO became a reality in 1969, Ford management saw it as the ideal opportunity to separate the customers from the factory rallying effort. There was, after all, plenty of space at the Aveley site. In spring 1987 rows of undelivered RS200s, plus their cannibalized cousins, set aside for spare parts, were accommodated in just one small corner of the vast engine shipping warehouse.

As FAVO developed, so did the sale of what were now called 'Rallye Sport' components. For the record, 'Rallye' was always spelt the Continental way in this division, though abbreviated to RS in the 1980s and spelt without an 'e' in some other company publicity material. The list of RS parts and accessories to support the Escort line — particularly the RS1600, Mexico and RS2000 in their early 1970s form — really did seem to multiply by the week. You could buy anything from a complete Type 49 heavy-duty Escort body, with the works wheelarch extensions mounted and primer coated, down to individual RS lamp covers.

A substantial department developed to deal with all this at Aveley, managed by Keith Verran.

Period studio shot above serves both to recall the Twin Cam Cortina and Escort parenthood of the RS line and to illustrate the wide range of speed equipment available back in the late 1960s and early 1970s. Deep dished steering wheel, right of the two examples shown, was fitted to many early RS1600s and Mexicos. RS1600, right, epitomizes the first approach to sports part marketing under the RS label, with quadruple Cibiés, extended steel arches, Minilites and fat Goodyears. FAVO-engineered four-spoke wheel, below, became popular both as an aftermarket item and as original equipment on many RS Fords and some specials like the Escort Harrier.

To the relocated Boreham stock was added a rapidly developing line of RS items aimed as much at the high street as the special stage.

Particularly popular RS lines were the simple four-spoke alloy wheels; Tech Del Minilites were a much more expensive alternative that were freely available in this period for factory team use, other committed rallyists or wealthy poseurs. Replacement custom or sports seating also became popular, as did auxiliary lighting and front spoilers. Some such items, notably the earlier Escort RS steel wheelarch extensions, are still stocked.

So long as we can easily get a component made up, and so long as there is a strong enough demand, we'll continue to stock it, Charles Mead explained. *However, if the tooling fails it is no longer a question of £5,000 to £8,000, as it was in the 1970s. Now we could be talking about £30,000 and that would make prices uneconomic for all concerned. When we get to that stage I advise the enthusiasts, like those in the owner clubs* (he is a vice president of Ford RS Owners Club) *to find a cheaper, yet safely-engineered, alternative manufacturing method.*

You would be surprised just how ingenious the owners of older RS Fords are. When supply of the centre consoles of the RS2000 dried up, owners naturally wanted to keep their cars original. As a result of their efforts the original supplier was found. The missing console tooling was discovered in a shed behind his house!

Similarly, the big decals for the RS2000 had a limited shelf life and 3M could not supply, so the RS Owners Club got together. Now a club-approved company called RSR is able to make them up to the authentic pattern.

Unfortunately life is not always that simple. Special bracketry was an inevitable part of the RS car. The tooling might well last 10-12 years, but when it goes, so does the likelihood of our paying to replace it. At some point you have to make way for the new developments such as the Sierra Cosworth, for which we have just ordered 600 Bilsteins. That leaves us with little alternative but to ask the enthusiasts to get their own parts hand-fabricated rather than us redoing the tooling and charging £100 each for brackets!

The FAVO production lines were mothballed in the winter of 1974-75 and have now been replaced by a Robotics development facility, whilst the FAVO paint ovens have been acquired by the Pilot Build facility that shares this site with diverse operations such as Body Assembly, Ford Photographic, Industrial Engines, and so on.

The closure of FAVO did not mean the end of RS parts, for the Competitions people and some ex-FAVO staff such as Bill Meade carried on developing performance components in association with their German counterparts. The late 1970s saw a vigorous advertising campaign featuring Bjorn Waldegard — World Champion in a 1979 Ford Escort RS1800— and the X-pack or Series X components.

Series X drew on an amalgam of proven competition hardware suitable for road use — such as the twin-carburettor Group 1 RS2000 conversion and associated uprated chassis equipment — and new body, wheel and tyre combinations. Most dramatic were the Capri and second-generation RS2000 fitted with 225/60 tyres on 7.5in wide rims.

There were also Series X kits for the Fiesta, Cortina and plainer Escorts. That is besides the well remembered triple-carburettor Capri V6 and numerous bits for the fashionable RS2000 which could be said to have paved the way for the obsession with body kits in the 1980s. These Series X kits were heavily promoted, proved successful and led directly to some limited edition Fords sold from new with external cosmetics like wheelarch extensions and appropriately fattened wheel/tyre combinations...the Fiesta Sport, for example.

Public interest in Series X also prompted within Ford mainstream management the idea of separating serious motorsport component supply away from both cosmetic items such as body styling kits (spoilers, wheelarch extensions and so on) and the straightforward service replacement parts needed to run an RS model.

The result was that the manner in which customers are served had changed considerably when I called in 1987, and further exciting developments were on the secret list at that time. Charles Mead outlined how the current system had evolved: *Originally there were two competition departments and two parts stores. Then Ford Motorsport in Germany closed their stores operation. On analysis it was found that the German Ford RS/Motorsport departments were meeting a demand of 90% for cosmetics such as body kits and 10% hard competition stuff. In Britain we had almost exactly the reverse situation.*

However, even in the UK it was obvious that the body kit business was growing too big to handle alongside competition components. Our attitude was completely different: we'd take in something like the Zakspeed competition wheelarches and sell them to convert a road car, whilst the Germans would develop equipment specifically for road cars.

RS parts are now a separate entity under the appropriately initialled R. S. 'Ron' Fischer in Germany and can be purchased from any Ford dealer in Europe. They continue to develop equipment specifically for road cars, whilst we deal with competition demand. Originally that type of business was worth about $3 million annually to us; in 1986 they did $14 million a year! You can see why the company restructured this side of the business. . . said Charles Mead thoughtfully. For comparison, by 1990 the Boreham-based stores held an inventory of $10 million and was selling around $6 million in race and rally parts annually; 50% went overseas.

A look through the German RS Sport Accessories catalogue — or its English equivalent — reveals that they cater for models right across the Ford range (including the obsolete Granada and Capri) with items like spoilers, side sills and wheelarch extensions. Fancy wheels both for steering and to support low-profile tyres are a natural part of this RS approach. The accent is cosmetic but I also found that the 1987 British catalogue listed a comprehensive spring and damper 'sports suspension/lowering kit' for the Sierra. And Ford had even got to the stage of offering alloy wheels for the new Transit.

So two of the three categories into which RS parts broadly divide, the mainly cosmetic RS Sport Accessories, and running replacement components for RS models, current and obsolete, are now handled by the mainstream parts operation, Ford Motor Company Ltd, Parts Operations, Royal Oak Way South, Daventry, Northants NN11 5NT. Colloquially known simply as Daventry, this massive centre handles all mass-production Ford spares business in the UK and has a counterpart at Merkenich in West Germany.

For the RS enthusiast fearful of a loss of prestige in all this I can offer some crumbs of comfort. Experienced owners of the older models know they will not be able to get interior trim more than a couple of years after Ford have ceased production, but they have usually worked their way around

such problems, as mentioned earlier. The ingenuity of the enthusiast is an essential element that has seen so many models preserved against all odds from far more unlikely marques than Ford.

On the mechanical side even the oldest RS types are reasonably well supplied, with more or less instant parts availability inside or outside the Ford network, particularly in the case of the simpler Mexico and RS2000 single-camshaft engines. The twin-cam BDA engines can also be kept running in 1987, but it is fair to say that they will cost a lot more to maintain for only a small performance advantage, unless advantage is taken of the fact that these 16-valve units can be tuned to produce more power than they do in standard trim, in which case there are plenty of specialist services ready to help.

Turning to the third category, parts specifically for competition use, it is evident that rear-drive Escorts are still performing with great brio at the club levels of British motorsport in the 1990s, and while that kind of 'customer base' exists the enthusiast will be able to keep even the more exotic RS types hale and hearty — though possibly at a price more akin to that of running a prestige West German marque!

Touring the stores shelves of Ford Motorsport it became obvious that some popular competition items are still available for older Escorts and also that there is still a degree of overlap between those three categories in the Ford parts operation.

Charles Mead again: *There are occasions when a man is going to need a combination between service replacement bits and full-blooded competition parts. It will probably serve the customer best if he goes to one of our RS Dealers because such a dealer can order up from ourselves at Motorsport and from Daventry.*

Incidentally, all the parts needs for the RS200 are met from Ford Motorsport's resources, for that really is a special case, and there was still a limited selection of Boreham's factory competition goodies for the supercar available in the spring of 1990.

Amongst the many different competition engines I saw warehoused, from FF1600s with slave tin sumps and no carburettors to complete RS200 BDTs, were the remaining 42 boxed RS500 motors. At the other end of the scale, simply manufactured items from the past, such as single-leaf rear springs and uprated front coils for the RS2000 were still regularly kept in stock.

To see how the Motorsport parts operation tries

Success of the 'Series X' kits in the late 1970s led to changes in the way RS parts were sold. Though advertised with strong links to Ford's competition achievements, and including uprated mechanical components, what 'Series X' did was to reveal the potential market for modifications more purely concerned with style, like the body parts fitted to this Capri.

Jackie Stewart stands alongside an Orion more typical of today's use of the RS logo in the market place. This kit of body parts, spoilers and seven-spoke alloy wheels exemplifies the work carried out in Germany, a rather different activity from the Motorsport department's concern with competition equipment.

to advise customers today, let us imagine you are preparing a competition Escort or Sierra. If you are not too proud to take advice, begin by reading *Ford Escort Rally Preparation,* by former rally manager Charles Reynolds and Mick Jones with further Group 1 research by former driver Henry Inurrieta; it has sold well over 10,000 copies. This update of the old Rallye Sports Club Technical Leaflets is a must for anyone working on the rear-drive Escorts. It has limitations: no engine advice is proferred, nor anything likely to set a car up for tarmac stages, never mind racing, but it is a good starting point, complete with drawings and suggestions that really were discovered the hard way.

For the front-drive Escorts, Ford Motorsport sold *How to Prepare the Escort RS Turbo for Rallying.* This covers some general preparation points of interest to RS1600i drivers too, including an endorsement of the 1600i's spoiler as more robust than that of the RS Turbo. This book also reiterates the importance of that mid-1983 calendar year change to the front suspension top mount on the Escort line. RS or otherwise, *All Escort bodyshells accept the parts listed in this booklet,* is the proud introduction. Since this means up to 150bhp in Group N or 230bhp for rallying in Group A it is not surprising that some really expensive replacement transmission parts (gear-

Sierra Sapphire with RS body styling kit comprising front spoiler, side extensions, back bumper and rear spoiler: none of these parts is the same as those fitted to the Cosworth-powered cars, three or four-door.

These parts racks were just a small part of the warehousing facility for RS components which was rapidly expanded at Aveley in the 1980s. The whole operation has now been transferred to the Boreham site which it shares with the Motorsport department.

box and Viscous Coupling) are advised.

The 'How to' Ford Motorsport series also included the general purpose **How to Prepare a Car for Rallying,** applicable to many marques. The original authorship was by Gerard Sauer but there was additional information from Charles Eveson, drawing on Hartford Motor's vast practical experience.

How to Prepare the Sierra for Rallying, first published in June 1986, was developed into a guide more detailed than that for the Escort Turbo. A **Sierra Competition Parts** leaflet became ever sturdier with comprehensive updates from Ford expert Graham Robson; it is now in its eleventh edition! Graham also runs **Performance News** to keep genuine competitors in touch with the works competition and components activities.

It was reassuring to find Mead and his parts team tackling the demands of today's advanced engineering while still co-operating with the owners of previous generation RS cars. The ever-increasing use of high technology could mean that the supply of RS and Motorsport components may yet have its most exciting era about to dawn. Charles Mead concluded drily: *When everything has an engine at each corner and active suspension, I intend we should be ready for them — even if I have to allocate the parts from my deckchair in Eastbourne!*

16

RS driving

For twenty years, from a pre-production RS1600 in 1970 to the factory pre-homologation Sierra RS Cosworth 4 × 4s, the Ford RS types have all been licensed to thrill. By 1990 the arrival of four-wheel drive had changed the nature of RS motoring for ever; the constant was the grin-inducing pleasure of driving both road and competition RS Fords. But when I first came to look back over my RS experiences, more than 17 years after Ford had delivered a long-term test RS1600 (GNO 420H, converted from an Escort Twin Cam) for me to pass on to Bill Boddy of *Motor Sport,* I was surprised how many links there were between the first RS types I drove and those of the late 1980s.

That first RS was a rear-drive 16-valve car with MacPherson front struts and rack-and-pinion steering — and the same could be said of the 1987 Sierra RS. On the other hand, the latter vehicle fairly bulged with more recent technology. Things like independent rear suspension, a Viscous Coupling limited-slip diff, turbocharging and electronic fuel injection, four-wheel disc braking, a five-speed gearbox, and luxuries like power steering and electric windows as standard equipment were the evidence of changing times.

When that plain white RS1600 arrived in West London in the spring of 1970, BMC still led the British market with their innovative 1100/1300 series, under increasing pressure from the Cortina Mk2. During the spell I was employed at Ford (1972-75) the company overcame the handicap of my presence to seize overall British market leadership with the Cortina Mk3. The Escort continued Ford of Britain's sales leadership during 1982-87.

Whilst the RS1600 was born into an era when rear drive was common and therefore unremarkable, Ford's decision to build the Sierra with rear drive was courageous in the face of almost universal use of front drive by the opposition, particularly the GM Ascona-Cavalier series. Such a decision was directly responsible for allowing the Sierra RS Cosworth to become such a powerful race and rally competitor. The thought of passing over 400bhp in a Group A car through the front wheels is enough to underline the wisdom of that choice. From a rallying viewpoint, of course, four-wheel drive would have been even better, but that had to wait until 1990.

Back in the 1970s the RS1600's belt-driven DOHC, 16-valve engine was well in advance of what could be purchased from the production lines of BMW or Alfa Romeo, never mind the Japanese, who had only shown the Americans (with Nissan-Datsun's 240Z) a taste of what would happen when they got serious about performance cars. By the late 1980s, Ford were having to compete against much tougher and more technology-orientated opposition, both in motorsport and in the market-place. The Sierra Cosworth shared the rear-drive layout and the classic 16-valve engine design, yet it was the technical progress made in those 17 years of RS production that was so impressive.

Official *Autocar* performance figures are collected together in the appendices, but it is relevant in this personal recollection to add that I tested both the RS1600 and the Sierra Cosworth in pre-production trim at race tracks. In both cases a fifth wheel was used, albeit the 1986 *Performance Car* outfit spat out data from a microprocessor and miniature printer, rather than the reliance on an electronic speedometer, wind-up stopwatch and grubby notepad, which was how it was done in 1970.

At Silverstone GP circuit the RS1600 averaged 0-60mph in 9.3sec, was credited with a maximum slightly over 110mph in my hands, and returned 21.1mpg overall. Following our tests at Mugello, Italy, in the 1986 Sierra RS, the results I recorded showed 6.7sec for 0-60mph, easily bettered when testing commenced over flatter terrain in Britain. A German TUV-timed 149mph at 6,576rpm was quoted as the pre-production maximum speed (*Motor* and *Autocar* got 145mph) and over 2,300 miles C232 HVW averaged 23.35mpg.

The figures tell us what 204bhp and an 0.34Cd drag factor produced in terms of Sierra speed compared to 120bhp and about 0.4Cd in the Escort. However, behind the wheel those plain white Fords did manage to convey a feeling of belonging to the same family.

Although the 1986 RS burbled quietly through traffic and swooped along southern *Autostrade* at a sustained 130mph, its nervous, darting feel at speed over B-road cambers and bumps was an instant reminder of the live axle 1970s RS. Also nostalgic for this driver was the characteristic whine of 16 valves, two overhead camshafts and associated drive belts, though the carburated gargling and spitting was replaced by the Garrett AiResearch turbine whistle extracting 102.4bhp per litre instead of 75bhp per litre in the naturally aspirated twin-choke sidedraught days.

There was another link: my original RS1600 had Weber carburation and the Sierra RS had Weber-Marelli electronic injection management. Mathematicians will also be quick to spot that the RS1600's price was around £1,500 when I first drove it and that the Sierra RS was over ten times as much — £15,950 at launch.

I rated the RS1600 as supremely entertaining road transport, experiencing at least four examples. These included a tatty LHD survivor that

Mike Smith's dad, Reg, lent me to ensure I could get to and from the car company who did not supply me with a vehicle on initial employment!

There were works RS1600s in 2-litre trim that I have written about in earlier work, and I am unlikely ever to enjoy a sunny Silverstone day more than I did with Ralph Broad's 138mph 1971 Group 2 racer. Timed on the Club straight it returned 0-60mph in 4.8sec — full figures are in the appendix.

The first Mexico was vital to FAVO's welfare as well as to many such as myself who could not operate an RS1600 regularly on grounds of cost and doubtful durability. Mexicos certainly proved durable enough to sustain the punishment of my second sortie on a circuit and subsequent unsuccessful Mexico racing outings (it was a 1300 Sport, visually similar, that brought honours to Janspeed and myself in the equivalent of today's Group N production saloon car racing). For road use I found the Mexico's tail-happy handling, formidably accurate steering and disc/drum braking more than adequate to make full use of the crossflow horsepower in enjoyable safety.

The three Mexicos I remember best all completed thousands of road miles sturdily and quickly. PEV 805K was a flared-arch Special Build model that had started out wearing RS1600 badges: I owned PEV and it was sold for £950 in October 1973, by which time it had covered 29,800 miles, mostly in my hands. That its reliability occasionally faltered was due to constant changes being made for show/photographic purposes and my initial use of an inept corner garage. Once properly sorted, PEV provided Mexico motoring with extra flair.

Then Ford provided the first of my company cars, always of RS type to go with my job as the Competitions and FAVO press officer. The first one was a bronze Clubman-spec Mex registered YOO 633L, passed back into the Ford system at 12,000 miles. A Custom Pack, wood trim and detectable extra refinement made the next one,

This is John Fitzpatrick at work in the Broadspeed RS1600 which I tested so enjoyably for *Motoring News* and *Motor Sport*.

NHK 272M, my yellow pride and joy during one Welsh holiday and for much of its 8,000 miles before it was sold to Tony Dron.

My final staff car was the best of all, a silver RS2000 to full Special Build flared-arch specification. Registered TWC 679M, it had 4,160 miles recorded when it was passed to me in December 1974. I did not get the chance to do much over a thousand miles in this smooth wide-wheeled example before leaving the company: I took the car with me, but it was sold to Gerry Marshall in February 1975 for £1,400 when my return to **Motoring News** and **Motor Sport** brought another staff car.

The RS2000 seemed an enormous advance at the time, combining 90% of an RS1600's speed with Cortina servicing bills. It was an excellent product with far better motorway manners than the less powerful, reverberating Mexicos, but the second, 'Beak Nose' RS2000 was just as big an improvement over the first one as that had been over the Mexico.

Naturally, RS2000s first came along in LHD during their introductory period in Germany. It was particularly noticeable how FAVO had upped the interior specification, especially the seating and the use of carpets as standard compared with the crinkled plastic trim and starkness of a basic RS1600 or Mexico in 1970-71.

Competition Mk1 RS2000s were highlighted for me by the chance to lay out an autocross course at Beaulieu, using PVX 446M, the Escort 2000 with twin Solex carburettors so skilfully employed by Roger Clark to win the 1974 Tour of Britain. That car, produced in RHD, had lost little of the mid-range wallop that distinguished the RS2000 from other contemporary RS types, but the top-end power was no match for the later RS2000 Group 1 conversion with double down-draught Webers — it had 138bhp against 160-165bhp for the later kit with replacement camshaft, valves and so on. It was a lot easier to drive than my other temporary mount for the afternoon, 000 96M, a full works 2-litre RS1600 that had finished second on the previous year's RAC Rally. However, I'll not deny that the full-house works cars were more at home elsewhere than on my restricted half-mile figure of eight!

The launch of the second-generation Escort was one highlight of January 1975, and the RS1800 show rally car attracted much speculative comment as to whether it could maintain the sporting record of the RS1600. As to the single-carburettor roadgoing RS1800, that was far more promising than its RS1600 equivalent.

I had two cracks at the car in 1975-76, first alongside the RS2000 and RS Mexico Mk2 for **Motor Sport** and then a solo encounter. Much more recently, I got in touch with RS1800 owner Colin Beverley and went for a ride in his Irish-registered example. Then I found he also had the second press demonstrator, Mick Collard's ONO 840P, in his care for a full restoration — a memorable day. . .

The restoration of that car to complete road-worthiness was still progressing when I called, so our outing concentrated on KIA 9922. This 49,000-mile RS1800 was prepared to standards well beyond those of 1975-76, when Ford had hurriedly assembled some roadgoing RS1800s to provide a credible background for the competition success.

Most impressive single facet was the engine. Rebuilt by Dick Langford in Northampton (better known as Langford & Peck in F3000 circles, for which they prepare effective Cosworth V8s) it soared from 3,000 to 5,000rpm with the kind of solid power that foreshadowed what the Japanese would offer us a decade later!

The 1.8 litre engine was quite happy to go to 6,000 or 6,500rpm, but generally it was the taut assembly of this RS1800, its tug-free rear-drive manners and flat handling which reassured me that the RS legend was founded on fact, not fond memories. The car in action was better than remembered, and this one was presented with a professional pride that you might expect if a regular Formula 1 mechanic decided to restore a decade-old road car. I could go on about this machine for ages, but we have others to recall.

All the restoration projects I looked at and heard about in preparing this book have given me a great admiration for the tenacity and dedication of those who recreate pristine RS Fords like those submitted to our lenses to brighten up these pages. Even before-and-after pictures of hopeless, once-abandoned bare shells transformed into concours challengers can't supply a full comprehension of the tasks restorers set themselves on the way to their personal homage to a fondly remembered machine. My own dismal memories of the midnight hours spent grubbing around my own motor bikes and a variety of Fords give an inkling, but it is not the same as suffering the maniacal pursuit of total perfection through the disruption of domesticity that so many such projects seem to encourage. My respects to all those who overcome such obstacles and still find time to smile and chat about their experiences!

The Mk2 RS2000 was arguably the best rear-drive performance Ford of all, balancing affordability against performance in a manner that keeps secondhand prices buoyant seven years after production ceased. Most of the examples I see nowadays are decently maintained. Compared with the earlier RS2000 it was a more civilized choice in terms of ride and cabin noise levels that sacrificed little in driving joy: when will Ford make such precise steering and slick gearchanges again?

If I liked the RS2000 as a road car — and some examples used by photographer acquaintances supported my suppositions of reliability at 60,000 miles and more — the Group 1-engined example I rallied for half a season in 1976 was the personal favourite. Assembled by AVJ in Pershore (Aston Martin service agents), it was a package of sweetness in traffic, Capri-killing straightline speed and a wide torque spread which I thought simply superb. I would still climb over a front-drive Escort, RS or otherwise, to drive an RS2000 like that. However, put me beside a Sierra Cosworth, particularly the RS500, and it would be a different story. . .

Close cousin to the Mk2 RS2000, the second Mexico managed 26 to 28.3mpg for me during a **Motor Sport** appraisal, but I'd also been impressed with its sheer enthusiasm for changing direction with a confident chassis balance during a preliminary encounter whilst attending the Ford rally school.

The RS1600i has a strong percentage of RS Owners Club loyalty, but I'd be a hypocrite if I said I liked the original very much: after all, I bought an XR3i when faced with a direct choice. Now my feeling, based on some short rides in later 1600i Escorts, is that the suspension revisions have improved it to the point where I could see its other attractions. Richard Longman's Group A RS1600i was driven at Donington and was beautifully presented, but needed delicate precision for sensible lap times, its engine, only recently settled from a record of mechanical carnage, exhibiting an amazing liking for life above 7,000rpm.

Perhaps the most positive memory I'll keep of the RS1600i is that, on its own, it showed Ford that

The 1974 RAC Rally winner of Timo Makinen and Henry Liddon (GVX 883N) was at home on this wild tank-testing terrain, and quite manageable in Brentwood High Street too. Works team lore, below: the late Norman Masters patiently explains the preparation of a factory rally car to a suited author at Boreham in 1974. Norman built the 1959 RAC-winning Zephyr for Gerry Burgess, as well as Roger Clark's winners.

Rallying an RS2000 in 1976. It was an extremely competitive car — though I stretched Barclay's credit limits spending non-existent cash to prepare it — and I count the experience amongst the most pleasurable in twenty years of active motorsport.

the RS reputation could live on commercially in the front-drive turbo era. But for that revelation, this book and the Fiesta RS Turbo would not exist. . .

I got a lot more miles in the RS Turbo Escorts of both shapes. We started off on the wrong pedal with the first road-test car (B905 BTW) hicupping into silence at GM's Millbrook test facility. There was plenty of sneering from the GM contingent as Ford personnel arrived with a second example (B932 AAR), but most other manufacturers would simply have ignored the chance that we might still meet press deadlines. We completed the test, including a timed maximum fractionally above 126mph, and a third, white example of the RS Turbo made the cover picture of the July 1985 *Performance Car.*

I was not fortunate enough to drive a Group A racing or rally Escort Turbo, but I drove one of Mike (BBC) Smith's two Ilford Turbos after it had won the 1986 Willhire 24 hours. We suspect it was the same car I drove again in 1987, by which time Karl Jones was driving it to consistent class successes with BF Goodrich tyres replacing the Dunlop D4s Smith and Lionel Abbot had used to win in Norfolk. Either way it was a neatly consistent machine capable of holding and beating the 16-valve supersaloons from BMW and Mercedes. As you'd expect, the 1987 edition was faster, mainly because the chassis had lost much of its 1986 understeer. The weak link was the brakes, virtually non-existent on the first Turbo even when fresh.

The second edition RS Turbo was widely condemned by RS enthusiasts and the press as a bit bland and boring compared to the original, an opinion summarized by the comments I received from more than one correspondent: *It's just an*

XR3i with a turbo on! As you will have read, that does the car a real injustice — aside from 132bhp where 105 existed before, there is the VC differential, unique wheel diameters and widths and far better braking, never mind a standard SCS anti-lock system — but its appearance lends weight to the argument. You have to spot the bonnet vents, side body-kit extensions and colour-matched rear spoiler, because the bigger wheels are deliberately styled like those of a 1986 XR3i, which seems strange after years of separate identity.

I used the RS Turbo as a road car for a week, much of it snowy, and drove it on the launch, where I shared with Tony Dron. The impression left behind was of a supremely competent front-drive RS that lacked the original differential steering quirks, the Dunlop D40s remaining poised under the challenge of some really fast driving from my skilful and internationally competitive partner.

Unfortunately the road tests all spoke of performance losses, some recording over 9 seconds to 60mph rather than the 8.1sec I filed for *Performance Car* in 1985. That magazine recorded a similar 8.2sec for the second Turbo's 0-60mph dash, but we were down to 122mph for the maximum rather than the 125mph-plus we could obtain easily with the first car.

For what it's worth my unfashionable coolness toward the RS1600i is accompanied by an equally unpopular regard for the second Escort RST as a far better sorted road car than the original.

An RS2600, with fuel injection, rather than the carburettor-equipped hybrid I had, remains a personal ambition. The RS3100 turned in some fine mileage for me at launch time — including following the fuel crisis RAC Rally of 1973 with four aboard — and I was very pleased that Dennis Sellars felt able to entrust his concours-winning example to me just after an engine rebuild in spring 1984.

Here is my diary entry for February 10, 1984, when I took *Performance Car's* Treser-tuned Audi Quattro along to meet the RS3100: 'To Chigwell to meet Peter Williams and AVO Owners Club Capri wizard Dennis Sellars. Car absolutely sparkling, inside and out, but looked like a narrow boat alongside a powerboat when we were out photographing it from the Quattro. In fact the picture session was a real pain, getting chased out of the various teaming slums the new photographer wanted. But Dennis certainly made the Capri move within the restriction of a 3,500rpm running-in limit and the photographer turned in some great stuff. Nostalgically overwhelming to see those big dials again, sitting surrounded by loads of black plastic. Great thing was the instant response compared with the power-steered cars we get now. Better than I thought it was in the 1970s.'

More recent RS models I was able to sample include the RS200, at its best on a muddy or loose-surfaced lane, preferably closed to other traffic.

Escort RS Turbo, above, during testing at Millbrook for *Performance Car* in 1985: quick and full of quirky character. Long-distance runner, above right: the Sierra RS Cosworth honourably bespattered during its hectic trip to Italy and back.

His and hers? Alas, the RS200 was only an overnight visitor, though perhaps the most memorable RS of all.

Nothing, nothing outside the purpose-built rally cars of the Group B era, came close to it for sheer efficiency and pleasure under such circumstances. Pity that the civilized ride and all its other admirable qualities were haunted by a piggy gearbox and clutch, but even so that has to be the ultimate RS excitement.

Running it close, though, were the Cosworth-powered Sierras in several forms. I truly enjoyed David Morgan's TCCs computer company-backed Sierra RS Cossie at the 1987 Willhire 24-hour race at Snetterton. It was running third overall even for me, some 3½ hours into the event, when an obscure module-side 20A fuse blew. We had a lot more troubles in the long struggle to finish. Yet the memory of its speed in practice and its friendliness, particularly the outstanding rear-end traction in the soaking night practice session, survives.

In the autumn of 1987 Ford let me bring my Sierra knowledge right up to date, beginning with the three-door evolution car, the RS500. At first I was extremely disappointed. As the RS500 plodded out into West London traffic the lack of mid-range power compared to the smaller-turbo 204bhp power train was immediately obvious and the ridge of the rear wing could actually obscure a complete car's presence, a factor that may have cost somebody their driving licence by now!

I had the 5,000-mile-old car from Friday to Monday, and it was only when I learned to wait for an extra 1,000rpm in each gear, or a minimum 4,000 revs if I really wanted to motor, that I grew to appreciate its qualities. These lie in two principal areas of improvement over the original Cosworth: speed and stability.

The RS500 was uncannily at ease with high speeds, ready to cruise at 5,600rpm and 125mph with more boost awaiting your command for a genuine maximum beyond 145mph: the consensus of UK magazine test results was in the 146mph band.

The engine's usual 4,000 to 4,250rpm roughness and resonance was easily avoided by taking advantage of the power bonus beyond this point. I did not encounter a cutout action, even when the needle was pressed to 7,000 rpm.

The feeling of continuing power beyond 5,000rpm in the roadgoing RS500 was quite a contrast to the midrange muscle of the earlier Cosworth specification, but I think few road-car users would put up with the RS500's poorer low

Unfortunately I lack the sheer talent Franklyn 'Karl' Jones displays in the ex-Mike Smith Escort RST racer, above, but I though it the best turbo Escort I've driven, with only moderate understeer, though handicapped by poor braking. Taking over the RS Cosworth, below, from regular Uniroyal production racer Dave Morgan provided a stern personal challenge during the 1987 Willhire 24 hours. Shared also by Sean Brown and Rod Birley, this Sierra was certainly fast, but had a troubled run to the finish.

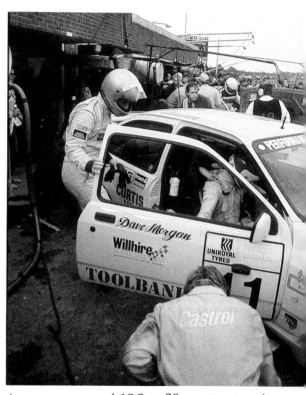

down manners and 18.9 to 20mpg in return for these illicit thrills.

Perhaps the ideal combination would be RS500 spoilers (preferably with a transparent section to the top deck!), the 204bhp power train and the later suspension, for the RS500's unchanged 1986 chassis exhibited wicked bump-steer under braking and had more bumping and thumping than I remember from the 1986 cars.

The Sapphire-bodied car I drove was in its fully-

One of the fastest weekends in my life passed at the wheel of this press fleet RS500. Initially disappointing for loss of mid-range puff, it came into its own over 3,500rpm and demonstrated awesome high-speed cruising capabilities and enhanced stability. Note that this Ford-owned vehicle was delivered with the lower auxiliary lamps in place, rather than the official specification of open duct grilles next to the indicators.

developed form except for a possible damper re-rate to overcome low speed washboard rowdiness and its door trim panels needed changing to a later Ghia pattern. Immediately after the RS500 it seemed slightly breathless and strained over 5,000rpm, but I soon got back to appreciating the stream of torque between 4,000 and 5,000rpm even if I could not analyse boost characteristics because SVE had happily dispensed with the boost gauge that was featured on hatchback models.

Most of the gains on the four-door car were to do with civilization, the body quietening the detail modifications made on the power unit, whilst the suspension balance chosen put the RS500 to shame. The car tracked into bumpy corners, with brakes applied, almost nonchalantly and the ride was firmly biased toward sporting control. I deliberately tried the low-speed aspect over the most decrepit surfaces Essex offers outside Bore-ham's test track infield and I could hear why they might change the damper spec for quieter shock absorption: it certainly wouldn't bother me unduly, but as it stood an Audi offered better low-speed ride with equal high-speed control. I should imagine Ford's comparison trials with other marques had shown them they were 90% there, but with room for detail development in the limited time still available.

The car cruised at 4,000rpm and an indicated 95mph with significantly lower noise levels than the RS500 or the 1986 Cosworth, but a third-generation Alfred Teves ABS anti-lock braking system exhibited a boring tendency to buzz as it pumped replenishment hydraulic pressure at every halt. *They all do that* was the reaction but I don't recall my similarly equipped Sierra XR4 × 4 doing anything of any sort.

By the late 1980s I had been spoilt for track and field time with the 'Cossies'. Rally days included a sodden morning in 1988 at Weston Park with Stig Blomqvist in the Texaco-backed three-door Sierra RS that he took to third on that year's RAC Rally; a dry day at Pembrey driving and riding alongside Group N champion Gwyndaf Evans for the **Motoring News** RAC Rally preview; and — an all-time high — a day at Boreham in the rain with Didier Auriol's historic Corsica-winning D372 TAR and engineer John Wheeler.

On top of all this was a 1988 season in production racing saloons with Janspeed, sharing all the long-distance events with Kieth Odor who went on to win the 1989 Firestone series. From four events we netted a third and a fourth overall, and I have to say that driving 287bhp on 205-section road tyres was wilder than any Cobra or GT40 track test that I have experienced. It was an animal when the boost came in — 20psi or more — and set fire to the rear BFGs. I retired from racing at the close of the season, but I would not have missed a single second of that compelling acceleration or of the unique view I had of those smoke-puffing, wheel-lifting 'showroom' saloons.

In 1988 there were two journalistic outings in full-blooded Group A RS500s, which proved ultimates for the sheer speed of the cars. One was as driven by Andy Rouse for Kaliber, tested for **Performance Car**, and the other the Karl Jones yellow-and-green Duckams/Asquith Motorsport machine which appeared in **Motoring News**, courtesy of Honda who had booked Snetterton for the day and let the 500bhp Ford ground-to-ground missile out amongst their 130bhp CRX one-marque racers.

The RS500s were both remarkably docile in the paddock, the Rouse car, with its Zytek engine management, completing twenty minutes in first gear for the photographers after providing the Silverstone Grand Prix driver's eye view of what it means to reach over 155mph amongst the Armco. The oversize replacement discs killed speed as dramatically as the cannonade from the side exhaust under boost (a little over 1.5bar for the test) built it up. Coming away from the Bridge complex in second, third and fourth is one of the abiding memories of the Rouse car because it seemed to accelerate as fast as you could whip the Getrag changes through, and that was seriously quickly. The only pause in forward motion came when you overdid the throttle in second gear and it turned the rear Dunlops into blue smoke, hanging fire like a dragster doing burnouts. Magic!

The Jones car was little adrift on Rouse power at that demo — if at all — because we ran about 1.8bar boost for the day so that Karl Jones could do realistic times. The abiding memory was of Karl flat-footing an already errant Cosworth around Coram with ever more vigour as the screen recorded our increasing angle of tilt (it had uprated rally suspension) and the necessary lesson was that braking and down-changes should be so late and rapid by mortal standards that it simply does not seem possible that the car can go from 140mph in fifth to 40mph in second in *that* dissolving space!

Another ride to remember came alongside Blomqvist in the moody black works RS. In a downpour the main concerns were finding any traction at all, and Stig had to reverse up to the BBC crew to film an interview in the car because we could get no traction travelling forward up a mild but grassy slope! However, once the car was moving it had shattering performance, speed born mainly of immense torque and prompt turbo response rather than high-rpm racing horsepower. Blomqvist's commitment at 40-something was a revelation, and each time we squirted from gateway into splashy ford he picked up time and eliminated as much sideways travel as possible in pursuit of elusive traction. On the 1987 RAC he was credited with second overall, a place ahead of Jimmy McRae, but both had been promoted in pursuit of victor Markku Alen (Lancia Delta) because Per Eklund and his Audi were disqualified over an inlet manifold irregularity which everyone agreed had no significant effect on performance. Both Lancia and Audi, though, did have the advantage of four-wheel drive.

When it was my turn to drive the Auriol car (D372 TAR, a plate still used by Boreham: the car was badly savaged within a month of the 1987 *Motor* test appearing) I could have wished for 0.5% of Blomqvist's slippery surface techniques. Never have the tight and cone-filled infield spaces of Boreham seemed so narrow, but considering the awful conditions the car performed superbly. Using Motorsport development engineer John Wheeler's driving talents and a set of super sticky Michelins *Motor* staffman Ian Sadler recorded some blinding two-way averages, including 0–100mph in less than 11 seconds and 0–60mph in 4.8 seconds.

As a driving experience a lot of the time was spent sideways or bobbing over the small artificial concrete yump. John Wheeler and Steve

My last race (left) was in October 1988 in the RS Sierra of 1989 Firestone Production Saloon Car Champion Kieth Odor. We finished fourth on my favourite driving track, the Brands Hatch GP circuit. Plenty of testing still to come, though, including the works Sierra (above) that Didier Auriol used to win the 1988 Tour de Corse: great fun in the wet, and the performance figures (see appendix) were sensational.

Woolmington, then sports press officer, both 'co-drove' which was a little less daunting than a subsequent 4 x 4 outing with Jimmy McRae growling softly, *remember: I scare easily!*

As with the racing outings, there was a lot of pleasure to be had from the sheer rate of acceleration and the positive speed of the Getrag gearbox (first closest to a LHD pilot). The rallying difference was that you could slide the car at speed — during the timed runs they were getting the legendary wheelspin in fifth over puddles — whilst the racers need to be kept reasonably tidy to conserve comparatively modest tyres. Karl Jones proved you *can* slide a racer about all over the place, but a gentle approach to tyre life generally paid racing dividends in the RS500.

I want to contrast the Fiesta RS Turbo with those RS500 experiences because my RS story begins and ends at Ford Motorsport, Boreham . . . saving the best to last.

Ford were in benevolent mood when we were updating this publication and I drove three pre-production turbocharged Fiestas, two at the Lommel track in Belgium and one for two hours solo on Essex roads. Remember, the turbocharged Fiesta was not due even for production until May 1990, months after our press date, and you will understand why we had no feedback from any market when these notes were written.

That Ford offered such good access and that SVE were allowed so radically to alter the handling of the turbocharged Fiesta was due, in my view, largely to *Car* magazine of January 1990 and their headline *XR2i: another duff fast Ford*. As I hope you have seen, Ford and their SVE offshoot did take that seriously and I have to say they needed to. It is not enough to take the 'XR plus a turbo' approach to either Escort or Fiesta to produce a genuine RS version, so that arrogantly influential glossy magazine did all RS customers a favour by showing the company they were unlikely to get away with that philosophy in the market-place.

At the wheel, the practical effect was that the RS turbo Fiesta improved enormously in development from 1989 to 1990. Steering feel was transformed and feedback grew close to that of the much praised Peugeot 205 GTI, without the penalty of severe lift-off oversteer; it would slide, but on the Escort-length wheelbase the transition from under to oversteer was milder than in a Pug. I believe journalists (myself included) ignore this aspect of Peugeot handling; it may be fun for a really good driver, but I have seen some of the best in the business spin 205s, especially in the wet, and I do not believe either Ford or GM, with their safety conscious US masters, would ever release a vehicle with these characteristics.

RS steering was slightly quicker in 1990 — dropping from over 4 turns lock-to-lock to nearer 3.7 turns — but I would have liked even higher-geared steering. Because of the engine's flat power and, more particularly, torque curves, wheelspin was a constant problem. I learned to drive with restraint on dry roundabouts or second-gear U-bends, but I was honestly not over-impressed by this aspect in comparison with Golf and Peugeot GTIs.

Outright performance was excellent. No, I did not benefit from more than the advertised horsepower, all the prototypes were around 130bhp, but the torque really punched them forward, showing higher speeds than rival Peugeot and Volkswagen products in back-to-back testing, but you should note the Golf had 129bhp with 16 valves and catalytic converter, and the Pug was a 1.6-litre of under 120bhp. The motor, like too many 1980–90 Fords, was at its best in the mid-range. That meant the Fiesta turbo really hauled along without fuss in the 50 to 90mph fifth-gear band (2,300–4,100rpm) and could be cruised at 100mph (4,600rpm) with less fuss than any class rival. Taking it much beyond 5,000rpm, never mind the 6,500rpm limit, induced the CVH coarseness that has bugged the motor since 1980. The turbocharger may quieten it fractionally, although you really do not register that it is turbocharged until a slight moan at 2,500rpm heralds the arrival of a significant proportion of

the modest boost that gives such relaxed and well managed manners.

Press and public had still to deliver their verdicts on the latest in RS motoring when this was written. My verdict was that SVE had done a patchy job on the chassis (although I would have liked to increase front-end traction) and made the best of an obstinate engine. It was much more of an RS Ford than the contemporary Escort but neither inspired me, partly because they had no motorsport reason for existence. Provided it is sensibly priced, at least £1,000–£1,500 less than the equivalent Escort, I am sure Ford will sell their modest forecast over the limited production period envisaged. I liked it better than the second generation Escort RS Turbo and a lot better on second acquaintance over British roads, when the remarkable ride and the stability conferred by the (prototype) large rear wing at motorway speeds were most impressive in severe gale conditions.

Now for something completely different. Here are some excerpts from **Motoring News** recording how I felt about the 1988 and 1990 four-door Sierra Sapphire RS Cosworths. *More civilized, more future*, ran our heading for the critique of the rear-drive car, which began: *The 204bhp Sierra RS in four-door form will come*

comprehensively equipped with standard anti-lock braking complementing a predicted 150mph maximum . . . It is a much better road car then the 1985/6 hatch, for it is built around the stronger and quieter post-87 Sapphire/ Sierra body panels.

Power oversteer, particularly on wet surfaces is dramatically reduced. The LHD demonstrators ran notable negative rear camber angles and the +2mm thickness of a replacement rear anti-roll bar design.

Built on a Ghia-trimmed base normally badged as Sapphire in Britain, the latest Cosworth has an effective and neatly trimmed cabin. One made more habitable by a pair of multi-adjustable Recaro seats, leather rim for the steering wheel (just 2.63 turns are needed for power-assisted lock-to-lock) and a legible instrument layout. Unlike the 1986 Cosworth, no turbo boost gauge is provided.

In the flesh the cars are considerably tougher than their executive-image handout pictures may suggest, the lack of Motorsport-required wheelarch extensions emphasizing rim widths . . .

We drove in Sicily; lots of rougher road made it obvious that the chassis engineers have

... and this is the 1990 Group A Sapphire 4 x 4 four-door prototype, with two-spoke OMP steering wheel, that I drove during an uforgettable test session at Boreham.

eliminated most of the 1986 car's spectacular handling traits in favour of an absorbent ride over 30mph (toward firm for this class at city speeds). The sensitive and rapid steering remains, but opposite lock is rarely necessary even when extending the capabilities of the Viscous Coupling limited-slip differential.

The stunning performance (0–60mph is believeably claimed in 6.1 seconds) is accompanied by Ford's best five-speed gearchange, one from Borg-Warner USA!

The short-stroke (90.82mm x 76.95mm) motor is well matched to the turbocharger and has better mid-range response than you would expect of a unit that routinely but harshly revs to 6,500 and beyond. Over 80% of peak torque can be deployed between 2,300 and 6,500rpm, concluded my 1988 **Motoring News** driving notes.

Looking back, with the benefit of later comparison sessions between the rear-drive three and four-door cars for production racing, I think these impressions were fair. Currently I feel the rear-drive Sapphire RS is the most undervalued RS of all, given that you accept £21,000 plus was a fair last list price. Private examples were on offer at £12,000 to £14,000 when this was written and there is the thought that this could well be the last rear-drive RS ever offered to the public . . .

My **Motoring News** notes on the Sierra RS Cosworth 4 x 4 were scrambled first time round, so that I ended up calling it — and some Bridgestone ER90 tyres — all the choice adjectives I had saved for a particularly venomous diesel Sierra spoof piece. Moral: don't try and be clever with printed media. Here are some excerpts from what I really said about those first German-

specification cars, as explained in the following week's MN . . .

The LHD specification differences over that intended in the UK (on sale during March 1990) centred on the twin-catalytic-converter engine and its emotively green cam cover, peak power just 250rpm further up the rev-limited 6,800rpm power curve. There was also the deletion of electric rear windows and no lumbar adjustment for the passenger in the car I experienced. For 1990 the Sierra adopted a number of range improvements, the main concern in an RS being that the steering column is now adjustable and complements both a new three-spoke wheel and (for our tests) optional leather-covered Recaros.

Unfortunately that was about it on the good cabin news. The glass sliding sunroof, central locking and so on all sound fine. Yet the new plastics proved unlovely, particularly around the centre console. Here there were 0.25in gaps to the upper, higher quality moulding.

The engine operated with electronically monitored precision at 800 or 6,800rpm, but the lightly co-operative gearchange of the MT75 has such a long throw that you could bark you knuckles on the 2–3 upchange, or fumble the downward 3–2 move, especially as the LHD pedals were not ideal for heel-and-toe operation. Malcolm Wilson will not face this problem with the Group A MT75, and neither should customers.

Initially it is the reduction in engine noise levels that is most startling. A lot of the 4,000rpm roughness and resonance has been subjectively removed, and it is not until you have driven several 4 x 4 hours that you appreciate it is still noisier than average around 4,000 (90mph), rowdier still if cruised at 4,600 to 4,800rpm (103 to 108mph). However, it is disconcerting how often one settles down beyond 90mph and the UK police may not share our admiration of the Cosworth's stable capacity for civilized travel at anything up to two miles a minute.

Acceleration feels slightly less spectacular than you might expect, owing to weight and 4 x 4 traction. Our demonstrators punched to 6,500rpm and the equivalent of 32mph in first; 60mph in second; 98mph in third and 120mph in fourth, all with plenty of enjoyable conviction. Top speed is unlikely to have exceeded an honest 140mph, even under favourable circumstances.

The killer punch from the Cosworth is the chassis, an obedient servant that fulfils the engineering objective of keeping the customer as safe as possible, for as long as possible. It is also extraordinarily satisfying to motor hard and not a bit boring as some exotica-sated journalists will report. Basic traits are the gentlest of understeer habits under pressure. You need loose surface, mid-corner bumps or a driver backing-off sharply in mid-corner to get the classic fast Ford posture of a tail-out oversteer slide.

It simply has the most grip with the least vices that I have encountered, a remark that embraces the 4 x 4 latest from Audi, Lancia and Toyota. Fantastic!

I was not keen on the lower speed ride over bumps — a bit bouncy compared with the 50mph-plus composure — but otherwise I thought the blend of steering speed and sensitivity and grip without tears was unmatched. It may be that Nissan's 280bhp GT-R is better, but the only place we Brits are likely to see that vehicle is production saloon-car races, ended my driving notes.

At press time for this book I had not driven a 4 x 4 on British roads, but I was privileged, just before the cars were scheduled to arrive in British showrooms (March/April 1990) to be invited to Boreham for a fabulous ride-and-drive session with Ford Motorsport and sponsors Q8. On a blustery but dry day they assembled Cartel winner Colin McRae in Cunico's three-door (registered with the nostalgic D372 TAR); Gwyndaf Evans in a brand new (one rally) Group N 4 x 4 RS and two Group

A counterparts of that 4 x 4 that were driven by Malcolm Wilson and a then scandalously under-employed Jimmy McRae. I rode with all but Malcolm Wilson (a genuine regret; I have always regarded Wilson and Pond as the quickest British practitioners of their respective eras), but the reason for missing out on Malcolm was simply that John Taylor flabbergasted me by saying, *right, it's your turn now . . . you drive Jim!*

My memory was already full of whirling impressions from the outings with McRae junior (one electrical cutout; one spin; one engine failure in one lap!) McRae senior — oh so smooth — and the brakeless but Mountune-quick Group N of the talented Gwyndaf Evans. Nevertheless it was the sheer commitment of McRae junior that lodged in my mind; he really gets stuck in and gives the car every split second of his considerable talents with a hunger that only youth supplies and with hair-trigger skills that are in the Vatanen crash-or-win mould.

Fortunately you needed no real expertise at all to get the Group A 4 x 4 under way and G687 BTW punched up to 1.5bar in each of the slick (short travel) MT75 ratios with stirring capability. It naturally felt a lot quicker than the other machinery, but most of that mixed-surface speed came from chassis grip, with braking and acceleration distances notably abbreviated.

The suedette rim of a simple two-spoke wheel took the inputs to beautifully graduated power steering, but there was no denying the extra understeer in slow corners; it was simply overcome in first through to third by extra power, when the tail would slither very gradually out of line, a stark contrast to the broadside travel of McRae junior in the 2WD car.

The fishtail exhaust was naturally sharper than the grunting (and occasionally pinking) Group N Cosworth and even my straightline speed was curtailed by needing to back off on the straights at 6,500 in fifth. By the end of the fiendish 'Boreham Stages', the Group A 4 x 4 RS, myself and 'Jimmy Mac' had covered first and second gear infield dirt, raised pavement third gear swerves and 100mph-plus straights in fifth. We all arrived back in the condition we set out, and I departed from Boreham hours later still with a stupid grin painted in place for the rest of the day. It had been a fitting way to close a twenty-year association with RS, the Faster Fords.

Appendix 1: Specifications, RS road cars

Ford Escort RS1600 1970-1974

Front engine, rear-wheel drive. Assembled initially at Halewood, Merseyside, then at FAVO, Aveley.

Body: Unitary steel two-door Escort Mk1 with Type 49 heavy-duty reinforcement.

Dimensions: Length, 156.6in/3,977.6mm; width, 61.8in/1,569.7mm; height, 54.5in/1,384.3mm; wheelbase, 94.5in/2,400.3mm. Weight, 1,920lb/870kg. Drag factor, approximately 0.43Cd.

Engine: BDA, in-line four cylinder. Cosworth 16-valve cylinder head with belt-driven twin overhead camshafts; initially on Kent series Cortina iron block; after autumn 1972, Brian Hart-developed alloy block. Capacity 1,599cc; bore × stroke, 80.97mm × 77.62mm (homologation figures, 1,601cc, 80.98mm × 77.72mm). Compression ratio, 10:1. Two twin-choke carburettors, initially Weber 40DCOE, Dellorto on some later cars. Output, 120bhp at 6,500rpm; 110lb/ft at 4,500rpm.

Transmission: 8.09in/205mm diameter clutch, hydraulic operation. Four-speed gearbox. Ratios: first, 2.97:1; second, 2.01:1; third, 1.40:1; fourth, 1:1. Live rear axle; final drive ratio, 3.77:1.

Suspension: Front, MacPherson struts, anti-roll bar. Rear, leaf springs, two radius rods, telescopic dampers.

Brakes: Solid front discs; diameter 9.6in/243.8mm. Rear drums; diameter, 9in/228.6mm; width, 1.75in/44.5mm.

Wheels and tyres: Standard steel rims, 5.5in wide × 13in diameter. 165 SR 13 radial-ply tyres.

Ford Escort Mexico 1970-1975

Front engine, rear-wheel drive. Assembled at FAVO.

Body, dimensions: As RS1600 except weight 1,964lb/893kg.

Engine: Kent series in-line four cylinder, as used in Cortina, Capri etc. All iron, pushrod overhead valve crossflow cylinder head. Capacity, 1,599cc; bore × stroke, 80.97mm × 77.62mm. Compression ratio, 9:1. One twin-choke downdraught Weber carburettor. Output, 86bhp at 5,500rpm; 92lb/ft at 4,000rpm.

Transmission, suspension, brakes, wheels and tyres: As RS1600 except clutch diameter, 7.54in/191.5mm.

Ford Escort RS2000 1973-1974

Front engine, rear-wheel drive. Assembled at FAVO.

Body, dimensions: As RS1600 except weight, 2,018lb/915kg.

Engine: Pinto series in-line four cylinder, as used in Cortina, Capri, Sierra etc. All iron. Belt-driven single overhead camshaft. Capacity, 1,993cc; bore × stroke, 90.82mm × 76.95mm. Compression ratio, 9.2:1. One twin-choke downdraught Weber carburettor. Output, 100bhp at 5,750rpm; 107lb/ft at 2,750rpm.

Transmission: 8.5in/215.9mm diameter clutch, cable operation. Four-speed gearbox. Ratios: first, 3.65:1; second, 1.97:1; third 1.37:1; fourth, 1:1. Live rear axle; final drive ratio, 3.54:1.

Suspension, brakes, wheels and tyres: As RS1600 except rear brake drums; diameter, 8in/203.2mm; width 1.5in/38.1mm.

Ford Escort RS2000 1975-1980

Front engine, rear-wheel drive. Assembled at Saarlouis, West Germany.

Body: Unitary steel two-door Escort Mk2 with added polyurethane nose and rear spoiler.

Dimensions: Length, 163.1in/4,142.7mm; width, 60.5in/1,536.7mm; height, 55.5in/1,409.7mm; wheelbase, 94.5in/2,400.3mm. Weight, 2,057lb/935kg. Drag factor, 0.383Cd.

Engine: As earlier RS2000 except output, 110bhp at 5,500rpm; 121lb/ft at 3,750rpm.

Transmission: As earlier RS2000.

Suspension, brakes: As RS1600.

Wheels and tyres: Initially alloy rims, 6in wide × 13in diameter; subsequently steel rims, 5.5in wide × 13in diameter, with optional alloys up to 7.5in wide. Standard tyre size, 175/70 HR 13.

Ford Escort RS1800 1975-1977

Front engine, rear-wheel drive. Batch of 50 converted from Mexicos at Pilot plant, Aveley; others, including rally cars, assembled at Boreham.

Body: Unitary steel two-door Escort Mk2, wih plastic front and rear spoilers.

Dimensions: Length, 156.6in/3,977.6mm; width, 60.5in/1,536.7mm; height, 55.5in/1,409.7mm; wheelbase, 94.5in/2,400.3mm. Weight, 2,016lb/915kg. Drag factor, approximately 0.45Cd.

Engine: BDA, developed from RS1600, all-alloy version. Capacity, 1,835cc; bore × stroke, 86.75mm × 77.62mm. Compression ratio, 9:1. One twin-choke downdraught Weber carburettor. Output, 115bhp at 6,000rpm; 120lb/ft at 4,000rpm.

Transmission: 8.5in/215.9mm diameter clutch, cable operation. Four-speed gearbox. Ratios: first, 3.36:1; second, 1.81:1; third, 1.26:1; fourth, 1:1. Live rear axle; final drive ratio, 3.54:1.

Suspension, brakes: As RS1600.

Wheels and tyres: Standard steel rims 5.5in wide × 13in diameter. 175/70 HR 13 tyres. Many alternative options.

Ford RS Mexico 1976-1979

Front engine, rear-wheel drive. Assembled at Saarlouis, West Germany.

Body, dimensions: As RS1800 except weight, 1,940lb/880kg.

Engine: As RS2000 except capacity, 1,593cc; bore × stroke, 87.67mm × 66mm. Output, 95bhp at 5,750rpm; 92lb/ft at 4,000rpm.

Transmission: As RS2000.

Suspension, brakes: As RS1600.

Wheels and tyres: Steel rims, 5.5in wide × 13in diameter, or alloy 6in wide × 13in diameter. Tyre size, 175/70 SR 13.

Ford Escort RS1600i 1981-1983

Front transverse engine, front-wheel drive. Assembled at Saarlouis, West Germany; engine from Bridgend, South Wales, with Ford Motorsport modifications.

Body: Unitary steel three-door Escort Mk3 hatchback with Ford Motorsport front and rear spoilers.

Dimensions: Length, 159.5in/4,051.3mm; width, 62.5in/1,587.5mm; height, 52.6in/1,336mm; wheelbase, 94.4in/2,400mm. Weight, 2,027lb/919kg. Drag factor, 0.38Cd.

Engine: CVH, in-line four cylinder, uprated from standard Escort. Iron block, alloy head. Belt-driven single overhead camshaft, solid lifters. Capacity, 1,596cc; bore × stroke, 79.96mm × 79.52mm. Compression ratio, 9.9:1. Bosch K-Jetronic fuel injection, overrun cut-off. Output, 115bhp at 6,000rpm; 109lb/ft at 5,250rpm.

Transmission: 7.9in/200mm diameter clutch, cable operation. Five-speed transaxle. Ratios: first, 3.15:1; second, 1.91:1; third, 1.27:1; fourth, 0.95:1; fifth, 0.83:1. Final drive ratio, 3.84:1.

Suspension: Front, MacPherson struts with leading-link location and separate anti-roll bar. Rear, independent, transverse arms, locating rods, progressive-rate coil springs. Koni dampers.

Brakes: Ventilated front discs; diameter, 9.5in/240mm. Rear drums; diameter, 7in/180mm.

Wheels and tyres: Alloy rims, 6in wide × 15in diameter. Tyre size, 195/50 VR 15 (Dunlop D4 for UK market).

Ford Escort RS Turbo 1984-1990

Front transverse engine, front-wheel drive. Assembled at Saarlouis, West Germany; engine from Bridgend, South Wales.

Details for second-generation cars, from 1986, where different, are indicated in brackets.

Body: As RS1600i plus side extensions. (Revised styling, twin bonnet vents.)

Dimensions: Length, 160.3in/4,071.6mm (159.3in/4,046.2mm); width, 64.5in/1,638.3mm (62.5in/1,587.5mm); height, 54.5in/1,348.3mm (53.1in/1,384.7mm); wheelbase, 94.4in/2,400mm. Weight, 2,136lb/971kg (2,247lb/1,017kg). Drag factor, 0.38Cd (0.36Cd).

Engine: CVH, dimensions as RS1600i, but compression ratio, 8.3:1 (8.2:1). Bosch KE-Jetronic fuel injection; Bosch-Motorola ignition/injection/wastegate management; Garrett T3 Turbocharger (water-cooled). Output, 132bhp at 6,000rpm; 133lb/ft at 3,000rpm (2,750rpm).

Transmission: 8.6in/218mm diameter clutch, cable operation. Five-speed transaxle. Ratios: first, 3.15:1; second, 1.91:1; third, 1.27:1; fourth, 0.95:1; fifth, 0.76:1. Final drive ratio, 4.27:1 (3.82:1).

Suspension: Front, as RS1600i (leading links deleted, location by anti-roll bar). Rear, as RS1600i plus anti-roll bar. (New spring and damper rates, revised ride height.)

Brakes: Ventilated front discs; diameter, 9.5in/

240mm (10.2in/260mm). Rear drums; diameter 8in/203.2mm (9in/228.6mm).

Wheels and tyres: Alloy rims, 6in wide × 15in diameter. (New 'turbine' styling.) Tyre size, 195/50 VR 15. Michelin MXV (Dunlop D40).

Ford Capri RS2600 1970-1974

Front engine, rear-wheel drive. Assembled at Cologne-Niehl, West Germany (millionth Capri, an RS2600, at Saarlouis).

Body: Unitary steel two-door Capri with flared front wheelarches.

Dimensions: Length, 169.4in/4,302.8mm; width, 64.8in/1,645.9mm; height, approx. 50in/1,270mm but varies with ride height; wheelbase, 100.8in/2,560mm. Weight, early homologation cars 1,980lb/900kg, typical production, 2,376lb/1,080kg. Drag factor, 0.39Cd.

Engine: 60 degree V6, all iron, pushrod overhead valves. Capacity, 2,637cc; bore × stroke, 90mm × 69mm. Compression ratio, 10:1. Kugelfischer mechanical fuel injection. Output, 150bhp at 5,800rpm; 165lb/ft at 3,500rpm.

Transmission: 9.5in/240mm diameter clutch; early, hydraulic; late, cable operation. Four-speed gearbox. Ratios, early: first, 3.65:1; second, 1.97:1; third, 1.37:1; fourth, 1:1. Ratios, late: first, 3.16:1; second, 1.94:1; third, 1.41:1; fourth, 1:1. Live rear axle: final drive ratio, early, 3.22:1; late, 3.09:1.

Suspension: Front, MacPherson struts, anti-roll bar, re-drilled Capri crossmember for negative camber. Rear, single-leaf springs, radius rods. Bilstein dampers.

Brakes: Early, solid front discs; diameter, 9.6in/243.8mm. Late, ventilated front discs; diameter, 9.75in/247.7mm. Rear drums; diameter, 9in/228.6mm; width, 2.25in/57.2mm.

Wheels and tyres: Minilite, Richard Grant or FAVO alloy rims, 6in wide × 13in diameter. Tyre size, 185/70 HR 13.

Ford Capri RS3100 1973-1974

Front engine, rear-wheel drive. Six prototypes assembled at Boreham, remainder built at Halewood, Merseyside.

Body: As RS2600. Deformable plastic rear spoiler.

Dimensions: As RS2600 except weight, 2,310lb/1,050kg. Drag factor, 0.37Cd.

Engine: Essex series 60 degree V6, all iron, pushrod overhead valves. Capacity 3,091cc; bore × stroke, 95.19mm × 72.42mm. Compression ratio, 9:1. One twin-choke downdraught Weber 38EGAS carburettor. Output, 148bhp at 5,000rpm; 187lb/ft at 3,000rpm.

Transmission, suspension, brakes: As late RS2600.

Wheels and tyres: FAVO alloy rims, 6in wide × 13in diameter. Tyre size, 185/70 HR 13.

Ford RS200 1983-1986

Mid engine, four-wheel drive. Prototypes built at Boreham, remainder assembled at Reliant factory, Shenstone.

Body: Glassfibre body panels over composite mono-coque structure of aluminium honeycomb. Panels and monocoque locally reinforced with carbon and aramid fibres. Tubular steel roll cage.

Dimensions: Length, 157.5in/4,000mm; width, 69in/1,752mm; height, 51.8in/1,316mm; wheelbase, 99.6in/2,530mm. Weight, 2,607lb/1,184kg. Drag factor, approximately 0.4Cd.

Engine: BDT, in-line four cylinder. All-alloy BDA derivative originally developed for Escort RS1700T project. 16-valve head, belt-driven twin overhead camshafts. Capacity, 1,803cc; bore × stroke, 86mm × 77.62mm. Compression ratio, 8.2:1. Ford EEC-IV electronic ignition and injection management. Garrett T03/4 turbocharger. Output, 250bhp at 6,500rpm; 215lb/ft at 4,000rpm.

Transmission: 7.3in/185mm diameter twin-plate clutch. Five-speed front-mounted transaxle incorporating front and centre differentials. Hewland gears, ratios: first, 2.692:1; second, 1.824:1; third, 1.318:1; fourth, 1.043:1; fifth, 0.786:1. Primary drive ratio, 0.864:1. Final drive ratio, 4.375:1. Viscous Couplings to Ferguson patents in front, centre and rear differentials.

Suspension: Independent by wide-based wishbones all round. Twin dampers and provision for twin coil springs at each corner.

Brakes: Four ventilated discs; diameter, 11.2in/285mm; thickness, 1in/25mm. No servo.

Wheels and tyres: Alloy rims, 8in wide × 16in diameter. Tyre size, 225/50 VR 16. Pirelli P700.

Ford Sierra RS Cosworth 1985-1986

Front engine, rear-wheel drive. Assembled at Genk, Belgium. UK-built Ford-Cosworth engine.

Body: Unitary steel three-door Sierra hatchback, with polyurethane nose and spoiler, twin bonnet vents and intake between headlamps, special single-pole rear wing.

Dimensions: Length, 175.5in/4,457.7mm; width, 68in/1,727.2mm; height, 54.2in/1,376.7mm; wheelbase, 102.7in/2,608.6mm. Weight, 2,651lb/1,205kg. Drag factor, 0.34Cd.

Engine: In-line four cylinder. Pinto series iron block with Cosworth 16-valve alloy head. Belt-driven twin overhead camshafts. Capacity, 1,993cc; bore × stroke, 90.82mm × 76.95mm. Compression ratio, 8:1. Weber-Marelli ignition/injection/wastegate management. Garrett T03 water-cooled turbocharger with intercooling. Output, 204bhp at 6,000rpm; 203lb/ft at 4,500rpm.

Transmission: 9.5in/240mm diameter clutch, cable operation. Borg-Warner five-speed gearbox. Ratios: first, 2.95:1; second, 1.94:1; third, 1.34:1; fourth, 1:1; fifth, 0.80:1. Final drive ratio, 3.65:1. Viscous Coupling limited-slip differential.

Suspension: Front, MacPherson struts, anti-roll bar, twin-tube dampers. Rear, independent, semi-trailing arms, coil springs, anti-roll bar, single-tube dampers.

Brakes: Ventilated front discs; diameter, 11.4in/283mm; thickness, 0.94in/24mm. Solid rear discs; diameter, 10.75in/273mm; thickness, 0.4in/10.2mm. Alfred Teves GmbH electronic anti-lock system.

Wheels and tyres: Alloy rims, 7in wide × 15in diameter. Tyre size, 205/50 VR 15. Dunlop D40.

Ford Sierra RS500 Cosworth 1987

Front engine, rear-wheel drive. 500 Genk-built cars extensively reworked to 'evolution' specification by Aston Martin Tickford at Bedworth, Warwickshire.

Body: As Sierra RS Cosworth with revised front bumper and spoiler, secondary rear spoiler and 30mm extension to rear wing.

Dimensions: As Sierra RS Cosworth except weight, 2,734lb/1,240kg. Drag factor, see text.

Engine: Sierra RS Cosworth unit with revisions to induction and management systems, including provision for secondary fuel injectors used only on competition version. Garret T31/T04 turbocharger, enlarged and repositioned intercooler. Output, 224bhp at 6,000rpm; 206lb/ft at 4,500rpm.

Transmission, suspension, brakes, wheels and tyres: As Sierra RS Cosworth. Provision to relocate rear trailing arms for racing.

Ford Sierra RS Cosworth 1988-1990

Front engine, rear-wheel drive. Assembled at Genk.

Body: Unitary steel four-door Sierra Sapphire in Ghia trim, with new bumper/air dam, rear spoiler and sill extensions by Marley.

Dimensions: As for 1986 car except length, 176in/4,460mm; width, 67in/1,700mm; weight, 2,750lb/1,250kg. Drag factor, 0.33Cd.

Engine: As for 1986 car with detail changes for durability.

Transmission, suspension, brakes, wheels and tyres: Data as for 1986 car, detail changes to brake pad spec, spring and damper rates, etc. New style alloy wheels, width, diameter and tyre size unchanged.

Ford Sierra Sapphire RS Cosworth 4 × 4 1990

Front engine, permanent four-wheel drive. Assembled at Genk, Belgium. UK-built Ford-Cosworth engine. Ferguson patent 4WD and VC transmission components from Viscodrive.

Body: Unitary steel four-door Sierra Sapphire with special local reinforcement. RS polyurethane front and rear spoilers, sills and bonnet louvres.

Dimensions: Length, 176.9in/4,494mm; width, 66.8in/1,698mm; height, 54.2in/1,376.7mm; wheelbase, 102.7in/2,608.6mm. Weight, 2,822lb/1,280kg (add 10kg for catalytic convertor). Drag factor, 0.322Cd.

Engine: In-line four cylinder. Development of original Sierra RS unit with modified Pinto/RS500 iron block and stiffened aluminium alloy Cosworth 16-valve head. Belt-driven twin overhead camshafts, revised profiles. Mahle pistons. Capacity, 1,993cc; bore × stroke, 90.82mm × 76.95mm. Compression ratio, 8:1. Weber-Marelli ignition/injection/wastegate management.

Garrett TO3B turbocharger with lead seal for wastegate; enlarged intercooler. Many detail changes include: inlet manifold and fuel rail; exhaust manifold (no damper); oil and water pumps; head gasket; platinum-tipped Motorcraft spark plugs (AGPR 9O2P). Cast light alloy sump accommodates 4WD. Synthetic oils only. Output, 220bhp at 6,000rpm (6,250rpm with cat); 214lb/ft (290Nm) at 3,500rpm.

Transmission: 9.5in/240mm diameter clutch, cable operation. Ford MT75 five-speed gearbox. Ratios: first, 3.62:1; second, 2.08:1; third, 1.36:1; fourth, 1:1; fifth, 0.83:1. Final drive ratios, 3.62:1; 22.24mph/ 1,000rpm. 34/66% front/rear torque split via epicyclic centre differential with Viscous Coupling to limit slip. Front drive by Hi-Vo transfer chain (31-tooth chain wheels), propshaft, 6.5in diameter spiral-bevel final drive, free differential, equal-length drive shafts. Rear drive by propshaft, 7in diameter hypoid final drive, Viscous Coupling limited-slip differential.

Suspension: Front, MacPherson struts, thicker (30mm) anti-roll bar. Rear, independent, semi-trailing arms, coil springs, 18mm anti-roll bar. Spring rates as for 1988 car, 21kNm front, 51kNm rear. Single-tube gas-filled dampers.

Brakes: Ventilated discs all round. Front, 10.94in/278mm x 0.94in/24mm. Rear, 10.75in/ 273mm x 0.79in/20mm. Alfred Teves GmbH electronic anti-lock system and power assistance.

Wheels and tyres: Alloy rims, 7in wide x 15in diameter, design as for 1988 car. Tyre size, 205/50 VR 15, Bridgestone ER90 on test cars.

Ford Fiesta RS Turbo

Front transverse engine, front-wheel drive. Assembled at Valencia, Spain.

Body: Unitary steel three-door Fiesta XR2i hatchback base. RS modifications: bonnet louvres; front bumper and mounting cut away to clear cooling fan; colour-coded rear spoiler; Benetton Ascot interior trim; Recaro front seats; 240km/h (150mph) speedometer; unique three-spoke steering wheel. Badges: RHD, *Fiesta RS Turbo*; LHD, *Fiesta Turbo*.

Dimensions: Length, 149.64in/3,801mm; width, 64.17in/1,630mm; height, 52.20in/1,326mm; wheelbase, 96.29in/2,446mm; front track, 56.29in/ 1,430mm; rear track, 54.17in/1,376mm. Weight, 2,028lb/920kg.

Engine: CVH, in-line four cylinder, developed specification unique to model. Escort Turbo block, crankshaft and pistons. Capacity, 1,596cc; bore x stroke, 79.96mm x 79.52mm. Compression ratio, 8.2:1. XR2i/3i EFI cylinder head and camshaft, Escort Turbo camshaft pulley. Garrett T2 turbocharger with intercooler. Bosch KE-Jetronic fuel injection, Ford EEC IV electronic ignition and injection management. Output, 133bhp at 5,500rpm; 135lb/ft (183Nm) at 2,400rpm.

Transmission: 8.6in/218mm diameter clutch, cable operated. Five-speed transaxle. Ratios: first, 2.95:1; second, 1.94:1; third, 1.34:1; fourth, 1:1; fifth, 0.8:1. Final drive ratio, 3.82:1. Free differential.

Suspension: Front, MacPherson struts; replacement A-arms and ball joints unique to model modify camber and castor; 16mm anti-roll bar. Rear, semi-independent with trailing arms and torsion beam, coil springs; 20mm anti-roll bar; ride height 12mm lower than XR2i. Spring rates: front, 21kNm; rear 23kNm. Armstrong gas-filled dampers.

Brakes: As for XR2i, ventilated front discs, rear drums. Ferodo 3432 friction material. Optional anti-lock SCS.

Wheels and Tyres: Alloy three-spoke rims, 5.5in wide x 14in diameter. Tyre size, 185/55 VR 14; Uniroyal 240/55, Dunlop D8, Michelin MXV or Pirelli P600.

Appendix 2: Performance, RS road cars

Mph (sec)	RS1600	Mexico/1	Mexico/2	RS2000/1
0-30	3.4	3.9	3.2	2.9
0-40	4.8	5.8	5.5	4.8
0-50	6.8	7.9	8.1	6.9
0-60	8.9	10.7	11.1	9.0
0-70	12.4	14.5	16.2	12.8
0-80	16.1	20.2	23.0	17.2
0-90	22.6	-	-	24.2
0-100	32.3	-	-	34.5
¼-mile	16.7	18.0	17.8	17.1
50-70 (4th)	9.5	-	-	8.8
Max mph	113	99	106*	108
Test mpg	21.5	27.5	27.2	26.6
Kerb wt (lb)	1,920	1,964	1,991	1,978
Source	Autocar	Autocar	Motor Sport	Autocar
Date	30/4/70/	12/70	1/76	11/10/73

* **Manufacturer's figure**

Mph (Sec)	RS2000/2	RS1800	RS1600i	RS Turbo/1
0-30	3.0	2.9	2.9	2.9
0-40	4.7	4.7	4.4	4.2
0-50	6.4	6.6	6.2	5.7
0-60	8.6	9.0	8.7	8.1
0-70	12.7	12.4	11.8	10.8
0-80	16.9	16.6	15.0	13.1
0-90	23.1	22.0	20.3	17.0
0-100	33.6	32.9	27.9	21.2
0-110	-	-	39.5	30.2
¼-mile	16.7	16.9	16.7	16.2
50-70 (4th)	8.4	8.9	9.8	5.8
Max mph	109	111	118	128
Test mpg	24.7	26.5	28.3	26.8
Kerb wt (lb)	2,075	2,016	2,027	2,150
Source	Autocar	Autocar	Autocar	Autocar
Date	17/1/76	26/7/75	5/2/83	27/3/85

Mph (sec)	RS Turbo/2	RS2600	RS3100	Sierra Cosworth
0-30	3.0	2.8	2.7	2.5
0-40	4.7	4.0	4.0	3.5
0-50	6.1	5.6	5.4	4.9
0-60	9.2	7.3	7.2	6.2
0-70	11.4	9.8	9.6	8.5
0-80	14.1	12.3	12.5	10.4
0-90	18.5	-	15.8	13.3
0-100	23.0	20.0	21.2	16.1
0-110	31.0	-	-	19.4
¼-mile	16.8	15.0	15.7	15.5
50-70 (4th)	6.1	-	6.7	4.9
Max mph	125	126	125	149
Test mpg	27.4	23.5	22.2	21.4
Kerb wt (lb)	2,247	2,315	2,310	2,688
Source	Autocar	Road & Track	Motor	Autocar
Date	27/8/86	12/71	13/4/71	13/8/86

Mph (sec)	Sierra RS500	RS Sapphire	RS Sierra 4 x 4	Fiesta RS	RS200
0–30	2.4	2.2	2.1	2.8	2.4
0–40	3.3	3.2	3.4	4.4	3.1
0–50	4.7	4.4	4.8	5.9	4.8
0–60	6.1	5.8	6.6	7.9	6.1
0–70	8.4	8.1	8.6	10.1	8.7
0–80	10.5	10.1	10.9	12.7	10.6
0–90	12.9	12.8	13.4	16.4	13.8
0–100	16.2	15.8	17.1	20.2	17.0
0–110	20.1	19.5	23.1	27.0	21.5
¼–mile	15.1	14.4	14.3	16.1	15.0
50–70 (4th)	-	4.8	5.2	5.7	5.0
Max mph	154	142	146	132	140
Test mpg	-	20.3	21.6	23.6	16.6
Kerb wt (lb)	-	2,660	2,874	2,004	2.835
Source	Autocar	Autocar & Motor	Autocar & Motor	Autocar & Motor	Autocar
Date	19/8/87	17/2/88	11/4/90	20/6/90	19/11/86

Appendix 3: Performance, RS competition cars

Performance testing competition cars is a fraught business but, to their credit, *Autocar* went through much of their regular road-test ritual to produce these figures for two Boreham-built works rally cars, RS1600 and RS1800. Both were 2-litre alloy block models. The racing RS1600 is the Broadspeed 1.7-litre version which I put through the fifth-wheel procedure for *Motor Sport* and *Motoring News* in 1971. The figures were two-way averages returned by the car's regular driver, John Fitzpatrick, on the Silverstone club circuit. It should be remembered that the racing saloon was a lot lighter than a fully equipped rally car, and used slick racing tyres rather than the chunky forest tyres of the two rallycars assessed by *Autocar*.

For competition RS Capri figures, we have to go to the pages of the West German magazine *Auto Motor und Sport*. They tested two Weslake-engined RS2600s, in 1971 with 2,873cc and 265-275bhp, and in 1973 with 2,995cc and 295bhp. In 1974 they tried a Cosworth GAA-engined RS3100 of 3,412cc, that engine developing from 415 to 455bhp during its factory team career.

Their 0-100km/h (0-62mph) times were: 1971, 4.9sec; 1973, 4.6sec; 1974, 4.2sec. For the two later cars they also timed 0-200km/h (0-124mph): 1973, 14.3sec; 1974, 13.1sec. Comparison with the Broadspeed RS1600's time closer to 18 seconds for the similar 0-120mph sprint proves that cubic capacity really was vital in pre-turbo days.

Best estimates of maximum speeds for the three Capris, based on factory figures and my own reporter's notes at various contemporary race meetings, range from 158mph in 1971 and 160-170mph in 1973 to 186mph for the 3.4-litre RS3100.

Mph (sec)	1971 racing RS1600	1973 rally RS1600	1976 rally RS1800
0-30	-	2.9	2.5
0-40	-	3.9	3.4
0-50	3.8	5.5	4.4
0-60	4.8	7.0	6.1
0-70	6.4	9.0	8.0
0-80	-	11.9	10.2
0-90	-	14.9	13.5
0-100	12.0	20.3	16.6
0-110	14.5	-	21.8
0-120	17.7	-	30.5
¼-mile	13.4	14.7	14.5
Max mph	138	108	108
at rpm	9,000	8,500	8,500
Bhp	250	200	250
Mpg	8-9	8-10	10-12.5

Appendix 4: Performance, RS turbo competition cars

First, two sets of sensational figures, again courtesy of *Autocar*, showing the kind of dragster performance available from 16-valve turbo BDA power and four-wheel drive — yet the RS200 was tractable enough to use on the road. While I have used *Autocar* figures for direct comparability, I have seen the Zakspeed-engined Gartrac car run even faster: when I tested it for *Motor*, it recorded an average of 2.7 seconds for 0–60mph and broke the 7-second barrier for 0–100mph in two-way runs at Millbrook.

The 1988 works three-door Sierra RS Cosworth rally car was tested by me for *Motor*, but the performance figures record John Wheeler's driving at Boreham, using that magazine's equipment, and give us an excellent idea of just how quick the outwardly standard-looking Group A cars can be — with four-wheel drive still to come!

The two journals are now combined in the Haymarket group's *Autocar & Motor*, and I am grateful to the editor Bob Murray for permission to quote more recent figures.

Mph (sec)	Works rally RS200	Gartrac rallycross Escort	Cosworth Sierra ex-Corsica
0–30	1.2	1.2	2.4
0–40	1.8	1.7	3.1
0–50	2.2	2.2	3.9
0–60	2.8	3.0	4.8
0–70	3.8	3.8	5.9
0–80	4.8	4.7	7.5
0–90	5.9	5.9	8.9
0–100	7.3	7.1	10.8
0–110	8.7	–	–
¼–mile	11.4	–	13.3
Max mph	118	129	–
at rpm	8,900	9,200	6,500
Bhp	450	575	315/340
Kerb wt (lb)	2,315	2,222	2,433

Appendix 5: UK-market sales of RS cars, 1972-1987

Source: Ford and SMMT. Note that these figures begin in 1972 and therefore do not represent total sales of the two earliest models, RS1600 and Mexico Mk1.

	RS1600	Mexico*	RS2000/1	RS2000/2	RS1800	Year total
1972	163	1,206				1,369
1973	121	2,182	1,862			4,165
1974	29	2,517	1,414			3,960
1975	5	867	483	46	24	1,425
1976		672		1,153	23	1,848
1977		639		1,274	41	1,954
1978		971		2,070	21	3,062
1979		8		2,825		2,833
1980				2,581		2,581
1981				90		90
Model total	318	9,062	3,759	10,039	109	

*Mexico: Mk 2 introduced January 1976.

	RS1600i	RS Turbo/1	RS Turbo/2	Sierra RS Cosworth	RS200	Year total
1982	47					47
1983	2,545					2,545
1984	10	2				12
1985	4	3,993		10	2	4,009
1986	2	1,581	1,317	1,064	18	3,982
1987 (first quarter)			803	579	1	1,383
Model total	2,608	5,576	2,120	1,653	21	

Appendix 6: Sales (all markets) of FAVO-developed cars, 1970-75

Cross-referenced from several internal Ford sources. Figures for 1975 estimated only.

	RS1600	Mexico	RS2000/1	RS2600	RS3100
1970	161	70			
1971	307	1,802		752	
1972	410	3,414		1,360	
1973	183	3,079	987	1,188	
1974	47	1,537	3,337	178	248
1975 (est)	31	450	1,010	1	
Model total	1,139	10,352	5,334	3,479	248

Appendix 7: RS2000 and Mexico production at Saarlouis

These figures confirm the Mk2 RS2000 as the most popular RS type to date and were listed in a Ford internal memo of November 1981. The same document records that 1,162 Mk1 RS2000s for the German market were made at Saarlouis in 1973-74.

	RS2000 German market	RS2000 export	Total	Mexico
1975	176	225	401	
1976	3,520	3,431	6,951	
1977	1,753	2,891	4,644	740
1978	1,417	3,428	4,845	702
1979	1,242	5,498	6,740	
1980	212	1,845	2,057	
Model total	8,320	17,318	25,638	1,442

Appendix 8: RS addresses

Ford RS Owners Club
Membership secretary: Bob Dinnage, 18 Downsview Road, Sevenoaks, Kent, TN13 2JT.

Ford AVO Owners Club
Membership secretary: Gareth Richards, 54 Banners Gate Road, Sutton Coldfield, West Midlands, B73 6RU.
Secretary: Dave Hensley, 11 Sycamore Drive, Patchway, Bristol, BS12 5DH.

Capri Club International
Field House, Redditch, Worcestershire, B98 OAN.

Ford RS Owners Club of Australia
Secretary: Peter Burt, 13/12 Ronald Street, Harbord 2096, Australia.

Ford Motorsport Parts
Boreham Airfield, Boreham, Chelmsford, Essex, CM3 3BG.

TURBO TECHNICS and FORD

A formidable blend of automotive attractions . . .

For drivers who demand a car that is more than just a means of locomotion, a vehicle that gives enjoyment in its use, Turbo Technics produce a staggering range of conversions with vivid performance, sure-footed handling, safety and reliability. Our long association with Ford cars has already given rise to many spectacular developments and it's hardly surprising that today, with Ford's comprehensive range of models, Turbo Technics offer immaculately engineered conversions for most of their cars. Escorts, Sierras, Granadas and Scorpios - yes even the Clubman's Cosworth, all benefit from our attentions. Let no one be confused - our modifications are not merely 'bolt-ons'. They result from major engineering and development programmes undertaken to make good cars better, and must be fitted at our approved centres.

A Turbo Technics car is eloquent proof that whilst attitudes to motoring vary - our quality doesn't.

TURBO TECHNICS

Contact your nearest approved fitting centre, or head office, Northampton, and find out more about motoring 'First Class' with Turbo Technics

TURBO TECHNICS

Head Office, Research and Technical Centre, 17 Galowhill Rd., Brackmills, Northampton NN4 0EE. Tel 0604 764005
Fitting, Servicing and Race Preparation Centre, Holder Rd., North Lane, Aldershot, Hants. GU12 4RH. Tel 0252 331251

A rare instance of a car company not blowing its own trumpet.

"The best road car Ford has yet built."
CAR MAGAZINE

"The car is at its most impressive on a tough, twisty, pock-marked gradient. On this terrain the Cosworth felt utterly in command, sure-footed and safe.
You can drive very quickly with the reassurance of considerable reserves of grip and stability."
THE OBSERVER

"The most exciting road car Ford has produced since the GT 40."
SUNDAY EXPRESS

"Handling is super-sharp but always on the right side of twitchy. Cornering grip is nothing short of sensational by any standards, never mind by saloon benchmarks."
COUNTRY LIFE

"In the last three years the Sierra Cosworth has won the World Touring Car Championship and 26 rally championships. Think what it should now do with four-wheel drive."
AUTO EXPRESS

"The grip provided by the rubber band 205/50ZR15 Bridgestones
is phenomenal, and even accelerating hard over
'ball bearing' gravel, spread across a broken road surface,
doesn't provoke a hint of wheelspin."

WHAT CAR?

"Ford's supercar sets pulses racing."

SUNDAY EXPRESS

"The engine has been so extensively modified that 80%
of its components are different from those of its predecessor.
A stunningly accomplished performer."

THE OBSERVER

"The revisions to the engine really work.
On the Millbrook test circuit, a 0-60 mph time of 5.6 seconds was
recorded several times, and one of 5.5 seconds."

PERFORMANCE CAR

"The best four-wheel drive saloon car you can buy."

AUTOCAR & MOTOR

The Sierra 4x4 Cosworth.

PERFORMANCE ENGINEERING

POWER CHIPS & POWER PLUS PRODUCTS

With over 20 years experience in tuning high performance cars the company in the early eighties became one of the first to specialise on turbo charged engine conversions, and have since built up a reputation as the leading exponent in this field moving into a new modern workshop in July 1990.

Below is a list of conversions that are available at present and new kits will be developed for new RS models as they are introduced by the Ford Motor Company.

ESCORT RS TURBO	STAGE I	195BHP	£325
STAGE I + CAM & STAINLESS EXHAUST	STAGE II	215BHP	£820
STAGE II + ADJUSTABLE SUSPENSION	STAGE III	215BHP	£1425
RS SIERRA/SAPPHIRE/4x4	STAGE I	270BHP	£250
RS SIERRA/SAPPHIRE/4x4	STAGE II	320BHP	£995
RS SIERRA/SAPPHIRE/4x4	* STAGE III	340BHP	£1550
RS SIERRA/SAPPHIRE/4x4	* STAGE IV	360BHP	£1995
RS500	STAGE I	300BHP	£250
RS500	* STAGE II	360BHP	£1550
RS500	* STAGE III	375BHP	£1995
RS500	* STAGE IV	500BHP	POA

* Includes Stainless Steel Exhaust System
We manufacture our own Stainless Steel Exhaust systems
specially designed to reduce back pressure

ESCORT RS TURBO	£325
SIERRA, SAPPHIRE and SAPPHIRE 4x4 COSWORTHS	£470

ALL PRICES INCLUDE FITTING AND ARE CORRECT AS OF 1.12.1990

All remapping and programming of engine management systems are done inhouse, not bought in or copied and the end results have become the envy of other companies.

Comprehensive stocks of new and secondhand Ford standard and competition parts are carried.

Competition wiring is available for all makes of race or rally cars.

Service exchange Turbos are stocked and custom built units are available to order.

Suspension systems from Koni or Bilstein are tailored to suit the requirements of each customer.

Our own RS200 Evolution model has been modified extensively through the rigorous testing we have done on the race track which has enabled us to provide many parts for both standard or modified RS200's – Lightweight Kevlar body panels, large brakes, uprated dampers and springs, wheels and tyres.

From a service to building of Race or Rally cars we are only a phone call away and are always willing to give free advice to any prospective customer.

Official Agents for KONI, REVOLUTION and BRIDGESTONE

Unit 6, Greenfields Industrial Estate, off Back Lane, Congleton, Cheshire CW12 4TR.
Tel: (0260) 279604 Fax: (0260) 299208